SEATTLE SPORTS

SPORT, CULTURE & SOCIETY

DAVID K. WIGGINS, SERIES EDITOR

Other Titles in This Series

Seattle Sports

Play, Identity,
and Pursuit
in the Emerald City

Edited by Terry Anne Scott

The University of Arkansas Press
Fayetteville
2020

ISBN: 978-1-68226-135-4
eISBN: 978-1-61075-723-2

24 23 22 21 20   5 4 3 2 1

♾ The paper used in this publication meets the minimum requirements of the American National Standard for Permanence of Paper for Printed Library Materials Z39.48-1984.

Library of Congress Cataloging-in-Publication Data

Names: Scott, Terry Anne, editor.
Title: Seattle sports : play, identity, and pursuit in the Emerald City / edited by Terry Anne Scott.
Description: Fayetteville : The University of Arkansas Press, 2020. | Series: Sport, culture, and society | Includes bibliographical references and index.
Identifiers: LCCN 2019057753 (print) | LCCN 2019057754 (ebook) | ISBN 9781682261354 (paperback) | ISBN 9781610757232 (ebook)
Subjects: LCSH: Sports—Washington (State)—Seattle—History. | Athletes—Washington (State)—Seattle—Biography.
Classification: LCC GV584.5.S43 S43 2020 (print) | LCC GV584.5.S43 (ebook) | DDC 796.09797/772—dc23
LC record available at https://lccn.loc.gov/2019057753
LC ebook record available at https://lccn.loc.gov/2019057754

To Dad and Ricky

Contents

Series Editor's Preface

Sport is an extraordinarily important phenomenon that pervades the lives of many people and has enormous impact on society in an assortment of ways. At its most fundamental level, sport has the power to bring people great joy and to satisfy their competitive urges while at once allowing them to form a sense of community with others from various walks of life who embody diverse backgrounds and interests. Sport also makes clear, especially at the highest levels of competition, the lengths that people will go to achieve victory. It is also closely connected to business, education, politics, economics, religion, law, family, and other societal institutions. Sport is, moreover, partly about identity development and how individuals and groups—irrespective of race, gender, ethnicity, or socioeconomic class—have sought to elevate their status and realize material success and social mobility.

Sport, Culture, and Society seeks to promote a greater understanding of the aforementioned issues and many others. Recognizing sport's powerful influence and ability to change people's lives in significant ways, the series focuses on topics ranging from urbanization and community development to biographies and intercollegiate athletics. It includes monographs and anthologies that are characterized by excellent scholarship, accessibility to a wide audience, and thoughtful design. The series showcases work by individuals at various stages of their careers—sport studies scholars of outstanding talent just beginning to make their mark on the field, as well as more experienced scholars of sport with established reputations—who represent a variety of disciplinary areas and methodological approaches.

Seattle Sports is the latest book in this series that assesses the patterns, roles, and meanings of sport in a particular urban setting. Edited by Terry Anne Scott from Hood College, *Seattle Sports* examines, through ten thoughtful and interpretative essays, how, over time, sport has changed and impacted the city that had been known for more than one hundred years as the "Queen City," and that has since come to be variously referred to (for obvious reasons) as the "Emerald City," the "Rain City," "Gateway to Alaska," and "Jet City." As Scott notes in her introduction, a large portion of the book deals with a critical interpretation of the interconnection among race, sport, and culture in a city that, irrespective of the titles given it, has largely been underappreciated and that has never received the attention paid to Chicago, New York, San Francisco, Philadelphia, or Los Angeles (among others).

Although space did not allow for coverage of every sport and player or coach that significantly influenced the city, this volume covers a wide range of topics. The essays explore, for example, the great swimmer Helen Madison, Japanese American sports during the interwar years, Lenny Wilkens and the 1978–79 world champion Seattle Supersonics, the history of the Seattle Mariners between 1977–94, and the story of the gay Emerald City Softball Association. The essays collected here demonstrate the vibrant sporting life that has been extraordinarily important in bringing people together and fostering communal pride in the beautiful city in the Pacific Northwest.

David K. Wiggins

Acknowledgments

Who knew a simple phone call to David Wiggins, one of the foremost sports historians in the country, would result in the writing of this book? I contacted David one spring afternoon to discuss the many works he had published that served as useful texts in my sports history course at the University of Washington. The exchange led to a series of planning conversations that culminated in the writing of *Seattle Sports: Play, Identity, and Pursuit in the Emerald City*. I am forever grateful to David for his wisdom, his guidance, and the opportunity to co-contribute a volume to the University of Arkansas series Sport, Culture, and Society.

Many insightful, dedicated scholars and sportswriters contributed to this volume. The diversity of their work, together with the passion that drove their historical inquiries, made this book both possible and pioneering. They all deserve quite a debt of gratitude due in large measure to their hard work, patience, and willingness to undertake projects that required exhaustive research and unwavering dedication to their craft. I am grateful for their commitment to the history of sports in Seattle. Thank you as well to the incomparable Matthew Roumain, Jordyn Schulte, and Ezri and Oni Scott for their invaluable work as researchers and, on occasion, as reviewers.

This book would not have been possible without the editorial staff at the University of Arkansas Press. Thank you to all of those involved in making this book a reality. David Scott Cunningham, the editor-in-chief, provided invaluable direction as this project came to fruition, as did Jennifer Vos and Molly B. Rector.

The Museum of History and Industry (MOHAI) in Seattle has proven instrumental to the completion of this book. Many of the photographs used in the chapters are housed at MOHAI. Adam Lyon was particularly helpful in locating and suggesting photographs that truly capture the wonderful nuances of sports history in Seattle.

My dear husband, Warren, and my brilliant and determined daughters, Ezri, Oni, and Zahar, deserve immeasurable thanks for lending me support in all phases of this project. Thank you also to my parents, William and Micheline Schulte, for their delight and excitement over my work.

SEATTLE SPORTS

TERRY ANNE SCOTT

Nestled in the nucleus of mountainous terrain and the serenity of the Puget Sound, Seattle exists at a juncture between metropolitan obscurity and a continuous longing for preeminence. It has yet to be considered alongside New York, Chicago, or Los Angeles in discussions of America's great sports cities, but Seattle's sports history—together with the advent of its most recent athletic triumphs, emerging leagues, and locally bred sports heroes—increasingly suggest that perhaps it should be placed on that preeminent list. Seattle's moments of sports success have been admittedly intermittent, but nonetheless remarkably significant since early in the twentieth century. From the 1917 Stanley Cup victory, three Olympic gold medals captured by hometown swimmer Helene Madison in 1932, and the gold earned in Berlin by the University of Washington (UW) men's rowing team in 1936, to father and son baseball greats as well as a National Basketball Association (NBA) Championship later in the century, Seattle's heralded moments of athletic accomplishments have certainly been sweet and successfully engendered civic pride but have failed to secure iconic status for the city. Even a Super Bowl Championship as well as a Fédération Internationale de Football Association (FIFA) Women's World Cup victories by a local goalkeeper and midfielder, both secured early in this century, have only worked to marginally elevate the city's profile in the world of sport.

Indeed, Seattle has long been cast aside as mildly inconsequential in the hierarchy of urban centers. The city has achieved national or international recognition only briefly during, for instance, February 1919 when 65,000 striking shipyard workers halted the city's operations for nearly one week. Seattle would achieve momentary distinguishability once again when, more than four decades later, nearly ten million visitors ascended upon the Emerald City to attend the Century 21 Exposition, also known as the World's

Fair—an event that would bequeath the Space Needle to the metropolis as its enduring legacy of international prowess. In a city heralded or admonished (depending upon one's political leanings) for its progressive politics and environmental regulations, there is much that has provided a basis for local pride while working to make Seattle increasingly visible. Music great Jimi Hendrix, the sagacious electric guitarist and songwriter whose genius has rightfully allotted him epic status, was born in Seattle's King County Hospital in 1942 and raised on Jackson Street, where Quincy Jones and Ray Charles played to adoring audiences. By the 1980s, Seattle had given birth to grunge, an underground, alternative rock subgenre that intriguingly blended cultural aesthetics with groundbreaking musical performances. Grunge's most prominent artists—Pearl Jam, Nirvana, Soundgarden, and Alice in Chains—have surely lent credibility to Seattle's notions of relevance. In recent years, Starbucks, Boeing, and Microsoft have allowed the young city to forge a global presence, which has worked to make the companies nearly synonymous with the city's name. Sports, however, just as much as any triumphant company or legendary musician, have rendered Seattle noteworthy, important, even exceptional. Much is changing in the picturesque northwestern city. From the Seahawks' rise to global stardom ("We're all we've got!" "We're all we need!" "Go Hawks!") to the dawn of ultimate and the Seattle Sounders Major League Soccer (MLS) Cup Championship, sports in Seattle promise to create and maintain global visibility for a city whose sports preeminence has historically been denied, dismissed, or disrespected. Despite a constant struggle for credibility, Seattle exists as a preeminent sporting center, which is clearly demonstrated by the groundbreaking essays included in *Seattle Sports: Play, Identity, and Pursuit in the Emerald City*.[1]

Seattle is a space where a torrential rain in the midst of an outdoor sporting event is shrugged aside by local players and fans as a mere drizzle. Only nearby lightning will interrupt play. While the players may retreat to a locker room or some other covered space via the commands of their coaches should the lightening become ominous, the fans will wait until play resumes. They will weather the storm, quite literally, and remain in position to cheer, whether watching a professional, college, or youth team compete. On any particular weekend across the city, parents, grandparents, siblings, other family members, and friends dredge through muddied local soccer fields, toting collapsible, monochromatic canvas chairs and perhaps even an umbrella (certainly not a given in Seattle) to watch their children compete in a seemingly endless series of matches. Indeed, even local children learn to play in the rain because few sports, if any, occur during a season that is exempt from Seattle's wet weather, considering *rain* is an unofficial, seemingly perpetual season in the city. Seattle fans will tirelessly search for the listed field number—no matter how obscure its location—and calmly stake their space in the narrow strip of grass between fields, despite the weather. Once they have unfolded their chairs, laid their blankets, or comfortably occupied their assigned seats at any given sporting event, they will then roar like a lion that has settled into its den.

The bellows of these resolute local sports devotees have been known to register seismic activity in the already earthquake-prone city. The so-called "Beast Quake," for instance, unleashed its tremulous clamor on January 8, 2011, at the conclusion of former Seattle Seahawk Marshawn Lynch's sixty-seven-yard touchdown. The magnitude one earthquake ignited by the "12th Man" after that infamous touchdown drive against the reigning Super Bowl champion New Orleans Saints demonstrated, among other things, that Seattle fans *will* release an earthshaking scream. Fans would shake the ground once again just a few years later when Lynch plowed through five broken tackles as he figuratively transfigured the gridiron into a medieval battlefield. There Lynch appeared, agile, fierce, quick-witted, continuously evading his captors like some majestic medieval knight dodging foot soldiers and pikemen, usurping his enemies of all energy and ability—simply amazing. Lynch—the soft-spoken, hard-hitting running back (and quiet humanitarian) with a style of play and dogged determination reminiscent of the great Jim Brown—embodies Seattle's unobtrusive yet resolute pride in its athletic leagues, franchises, and local heroes. The image of Lynch perched atop his personal motorcade during the 2014 Super Bowl victory parade, joyfully tossing candy to an adoring crowd, will linger in the hearts and minds of Seattleites for, perhaps, an eternity.[2]

Local sports fans still reminisce about the SuperSonics' 1979 NBA Championship, with three-time Naismith Memorial Basketball Hall of Fame inductee Coach Lenny Wilkens at the helm. Much like Wilkens, the SuperSonics were not expected to succeed. Wilkens grew up in a Bed-Stuy tenement before the Brooklyn neighborhood played host to the trending interests of new-moneyed hipsters. Born in 1937 to a working-class Irish mother and African American father, Wilkens would encounter racial discrimination in a racially divided America. Despite their varied obstacles, including the death of Lenny Sr. when Wilkens was only five years old, Wilkens's mother ensured that her children would flourish. "She would tell me, 'let your integrity and honesty define your character,'" the legend fondly remembers.³ Wilkens rose to sporting fame and became a philan- thropic hero along the way. His success reminds us that the contours of our encounters can either slowly lower us into an abyss of insignificance or inform our perseverance, our aspirations to fashion a world of acceptance and parity from the cruelty of our experiences. Wilkens worked tirelessly to be the best, determined to overcome any obstacles he encountered through- out his lifetime, and to bring about equity for others in the process. His unexpected success mirrors that of the SuperSonics, a team that had never seriously been in the conversation for an NBA championship previous to Wilkens's second tenure with the team in 1977 (he was a player-coach earlier in the decade before leaving for Cleveland). The SuperSonics won their first division title at the end of the 1978 season but lost to the Washington Bullets in the championship. The following year, the SuperSonics would face the Bullets once again and clinch the NBA championship in Game Five, winning 97–93. Fans present at the unprecedented citywide celebra- tion that followed continue to wear thinning, faded championship T-shirts that bespeak an enduring pride. It was an unexpected championship that fleetingly cast a sleepy northwestern town into national stardom. As one Seattleite once admitted, the 1979 championship series was so important to local residents that she rescheduled her wedding reception, so it would not conflict with a game in the series. Clearly, local sports fans defer to and herald their precious sporting moments. They cup them in their palms and gently press them against their chest. The moments are emblazoned into their memories and carried in their hearts—perhaps not as much as, for instance, the birth of their child but certainly a close second.⁴

The intense reverberations and steadfast admiration of the city's sports enthusiasts should not be interpreted as evidence of collective insanity. Seattle fans might not don menacing black-and-silver costumes covered with spikes and chains traversing one another in a startling pattern that promises sure destruction (*read* Oakland Raiders fans). Nor are they likely to hurl their ire, objects, and gratuitous death threats at an unsuspecting spectator who, in a moment of overwhelming excitement, reaches over the rail to catch a baseball (Cubs fans, do you have anything to say?). That typically happens elsewhere, not in Seattle. Furthermore, they will probably not be heard impudently pitching racial slurs at visiting players (Boston fans?). Seattle fans are urbane, self-assured, measured—or so they tell themselves and others. To be sure, there is hardly anything portentous about the neon-green, fuzzy wigs seen bobbing along the crest of a crowd at Sounders matches or Seahawks games. Similarly, the UW Huskies paraphernalia featuring a fluffy Alaskan Malamute and flaunted by the athletic program supporters is simply adorable. But while the tempered emotional and aesthetic expressions of local sports enthusiasts may keep them largely buffered from arrest or embarrassing news coverage, they are nonetheless committed and passionate while, of course, remaining nothing shy of socially appropriate. This is evidenced best, perhaps, by an incident involving a locally esteemed professional football player.

Race has historically been a complex centerpiece of sports in Seattle and across the nation. Thus, it will not surprise readers that several of the essays in this volume offer critical analyses of how the intersection of race and sports functions as a microcosm of macrosocial and macropolitical issues, challenges, and triumphs. More recent events involving some of the most illustrious personalities in the history of Seattle sports belabor this point. When extolled Seattle Seahawks cornerback Richard Sherman tipped a deep pass intended for San Francisco 49er Michael Crabtree during a 2013 playoff game, the move—replete with Sherman's sharp, postgame commentary in which he claimed that he was "the best corner in the game" then questioned Crabtree's "mediocre" abilities—would send both the team and the city into national view once more.[5] The importance of the Seahawks' Super Bowl Championship that followed within weeks could hardly compete with the attention, even obsession, allotted to Sherman's monologue. He would be the victim of implicit bias, and perhaps racism, from people who sought to characterize his bombast as nothing more than the platitudes of a common "thug." The scene that featured Sherman shaking hands with Crabtree and exchanging what seemed to be a kind word would not be played with nearly the intense frequency that Sherman's self-possessed declarations would experience. Members of the media enjoyed exploiting the poised player's comments while mischaracterizing his confidence and dreadlocks (and denying his intelligence—he is, after all, a Stanford graduate) as something menacing. The media intelligence organization iQ Media reported that "thug" was used at least 625 times on US television the Monday following the game, which exceeded any single day during the previous several years.[6]

Accusations of threat, signifiers of racial othering, and commentaries that sought to portray Sherman as a ruffian revealed much about the continued conflations of race and criminality in American society. Belying his critics' claims of innocuousness, the outspoken, erudite player expressed his disappointment in pundits' characterizations of him at a press conference held just days after the incident: "I was on a football field showing passion. . . . I wasn't committing any crimes and doing anything illegal."[7] When asked by a reporter if it bothered him that many on social media had referred to him by the disparaging appellation of *thug*, Sherman's answer alluded to the racialized nature of the accusations. His response also took critics to task for the glaring bias that placed in sharp relief how race informed their opinions:

> It bothers me because it seems like it's an accepted way of calling somebody the N-word now. It's like everybody else said the N-word and then they say 'thug' and that's fine. What's the definition of a thug? Really? Can a guy on a football field just talking to people [be a thug?] . . . . There was a hockey game where they didn't even play hockey! They just threw the puck aside and started fighting. I saw that and said. . . . I'm the thug? What's going on here?[8]

Sherman's blunt observations and rhetorical questioning would be echoed by local fans. Social media posts from around the city admonished the presence of racial undertones in critiques offered by sports journalists and commentators. Fans appeared on news programs defending their beloved Seahawk and posted reminders about Sherman's Stanford University education, as well as his charming and kind disposition. Seattleites stood by Sherman, supported him through the media frenzy that sought to diminish his character and upset the season's momentum. They refused to allow one of their own to be chided by cynics; distractors would have to take that nonsense elsewhere.[9]

Seattle is a city where diversity and social progress are indeed reflected in, and reinforced by, the history of play. The included narratives of many lesser-known individuals and team sports in this anthology will provide the reader with a more comprehensive understanding of how the city's historical diversity related to race, ethnicity, sexuality, and gender have defined and refashioned local play. The history of Seattle roller derby teams, for instance, and the fierce women who have risen to local stardom have been largely dismissed until now. A truly pioneering examination of gay softball leagues appears in this volume, as does an essay on the centrality of athletics to the cultural and communal development of local Japanese communities during the interwar years. Collectively, the topics covered by scholars, sportswriters, and others in *Seattle Sports* undeniably run the breadth of the relatively young city's diverse, fascinating—at times forgotten or simply devalued—sports history. They investigate a wide range of teams, leagues, characters, and moments that offer a glimpse of how Seattle has functioned as a preeminent sporting center. Of course, the city's renowned sporting empires, including the Seattle Seahawks and SuperSonics, are thoroughly explored; however, the reader will find the lauded victories as well as previously unexamined nuances of those teams' existences included in the following pages. The centrality of some Seattle high schools in the making of NBA greats is also chronicled and will likely challenge those readers who had previously disregarded the city as a basketball trendsetter. Thus, from national championships to intra-communal play and the elimination of racial, ethnic, and gender barriers, the following essays explore the city's highly visible as well as more clandestine sporting moments.

Seattle Sports is not intended as a comprehensive investigation of the city's remarkable sports' history. Despite the expanse of individuals, organizations, and ideas explored in this volume, much remains absent, as with any anthology. The UW's significance in the city's history of sports is certainly included, but not in the manner readers who are even marginally familiar with the city's history might expect. In short, the story of UW's gold medal eight-oar rowing team has been beautifully documented in Daniel James Brown's *Boys in the Boat: Nine Americans and Their Epic Quest for Gold at the 1936 Berlin Olympics* and, therefore, is largely absent in *Seattle Sports*. The story is nonetheless powerful in both its historical significance and the legacy it imparts to the university and the city, in large measure because Adolf Hitler's passage of the anti-Semitic Nuremberg Laws—together with the burgeoning alliance of the Axis Powers—called into question the virtue of participation in the games. Brown explores the complicated and politicized saga of the mainly working-class student-athletes and the city that rallied around them to support their efforts and pay their passage to Germany. "People in the city felt they were stockholders in the operation," recalls Gordon Adam, a member of the team.[10] Those local investors tuned their radios to the Central Broadcasting Station (CBS) the morning of August 14 and listened to their hometown team defeat Germany and Italy while striking blows at fascism and Nazism in the process.[11]

The absence of a chapter on soccer in this volume should not be interpreted as a dismissal of the sport's importance in Seattle. Soccer has enjoyed a steadily increasing presence and popularity in the area since the late nineteenth century. In the 1880s, Irish immigrants organized a soccer league as a retreat from the grueling nature of work in the coal mines. By World War II, multiple local ethnic groups established soccer teams. The sport experienced an upsurge in interest both nationally and locally following the 1966 FIFA World Cup final. By the end of the decade, numerous youth soccer leagues emerged locally and the number of youths playing the sport in the metropolitan has since grown exponentially. Several of those local youth have risen to international stardom. Born in Richland, Washington, goalkeeper Hope Solo, for instance, played soccer at UW before becoming an Olympic gold medalist. Solo also played for several professional teams, including the local Seattle Reign. In 2015, she helped lead her women's national team to FIFA World Cup victory. The popularity of soccer in Seattle is further evidenced, at least in part, by attendance at Sounders matches. Since the team joined MLS in 2009, the Sounders have attracted local interest that far exceeds that experienced by other MLS teams. In 2015, attendance averaged 44,000, approximately twice the average for the league. "Seattle is a place where we know [residents] are going to be 1,000 percent behind us and push us," insisted Jurgen Klinsmann while head coach of the US men's national team.[12] Seattle native and former Sounders defender DeAndre Yedlin echoed Klinsmann's sentiments: "The fans have such a passion for the game and understand the game. They don't stop cheering you on."[13] (In 2015, Yedlin joined the ranks of a small number of Americans to play for the English Premiere League.) From its popularity among local youth to exceptionally well-attended Sounders matches and a highly supportive fan base, soccer is an essential part of the city's identity.[14]

Other, less investigated narratives are also absent in *Seattle Sports*. Alas, an analysis of Elgin Baylor's storied basketball career at Seattle University would certainly have been an exciting addition to this pioneering volume. His story is saved for another time, as are biographical essays on the extraordinary careers of Bruce Lee or Seattle Mariners Felix Hernandez and Ichiro Suzuki. Despite what is not included, *Seattle Sports* will delight readers with the authentic voices, examples of perseverance, and previously veiled stories that fill the following pages.

Authors in this volume abstain from any dabbling in hagiography and reject the lure of revisionism. Their inquiries are honest and refreshingly original while appealing to the broader contours of readers' varied interests. To be sure, the largess of some of Seattle's renowned sporting heroes may be challenged by the research and analyses of contributors to this volume. But the pioneering work that appears in *Seattle Sports* will inspire hope, humor, and resolve.

Today, the city proper boasts a population under one million. Seattle is still a midsize city by most measures, but its sporting prowess is increasingly impressive and should be considered alongside that of America's largest cities. The contributors to this anthology certainly make this case. *Seattle Sports* urges a reconsideration of how we qualify and interpret greatness and define success. "A history of Seattle can be nothing more than a chapter from an uncompleted volume," reasoned Frederic James Grant late in the nineteenth century.[15] The straightforward yet complicated pronouncement made by the state legislator and editor of the *Seattle Post-Intelligencer* reminds us that, no matter how magnificent the relatively young city's history has been thus far, there is much more to come. Sport in Seattle is no exception. Its history has simply been one superb chapter in a volume that promises to be rich with victory and intrigue. Enjoy.[16]

CHAPTER ONE

Winless in Seattle

A History of the Seattle Mariners, 1977–1994

CHRIS DONNELLY

"I also don't think this is a town that will ever draw 25 or 30,000 regularly. It's a town that's much more concerned with culture than athletics."

—Jim Bouton, referring to Seattle in Ball Four

In 1969, there was scant evidence of the skyscrapers that would dot the city streets of Seattle in the years to come. From Puget Sound, one could see the world-famous Space Needle hovering above the city's northern side. To the southeast, with Mount Rainier towering behind it, lay Sick's Stadium. At Sick's, minor league baseball had thrived in Seattle for decades. The Rainiers of the Pacific Coast League had played there since 1938 under the management of such baseball superstars as Rogers Hornsby, the Hall of Fame second baseman, and Lefty O'Doul, who once collected 254 hits in a season for the Philadelphia Phillies.[1] Throughout the years, the Rainiers had been affiliated with several Major League teams, including the Tigers, the Reds, the Red Sox, and the Angels. Because of this affiliation, the Seattle community saw its share of future major leaguers. But decades of local minor league baseball had left a yearning in the Emerald City for a Major League team. When Major League Baseball (MLB) announced that it would be expanding, Seattle—led by King County officials and Washington senator Warren Magnuson—decided to take a shot at receiving Major League affiliation. As would occur so many times throughout the next thirty years, politics played a crucial role in Seattle baseball.[2]

In 1967, the Athletics moved from Kansas City to Oakland, infuriating Missouri senator Stuart Symington. He threatened the American League (AL) with a lawsuit, and the owners decided to quickly appease the senator by agreeing to add two teams to the AL.[3] One would be located in Kansas City while the other would be placed in another not-yet-determined city. Hoping to snare the other team, Seattle sent a delegation led by Senator Magnuson to the 1967 winter meetings of the AL team owners to plead the city's case. Convinced of the viability of baseball in the Pacific Northwest, the owners agreed to award the other team to Seattle based on two conditions. First, Sick's Stadium, which had been simply a minor league park, had to be renovated and enlarged from 11,000 seats to 30,000 seats. Sick's would serve as a temporary home to the new team. Second, the owners demanded that a new stadium be built. A $40 million bond issue to build a domed stadium, with construction beginning no later than December 31, 1970, had to be voted on and passed by residents of Seattle. Dewey and Max Soriano would be the owners of this new team, spawning the birth of Major League Baseball in Seattle.[4]

In February 1968, due largely to a local media blitz and visits to Seattle by baseball players like Mickey Mantle, Carl Yastrzemski, Ron Santo, and Joe DiMaggio, voters approved the bond referendum for what would eventually become the Kingdome. Renovation of Sick's Stadium began and the ball club, named the Pilots, set about building a team for the 1969 season. During the expansion draft, the club acquired such players as Tommy Davis, Diego Segui, Tommy Harper, Don Mincher, Jim Bouton, and rookie Lou Piniella. Expectations for the Pilots were not great, but still, as the 1969 season approached, there was a high level of anticipation from the Seattle community. Once the season began, the ambience surrounding the Pilots disappeared nearly as fast as it had been created.[5]

The Pilots won their first game on April 8, defeating the California Angels in Anaheim, and three days later they would even win their home opener in Seattle. These victories, however, represented the few successes of the franchise. The Pilots were 4-4 after eight games and never reached .500 again. The team suffered from a multitude of problems, not the least of which was a simple lack of talent. The roster featured an assortment of has-beens and never-would-bes. Former All-Stars like Tommy Harper dotted the lineup, but their best years were far behind them. The team's manager, Joe Schultz, referred to as "a short, portly, bald, ruddy-faced, twinkly eyed man" by Jim Bouton in *Ball Four*, had little to work with and he knew it.[6] As the season went along, the team's record and performance gradually worsened.[7]

The Pilots' home facility added to their inaugural season woes. Opened in 1938, Sick's originally seated only 11,000—adequate for a minor league facility but paltry for a Major League park.[8] It consisted of only a single level of seating and was a colorless, unpleasing structure, lacking any of the frills or aesthetic pleasures of a Fenway Park, Yankee Stadium, or Wrigley Field. Charlie Finley, owner of the Athletics, once referred to Sick's Stadium as a "pigsty."[9] Perhaps the only benefit of its small size was the intimacy it created for the fans, who had a superb view of every play. Once Seattle was forced to expand seating capacity after being awarded the Pilots, construction crews set upon Sick's to add another 14,000 seats. A problem arose, however, when the expansion was not completed in time for the start of the 1969 season. On opening day in Seattle, construction workers took breaks to enjoy the action on the field, and those without tickets could leer through holes in the left field fence where seats were planned but not yet added.[10] Even worse, Sick's water pressure was so poor that opposing players preferred to shower at their hotels, and when crowds exceeded 10,000, the toilets stopped flushing.[11]

Adding insult to injury, the Pilots sported the oddest and least attractive uniforms in baseball. Modeled after maritime and aviation uniforms, the team's logo was a ship's wheel surrounding a baseball from which gold wings extended. This logo was sewn onto the chest of both the home and away uniforms. But the most interesting aspect of the uniform was the hat, which featured a single gold *S*. Underneath the *S* was a gold braid and "scrambled eggs," military parlance that refers to leaf-shaped emblems. In essence, the hat mimicked those worn by pilots in the armed forces. "They're so gaudy," wrote Bouton. "We look like goddamn clowns."[12]

Poor performance on the field, a deficient stadium, and ridiculous uniforms were more than enough to keep the fans away. Despite a large ceremony downtown before the Pilots' home opener, which included receiving ceremonial keys to the city, public interest in the team sharply declined within weeks. The Pilots had no television contract and were barely heard on the radio, so unless fans were attending games, there were few ways to follow the team.[13] The poor attendance and lack of a television deal meant the team was losing revenue and could not pay its bills. It was evident as the initial season came to a close that the Pilots were in financial trouble. They needed to draw 850,000 during the 1969 season to break even but only attracted 677,944 spectators.[14] Rumors spread that baseball would not survive in Seattle, but 1970 began without any indication that the Pilots would be playing anywhere else. The team reported to spring training that year. The new manager, Dave Pristol, and his players even posed for their Topps trading cards.[15] As late as March 1, the *Seattle Post-Intelligencer* was still holding a contest to become a Pilots batboy for the summer.[16] Then, everything changed.

Unbeknownst to many, MLB owners had been expressing their disappointment with the situation in Seattle. The Pilots' poor attendance numbers and financial troubles convinced them that baseball would not thrive there. In the middle of spring training, AL officials announced they would have to take a "serious second look" at whether to keep the Pilots in Seattle. On March 31, merely six days before the 1970 season was to start, the Pilots were officially sold and moved to Milwaukee, where they became the Brewers.[17] After just one year, MLB was officially dead in Seattle. But some Seattleites refused to let baseball leave without a fight.

For the first of many times, Slade Gorton stepped in to save baseball in the city. As Washington State's attorney general in 1970, Gorton was livid over the Pilots' departure and moved to sue the AL for breach of contract, claiming they had welshed on several agreements with Seattle by letting the team move to Milwaukee. Gorton, who argued the case with lawyer Bill Dwyer, sought to collect $32.5 million from the league, specifically for funds that Seattle had expended to fix Sick's Stadium and to begin construction on the Kingdome.[18] The lawsuit was not originally intended to bring a Major League team back to the region. When the issue finally went to trial in 1976, a seemingly flabby case against the AL instead backed the owners into a corner. The trial revealed various types of deceit on the owners' behalf, shining a particularly negative light on Oakland A's owner Charlie Finley and former Washington Senators owner Bob Short.[19] Realizing they were on the losing side of the argument, the owners agreed to expand yet again, adding two teams to the AL. One would be located in Toronto and the other in Seattle. In response, Gorton dropped the lawsuit.[20]

Baseball was back in Seattle. Four local businessmen—Stan Golub,

Walter Schoefeld, Jim Walsh, and Jim Stillwell—joined with recording executive Lester Smith and entertainer Danny Kaye as the owners of the new franchise. Housed in a new state-of-the-art facility, the team, called the Mariners, began play before 57,762 at the Kingdome on April 6, 1977.[21] Despite the team's shutout that day by the California Angels, the crowd and the city were elated to have baseball back. The elation, much as it had been for the Pilots, was short-lived. The new baseball team in Seattle would be no different from the old one. Poor upper management, marginal talent, and a subpar playing facility handicapped the Seattle Mariners for years to come.

The 1977 Mariners were shut out in their first two games before winning their third game, one bright spot during a season that saw them lose ninety-eight games. The poor performance could be easily written off as the jitters of an expansion team in its first year. Seattle's problems, however, were more complex than that. In an effort to assemble a team that would win fast and keep fans coming to the ballpark, the ownership had selected the best proven players available during the expansion draft, instead of opting for younger players whose full potential wouldn't blossom for a few years. "They [the other teams] froze all the good players," recalled then-owner Lester Smith. "What were we going to do?"[22] The Mariners ended up with an abundance of players whose best years were long since gone or who would never muster stellar careers. In their initial season, Seattle used an astounding seventeen different starting pitchers, only one of whom won more than eight games.[23] Their top five starters that year—Glenn Abbott, Dick Pole, Gary Wheelock, John Montage, and Tom House—won a combined total of just 146 games in their Major League careers. Frank MacCormick, who began the season in the Mariners' starting rotation, lasted only three starts and was back in Single-A ball before the year was over.[24] The Mariners' inability to draft a substantial amount of young talent, particularly pitchers, would cripple the franchise for years. Instead of progressing through the early years, even by just baby steps, the Mariners were as bad or worse in the seasons after 1977. They lost 98 games in 1977, 104 in 1978, 95 in 1979, and 103 in 1980. Excluding the truncated schedule of October, the Mariners did not have a month in which they posted a winning record until June 1979.[25] The failure to show even a hint of improvement pushed the fan base away in droves. After drawing over 1.3 million to the Kingdome during the initial season, attendance fell to just 836,000 in 1980, a disastrous 36 percent drop in just four seasons.[26] The lethargy extended to the media. In the late

1970s, *Seattle Times* sports editor Georg Meyers informed Mariners public relations director Randy Adamack that he had "no interest in baseball" and that Adamack would not see him at any games.[27] Who could blame Meyers? Editors, writers, and fans had little reason to show up, outside of witnessing the purely entertaining ways the Mariners found to lose.

During a July 10 game against the Twins in 1977, Mariners starting pitcher Stan Thomas attempted to hit the Twins' Mike Cubbage due to a long-standing feud between the two. Thomas threw at Cubbage four times with the intention of hitting him and missed each time. The Mariners lost that game 15–0, and Mariners manager Darrell Johnson hit Thomas with the highest fine he gave a player in his managerial career.[28]

In September 1979, the Mariners started a rookie pitcher named Roy Branch against the Texas Rangers. The first pitch Branch threw in the Major Leagues was hit for a home run by Mickey Rivers, making Branch the first pitcher in seven years to have accomplished such a feat.[29] The Mariners lost the game 5–2, and Branch made only one more start in the Major Leagues. Byron McLaughlin, who pitched for the Mariners from 1977 to 1980, once missed a start because he mistakenly thought the game, which began in the afternoon, was scheduled to start at night. In 1980, pitcher Rick Honeycutt was ejected from a game and eventually suspended for using a thumbtack bandaged to his finger to scuff the ball.[30]

There was also Mario Mendoza, a light-hitting shortstop whom the Mariners acquired from the Pittsburgh Pirates in 1979. During his first season in Seattle, Mendoza mustered only a .198 batting average. It was one of the worst single-season averages in baseball history for a full-time player.[31] Eventually, the Kansas City Royals' George Brett was glancing at player's batting averages in the newspaper and quipped, "I knew I was off to a bad start when I saw my average listed below the Mendoza Line."[32] The expression stuck, and from that point on, any player who failed to hit higher than .200 was said to be below the "Mendoza Line."

It was all part of the Seattle legacy of embarrassment, and by 1981, the original owners had had it. The team was no better than the expansion team of 1977 and had not drawn more than a million fans in any season since then. Facing extreme financial hardships, the owners decided to sell the team to George Argyros. Born in Detroit to second-generation Greek Americans, Argyros had moved to Pasadena with his family when he was ten. He had attended Michigan State University and graduated from Chapman College, where he majored in business and economics.[33] By 1981, he was a wealthy real estate developer who had purchased the former San Clemente home of President Richard Nixon.[34] The opportunity to buy the Mariners came his way thanks to Hall of Famer Harmon Killebrew, who notified him of the team owners' intent to sell.[35] He made an offer to buy the team and the owners accepted. Argyros paid $10.4 million for an 80 percent share of the team. Original owners Golub, Smith, Schoenfeld, and Kaye each maintained a meager 5 percent share. When asked why the AL would allow someone outside of Seattle to purchase the club, league president Lee MacPhail's response was telling of the type of future the team had in store. "There was nobody around willing to purchase the club locally," said MacPhail.[36]

Argyros was originally received as a savior in Seattle. He would keep the team in the city, and since he was a wealthy business owner, it was believed he could run the club with more structure and acquire better talent than the previous ownership. The honeymoon was short-lived. Though acquaintances would refer to Argyros's big heart and point to his various acts of small kindness and courtesies—including contributions to the Boy Scouts, programs for abused children, and cultural activities—his legacy in Seattle would be that of a penny-pinching owner who presided over the worst trades in club history, allowed some of the best players to sign with other teams, hired and fired managers on impulse, and generally ran the club with little knowledge of the actual game itself. It all went downhill from the beginning.[37]

In fairness to Argyros, he walked into an extremely difficult situation. As the New York Times wrote in a 1981 team preview, "People who have watched the Mariners in spring training suspect they could be a disaster."[38] "We needed to start from scratch," said Argyros. "The Mariners had gotten short-changed in the expansion draft. We had to expand the farm system, develop players, and it wasn't easy."[39] In a strike-shortened season, the team finished 45-65 and placed next to last in league attendance.[40] Part of the reason for the disaster was the team's manager at the beginning of the year, Maury Wills. Wills had been hired in 1980 to replace Darrell Johnson, but unbeknownst to Seattle management, Wills was battling a serious drug problem. The result was a series of strange and erratic decisions that drew further ridicule upon a team already on pace to be perennial losers. Asked before the start of the 1981 season who his center fielder would be, Wills replied, "I wouldn't be surprised if it was Leon Roberts." Apparently Wills did not know or did not remember that

Roberts had been traded from Seattle weeks earlier.[41] During a spring training game in 1981, Wills went to the mound and signaled for a right-handed
pitcher, but there was no right-hander warming up.[42]

The biggest gaffe Wills committed, however, couldn't be blamed on a
simple verbal mistake or inattention. It was just downright cheating. Before
an April 25 game against the A's at the Kingdome, Wills instructed the
Mariners' grounds crew to make the batter's box six inches longer in front
than normal. The purpose was to allow Tom Paciorek, a Mariner outfielder
who liked to stand near the front of the box, a little more room. Paciorek
had recently been called out for stepping outside the box on a swing and
Wills thought the box extension would give him an advantage.[43] Inexplicably,
Wills did not think that either the umpires or the opposing players would
notice the extra length. Sure enough, before the game even started, A's
manager Billy Martin noticed and brought it to umpire Bill Kunkel's attention. Kunkel measured the box and saw it was too long.[44] Wills was fined
$500 and suspended two games for the stunt.[45] In his autobiography, Wills
shirked responsibility and blamed the entire incident on his grounds crew
for informing Billy Martin of the extra distance.[46] The Mariners got off to a
6-18 start under Wills in 1981, and he was finally fired.

Wills had not been George Argyros's hire, so there was no blood on his
hands for Wills's actions. The firing allowed Argyros to make his first managerial decision, and he did—sort of. On the advice of a beat writer from
the *Seattle Post-Intelligencer* named Tracy Ringolsby, Argyros hired Rene
Lachemann.[47] The move appeared to pay off. Although the Mariners floun-
dered through the rest of the 1981 season, they played well throughout the
early part of 1982. Finally armed with a capable starting rotation—featuring
pitchers such as Floyd Bannister, Gaylord Perry, and Jim Beattie—the
Mariners were three games over .500 on July 28 and only five games out of
first. The team then fell apart, going 25-38 the rest of the year and finishing
seventeen games out of first place. The Mariners played their final home
game of the year before only 6,742 people.[48] In fact, despite drawing over one
million fans for the first time in five years, the Mariners' attendance had been
a particular source of embarrassment for them in 1982, thanks to a bizarre
promotional giveaway. In 1981, Tom Paciorek had filmed a commercial for
the Mariners, falsely claiming there would be a Funny Nose Glasses Night
at the Kingdome when it was actually Mariners Jacket Night. As a result of
the commercial, however, the Mariners decided to have Funny Nose Glasses

Night on May 8, 1982 during a Saturday night game against the Yankees. Players, fans, and even Argyros sported a pair as nearly 37,000 people filled the Kingdome that night for the kooky promotion. Two nights earlier against the Yankees, with Gaylord Perry on the mound looking for his 300th career victory, the Mariners had drawn only 27,000 fans. A player making baseball history attracted 10,000 fewer fans than the plastic-nose giveaway.[49]

By 1983, the relationship between George Argyros and his manager was crumbling. Some owners took a hands-off approach to their team, but Argyros was a constant second-guesser, and it was common for him to call down to the dugout during a game. The behavior wore on Lachemann, who didn't hide his displeasure with his boss. Of Argyros, Lachemann once remarked, "He was just a fan, one who didn't know the game."[50] During an eight-game losing streak in the middle of 1983, Lachemann was let go with the team's record at 26-47. The firing did not endear Argyros to the Mariners' clubhouse, where Lachemann was known as a players' manager. "There were a lot of guys with tears in their eyes," said Mariners relief pitcher Bill Caudill after the announcement. "This is like losing a best friend . . . it was heaven playing for Lach."[51]

Lachemann would be the first in a series of Seattle managers to come and go under Argyros. All told, eight men would serve in that position during the eight years Argyros owned the team. None would last more than two full seasons, and none would leave with a winning record. "We had one-day managers, one-month managers, one-week managers," said Julio Cruz, who played second base for Seattle for six seasons.[52] Replacing Lachemann was Del Crandall, a former manager of the Brewers whose most recent managerial job had been with the Albuquerque Dukes of the Pacific Coast League. "We are a young franchise and a young franchise needs careful handling. I believe Del Crandall is a winner and a leader," said George Argyros after the hiring.[53] But Crandall was unable to guide the Mariners toward success. They went 34-55 the rest of the 1983 season, finishing in last place in the AL West. They were no better in 1984, posting a 55-76 record before Crandall was let go.

Argyros made an internal hire next when he replaced Crandall with Chuck Cottier, the Mariners' third base coach at the time. Under Cottier, the Mariners went 15-12 to finish the season, offering a possible glimmer of hope for 1985. The hope faded as the Mariners went 74-88 in 1985 and finished in sixth place. When the team started the 1986 season slowly, Cottier was fired.

Cottier had the highest winning percentage of any manager in team history at .452, but the Mariners had not gotten any better in the season-and-a-half he was at the helm.[54] Cottier also had the unfortunate distinction of having to watch two of the more embarrassing moments in Mariner history. The first came on July 10, 1985, when the Mariners had two runners thrown out at home plate on the same play. Playing at the Kingdome against the Blue Jays, Phil Bradley tried to score from second base on a single to right field and collided with catcher Buck Martinez at home. Bradley was called out, but in the process, he dislocated Martinez's ankle. Martinez, still on his back, threw to third base, trying to nail an advancing Gorman Thomas. The throw went wild and Thomas headed home, but the Blue Jays quickly recovered and threw to Martinez who, still lying on the ground, scooped the ball and tagged Thomas out on the leg for an unconventional 9-2-6-2 double play.[55]

The second embarrassment came on April 29, 1986, when Boston Red Sox pitcher Roger Clemens set a Major League record by striking out twenty Mariners in a nine-inning game. It was not long after Clemens's performance that Cottier was let go. Before a permanent replacement for Cottier was found, Mariners third base coach Marty Martinez was named acting manager for one game. The Mariners lost that game, 4–2. Even a one-day manager had a losing record for Seattle.[56]

The day after that loss, the Mariners hired Dick Williams, a well-established and successful manager. Williams, who had previously led three different teams to the World Series, was an old-school hardcore manager. Unlike Crandall or Lachemann, he was not regarded as a player's manager.[57] "I'm demanding," said Williams at his initial press conference. "I'm not hired to be a nice guy."[58] As with previous managers, Williams received praise from his new boss. "In Dick Williams, the Seattle Mariners will have an experienced manager who is an established winner," said Argyros. "He is a World Series championship manager." But the Mariners were not a World Series team, and they finished last in 1986—their fourth last-place finish in ten seasons. They improved in 1987 as Williams led them to their best finish in history. But for the Mariners, best finish was a relative term as they still lost eighty-four games and finished in fourth place. In 1988, they got off to another sluggish start and rumors swirled that Williams would be let go. With the team at 16-22, Argyros tried to downplay any such talk. "Dick is an experienced manager and if anyone can turn this team around, he can," the Mariners owner told the Associated Press.[59] Apparently, then, no one could turn the team around because after that statement, the Mariners went

7-11. By that time, it was a badly kept secret that many players were unhappy with Williams's management style. Pitcher Mark Langston had been critical of Williams, telling the media that "leadership starts with the manager and if it's not working, then something has to be done. This team is going in the wrong direction and we've worked too hard for that."[60] The day after Langston's comment, Williams was let go, though all involved said Langston's remarks had nothing to do with the move. "I think Dick had lost control of the club," remarked Mariners general manager Dick Balderson on the day of the firing.[61] Though he offered nothing but praise for his newly departed manager, Argyros was blunt about the state of the team: "I'm disappointed and I'm tired, tired of this losing."[62] The losing would continue under interim manager Jim Snyder as the Mariners finished the season last in the division, thirty-five games behind first-place Oakland.

During the off-season, Argyros hired Jim Lefebvre, the last of eight men to serve under him as manager. Lefebvre "was our No. 1 choice because he's a winner," declared Mariners executive Woody Woodward the day Lefebvre was hired.[63] For Mariners fans, it was an all-too-familiar declaration. For all the talk about hiring managers who were proven winners, Seattle had nothing to show for it. By 1989, the Mariners had been in the AL for twelve seasons without once finishing .500 or better. Their best season had only resulted in a fourth-place finish. By contrast, the Toronto Blue Jays, who had entered the AL with Seattle in 1977, had finished higher than .500 six times, made the playoffs in 1985, had only four managers in their history, and were perennial contenders in the AL East.

Under Argyros's management, Seattle also became infamous for constantly trading away its best players or allowing them to walk via free agency. Argyros was notoriously tightfisted and did not believe in signing players to long-term contracts.[64] "Costs were so high, and we had a poor lease with the stadium. There just wasn't enough revenue to support baseball," said Argyros.[65] The result was a series of teams that played below-average baseball, a fan base that had no desire to witness it in person, and a feeling around the league that flourishing as a player in Seattle wasn't possible because you'd simply be traded away. "If you were a good player with a rising salary, they said, 'We're going to lose [him] anyway; let's get rid of him,'" said Dave Henderson, who would himself be a victim of Seattle's purging of talented players.[66]

"Ownership was unstable," recalled Ken Phelps, who played with the

Mariners from 1983 to 1988. "You wondered who would be around for the next season. There were never any three- or four-year contracts. Most contracts were year-to-year."[67]

"In my heart, I truly believe we could have been as good as Oakland was in their heyday," said Chuck Cottier, referring to the loss of quality player after quality player. "You saw what happened to them when they went to other organizations. They had nice careers and wound up as millionaires with other teams."[68]

"We'd start to make progress, but then we wouldn't make it all the way and changes would happen," recalled Phil Bradley, a Mariners outfielder for four seasons who was eventually traded away to the Phillies. "The Angels would start the year with twenty veterans and five rookies, but we'd start with twenty rookies and five veterans because of the trades. I can't recall a person actually becoming a free agent. They'd always be traded first once they became too expensive."[69]

The legacy of failed transactions and of the inability to retain players began on October 23, 1981, when the Mariners traded away a player to the Kansas City Royals for Manny Castillo. Castillo played one full season with Seattle in 1982, batting just .257 with 3 home runs. Perhaps his greatest notoriety came when the Mariners had him pitch in a game against the Blue Jays. Castillo gave up 7 earned runs in less than three innings.[70] After 1983, he never played another game in the majors. The player traded away in the deal was pitcher Bud Black. Black would have a respectable career, winning 121 games and helping the Royals to their first world championship in 1985.

Floyd Bannister was the Mariners' most consistent pitcher from 1979 to 1982, averaging 10 wins a year and striking out 209 hitters during the 1982 season. A free agent at the end of that season, Bannister left Seattle and signed with the White Sox, where he won seventeen games and led them to the postseason. He went on to win ten or more games during each of the next six seasons after he left Seattle.

Before the start of the 1986 season, the Mariners traded Darnell Coles to the Tigers for relief pitcher Rich Monteleone. Coles hit 20 home runs and drove in 86 runs for Detroit that year while Monteleone pitched only three games for the Mariners before being released. The Coles trade was merely a preview of the fire sale that would occur in Seattle during 1986. On June 26, Seattle sent a player to the White Sox for Scott Bradley. Bradley was a light-hitting catcher who went on to play several seasons with the

Mariners, but his offensive production tended to be marginal as he never hit more than 5 home runs in a season or batted higher than .278. The player sent to the White Sox was Ivan Calderon. Calderon was an outfielder and had batted .286 for Seattle in 1985, making minor contributions. After moving to Chicago, he burst out with 27 home runs in 1987 and made the All-Star team in 1991, just a year before Bradley retired.

Following the trade of Calderon, the Mariners pulled off one of the most disappointing moves in team history when they sent outfielder Dave Henderson and shortstop Spike Owen to the Red Sox for cash, infielder Rey Quinones, and three other players. The trade, done to dump high-profile players to a team that was contending, proved to be a disaster. Henderson, the Mariners' first-ever draft pick, had been one of the few legitimate stars in Seattle during the early eighties, and he was shocked by the move. "When you get traded from the organization that drafted you No. 1 and was going to build around you, it hits you right in the stomach," he remarked about the trade.[71] Henderson went on to hit one of the biggest home runs in post-season history that year for the Red Sox, propelling them into the World Series. He also won a championship with Oakland in 1989.

Spike Owen, though not one of the game's elite shortstops, was a steady force defensively and had a respectable career with several teams before retiring after the 1995 season. The players the Mariners received in return made no significant contributions to the team. Quinones, though an offensive upgrade over Owen at shortstop, played only two seasons with Seattle before being traded to Pittsburgh. He was out of baseball by 1989. The three players Seattle received later were all playing for different teams by 1988.

The final disaster of 1986 came in December when the team sent Danny Tartabull and a minor leaguer to the Kansas City Royals for pitchers Scott Bankhead and Steve Shields and outfielder Mike Kingery. Tartabull had risen through the Mariner system as an infielder though he eventually moved to the outfield. In 1986, he hit 25home runs and drove in 95 runs. Instead of embracing this newly found offense, the Mariners traded him. The next year in Kansas City, Tartabull hit 34home runs. He would have five 100-runs batted in (RBI) seasons in his post-Seattle career. Bankhead had enjoyed moderate success in Seattle, including a career year in 1989, but injuries and pitching in a hitter's park took their toll on his statistics. Shields pitched twenty games for the Mariners in 1987 and posted an earned run average (ERA) of 6.60. He left via free agency after the season was over. Kingery had a respectable 1987 season but was regulated to mostly part-time or pinch-hitting duties in 1988 and 1989 before leaving the team. The Mariners had traded away hundreds of RBIs and received little in return.

Phil Bradley was an exceptional athlete who showed flashes of power and speed. He hit over .300 for Seattle in 1984, 1985, and 1986. In 1987, he stole over 40 bases and scored 101 runs. Those attributes made him increasingly more expensive as the years went by. Bradley had beaten the Mariners twice in arbitration, which he believed irritated the team's owners. Rather than resort to arbitration a third time, they traded him to the Phillies on December 9, 1987. In return the Mariners received outfielder Glen Wilson, pitcher Mike Jackson, and a minor leaguer. Wilson flopped in Seattle and was traded during the 1988 season. Jackson turned out to be a key acquisition for the Mariners, but he too would eventually be shipped to another team in possibly the worst trade in franchise history.

After the 1988 season, Mike Moore, considered one of the team's best right-handed starters, left via free agency and joined the Oakland A's. Moore won nineteen games for the A's in 1989 as they went on to a world championship. Black, Coles, Calderon, Henderson, Owen, Tartabull, Bradley, and Moore. Though not a list of Hall of Famers, they were all good players who went on to make major contributions after leaving the Mariners. The continuing parade of managers and loss of talented players fueled Mariners fans' animosity toward Argyros. Perhaps no move, however, infuriated fans more than Argyros's attempt to buy the San Diego Padres in 1987.

In March 1987, Argyros was fighting with the city over a new lease for the Kingdome. He had just announced that the Mariners were close to signing free agent Tim Raines, the National League batting champion (though Raines's agent announced that Argyros knew Raines had ruled out going to Seattle months ago).[72] Suddenly on March 26, Argyros announced that he was putting the Mariners up for sale and purchasing the San Diego Padres. He said that personal issues required him to spend "an ever-increasing amount of time in Southern California."[73] Although he pledged to sell the team to a local owner, thus preventing the Mariners from moving out of Seattle, Argyros's announcement made him Public Enemy Number One in the Pacific Northwest. He was booed heavily on opening night at the Kingdome, and a police escort led him from the stadium.[74] Fans in the Kingdome began to cheer any time it was posted that the Padres were losing and referred to San Diego as "George's Other Team."[75] Things got worse for Argyros when on April 16 he called Padres manager Larry Bowa to congratulate him on San Diego's victory over the Dodgers that night. Argyros was still the owner of the Mariners, and he had been warned not to contact any player, coach, or the manager of San Diego. Argyros's call might have gone unnoticed had National League president Bart Giamatti not been sitting in Bowa's office at the time of the call. Giamatti reported the incident to Commissioner Peter Ueberroth, who in turn slapped Argyros with a $10,000 fine.[76] Within weeks, the deal to buy the Padres fell apart. Argyros was no closer to home, stuck with a team he apparently didn't want, and surrounded by fans who apparently didn't want him.

By the winter of 1989, Argyros had had enough of Seattle baseball. The team had not improved since he had taken over, and the fans were not coming to the ballpark. The Mariners had finished last in attendance in 1988, further fueling the idea that baseball could not exist in Seattle. To some, the region would never support a team, even a successful one, because Seattle people simply were not interested in the sport. This theory was supported by the absence of any local interest in purchasing the club when Argyros put it up for sale that winter. The threat of the team leaving, just as the Pilots had, hung in the air. Then came Jeff Smulyan, another wealthy businessman who appeared to be the savior of the Mariners. Like Argyros, Smulyan was an out-of-towner, coming from Indianapolis, where he had made his money as a radio mogul. He purchased the team for $76 million.[77] Despite the lack of success that had occurred on his watch, Argyros sold the team for $76 million, earning himself a $63 million profit. In retrospect, some of the harshest criticisms of Argyros may not be deserved. "He was portrayed as trying to extort the community, but that was not true. The columnists were always pointing out that he lived out of town. You couldn't blame George for all the difficulties, but after '87, the community couldn't think well of him," said George Armstrong, who served as the Mariners' team president under Argyros.[78] While Argyros certainly pinched pennies wherever he could, the fiscal condition of the team left him little choice in terms of keeping or signing high-quality players. Of course, the large profit he pocketed despite the team's financial straits and lagging attendance can also cause one to ask why more money was not available to improve the team.

"There will be more promotions, more fun, and a better team," said Jeff Smulyan shortly after buying the team.[79] Like Argyros, Smulyan was greeted as a hero in Seattle. He announced his intention to go after marquee play-ers and even to move the fences at the Kingdome back to make the field more pitcher-friendly.[80] But as it was with Argyros, the honeymoon was short-lived. Smulyan proved no different in terms of acquisitions. Under his ownership, Seattle made the worst trade in franchise history when the Mariners dealt pitchers Bill Swift, Dave Burba, and Michael Jackson to the San Francisco Giants for outfielder Kevin Mitchell. Mitchell would play one season in Seattle, during which he hit only 9 home runs and became a clubhouse problem.[81] Eventually, rumors swirled that Smulyan was simply biding his time in Seattle before he could move the team to another city. By the winter of 1992, the Mariners remained unprofitable. Smulyan, who reportedly still owed creditors $39.5 million for the purchase of the Mariners, was forced to put the team up for sale. Luckily for Seattle, the team's lease with the city had a provision that said if the team was put up for sale, a 120-day window had to be left open for a local buyer to be found.[82] That clause probably saved Seattle baseball.

In 1991, the Mariners finally finished over .500. It was a joyous moment for a team that had known nothing but losing. Still, it was an example of how badly things had gone that the team was actually celebrating a .500 record as if they had made the playoffs. Shortly after the season ended, manager Jim Lefebvre was fired, and Smulyan put the team up for sale. The joy of finally producing a winning season was washed away by the turmoil of off-season events. But the sale of the team, which some thought would spell the immi-nent demise of the Mariners, proved to be a blessing in disguise. The sale, along with other behind-the-scenes factors, would turn the Mariners from a laughingstock into the 1995 AL West champions.

During the winter of 1992, the prevailing belief was that the Seattle Mariners were headed out of town. Jeff Smulyan was informing other Major League owners of his plans to locate the team elsewhere—possibly Tampa, Florida—believing that no local buyer would risk the asking price for the team: $100 million.[83] In Seattle, a small group of people was banding together to try and save the club and was not having much luck. A group of local business owners appointed Herman Sarkowsky, the former part-owner of the Seattle Seahawks, to head up a committee to find a local buyer for the Mariners as well as to drum up local business support to increase revenue. "It was difficult," recalled Sarkowsky. "We formed a committee and contacted businesspeople and some promises were made that they would buy commercials." But the deals fell apart in the end.[84] Trying to find a local buyer was even worse. Microsoft and Boeing were in the Mariners' backyard, but neither corporation showed any interest in purchasing the team. Finally, Slade Gorton, now a US senator, thought outside the box. He went searching for an investor and found someone who had never seen a Mariners game in his life yet was willing to buy the team.

"When it became obvious that Smulyan was selling the team to Tampa, I thought of reaching out to Japanese investors," said Gorton, looking back at one of the most critical moments in Mariner history. "I'd thought of them before when Argyros was going to sell the team after he'd bought the Padres. I thought of Nintendo and had my secretary set up the meeting."[85] By 1991, Nintendo was a hugely successful Japanese video game company that had an office located in Redmond, just outside of Seattle. The president of the American branch company was Minoru Arakawa, who just happened to be the son-in-law of Hiroshi Yamauchi, head of Nintendo Company Ltd. Arakawa, along with his senior vice president, Howard Lincoln, agreed to meet with the senator, though Arakawa was not particularly interested in baseball.[86] Gorton explained to them that the community had exhausted all possibilities and that, while some local parties were interested, none of them could do it by themselves. Gorton was looking for potential Japanese investors to buy the Mariners and hoped they could inform him of anyone they knew who might be interested.[87] When Arakawa relayed this message to Yamauchi, his father-in-law advised him to look no further, telling him, "I will do it."[88] Arakawa relayed the message to Lincoln, who had been a Mariners fan for years. Lincoln was flabbergasted. "You've gotta be out of your fucking mind," Lincoln replied. "Do you know what it's like to own the Mariners? He'll [Yamauchi] be greeted as a hero at first, but once the team goes downhill, he will be vilified."[89] Yamauchi did not care. To him, it was a public relations gesture. The region had been very good to Yamauchi and his business, so he decided to give them something in return by keeping the Mariners in Seattle. On December 23, 1991, a very sick Slade Gorton got a phone call from Arakawa, informing Gorton that Arakawa's father-in-law would purchase not just part of the team but the entire $100 million asking price. "It was the greatest Christmas present I got in my life," said Gorton, who even sixteen years later still grinned from ear to ear just thinking about that moment.[90]

Gorton knew, though, that once the other baseball owners got a whiff of Yamauchi's proposition, they would try to stop it. Allowing a Japanese businessman to purchase a Major League team would be allowing someone into an extremely exclusive club that didn't particularly want him. There was a large concern, particularly at that time in the United States, that Japan was conquering certain aspects of the business world and threatening American supremacy in various areas. If one Japanese owner was allowed in, how soon would it be before others followed suit? How long would it be before all American teams were Japanese-owned? Another concern was Yamauchi's vast wealth, estimated at over $1 billion, and whether he would use this personal fortune to begin purchasing the game's best players.[91] Hoping to quell these concerns, Gorton met with Arakawa and Lincoln and informed them that they had to find local buyers to join Yamauchi, or it wouldn't work.[92] They all agreed, and so John Ellis, CEO of Puget Power & Light Company and a friend of Gorton's, was asked to become a part-owner. "I told them I wasn't a baseball guy and I didn't have that kind of money," said Ellis. They moved on, but shortly thereafter, they approached Ellis again, this time asking that he represent the group that intended to purchase the team. By now, the group included Yamauchi as majority owner, along with several other people as minority owners. Ellis agreed, mostly out of civic duty and because he didn't think it would be a long commitment. "But weeks turned into months," said Ellis.[93]

After a meeting with Commissioner Fay Vincent was canceled, the group of would-be owners decided it needed to get the public on its side and put pressure on the rest of the MLB owners. The group scheduled a press conference on January 23, 1992, in the ballroom of the Madison Hotel in downtown Seattle. There, John Ellis announced to the world "his" group's intention to purchase the Mariners. "I had never been in a meeting with so much press before," recalled then–Seattle mayor Norm Rice, who had also been involved in the search to find a local buyer. "They hung on our every word. That news conference really did bring on so much attention to the issue."[94] It especially caught the attention of the other Major League owners and Commissioner Vincent, who issued a statement that same day declaring that baseball "has a strong policy against approving investors from outside the U.S. and Canada" and that the chance of the deal going through was unlikely.[95] Public backlash against the MLB owners and Vincent was harsh as they faced charges of big-otry and racism. They eventually eased their position and made clear that they wouldn't oppose involvement of a foreign investor. The only question was how much involvement they would tolerate. Several of the would-be owners met with the MLB ownership committee in April, and the committee made it clear that no one with even a connection to Yamauchi would be allowed to have control of the team. That included Arakawa and Lincoln. "It was made clear to us that they would only accept limited Japanese ownership," said Lincoln. "On the flight back from the meeting I thought of using John [Ellis] because they trusted him. That broke the dam and was considered accept-able."[96] Ellis would become the team's general managing partner, although MLB required that Ellis invest $250,000 in the purchase of the team. Lincoln accepted Ellis, who had merely agreed to be the titular head of this group because he felt it was a civic duty that would not take up too much of his time, was now going to be in charge of the Mariners.

In the end, various aspects of the original deal were changed. Yamauchi reduced his ownership share to 49 percent and shifted part of his investment into a $25 million fund for the new owners to use for capital improvements. Lincoln, Arakawa, Ellis, Chris Larson, John McCaw, Craig Watjen, and Frank Schrontz would form a seven-member board of directors, and ownership was divided up in such a way that prevented Yamauchi from having a majority control of operations.[97] Chuck Armstrong, who had been president of the Mariners from 1983 to 1989, returned to that position. By July 1992, the sale was official. "Yamauchi accepted all these restrictions with an 'OK' atti-tude," said Lincoln.[98] Yamauchi's attitude was remarkable, considering the xenophobia he faced for making what he considered a gesture of goodwill toward Seattle. Regardless, after fifteen long years, the Mariners now had a solid, locally based ownership that was going to change the way things happened in the Kingdome.

"We concluded that all of the owners had to be treated as equal partners," said Howard Lincoln. "We held monthly ownership meetings where every-one would be heard from and free to express their views. We had new-owner syndrome where we all thought 'We can turn this team into a winner.'"[99] One of the first ways they decided to start becoming a winner was by getting a new manager.

Despite finishing .500 in 1991, the Mariners endured a horrific 1992 season that saw them lose ninety-eight games and attendance dropped by 500,000. Manager Bill Plummer was let go after just one season, and the new ownership began a search for its first manager. John Ellis approached Chuck Armstrong and General Manager Woody Woodward with a proposition. "I asked them to give me a list of their top ten choices for manager," said Ellis. The two were not to discuss or compare their lists to one another's before submitting it. Armstrong and Woodward complied, each listing ten choices. Only one name was on both their lists, and coincidentally, they both had it listed as their number one choice: Lou Piniella.[100] Not only was Piniella a proven manager who had taken bad teams and turned them into winners, but he was someone with credibility. Hiring him would show Mariner fans that these new owners were serious when they said they wanted to create a winner. Piniella wouldn't just make the team better—he would get people in the seats, too.

Like so many others, Piniella did not distinguish himself as a player in his short time with Seattle, although he had a very successful career after leaving the city. He had been on the 1969 Seattle Pilots club but did not make it out of spring training before being traded to the Kansas City Royals. There, he won the 1969 Rookie of the Year award, and he eventually made his way to the New York Yankees and became a key component of the "Bronx Zoo" era teams. Piniella played hard and was fiercely dedicated to winning. He had a penchant for clutch hits, including a ninth-inning game-winning single during the third game of the 1978 World Series. His playing career ended with the Yankees in 1984, and he became their manager two years later. Piniella's first go-around as a manager was not easy as he became one of a string of managers that had to contend with the intricacies of Yankees owner George Steinbrenner. Piniella made it through two complete seasons—no small task at the time—before being replaced by Billy Martin for the start of the 1988 season. Martin was fired halfway through the year, and Piniella returned to the dugout to finish out the season. He did not return in 1989, instead taking another position within the Yankee organization. In 1990, Piniella accepted a managerial position with the Cincinnati Reds. It was in Cincinnati that he cemented his reputation as a successful manager, leading the Reds to victory against the heavily favored A's in the 1990 World Series. He also cemented other aspects of his managerial style. Piniella engaged in a clubhouse fight with Reds relief pitcher Rob Dibble, and the entire incident was caught on camera. He was legendary for his outbursts at umpires, but his fight with Dibble displayed to the public what those who had played for him already knew: Piniella did not take shit from anyone, not umpires, not coaches, and certainly not his own players. He could be especially hard on catchers. His dislike for pitchers, particularly those who could not find the plate, was also well known.

Though they slipped in 1991, the Reds rebounded to win ninety-two games in 1992 but fell short of making the playoffs. Piniella, in the final year of his contract, was hugely popular in Cincinnati and easily could have returned.[101] The Reds offered him an extension, but his mind was focused elsewhere. Unfortunately for Piniella, a series of business interests had soured during the course of the early nineties, and many of his partners went bankrupt. He felt he had to leave baseball for a while and return to his home in New Jersey to get his finances in order.[102] Little did he know that on the other side of the country, a few men were plotting to thwart his plans. After receiving both Woodward and Armstrong's managerial choice list, Ellis and others began making their play for Piniella. Woody Woodward knew Piniella from his days as a Yankee executive and asked him to come to Seattle to meet the new owners. "I'll come out," Piniella told Woodward, "but I have no interest in the job." Piniella told his wife, Anita, the same thing. He was only going out there as a courtesy.[103] Piniella met with Ellis, Woodward, Armstrong, and part-owners Chris Larson, Jeff Raikes, and Craig Watjen at Salish Lodge, a restaurant approximately thirty miles outside Seattle. "Some of the guys really grilled him," said a somewhat embarrassed Ellis, "but Lou handled it all well."[104] After dinner, Ellis told Piniella they really wanted him to be their manager. Piniella wasn't convinced yet. He liked Ellis, but he had committed himself to taking care of his financial obligations and knew his wife would not approve.[105] The next day, after Piniella had flown back home, Ellis called to tell him, "We would really like to see you as manager, but I'm not convinced this would be anything but a short-term job." By implying he didn't think Piniella could turn around the Mariners, Ellis was indirectly challenging his ability as a manager. The tactic worked. Piniella took the bait and, much to the disapproval of Anita, accepted the job. "I made him so mad that he would show me that he was up to it," said Ellis.[106]

"When Lou came in, you noticed the change immediately," said Jay Buhner, who had been with the Mariners since 1988.[107] Buhner had come from the Yankees, where winning was expected day in and day out. His experiences once he arrived in Seattle had shocked him. Not just the losing but the attitude around the team and city that losing was okay. That changed when Lou Piniella arrived in the spring of 1993.

"Lou was very instrumental in [my] signing with the team," said Chris Bosio, a starting pitcher who had signed with the Mariners before the 1993 season. "I felt the team could win quickly [with Lou there]."[108]

Piniella swept into training camp like a hurricane, immediately making clear that the misgivings and sins of Mariners teams of the past would not be tolerated. After an early spring training loss, he ordered the food room in the Mariners clubhouse to be locked up. When players began griping about it, Piniella exploded. "I'm tired of this," he yelled in one of many memorable clubhouse tirades. "This isn't a fucking country club. We got the motherfucking sandwiches and the motherfucking pizza. We got the fucking mini-bars. I'm sick and tired of this shit."[109]

The tirades continued. The Mariners had to play all of spring training on the road in 1993 because their complex in Peoria would not be complete until the next year. Constantly being on the road did not ease the pressure. Neither did an early spring training-losing streak that culminated when the Mariners lost a game in the ninth inning. On the bus afterward, Piniella sat up and, to no one in particular, began muttering out loud, "I can't believe this. There is no way these guys are this fucking bad. No way." As he kept muttering, Piniella spotted some kids playing baseball in a sand lot. "Stop the motherfucking bus!" he shouted. "You see those guys, those guys can play the game. Maybe we could beat these motherfuckers!"[110] The tirades continued into the regular season. Some bordered on the comical, such as the time Piniella pushed over a postgame spread and the clubhouse carpet caught fire. Piniella kept yelling and didn't notice the flames before players doused them with milk.

But even the comical moments got their point across. Piniella was obsessed with winning, and he instilled that type of attitude into his players. "Lou came in [during] spring training and said, 'Within three years, we will be in the playoffs,'" said Mariners trainer Rick Griffin. "That started people thinking not about .500, but about the playoffs."[111] It was an attitude that had been lacking in the Mariners' clubhouse for fifteen years. "We're not going through the motions," Lou told his players. "I'm going to weed out everyone who does, and I promise you your ass won't be here."[112]

The attitude paid off, as the Mariners finished 82-80, an impressive eighteen games better than 1992. They lost the division to the Chicago White

Sox, who clinched the title at home during the end of the season. That night, as the White Sox celebrated, Piniella gathered his players in the clubhouse. "What you are seeing and what you hear, that's why you play. That's never gonna happen again while I'm here," he told them.[113]

Almost as important, over two million fans came to the Kingdome that year. The new ownership and the new manager had created a buzz around Seattle. But there was another element that contributed to the new Mariners.

The foundation for the Mariners' success was laid many years before 1993. Seattle's new owners and manager were able to cultivate the seeds that had been planted, oddly enough, by the previous owners and personnel of the team, who almost caused its ruin. The biggest seed was Ken Griffey Jr. "Junior" was the seventeen-year-old son of Major League outfielder Ken Griffey Sr., and in 1987, he was crushing the competition as a player at Moeller High School in suburban Cincinnati. That year, he hit .478 with 7 home runs and 26 RBIs in just twenty-four games.[114] "He was the best player I ever had in forty years of coaching. Junior would make a play, and [opposing] players collectively would go, 'Oh my God.' You never heard that about other players," said Mike Cameron, Griffey's high school baseball coach.[115] Scouts were all over him and for good reason. "The major league scouting reports all said the same thing about this kid—tremendous tools, a man in a kid's body, the sky is the limit," said Mariners scout Tom Mooney.[116] The upside of all the Mariners' abhorrent finishes was continuously having the top-five pick in the amateur draft, and in 1987, they had the first pick. The Mariners had not squandered their first picks in previous years, but those players became too good for Seattle and would be traded or allowed to leave. The Mariners knew what they were doing in terms of scouting, yet because of the complicated state of the team, they almost passed on Junior. George Argyros was in the middle of trying to sell the Mariners and buy the Padres. To avoid possible conflicts of interest, Commissioner Ueberroth had stopped Argyros from managing the day-to-day operations of the team and allowed him only one phone call a day to club president Chuck Armstrong, but only if there was a witness in the room.[117] Argyros had hinted that he didn't want the talented young outfielder. Griffey had not done particularly well in school, and there were questions as to whether he had the psychological makeup to be a big leaguer. Instead, Argyros wanted to pick Mike Harkey, a pitcher from Fullerton State. Shortly before the day of the draft, Armstrong and Argyros had their daily call, this time with Commissioner Ueberroth listening in. Armstrong pleaded his case and Argyros relented as long as Griffey wouldn't cost them too much money.[118] As fate would have it, Junior was more interested in being the first pick than in having a cushy contract. The Mariners and Griffey came to an agreement, and he was selected first overall.[119] Mike Harkey was selected fourth by the Cubs.

Griffey's selection altered the course of Mariners history. After just a year-and-a-half in the minors, he joined the big-league club and began dazzling fans with his abilities. The scouting reports turned out to be accurate, as Junior developed into the best all-around player in baseball. In the outfield, the grace and the sheer easiness with which he tracked down fly balls amazed fans across the country. At the plate, he had the smoothest left-handed stroke that many people would ever see. He swung with no extraneous motion, using no leg kick and little movement of his hands or arms. As the pitch came, he smoothly brought the bat through the strike zone before it quickly exploded, sending balls high and deep into the Kingdome's third deck. By 1990, just his second year in the league, he was a *bona fide* star. That season he took part in one of the more poignant moments in baseball history when he played alongside his father in the Mariners outfield, the first time a father and son had ever played on the same team. In a magical moment at the "Big A" in Anaheim, the two hit back-to-back home runs.[120] Junior was named to his first All-Star team in 1990 and would be selected every year for the rest of his Mariners career. He broke out in 1993, hitting what was then a club record 45 homers. During the season he tied a Major League record by homering in eight consecutive games. Junior wasn't just the game's greatest player; he was the face of baseball in Seattle. With Griffey, the Mariners finally had someone that the team could build the franchise around. This was not just because of his playing ability. He also had an infectious smile that became just as much a part of his legacy as his statistics. Still young, he was, by many accounts, a big kid at heart. "He played [video] games in the hotel room. He ate jawbreakers, licorice. There wasn't a mean bone in his body," said teammate Chris Bosio.[121] His attitude, which could give off an aura of entitlement, sometimes drove a wedge between him and his teammates, but there was no doubting his ability and dedication to the game.

"There was always something he did a couple times a game where you went 'Wow,'" said former teammate Darren Bragg.[122]

In addition to Griffey, the Mariners made other well-timed draft picks, including Edgar Martinez in 1982 and Tino Martinez in 1988. Not every trade made was a disaster, either. In 1989, they had shipped away their best pitcher Mark Langston to the Montreal Expos, a move decried in Seattle as just another money-saving trade that would not benefit Mariner base-ball in any way. As part of the deal, the Expos threw in a tall starter with horrible control problems, but by 1993 Randy Johnson had worked out his issues and become the game's most dominating left-handed pitcher. With Junior, Edgar, Tino, Johnson, and others (such as Buhner, Bosio, and Mike Blowers), the 1994 Mariners were poised to capture the AL West division title. The season got off to a disastrous start, however, and after several tiles fell from the Kingdome ceiling, the team was forced to go on an extended road trip that lasted weeks. But the road trip invigorated the Mariners, who had the benefit of playing in baseball's worst division. On August 11, they had a 49-63 record but were miraculously only two games behind the divi-sion-leading Rangers. The possibility of playoff baseball in Seattle was real for the first time.

Crowd during parade in Seattle, Washington on June 4, 1979, in honor of the Seattle SuperSonics after they won the NBA championship. Credit: MOHAI, *Seattle Post-Intelligencer Collection*, 2000.107.240.01.01

Inconceivable Victors

Lenny Wilkens and the 1978–1979 Seattle SuperSonics

TERRY ANNE SCOTT

The boisterous clamor produced by scores of excited people honking car horns in Seattle's streets on the evening of June 1, 1979 was beautifully immutable. Seattle's skies were clear—a seeming rarity for early June in the city—but the air was warm, heavy, even muggy. Friday evening's uncomfortable conditions did nothing to dissuade local residents from throwing an impromptu party that spanned from the southeastern reaches of the Cascade Mountains to the northern stretches of the San Juan Islands. One observer noted that such a celebration had not been seen in the "Pacific Northwest since . . . the end of World War II." "We did it. We did it. We really won the thing," a young fan howled as he scuttled toward Pioneer Square from First Avenue in downtown Seattle. "I've been following the Sonics ever since they came into the National Basketball Association (NBA) twelve years ago and it's finally happened. We're number one," he joyfully added with a near disbelief that echoed throughout the area. The Seattle SuperSonics reigned victorious for the first time since the team's inception in 1967—they were the world champions, the downtrodden underdog finally able to emerge from a haze of derogation, a saluted redeemer of the accumulated disappointments that defined the team and plagued its fans. It became unavoidably apparent that evening during Game Five of the NBA championship series that the SuperSonics were "Bullet-proof," as some would later utter in jest, a clear reference to the Washington Bullets' inability to stymie the SuperSonics' playoff momentum *this* time. "Champions of the world, dig it!" a local journalist jubilantly proclaimed the next day. As the newspapers laid prone on driveways across the metropolitan area and in the far corners of the country Saturday morning, featuring headlines that bespoke a historic moment, 15,000 fans—or perhaps double that number, according to some estimates—gathered at Sea-Tac Airport to greet the returning team. Players and coaches descended the plane, many donning white T-shirts that featured the simple yet majestic phrase "World Champions" scrolled across the front. Fans smiled, prattled, and cheered as they reached their hands forward to make sure the imagined was real, tangible, to perhaps touch even a wisp of their heroes' hair. But while the numbers assembled were so foreboding that the plane had to be rerouted to a less congested area of the airport, they were hardly comparable to the throngs of fans who would fill the downtown streets the following Monday for a celebration that rivaled any festivity ever witnessed in that region of the country.[1]

On the morning of the parade, Leonard "Lenny" Randolph Wilkens II—clad in a tan suit jacket, white button-down shirt, and slacks—climbed into his car with his beautiful wife, Marilyn, and their three children and headed toward the Kingdome in downtown Seattle. Leesha, Randy, and Jaime Wilkens, together with an estimated one-third or more of other school children in the Puget Sound area, missed classes that historic day. The Wilkens scions would instead receive a lesson in the expanse of the adulation heaped upon their father by a city fully immersed in an unbounded trust for him, a city that had finally relaxed into a jubilation that SuperSonics fans had longed for since the team's beginning. Some schools simply canceled classes altogether, so their students, much like the Wilkens children, could witness firsthand the impact of the victory on the city. The entire student body of Seattle Preparatory School was dismissed to watch the parade, for instance. Rev. Thomas Healy, the school's president, told reporters, "We've always stressed the importance of being involved with the community in our program. We think Lenny Wilkens and the Sonics have done a lot for the community, and we want them to know that we support their efforts."[2]

When the family arrived at the start of the parade, they had to be escorted by police to help them make their way through the dense crowd. Wilkens and his family accompanied Seattle's mayor, Charles Royer, in a convertible that would join the procession of cars carrying members of the SuperSonics franchise. An estimated 250,000 to 400,000 people lined the streets that served as the theater for this celebration. People hung from the windows of buildings that dotted the route as they tossed confetti onto the masses of onlookers. Some were precariously perched atop light posts as they awaited the arrival of their team. The cheers were almost deafening, but the crowd remained orderly. They wanted nothing to disrupt the momentous occasion that celebrated what starting point guard Gus Williams referenced as a "sleepy town's" rise to fame. The Wilkens family finally arrived at a makeshift stage erected at Fourth Avenue and University Street. Standing atop that stage while holding his toddler son was team captain "Downtown" Freddie Brown. "It has been a long time coming, and I know how all [of] you feel and I feel the same way that you do," he told the crowd. His confident and demure demeanor sent ripples of esteem throughout the listening mass—they were proud of Brown and the words he would impart to them that day. Brown, the six-feet-three-inch guard from the University of Iowa who had earned his nickname because of his proclivity for shooting far from the basket, sunk 4 out of 5 shots in the last thirteen minutes of Game Five. "Thank you very much. We deserve it," he added in closing. The sincerity of Brown's final comment demonstrates a recognition of the collective efforts of a team and city that worked to forge a historical outcome. Standing to Brown's left was Wilkens—the famed player, coach, and front office executive—who took a faltering team (they were 5-17 when Wilkens reassumed his role as head coach) and made them the champions of the world over the course of one-and-a-half seasons. Other members of the SuperSonics organization settled into nearly every available space on that platform, standing in a victor's pose, yet humbly accepting the palpable exaltation that occupied the day.[3]

Neither Wilkens nor the SuperSonics were supposed to succeed. The latter were cast aside by sportswriters, naysayers, and even some of the team's fans as consistently floundering and fated to fail. But they were rendered triumphant by the unwavering confidence and basketball acumen of the team's new head coach, who would be at the forefront of change for the franchise, together with the resolve of players who harbored an unusual synergism defined by Williams as an "all for one and one for all" stance. The achievements of Wilkens mirror those of the SuperSonics, an organization that had never seriously been in the conversation for an NBA championship prior to Wilkens's second tenure as coach with the team in 1977. The parallels between the team and Wilkens are captivating: with origins separated by time and space, both would unpredictably rise to stardom and forge a new reality out of a seemingly indomitable set of circumstances.[4]

Lenny Wilkens: From Bed-Stuy to Stardom

Lenny Wilkens was not expected to do well in basketball, much less in life. The future three-time Naismith Memorial Basketball Hall of Famer (inducted as player, coach, and member of the 1992 Dream Team coaching staff) grew up in tenement apartments in the Bedford-Stuyvesant, or "Bed-Stuy," section of Brooklyn. Trouble loomed large in the urban complex by the time of Wilkens's birth on October 28, 1937. Situated in the north central portion of New York's most populous borough, Bed-Stuy was home to gangs, violence, and other perils attendant to economic hardship. "I know what it means to be on welfare," Wilkens once averred. "I know what it means to have a stranger in the house, snooping around, checking to see if you are hiding something." When Wilkens was five years old, his father, a chauffeur, passed away. Wilkens's mother had to raise four small children on her own while working at a candy factory. "No matter how hard she worked," he remembered, "there was never enough money, enough time, enough energy."[5]

Despite his humble beginnings and less-than-spectacular entry into basketball (he only played half of a season for his high school team), Wilkens became one of the greatest players and coaches in NBA history but not by his own admission. His seemingly innate humility forbids such a boasting. It is this unique self-effacement that defines his character in ways constantly revealed and almost always surprising. The former US Army officer (yes, he accomplished that as well) possesses an uncanny resolve to succeed in all things. Seattle sportswriter Gil Lyons once ribbed that the "first page of Lenny Wilkens' playbook [reads] 'Never give up.'" His former assistant coach, Tom Meschery, described him as "such a good person, such a dignified man." Wilkens's son characterized his father as the consummate family man who included his family in all his professional moments and never forgot that being a father came first. A thirteen-year-old Randy once asked his father for $1 to purchase a hot dog—an ostensibly benign request; however, one that was presented during a game against the Los Angeles Lakers. Randy's original plan was to ask his father for the money during halftime, but Wilkens was busy talking to his players. Halftime ended, and play resumed. The SuperSonics were up by two, and the ball was headed up court—a tense moment. Wilkens felt a tap on his shoulder. He turned away from the game to find his son asking for money. Wilkens pulled out his wallet and gave his son the dollar—always a father first. Later, however, there was a conversation between the two about timing.[6]

As a player, the six-feet-one-inch tall, left-handed guard was unrelenting in his pursuit of the basket. "No one was going to stop me. They could try, but they were not going to stop me," intoned an unwaveringly determined Wilkens. As a coach, he was nurturing when necessary, stern but fair in all instances, exacting on the court and a sage for players off it. His penchant for winning came second only to his desire to effect change among econom- ically marginalized individuals in his local communities. Wilkens believes his contributions to bettering the lives of young people matter the most. Over the past several decades, he spent much of his time raising money and awareness for the lack of health care that plagues many communities. "He shows up, he always shows up," Dr. Ben Danielson, director of the Odessa Brown Clinic, insisted in reference to Wilkens's steadfast desire to help the clinic's patients. Wilkens and his wife established the Lenny Wilkens Foundation in 1971 to fund the work of the clinic. Through the foundation, which is dedicated to extending free healthcare services to underprivileged children, the Wilkens have helped to raise tens of millions of dollars. "I always felt that young people should be entitled to health care without hassle, and when I was growing up it was a hassle, believe me," he affirmed, As a youth, he and his family "didn't have any health insurance and it was a struggle."[7]

I was determined to understand how a kid who was ranked number fif- teen on his high school basketball team of fifteen his freshman year—a poor black kid from Brooklyn, raised by a single mother and coming of age when racial discrimination was still sanctioned by the federal government—could become the great basketball Hall of Famer and quiet philanthropist, Lenny Wilkens. For our first several conversations, I met Wilkens at a coffee house near his home in Medina, an affluent suburb across Lake Washington from the city of Seattle. It was a quaint shop with a fireplace in the far corner of the standalone building that created a warm, comfortable setting—an unostentatious space where Wilkens felt content. Everyone present knew who he was despite the cover of his low-sitting baseball cap that lent partial asylum to his identity. He was recognized and respected—both would fall from the lips and show in the demeanor of local admirers every step Wilkens took. I was enthralled by the deference and adoration shown to him: "Hi, Coach." "Hey, Coach." "Mr. Wilkens, you don't know what you mean to me." The esteem was endless, and with each stream of love, each expression of reverence, Wilkens maintained the same quiet humility and reciprocal respect: "Thank you." "How are you today?"[8]

It was in a corner of that picturesque shop, with unassuming artwork don-ning the walls and accenting the unique sameness that defines so many small, corner cafes, that I first queried Wilkens about the origin of his resolve, the root of his inestimable perseverance in the face of cruel obstacles. Through his lingering Brooklyn accent that dropped the *–er* in favor of a warmer *–uh*, Wilkens insisted that his *mothuh* imbued his character with an unshakable determination to persevere. His success was expected—Wilkens's mother made sure that he and his siblings fully understood that. The line of inquiry I pursued during this early conversation ignited something in him. As we sat across from one another, I observed his countenance shift from guarded, with hands folded, leaning slightly over the back of his chair, to engaged as he carefully moved his chest forward, rested his forearms on the table, and began to speak endearingly about his mother through a self-assured chortle.

As he reminisced, I could not help but think about an interview I once watched with acclaimed author Alex Haley. Recounting his many conver-sations with El Hajj Malik El Shabazz (at the time, Malcolm X) while pre-paring to ghostwrite the now famous *Autobiography of Malcolm X,* Haley revealed that El Shabazz's demeanor shifted from nearly methodical and determinedly sycophantic in his praise for Elijah Muhammad to sweetly reflective when Haley asked about his mother. The memory of Wilkens's mother similarly evoked a return to a space of reflection that seemed to cast out all else as meaningless. Unlike Shabazz, there was absolutely no obsequious bowing to any seemingly undeserving figure before Wilkens beamed endearingly about the memory of his mother. There was a certain reluctance, however, born from an unfamiliarity with me and my objectives, born from a necessary guardedness that he developed over the course of his lifetime. It was a prudent caution I would come to know as part of what made Wilkens wise, distinguished—a man with a discerning skepticism. He is a man who, despite the humility that wholly accentuates his deportment, did not ever tolerate disrespect from others. There he sat, leaning closer to the edge of the table with each recollection, sharing stories about his mother, about some of the best parts of his past existence, the stories that collectively made him great. As such, Wilkens's story begins with his mother and her efforts to thwart the potentially devastating impact of a childhood interrupted by death.[9]

Henrietta (Cross) Wilkens expected that her four children would represent the family and themselves well in all things. They were required to allow their "integrity and honesty to define" their character and dictate their actions, Wilkens disclosed. Henrietta harbored a profound intolerance for a lack of accountability or disinterest in trying. Wilkens insisted that she spent much of "her time trying to get us to concentrate on what we did have, not moaning about what was missing." "Don't make excuses, you can accomplish whatever you set your mind to, you're as good as the next person," she would tell her children. [10]

An Irish Catholic woman born in Brooklyn, Henrietta went to mass every morning. His mother was "what we call a daily communicant," Wilkens divulged, "She prayed more than anybody I knew." If she could not attend mass at Holy Rosary Catholic Church because illness or a pressing obligation rendered it difficult, then a *novena* would substitute. "The Catholic Church was the answer to my mother's prayers," Wilkens insisted, adding that his mother's devotion to God shaped his existence in multiple ways. He attended mass and school at Holy Rosary. The regimen associated with Catholic school helped to create an environment where transgressions were not tolerated. It served as a "place where her children could receive extra discipline," Wilkens noted, "a place where there were strong male role models—critical for kids being raised without a father."[11]

During his father's funeral, a nun in attendance took Wilkens into her arms and lovingly yet forthrightly informed him of his new reality: "You are the man of the family now." His father died of a bleeding ulcer that was mistreated at the hospital. Wilkens was only five years old. "How was I supposed to know what it meant to be the man of the house?" he rhetorically wondered. Despite any confusion and trepidation, his life would be unimaginably affected by both the death and the dictate: "I was the man of the family. I had no idea what it meant, I just knew that on the day my father died, everything had changed. . . . More was expected of me. . . . His absence had a far more profound impact on me than his presence, because his being gone meant that I had to grow up."[12]

The death of Wilkens father in 1943 and the attendant financial struggles forced the family to move into a series of cramped, multi-family dwellings. During the 1920s and 1930s, many Bed-Stuy homeowners converted single-family dwellings into apartments, a financially astute move that accommodated the influx of working-class migrants and immigrants into the area. Despite any shortcomings in the small and cramped living areas, they were home for Wilkens—the stark, sturdy architecture of the late-nineteenth century housed his daily play, his memories of a childhood in which his struggles were often somehow mitigated by the wafting bouquet of fresh bread and sweet pastries from a local bakery. Wilkens felt a sense of community in his portion of Brooklyn, regardless of financial hardships. There was unity produced by the shared experience of poverty, by the reality that "we were all poor."[13]

By the turn of the twentieth century, Bedford was a neighborhood of old-monied white Protestants, many of whom were Dutch or German. Stuyvesant, however, was populated primarily by European immigrants who had achieved a *nouveau riche* status. By the 1920s, southern black migrants and Afro Caribbean immigrants poured into the areas at unprecedented rates, causing a level of 'white flight' that steadily transformed the racial composition of what became known as the Bedford-Stuyvesant neighborhood, or "Bed-Stuy." Middle and upper-class white residents absconded from the neighborhood as deflated prices attracted increased numbers of working-class southern black migrants, West Indians, Italians, Irish, and Jewish people. Leonard Randolph Wilkens was among those migrants. He followed the wave of other southern African Americans who escaped the Jim Crow South for a less racially oppressive North. Born in North Carolina, Leonard Sr. arrived in Brooklyn to flee racial segregation, racialized violence, and the poor economic opportunities of his place of birth.[14]

Although Leonard Sr.'s children were born to an Irish mother, they would largely be defined by the race of their father. "When my mother would take us shopping, we were the color of the rainbow," Wilkens jeered. "People would look," he recalled. "She would turn around and ask them what they were looking at." His mother, never one to tolerate disrespect—much like her son—understood that her children would encounter discrimination in a racially oppressive America. She made sure that Wilkens was fully aware that he was growing up as a black man in a racially oppressive society, despite his Irish heritage. A priest once queried Wilkens about his racial heritage: "What's it like to have a foot in both worlds?" The question seemed somewhat odd to Wilkens. He was fully aware at a young age that he was biracial, but when asked to fill in his race on a form, "I'd write I was African American." He knew (perhaps subconsciously, even instinctually, at first, but with intentional fortitude as he grew into adolescence) that he could either relax into a nihilistic existence in which a debased, racialized status was internalized, only to become crestfallen and discouraged, or he could emerge as a victor in all things. He chose the latter. Wilkens worked tirelessly to be the best, determined to overcome any obstacle presented to him throughout his lifetime and to bring about equity for others in the process. [15]

"On my desk, there's a picture of my father," Wilkens once mentioned. His admiration for his father eclipses all time and space, serving as both prologue and primer for Wilkens's life: "He's a man I never really knew, yet a man who feels very much a part of me today. The man staring at me is always about thirty-five, always in the prime of life, dark-skinned, strong, healthy. He's the father I wished was there when my team in Seattle won the 1979 NBA title, the father I wanted with me when I was inducted in the Basketball Hall of Fame. . . . He's the father I wished could see my children and meet my wife, Marilyn." Over the years, Wilkens's extended family has found parallels in his disposition and that of his father: "I [am] in control, calm. I [don't] get too excited about things but always [seem] to be in control of what I [am] doing." Even in his absence, Wilkens's father shaped him in enduring ways. [16]

Wilkens's mother raised her four children after Leonard's death but not entirely on her own. Henrietta's and Leonard's siblings provided tremendous support throughout Wilkens's childhood. Her parish, Holy Rosary, would also lend a hand. A young priest with a humble proclivity for helping the neighborhood children would unexpectedly change the course of Wilkens's life. Father Thomas Mannion was an average-size man, about five-feet-eight-inches, with a medium build, but he seemed of enormous stature to the young Wilkens, a testament to the admiration and respect he harbored for the priest. Mannion cared about all the children in the neighborhood but saw something special in Wilkens—a resilience and insightfulness that defined the young boy's character. As such, Mannion took a keen interest in making sure that Wilkens stayed on a particular path. When Mannion feared that Wilkens might succumb to the pressures of his surroundings, he would boldly and rhetorically demand to know, "who promised you? Did someone promise you it was going to be easy?" "He was like a big brother," Wilkens disclosed of the man who would eventually help to secure opportunities that altered Wilkens's very existence. [17]

Wilkens had played basketball with friends in the neighborhood and considered himself a decent ball player by the time he became a teenager.

In most other cities, Wilkens would likely have been a starter on a high school team, but talent was deep in New York, and Boys High School was no exception. There were fifteen boys on his freshman team, and Wilkens was the fifteenth one, which meant that he spent most of his time during games on the bench. The ranking left little hope for Wilkens to feel the hardwood against his soles; therefore, he left the team to work after school and help support his family instead. To satiate his desire to play basketball, Wilkens joined the Catholic Youth Organization (CYO) team at Holy Rosary parish during high school at Mannion's urging. Wilkens started for the team. His coach, Mickie Fisher, called his new starter a camera. Fisher observed that Wilkens had an astounding ability to scan the floor and instantly make note of everyone's location. He seemed to take a series of pictures in his mind that he instantly referenced as he charted each move on the court.[18]

After Wilkens left the Boys High team, he began to play more frequently on courts in local parks, where the competition level was historic. It was on those outdoor courts where greats like Wilt Chamberlain were created. Wilkens, too, would be among those who could list participation in outdoor pickup games around New York City as an impetus to an outstanding career. "The idea was to win the game, especially since the winners stayed on the court," Wilkens recalled of his days playing in the park. "Older guys taught younger players the value of moving without the ball, of always keeping your eyes open for a pass," he added. Next-level play occurred on the courts in places like Madison Street Park. For instance, "the pick-and-roll play, which remains one of the keys to scoring in the NBA was . . . an art form on the New York playgrounds of my youth," he fondly recalled. These courts were spaces where a young, starry-eyed neighborhood kid could watch in awe and develop a style influenced by a tradition and culture of play yet a style that was strictly his or her own. The courts were spaces of artistic physical expression that coalesced with a necessity to avoid embarrassment. Credibility and respect were at stake. In one particularly memorable moment, Wilkens played against the great Vincent "Vinnie" Cohen, the Syracuse All-American who had attended Wilkens's high school. As the sideline crowds watched their hometown hero, Wilkens, who was still in high school at the time, blocked one too many shots from Cohen. The crowd cheered. Wilkens then began to steal the local legend's ball. The crowd roared! These moves, replete with Cohen's misplaced frustration and taunting from the gathered onlookers, caused Cohen to respond by slamming Wilkens into a pole.

There were no hard feelings following the incident. Both left the court on cordial terms, but only one had been defeated during play. This was a clear demonstration that Wilkens had reached another level. He would no longer be last on a team of fifteen.[19]

At the beginning of the basketball season during his senior year at Boys High, Tommy Davis, Wilkens's perennial friend and future Los Angeles Dodger, was relentless in his encouragement of Wilkens to try out once again. Wilkens was reluctant to relinquish his job at the local store because the money he earned helped to support his family. But Davis would not stop. He even enlisted Mannion in his mission, a move which proved eminently successful: "Father Mannion . . . came to me one day and said, 'Why don't you go out for the high school team?' That was the last shove I needed to take the plunge," Wilkens admitted. He had honed his skills on the city's courts and arrived a force this time. He not only made the team but also started. Wilkens scored 20 points per game and a memorable 35 points against Jefferson High School and their star player, Tony Jackson, who accepted a scholarship from St. John's University.

Wilkens graduated from high school one semester early in January 1956. He was an excellent student, and his work ethic enabled him to skip a semester. Graduating in January, however, meant that he was not allowed to complete the basketball season. It also meant that he was no longer visible to college scouts. It seemed that his basketball career was ending, despite stellar play the first part of that season. So, basketball seemed to be a fleeting moment in Wilken's life. He started working full-time at Montgomery Ward and planned to attend night school that fall to become a teacher. Mannion had alternate plans. He wrote to the athletic director at Providence College, a Catholic institute in Rhode Island with a basketball program. Father Bagley forwarded the letter to the team's head coach, Joe Mullaney, who invited Wilkens to try out for the team, an action that is now prohibited by the National Collegiate Athletic Association (NCAA) but was acceptable at the time. Impressed by both his academic and athletic performances, Providence offered Wilkens a full scholarship.[20]

Wilkens thrived academically while at Providence. Each term, students with the highest grades had their names posted in the hallways of buildings where classes were held. Wilkens was determined to have his name affixed to those walls, to demonstrate the fallaciousness of societal stereotypes that cast college athletes, particularly black athletes, as unsuccessful students.

His attempts were a success as his name was regularly featured on the walls in the hallways. An honor roll student, Wilkens insists, "most of my professors will tell you I wasn't afraid to question them on whatever they were teaching." He was a member of multiple organizations and made the elite *Who's Who* among college seniors nationwide. Wilkens was active in the Reserve Officers Training Corps (ROTC) during his entire college career. Participation was required at Providence for freshman and sophomores, but he chose to remain in the organization until graduation. He became vice president of the Cadet Officers Honor Corps, an exclusive ROTC branch, his senior year. He also served as treasurer of his class, a job quite suitable for an economics major. [21]

While a Providence Friar, Wilkens helped transform the basketball program into an enduring powerhouse. The agile, determined point guard with amazing court vision led the Friars his junior year to the 1959 National Invitational Tournament (NIT). This was the team's first appearance in the tournament. At the time, the NIT was the most prominent tournament for college basketball. It was, by most measures, equivalent to the modern NCAA championship tournament. The following year, the team returned to the NIT, and Wilkens achieved Most Valuable Player (MVP) honors. Wilkens was invited to participate in the prestigious East/West All-Star Game, an opportunity that promised exposure to NBA scouts. Shortly after Wilkens graduated in June 1960, he was drafted by the St. Louis Hawks. [22]

Highly visible athletic success typically affords one a certain notoriety, a lionized existence that allows the sports star to be treated as a celebrity. Yet the social mores of a particular historical moment are often reflected in the interplay between race and athletics. Therefore, even celebrity standing was not strong enough at particular times in our nation's history to overcome the debased status of blackness. This is why Wilkens could be cheered for in St. Louis's Kiel Auditorium during a game one evening but was unwelcomed at local restaurants the following day because of his race. Despite his light skin and dual racial heritage, people were fully aware that he was not white. St. Louis was a segregated city when Wilkens was drafted by the Hawks. The storefronts, however, did not don "For White Only" or "No Colored Allowed" signs as they did in other segregated spaces. Wilkens was somewhat familiar with such signs; he first witnessed them when traveling by bus through Virginia while playing for Providence College. He was also familiar with the rage and ridiculous fear engendered by his race. St.

Louis would nonetheless exist as a new world for Wilkens, one whose racial restrictiveness would align the city with many other areas across the country but would stand as something wholly apart from Wilkens's childhood home, where he was friends with children from various racial and ethnic backgrounds. He had felt the contemptuous stares of onlookers in New York when his mother took him to certain stores. He had dealt with racist school administrators who had warned him to stay away from white women. None of this was new to Wilkens, but within the boundaries that defined his part of Bed-Stuy, he had been largely removed from the abject racism extant across other parts of the country at the time until he was drafted by the Hawks. In the absence of Jim Crow signage, St. Louis's segregated mapping was accomplished through icy reception in public spaces, refusal to seat African American patrons at restaurants or serve them at stores, "white flight," and, not infrequently, violence.

While always insulting, the irony of racism in St. Louis was particularly glaring at times. "There was a cafeteria-style restaurant that had pictures of several Hawks players in the window, including me," Wilkens remembered. "Everyone knew the restaurant only served whites, but there was my picture. They thought I was good enough to be in their window and maybe help bring in business, but I wasn't supposed to eat there," he added while alluding to the galling hypocrisy. One evening, he decided to test the restaurant's gall and push against the boundaries of racism. He stood in line and waited to be served. Had they refused to serve him, he was ready to strike at the effrontery required to use him to solicit customers but refuse him service. The restaurant avoided any confrontation and instead served Wilkens. "Everyone was staring," he recalled, "but no one had the guts to challenge me."[23]

By his second season with the team, Wilkens and Marilyn were married and expecting their first child. They were ready to vacate their apartment and purchase a home for their growing family. By the time the Wilkens searched for a house in St. Louis, racial restrictive covenants that had once barred African Americans from living in various areas of the city were no longer legal. White residents who opposed the presence of African Americans in their neighborhoods would find other ways to register their contempt. The Wilkens purchased a home that had been repossessed by the bank in Moline Acres, a white, middle-class suburb established in 1949. Wilkens and a friend did the repairs on the home themselves without incident. None of the neighbors said anything to them as they worked. Wilkens reasoned later that they must have assumed he and his friend were simply construction workers and not their new neighbors. Then, the Wilkens moved into their newly purchased, renovated home, a move that prompted many of their white neighbors to abscond from a neighborhood that now had a black family in it: "The FOR SALE signs popped up, one after another after another," Wilkens recalled. "No one came to the house to meet us. No one knew, or cared, that I played for the St. Louis Hawks. It didn't matter that we'd put a lot of work into the house and had it in better shape than it had been for years." He shrugged. Nor did it seem to matter that he and Marilyn were college-educated. The neighbors were almost scornful of the fact that he and his wife had "solid values who just wanted a nice, safe place to live" and that they "could afford to buy the house," Wilkens noted. The seeming height of racism was reached when the Wilkens's collie, Duchess, was poisoned by neighbors. Instead of encouraging the couple to flee, the incident redoubled their resolve to stay: "No one was going to scare us, to run us off. We had as much right to live on that street as anyone."[24]

Despite the challenges presented by being African American in St. Louis and one of very few African Americans on the team, Wilkens ultimately garnered unprecedented success with the Hawks. But first, he had to struggle for time on the court. When Wilkens first started with the team, head coach Paul Seymour would remove him from the game for minor mistakes. During one particular practice, the coach yelled to Wilkens that he should play like that in the game. Wilkens retorted, "How would you know how I play in the game, I'm never in there long enough." The abrupt response caused a moment of pause in the gym. After practice, Seymour asked Wilkens, "What is on your mind?" Wilkens informed Seymour that when he made a single mistake, Seymour removed him from games. By contrast, he told Seymour, "these other guys make multiple mistakes and you leave them in." Seymour surprisingly responded, "You might be right, rook." He called Wilkens "rook," which was short for rookie. The next game, Seymour put Wilkens in early. Wilkens passed the ball over the head of a player and assumed that he would be put back on the bench, but Seymour left him in this time. Wilkens went on to help win the game. "From that point on, I became a starter," he remembered.

After his first season with the team, Wilkens was called into the US Army. He was stationed at Fort Lee in Virginia for eighteen months. Upon

his return to the Hawks, he resumed his starting position and would funda-
mentally alter the way the Hawks played the game of basketball:

In the early 1960s . . . a lot of teams ran set plays to get their stars shots.
When I joined the Hawks, we must have had twenty plays to get the ball
to [forwards] [Bob] Pettit and [Cliff] Hagan. As I played, I short-cutted
those plays. In other words, I saved us a pass or two and found a way to
get the ball directly to Hagan and Pettit, exactly where they wanted it.
Together, we improvised; rather than pass the ball left, run right and set a
pick, then run back and catch another pass and throw it to Hagan . . . well,
I'd just beat my man off the dribble, head to the spot to create the proper
passing angle, then throw the ball to Hagan. This saved time on the shot
clock, and created fewer chances for turnovers because the ball didn't go
through as many hands.[25]

When Wilkens first entered the NBA, neither players nor coaches were
given pensions. Wilkens stood at the helm of change while with the Hawks.
He was among a small group of player representatives in 1964 who secured
pensions for players by promising to boycott the All-Star Game in Boston,
Massachusetts, should the owners and commissioner refuse to negotiate.
Wilkens, together with a group that included Bill Russell, Bob Cousy, Tom
Heinsohn, and attorney Larry Fleischer, issued their demands just minutes
before the game was set to be played, a bold and impressive move that rendered their efforts successful. Years later, he would help to secure pensions
for coaches as well.[26]

Wilkens remained with the Hawks until 1967 when the team moved to
Atlanta. He would not make the move as he was traded to a franchise in
the seemingly distant Pacific Northwest. "For the first time, the National
Basketball Association has moved into virgin territory ahead of its football
and baseball competitors," noted *Sports Illustrated* writer Frank Deford. The
Seattle SuperSonics were a new expansion team, "and not a very good one,"
Wilkens recalled, but the team certainly needed him.[27]

Champions of the World

Samuel Schulman was, by most measures, a shrewd businessman whose
desire for grandeur frequently drove his financial decisions and brought into
stark relief his proclivity for making impetuous choices. Never one to shy

away from tough negotiations, he left some players feeling undervalued and underpaid. Although at times unwilling to pay many what they requested or deserved, Schulman nonetheless understood players' aspirations to gain as much as possible; he once stated, "If I were an athlete, I'd certainly be trying to get as much as I could." "Wouldn't you?" he then queried. When he truly coveted a player, however, he was prepared to offer exorbitant contracts that courted the ire of his stockholders. One offer extended by Schulman would change the very manner of how young players could profit from their skills for decades to come.[28]

Equipped with an undergraduate degree from New York University and a Master of Business Administration degree from Harvard University, Schulman led various business ventures previous to his entry into the relatively nascent world of the NBA. The New York native once revitalized a struggling bookbinding company, owned an insurance agency, and ran a savings-and-loan venture. Perhaps most notably, Schulman produced motion pictures. In 1966, the NBA awarded Schulman and Eugene V. Klein an expansion team to be located in Seattle. Schulman and Klein were already familiar with the business of sports; the two, together with a small group of investors, had purchased the American Football League's (AFL) San Diego Chargers in 1965. Klein would be a silent partner in the basketball venture until he sold his portion of the team to Schulman in 1972. Schulman, who was to serve as the new basketball team's director of operations, named the team after a plane that was in production at the Boeing Corporation, which was located in the area. Boeing had been awarded a government contract to construct the supersonic transport airplane (SST), the first domestic project of its kind. Schulman wanted his new team to possess all the innovation and glamour of its namesake.[29]

When Schulman asked Wilkens to take on the role of player-coach in 1969 and replace Al Bianchi, Wilkens harbored deep reservations about the move. Wilkens completed his first season with the SuperSonics as the runner-up Most Valuable Player in the NBA; Wilt Chamberlain secured the title that year. Wilkens was only thirty-two years old and, by his own estimation, in his "prime as a player." He had not asked for the position but was wary about dismissing the offer: "Who knew when the chance would come for me—or any black man—to be a head coach again?" he wondered. There had only been one African American head coach in the in NBA by the time Schulman made Wilkens an offer. Schulman and Wilkens agreed to a one-year contract (Seattle offered two years, but Wilkens declined because he was not entirely sure that he wanted the position) that granted Wilkens wide latitude on decisions regarding trades and draft picks. He continued to thrive as a player-coach. Of the last four home games during the 1969–1970 season, three were sellouts. This was the first time in franchise history that a home game sold out. But Wilkens, who scored 21 points in the 1971 All-Star Game and earned the game's MVP title, was in need of additional talent if the team was to secure a championship title. The SuperSonics had acquired Don Smith just before the beginning of the 1970–1971 season, but the star forward was forced to leave professional basketball due to a heart condition. Center Bob Rule suffered a season-ending tear of his Achilles tendon. In search of a big man, Schulman and Wilkens reached out to Spencer Haywood.[30]

Schulman offered Haywood a $1.5 million, six-year contract, a move that would prove duly prohibitive as Haywood's early departure from college complicated the acquisition of the star player. He had easily secured the American Basketball Association's (ABA) Rookie of the Year and Most Valuable Player titles in 1970. Haywood was an extraordinary player who averaged 30 points and 19 rebounds per game with the ABA's Denver Nuggets. However, his signing with the SuperSonics would violate the NBA rule regarding player eligibility at the time. Haywood, a former Olympian who had played for the US basketball team in the 1968 Mexico City Olympic games, left the University of Detroit after one year to play professional basketball. The rule dictated that a player must be out of high school for four years before signing with a team in the league. The six-feet-nine-inch Haywood graduated from high school in 1967, a mere three years before Schulman signed him. His already pricey contract became even more costly when the NBA sued Haywood and the SuperSonics to block Haywood's ability to play for the team. The case would work its way up to the US Supreme Court. In 1971, the court determined that the NBA affected economically disadvantaged players' ability to earn a living wage. Haywood was free to remain with the SuperSonics. "It was a matter of principle," Schulman told a local reporter years following the court case, "I couldn't see any logical reason for keeping a man from making a living. I thought it was unconstitutional."[31]

Haywood proved to be an invaluable player for the SuperSonics, but the financial cost of his acquisition did little to assuage the concerns of team stockholders. They had accused Schulman of extending large contracts to several players while the team was suffering financially from decreased ticket sales. Schulman then signed ABA player Jim McDaniels to a seven-year contract worth $1,870,000, which lent further ire to disgruntled stockholders who collectively owned approximately 30 percent of the team. It also ruffled the deportments of ABA team owners who harbored increasing resentment over NBA owners supposedly "raiding" the ABA for top players. Despite the ill feelings, the SuperSonics ended the 1971–1972 season with a 47-35 record. This marked the first winning season in franchise history. Then, in a move that shocked and upset many in Seattle, including Wilkens, the SuperSonics traded Wilkens to the Cleveland Cavaliers.[32]

The SuperSonics ended the 1972–1973 season with a 26-56 record. Tom Nissalke replaced Wilkens as head coach, but his tenure was short-lived. Nissalke, who had been named the ABA's Coach of the Year, was dismissed from the team when his record stood at a dismal 13-32. Season ticket sales were half the total from the previous season. Furthermore, several of the players had expressed interest in leaving the team for the ABA, something that happened with increased frequency at that time. Assistant coach Bucky Buckwater replaced Nissalke but fared little better. The former Seattle University head coach had led the SuperSonics to the third-highest scoring average in the league during their first season; however, his numbers were not enough to create winning seasons nor playoff runs. Buckwater was subsequently fired.[33]

The changes proved too much for already irritated shareholders from the SuperSonics parent company First Northwest Industries. They sued Schulman in 1973. The lawsuit charged that Schulman engaged in "an extensive course of unauthorized conduct" by acquiring Spencer Haywood, John Brisker, and Jim McDaniels and then by hiring and firing two head coaches in one season. Over the course of six years, Schulman had already gone through three general managers and four head coaches. In total, there were fourteen lawsuits against the franchise by 1973. The consummate and purposive businessman had incited the fury of investors by "running up large debts," according to William "Bill" Russell, Schulman's next fixation.[34]

By June of 1973, Schulman once again desired a new head coach following the release of Buckwater and contacted the unassailable Russell for recommendations. Russell, the six-feet-ten-inch celebrated Boston Celtics center, seemed a logical source for judicious endorsements—after all, he had led a storied twelve-year career in the NBA. Russell played college basketball at the University of San Francisco before earning a spot on the 1956 Olympic basketball team. The legendary Arnold "Red" Auerbach, then coach of the

Boston Celtics, chose Russell in the first round of the 1956 NBA Draft. A decade later, Auerbach named Russell player-coach, a role that would render him the first African American head coach in the NBA. After leading the Celtics to its tenth NBA championship since he joined the team, Russell retired in 1969. By the time Russell bid farewell to the NBA, he had settled into a life without basketball. That, however, would change when Schulman began calling Russell incessantly in search of a head coach for his struggling team. Russell detailed the exchange with Schulman in his autobiography:

> I gave him three or four names but he found something wrong with each one of them, When I said I couldn't think of anyone else, he asked, 'What about you?' 'No,' I said. I don't want to do it. 'Why not?' 'Well, everybody knows that you never let your coaches alone. You stay involved just enough to make a mess.' 'I'm not like that, I never interfere.' 'Well, I'm just not interested.' [35]

Notwithstanding Russell's clear disinterest in the position, Schulman was relentless and called the basketball virtuoso multiple times over the course of the following weeks. Russell reasoned that perhaps a seemingly outrageous set of contingencies would quell Schulman's interest in him. When Schulman called once more, Russell laid out his demands: the model of car he wanted waiting for him when playing teams in other cities, full control of the organization, a noninterference clause in his contract, and what Russell thought was an unreasonable amount of money. To Russell's dismay, Schulman simply replied, "okay." A conversation with Shulman that Russell perceived as a final shooing instead somehow transformed into a lucrative position that brought the former Celtic back into the game.[36]

Russell assumed his role as head coach and general manager of the SuperSonics just before the start of the 1973–1974 season. "My job was much more than rebuilding a bad basketball team," he declared with a certainty that clearly denoted the beginning of a massive undertaking. "It was also to rescue a franchise that was in shambles," he lamented. Zollie Volchok, the team's president, said of Russell, "We didn't just buy a coach, we bought a voice, a style, an image." That image was unrelenting in a pursuit of social justice and racial equality off the court. At times, however, Russell's comportment was demeaning to some of his players. Known for his abrupt honesty, the already legendary NBA veteran ruled with a heavy hand and, not infrequently, an intolerable reaction to perceived dissonance. When players were late to practice or meetings, for instance, the NBA created a standardized $1 fine per minute. Russell perceived such a fine as far too lenient; he changed the fee to $100 per minute. He was not to be crossed. "I'm a pretty direct man. You say something I like, I'll tell you so; you say something I don't like, I'll tell you also. A diplomat I'm not," Russell admitted in his 1969 retirement speech. It was a foreshadowing of sorts, an unintended warning issued to his future players.[37]

When Russell arrived in Seattle for the start of the 1973–1974 season, he found a team that he observed "was completely devoid of personality." "Whatever the opposing team wanted to do, we accommodated them," he insisted, "whether it was fast breaks or slowing the game down to a walk." Per his agreement with Shulman, Russell was granted full control of the team, which proved quite useful. During Russell's first season with the SuperSonics, they secured ten more wins than the previous season. The team's improvement was steadfast over the next two seasons. Russell helped to lead the SuperSonics to the playoffs at the end of the 1974–1975 season and then again the following year. Russell also signed two young players, one of whom, Dennis Johnson, would prove to be pivotal in the team's bid for the championship in 1979.[38]

Unfortunately, Haywood and Russell's relationship was fraught with disagreement and contentiousness, which ultimately led to Haywood being traded to the New York Knicks. Russell's issues with Haywood were not unique. Several players expressed concerns about Russell's overbearing, occasionally combative methods, which, at least in part, encouraged Schulman to ask for Russell's resignation. Russell himself had grown disenchanted with many of his players: "As is true with most losing teams, the Sonic players had fragile egos, and they spent a lot of time looking for reasons not to play, pointing fingers at each other and blaming everyone but themselves," he argued. Russell reached the pinnacle of his frustration with the players when they met alone to discuss the distribution of playoff money. They acted against prevailing methods and voted to withhold "even the complimentary amounts customarily given to such support people in the franchise as the trainer, people in the front office and assistant coach," Russell lamented. Additionally, they decided that two individuals who were hurt would receive nothing, and then they reduced the allotment to a third injured player. "I couldn't believe it," Russell jeered. The deed made it clear to him that he was no longer interested in continuing as head coach. In May 1977, Russell quit the franchise as coach and general manager. Schulman publicly declared that although Russell had always provided "110 percent," he was simply "too expensive." "Sam Schulman has a dream which I know he will fulfill to bring the N.B.A. championship to the wonderful people of Seattle," Russell told the press upon his departure from the team.[39]

Robert "Bob" Hopkins, Russell's assistant coach and cousin, was promoted to head coach. Schulman believed Hopkins deserved the opportunity after serving on the coaching staff for several seasons. Born in Jonesboro, Louisiana, in 1934, Hopkins—known by his players and colleagues as "Hoppy"—was a star at Grambling State University where, in 1955, he became the first college basketball player in history to score 3,000 total career points. Drafted by the NBA's Syracuse Nationals (now Philadelphia 76ers) in 1956, Hopkins had spent five seasons playing for the Nationals before embarking on a college coaching career. Hopkins resigned his position at Xavier University to take the assistant coaching job with the SuperSonics. His college coaching career was impressive by most measures. He finished his tenure at Xavier with an 85-45 record. Hopkins's team was 22-5 then 21-5 during the 1971–1972 and 1972–1973 seasons, respectively. It was at Xavier that Hopkins first met Donald "Slick" Watts, the Mississippi-born guard who would became a favorite player among Seattleites. The two were very close, and Watts was elated to once again work with his former coach in Seattle. ("Good, bad or whatever, he made me who I am," Watts told a reporter following the passing of his beloved coach in 2015. "I know a whole lot of people owe an awful lot to Bob Hopkins," he determinedly added.)[40]

In May 1977, Schulman approached Wilkens with an offer for a position in the front office. Wilkens had been fired from the Trailblazers in 1976 and had just finished one year of commentating for CBS, a new endeavor that he rather enjoyed. "The last thing I ever expected to be was a general manager, or as my official title stated: Director of Player Personnel," Wilkens admitted. He planned to return to CBS; the SuperSonics' needs, however, sidetracked his own immediate interests.[41]

When Wilkens arrived in the front office, he asked a simple question that would alter the structure and viability of the team: "Where are we?" He wanted to understand the team's plans for trades and draft picks and, by extension, the viability of the current lineup. When Wilkens learned that the organization had intended to trade Brown for Los Angeles Lakers Earl Tatum, he immediately thwarted those plans. "You better get a lot more than Earl Tatum for Fred Brown," Wilkens sharply contended. Brown was a standout shooter; "you don't just give guys like that away," Wilkens exhorted. He later discovered that the seemingly shortsighted move had much to do with Brown and Russell's tumultuous relationship.[42]

Wilkens also discovered that the franchise planned to trade seven-feet-four-inch center Tom Burleson. With an average of 6.7 rebounds and 9.7 points per game, his numbers were not extraordinary, but the benefits of his height were incomparable. Burleson could easily block shots, rendering him an asset for most teams. If they were going to trade him, Wilkens wanted to ensure that they gained a player similar to Burleson but better. Before Wilkens was brought into the front office, the original trade deal included signing Golden State Warriors' George Johnson, a good player but one who stood eight inches shorter than Burleson. "What about Marvin Webster?" Wilkens queried. Webster, a seven-feet-one-inch center who was playing for the Denver Nuggets piqued Wilkens's interest. Nicknamed the "Human Eraser" at Morgan State University because the Baltimore native averaged eight blocked shots per game, the long-armed Webster could also rebound and was unremittingly willing to take a back seat to his teammates on offense. Webster was never especially concerned with whether or not he scored but instead chose to focus on playing strong defense. Burleson had five years left on an expensive contract, which factored considerably into Wilkens's decision to trade him. Burleson for Webster, that was part of the deal Wilkens successfully proposed to Denver. The trade proved successful as Webster finished the 1977–1978 SuperSonics season with 289 rebounds and 58 blocks. "Webster emerged as a defensive monster," *Sports Illustrated* writer Jeff Pearlman proclaimed excitedly. Additionally, the SuperSonics new star player ended the season with a stunning 14 points per game, despite his proclivity for allowing his teammates to shine on offense.[43]

Wilkens also managed to secure Paul Silas in the trade. Great leaders discern talent more effectively than others, which is exemplified by Wilkens's acquisition of his former teammate. Wilkens had played with the six-feet-seven-inch forward in St. Louis. Silas was nearly thirty-four-years-old by the time Wilkens expressed an interest in signing him. He was quite ancient by basketball standards. Drafted in the second round by St. Louis, Silas had been in the league since 1964. He had joined the Denver Nuggets in 1976. Wilkens believed that Denver failed to correctly utilize Silas. "They wanted him to score," he charged incredulously. But Silas was never a scorer and would serve a team better as a shot-blocker and rebounder. "Most players around the league can't take contact," Silas once told a reporter, "they get banged once, twice, and the pressure gets to them. They have a tendency to give up. Me, I learned a long time ago that I want to win, and this is the way I have to earn my livelihood. It's become natural for me to go to the boards."[44]

Despite the new talent, the SuperSonics began the season by losing seven of their first eight games. Hopkins was resentful of some of the changes Wilkens made, a resentment that too frequently factored into his interactions with the players. Furthermore, some in the press were relentless in their assessments of the team's record, which angered the new head coach. Hopkins's increasing unease gave way to what some would call behavior unbecoming a head coach. He began to both privately and publicly disparage his players, which further alienated him from the players and the front office. Hopkins had taken to scapegoating certain players in response to queries about the team's dismal performance. His frustration had also started to bear upon his interactions with the players: "Hoppy was always howling," recalled Webster. Schulman wanted to fire Hopkins after those first eight loses, but Wilkens urged the owner to "give [Hopkins] a chance to pull the team together." "You hired him, so give him some time," he advised. But "time didn't help," Wilkens admitted. Schulman reignited chatter about firing Hopkins. Meanwhile, Volchok, at the urging of Schulman, was asking Wilkens to take over the head coaching position. Wilkens staved off the initial requests, but the record would just not improve. The team was 5-13, then 5-14. When the SuperSonics' record hit 5-17, Schulman reached the height of his frustration. The record was an embarrassment to the organization and left many in the city sullen, even cross. A local fan publicly issued a scathing yet quip indictment of the Sonics when he told a *Seattle Times* journalist before the coaching change: "They are playing on public property. They should be investigated for consumer fraud."[45]

Volchok, who was now running the business side of the operation, and Wilkens got on a flight and headed to Kansas City. It was November 30, 1977, and the team was last in their division. They had just lost to Denver, prompting Carl Scheer, Denver's general manager, to claim that the SuperSonics "were one of the worst teams he'd ever seen." A few of the Denver players openly shared his sentiment. Volchok and Wilkens met with Hopkins in his Kansas City hotel room shortly after the team arrived from Denver and informed him that he was no longer the head coach of the SuperSonics. Wilkens observed that Hopkins actually seemed pleased to relinquish his post as coach. "Bob Hopkins has been relieved of his duties as head coach of the SuperSonics," Volchok announced at an impromptu press conference in Kansas City that evening. "This is quite an emotional decision on both Sam's and my part, but it is based on a hope to improve the team's record," he added. "The stockholders feel the main thing is we've been losing at home and the crowd dwindled." Wilkens was somewhat reluctant to accept the position as head coach but accepted the offer with one contingency. "I took it only with the stipulation that I could go back as director of player personnel if I choose at the end of the season," he disclosed.[46]

Hopkins admitted to the press when questioned about the coaching change: "The bottom line is you got to win." "I think the Nets were the coup de grace," he admitted. The SuperSonics lost to the New Jersey Nets 99–96 just three days before Hopkins's firing. Some assessed that the Nets were possibly the worst team in the league at that time; therefore, a loss to them was particularly egregious.[47]

Despite his shortcomings, several of Hopkins's players maintained an unwavering level of respect for him following the transition. "I thought, and I still think, he has one of the smartest basketball minds in the world," Watts boasted of his former college and SuperSonics coach. He added that Hopkins was simply "too intense for NBA players." Wilkens too expressed deep regard for Hopkins. He had attempted to improve Hopkins's relationship with the players when he first became Director of Player Personnel, but it seemed the erstwhile coach was unreceptive to suggestions. Nonetheless, Wilkens and Volchok kept Hopkins in the organization as a scout for the remainder of the season.[48]

Wary of making any immediate changes without the opportunity to practice first, Wilkens left intact the starting lineup that Hopkins had used in Denver. This included Marvin Webster, Bruce Seals, Slick Watts, Paul Silas, and Fred Brown. The team was mentally discouraged and "badly in need of confidence," Wilkens admitted to a sportswriter days following the game. He described them as existing "in a bottomless pit." Instead of remapping positions, Wilkens worked to imbue a sense of confidence in his players: "I told them they did have talent. That I had confidence in them." His reassurance seemed to infuse the players with the vigor need to achieve a victory. They edged out Kansas City in Kemper Arena by a mere 2 points that evening, winning 86–84. It marked the first road win in twelve attempts. Wilkens understood that when a team experiences a coaching change midseason, there is "an immediate infusion of energy" that enables the team to win the first game following the change in leadership. He wanted to sustain that energy, to ensure that the victory was not a fleeting moment followed by a return to sullenness.[49]

Once the team arrived in Boston, Wilkens made some significant changes. He had two days to practice before the game, which would allow the team to do a run-through with a new lineup. He added guard Gus Williams to the starting roster, a move that made Brown the sixth man. Wilkens explained to Brown that he "would come off the bench shooting, instant offense." Although not entirely happy with his altered role, Brown was willing to trust his new coach. Wilkens made John Johnson, with whom Wilkens had played in Cleveland, and Jack Sikma starters. Dennis Johnson, the six-feet-four-inch guard who NBA Commissioner David Stern once described as "a man with extraordinary character" and "a tremendous passion for the game," replaced Watts as a starter. Watts, not entirely at ease with the decision, half-humorously said he would try it. Wilkens also granted a larger role to Webster, Silas, and Seals, all of whom would touch the hardwoods more during Wilkens's tenure. Sikma, a phenomenal rebounder, started in the game against Boston that evening. The changes seemed to work impeccably as the team beat Boston by 22 points. The SuperSonics went on to secure four additional victories in a row. "The NBA is flatly amazed by the Sonics," exulted sportswriter John Papanek. "You always expect a little surge after a coaching change, but this is too many wins to be a little surge," Wilkens furtively acknowledged.[50]

Local sportswriter Blaine Johnson pondered the success: "What did Wilkens have that Russell and Hopkins lacked?" Johnson reasoned that "more organization, maybe more communication, [or] maybe he wound up with the right blend of personalities," adding that "one thing is certain—he put all the necessary ingredients into the pot at the right time." He put the "Super in Sonics," Papanek mirthfully wrote. Wilkens "made it a point to never embarrass his players," Wilkens's son asserted about his father, pointing to this leadership style as largely responsible for his success. The previous coaches of the SuperSonics conducted the team with leadership styles that some interpreted as wholly demeaning. By contrast, Wilkens showed the players respect, an attitude that was reciprocated. This mutual veneration was a considerable part of Wilkens's algorithm for his nearly immediate success on the court after he assumed the head coaching position midseason.[51]

Gus Williams recalled that during many practices, Wilkens would take to the court and show his players how to execute moves. Williams was endeared to his new head coach by such actions: "To me, that was impressive and I could relate to him." Williams expressed some level of both disbelief and admiration that a Hall of Famer would do such a thing. According to Williams, who played college basketball at the University of Southern California (USC), the abrupt mid-season coaching change did not fluster him in the least.[52] The native of Mt. Vernon, New York, was used to adjusting as the circumstances required. After all, he had learned to play the sport he loved in less than ideal circumstances: "I used to lace on my sneakers and hitch a ride into the city, looking for a game. They were just pickup games, usually outdoors. The asphalt wasn't real smooth and there was broken glass around. The baskets didn't have nets and sometimes the hoops were bent and the backboards were dead."[53]

The SuperSonics finished the 1977–1978 season with a 47-35 record, which matched the team's best record set during Wilkens's 1971–1972 season before he was traded to the Cleveland Cavaliers. Perhaps more significant, however, since replacing Hopkins as head coach, the team's record with Wilkens at the helm was 48-18. They also led the league in attendance by the end of the season. "When the playoffs began, no one gave us much of a chance of winning," quipped Wilkens, a cynicism he took as a challenge. The SuperSonics opened the playoff series against the Los Angeles Lakers and their star player, Kareem Abdul-Jabbar. Despite doubts expressed by sportswriters and NBA fans, Seattle reigned victorious and moved on to the next round.[54]

In round two, the SuperSonics faced Wilkens's former team, the Portland Trailblazers. With a 58-24 record going into the playoffs, the Trailblazers proved determined foes, taking the SuperSonics on in six games before succumbing to their unexpected defeaters. Wilkens recalled that, "the Portland series brought some national attention to us." The SuperSonics were continuously astonishing sportswriters and fans, soliciting myriad speculation about what forces were at play to fashion such unprecedented achievement. "Was Seattle's Lenny Wilkens some kind of a) miracle worker b) faith healer c) just plain lucky?" posited a *Sports Illustrated* writer.[55]

The SuperSonics 106–102 victory over the Washington Bullets in Game One of the finals seemed to promise a championship at the end of the 1978 series. But by the last fourteen-and-a-half minutes of the game, the

SuperSonics trailed by 19 points. There appeared to exist little hope for the team that turned its fate from predetermined failure to victory. "I felt that if we could get it down to [ten] by the third quarter we could win it," Wilkens told a reporter following the game. His calculation was accurate. But, alas, in Game Seven, the Bullets defeated the SuperSonics. "Everyone predicted that a SuperSonic victory would turn the town upside-down, but it looks as though Seattle will stay right-side up for at least one more year," sportswriter Jack Broom prophetically lamented. Supporters of the team citywide echoed Broom's sentiment: "They'll be back next year," Andy Palmer correctly predicted. Palmer, together with approximately 14,000 other fans, left the Kingdome the evening of June 7, 1978, disappointed but optimistic for arguably the first time in many years. The SuperSonics lost to the Washington Bullets 105–91 in Game Seven of the 1978 NBA Finals. "Even though we lost, it's a great memory, getting that far," Webster recalled years later. "I remember the locker room after the final game—how the champagne was on ice, guys with tears in their eyes. I loved being on that team." Wilkens confessed that the loss stung "because it came down to the seventh game, a couple of key plays, a couple of crucial toots of the whistle. So close." The sting was redoubled for Wilkens as he shockingly received virtually no consideration for NBA Coach of the Year.[56]

A stunning, unexpected season and second-place finish would end with a heroes' parade in the downtown streets of Seattle, a monumental gesture that somewhat mitigated the pain of losing. "Number two and proud of it," read a billboard affixed to the back of a truck roaming the streets that day. One reporter observed that to the fans who filled the streets for the parade, the SuperSonics were "undeniably No. 1." At the parade's closing ceremony, Wilkens, the forty-year-old coach who had transformed a struggling team into a championship contender over the course of just half a season, stepped to a microphone perched atop a stage in the middle of the celebration and exclaimed, "It's been a fantastic year." He added with an unreserved pride that, quite likely, further endeared him to a city grateful for his success, "I thank God that I'm a Seattleite."[57] Fans dangled from windows along the parade route to catch a glimpse of their beloved team and the presentation of plaques to Wilkens, Schulman, and Volchok by Seattle's mayor, Charles Royer. The celebration, however, would fall desperately short of the stately merriment that would ensue the following year.[58]

The 1978–1979 season started without Slick Watts, who had been traded in January to the New Orleans Jazz for a first-round draft pick. Easily one of the city's favorite players, Watts had captured the adoration of Seattleites through his local youth basketball camps, unrelenting willingness to interact with fans, and, of course, his signature headbands. Fans often revealed their love for Watts by donning headbands to the games. Watts's decreased playing time after Wilkens had taken the head coaching position factored heavily into Watts's decision to request that Wilkens trade him to another team.[59]

Additional changes were made to the rooster for the start of the 1978–1979 season. Wilkens traded a first-round draft pick for Denver's six-feet-ten-inch, former Olympian Tom LaGarde to serve as a backup center. Webster, by that time a free agent, signed a five-year $3 million contract with the New York Knicks. In exchange for losing Webster, Wilkens selected Knicks player Lonnie Shelton to join the SuperSonics. The power forward known as "The Enforcer," Shelton would be a key player in the team's next bid for the championship by providing pressure on defense. The changes were successful. Seattle ended the 1978–1979 season with a 52-30 record. The team had learned one another's strengths, compensated for one another's weaknesses.[60]

They entered the playoffs with an indomitable resolve to achieve what was unattainable the previous year. Their playoff opponents dropped one by one—first the Lakers, whom they dominated in four of five games. Then the Phoenix Suns, whom they beat in Game Seven, once again securing a Western Conference victory. Sikma had double-doubles nearly every game. Brown would "[launch] jump shots from another area code," his coach happily noted. They were unstoppable, a force fueled by years of dismissive commentary, overwhelming disappointment, doubt. Alas, the Washington Bullets would be the team they played in the finals, a repeat matchup from the previous year. Despite Williams's 32 points, the SuperSonics fell to the Bullets in Game One. The seven-game series in 1978 ended without a victory but not this time. The SuperSonics went on to defeat the Bullets in the next four games, securing the only NBA championship title in franchise history on June 1, 1979. Dennis Johnson claimed the NBA Finals MVP honor, and Gus Williams secured the title of top scorer with an average of 28.6 points per game. "That the SuperSonics are now champions of the NBA might shock those who remember the circus act under the whip and whistle" of some of the coaches who predated Wilkens, sharply observed Papanek shortly following the 1979 victory. "Even after we were beaten in the first game, I was confident that we'd win," Wilkens recalled years after the historic series. "We were the right team in the right place at the right time"—a suitably selfless assessment advanced by a humble legend.[61]

Despite the successful season and astounding victory, Wilkens was once again not considered for NBA Coach of the Year. It seemed that title was not going to be allotted to a black head coach at that time, no matter how deserving. He would not be awarded the title until 1994. The dismissiveness, however, would do nothing to temper the excitement of a team and its sporting heroes.

The SuperSonics had accomplished the seemingly impossible. They were champions of the world; a team from a sleepy Pacific Northwestern town had reigned supreme. It seemed only befitting that the SuperSonics would be welcomed home from Washington, D.C., with a hero's parade, so a city cast aside as irrelevant could celebrate the exaltation engendered by a long road to triumph. Hundreds of thousands of delighted onlookers arrived in Seattle on the morning of June 4, 1979, a Monday, to demonstrate a collective exuberance, gratefulness. One reporter mocked that the streets were filled with children who "suddenly developed a fever" and could not attend class and businesspeople who "left the office early 'for my grandmother's funeral.'" Scores of fans lined the parade route along Second Avenue from the Kingdome sixteen blocks to a plaza adjacent to the Rainier Bank building and the famed Olympic Hotel. They climbed light poles and sat on rooftops to cheer for the city's golden sons from unfettered views. Some paradegoers held signs high in the air featuring myriad declamations. "Faster Than a Speeding Bullet," one sign read, a clear reference to the opposing team's inability to reign victorious. Another presented a brash commentary on long-held sentiments about Schulman's parsimony: "Pay to the order of Dennis Johnson, $500,000, Sam Schulman." Perhaps the simplicity of the sign that read "Sonics, No. 1" was most poignant. Wilkens, described by *Seattle Times* sportswriter Don Duncan as the "pied piper" who led a previously struggling team to victory, was perched atop the back portion of a convertible that was forced to crawl through the dense crowd. He proudly lifted the NBA championship trophy above the crest of that crowd in an extended moment of bliss. While Wilkens relished in the "euphoria" created by the unprecedented victory, he did not share the overwhelming astonishment that had befallen the city. When probed years later about the championship, he insisted with striking assurance, "As a coach, I wasn't surprised that we won because I believed that we could win." Moments following the final defeat of the Bullets, Wilkens took a brief hiatus from the exuberance that filled the locker room in the Capital Centre and told a reporter, "You've [got to] have confidence and believe in yourself."[62]

CHAPTER THREE

Play/Gay Ball!

The Emerald City Softball Association and the Making of Community

RITA LIBERTI

In 1985 Stuart Feil stepped, for the first time, onto a Queen Anne Hill District softball field to play the game he excelled at and loved since childhood. The day's other "first" for Feil on that morning was that he shared the athletic space with other gay men. The team's practice had already begun when Feil, both nervous and excited, approached the field. He wondered if the players were going to be skilled and competitive. Feil need not have worried. Impressed not only with the players' athleticism but also their good looks, Feil, as a single man, thought to himself, "this could be a lot of fun!"[1] Indeed, participating was enjoyable for Feil and many other gay men who played for teams within the Emerald City Softball Association (ECSA) during the 1980s and early 1990s, but it was so much more.[2]

In the early 1980s, members of Seattle's gay community took to the field, starting what would become the ECSA. What began as a small group of men playing pickup games on the weekends turned into an enormous enterprise with dozens of teams competing within several different divisions. It is little surprise, perhaps, that organized gay softball began in the early 1980s as the "closet" door was forced open by gays and lesbians demanding a visible claim to public spaces, including athletic fields. Fred Parham, whose gay softball career began in Seattle soon after the league got its start, describes the league's appeal to a diverse range of men: "All of us gay boys who were athletes" as young men but who did not dare "come out" and "all of us gay boys who were never picked [for athletic teams]" were eager to "create something for ourselves."[3] The players' skill levels may have differed but not their determination in establishing Seattle's gay softball league. In the decades since, the ECSA has grown into one of the largest and most long-standing gay softball organizations in the country.[4] In many ways, the origins of the ECSA have their start in a much broader program of recreation and sports within the gay community during the 1970s and 1980s.

The sporting histories of marginalized groups, including Seattle's gay athletes/experiences, are incredibly valuable sites to understanding not only the complexities of the past but also the diverse richness of a place. As a result, this chapter seeks to examine the ECSA's early years, as well as athletic activity more generally in Seattle's gay community from the 1970s through the early 1990s. Participants negotiated the realities of homophobia using sports as a vehicle to chart that path. Gay softball in Seattle was far more than mere amusement. Importantly, the league and softball, more specifically, created spaces in which gay Seattle residents could create community, assert agency, and define themselves and their masculinity in a broader world in which these privileges and avenues for self-representation were often denied them. A focus on the ECSA and sports within the gay community, more broadly, adds depth to Seattle's history as it affords us a unique and important lens through which to view the city's past and more fully understand its present.

Throughout the 1970s and 1980s, gay communities became much more visible and political in Seattle and beyond, helping give rise to much more expansive social networks and support systems. Athletic participation and the development of sports organizations, including the ECSA, were both products of these broader social changes and avenues through which increased demands for inclusion in public life by gays and lesbians occurred. Over the final three decades of the twentieth century, sports organizations, like the ECSA, became the largest gay community groups across American cities.[5] Nationally, organizations were founded and grew in size and complexity to accommodate and govern burgeoning gay sports teams and leagues. By 1977, the North American Gay Amateur Athletic Alliance (NAGAAA) offered its first "World Series" championship softball tournament.[6] The international scope of gay sports' popularity was in evidence just five years later when San Francisco hosted the first Gay Games, in which several nations and well over 1,000 athletes joined to compete in seventeen sports.[7] Athletics, once "hostile" to gay men, became a "haven" in this period.[8]

Some herald the summer 1969 Stonewall Riots in New York City as the impetus for many of the subsequent changes in the ensuing decades, including sports' growth in gay communities. Indeed, the resistive acts by Stonewall Inn gays, lesbians, transvestites, and drag queens leveled against police harassment and brutality did signal a significant turning point in gay freedom struggles. The Stonewall Riots served to raise communal and political consciousness among gays and lesbians as the acts bolstered existing efforts around the country in defense of the rights of sexual minorities.[9] Thus, the events at the Stonewall Inn are significant to US history, not as the start to gay liberation, however, for those roots are to be found around the country in cities like Seattle in the years leading up to the riots in New York City.

A share of the nation's strongest threads of gay resistance and liberation are woven into Seattle's history. These challenges to the status quo are set, some suggest, in a city whose progressive past and liberal leanings provided a welcomed site for civil rights agitation by/for marginalized Seattleites.[10] While it may be that Seattle's heterosexual population was more tolerant of sexual minorities than other places, I am careful not to draw too strong a conclusion. To do so runs the risk of minimizing and obscuring the homophobia that gays and lesbians endured throughout Seattle's history to date. A tolerant climate may have existed but not without tension.

Some of Seattle's earliest gay history can be traced back to before the turn of the twentieth century in Pioneer Square, where men frequented bars, gambling houses, and brothels. The area, characterized by some as "the lowest part of town in elevation and in morals," remained central to Seattle's gay community for years.[11] Ironically, it may have been the actions of many in Seattle's police department that gave rise to and fostered the vibrant gay nightlife in the city throughout the early decades of the twentieth century. An elaborate police payoff system grew, one in which officers permitted "more wide-open operations" in the bars in exchange for a few dollars or several hundred dollars a month in compensation from the club's owner.[12]

In 1966, after a police crackdown on the city's fifteen gay bars, M.E. Cook, the assistant police chief, noted, "word got out that Seattle is soft on homosexuals."[13] Far from something to be celebrated, the number of bars and the 12,000 gay Seattleites who might frequent them was cause for concern to city police chief Frank Ramon who cautioned, "we are not going to let this city get like San Francisco."[14] Unfortunately, for Ramon, the strength and size of Seattle's gay community joined with the rapidly changing local and national social environment in which marginalized and previously silenced segments of the population, more loudly than ever, forced their way into society's mainstream. By the end of the 1960s, Seattle's gay population was "speaking out," putting an end to the deafening silence of the largely invisible community.[15] Gays and lesbians in Seattle and elsewhere began to disrupt a dominant narrative that, according to Dudley Clendinen and Adam Nagourney, cast them as only "existing as a negative" and characterized them as "sinners, criminals, degenerates, and mentally ill."[16] As the decade of the 1970s progressed, gay men and lesbians were not satisfied with simply moving into view of the dominant society. Adopting more activist strategies, the gay community demanded greater participation in civil society and expanded legal protections. As we will see, Seattle sports was sometimes at the center of those advancements.

Claims about the city's openness toward sexual minorities continued in the 1970s and 1980s and came from those within as well as outside of the gay and lesbian community. Seattle "has progressed more than any other city in its acceptance of gay people," the editor of *The Advocate*, a gay publication, told the *Seattle Times* in 1976.[17] Testimonials to the city's inclusivity continued in the early 1980s, as a lengthy piece in the *Seattle Times* noted, "Most gays who live here give Seattle high marks as a comfortable place to live. San Francisco may be the 'gay mecca,' but as one lesbian put it, Seattle is as liberal as California . . . but without being flaky."[18]

Evidence in support not only of Seattle's vibrant gay community but also the city's hospitable attitude in response to that presence was no clearer than in the variety of establishments and organizations catering to sexual minority communities, according to a 1982 *Seattle Times* article. Over two dozen gay/lesbian bars, a bathhouse, a hotel, athletic groups, and even transvestite potlucks were offered up as evidence of the city's tolerance.[19] Far more than simply a checklist, the leisure spaces, such as those listed above, are at the core of gay men's social identities and formed the foundation upon which community was built.[20] By the 1970s, other recreational spaces in addition to gay bars, including athletic fields and courts, were, according to political geographer Michael Brown, "sources of community and strength upon which politics flourished."[21]

As early as the 1960s, for example, gay men occupied public space and in doing so found and built community in bowling leagues and hiking clubs in Seattle.[22] By the mid-1970s, Sunday afternoon bowling became the most popular organized athletic activity for Seattle's gay community, attracting 100 participants each week.[23] Those not wanting to compete were still encouraged to attend, as stated by Stephen Wells of the *Seattle Gay News*, even if it was only to "sit and figure out if anyone in the alley [was] straight."[24] The league's success led to the creation of the Blue Boys Bowl Classic by the early 1980s. The American Bowling Congress (ABC)-sanctioned event drew gay bowlers from around the country, vying for thousands of dollars in prize money.[25] Bowling and hiking may have been the earliest organized athletic opportunities for gay men and women in Seattle but were far from the only activities. Throughout the 1970s and 1980s, gay Seattleites were engaged in swimming, skiing, volleyball, boating, tennis, biking, running, soccer, and even ice skating.[26]

Those who promoted athletic participation for gay Seattleites argued that physical activities offered unique benefits to individuals and the wider community. In the lead up to the newly formed Seattle Gay Athletic Association's (SGAA) 1981 Expo, organizers who sought to "promote athletics in the community," according to Paul Kavata, the community affairs representative for SGAA, detailed a list of exhibitions, concerts, games, and entertainment scheduled for the weekend festival.[27] Kavata reminded gay and lesbian observers of sports' potential to bring good. The "Expo is different from other things we do," Kavata explained. "There is a real high burn out rate in the community but this is the place to play. This is an energy *giving* event."[28] Like Expo organizers, the unique benefits that sports provided to longtime ECSA athlete Ron Fox were clear. Gay softball, according to Fox, provided "a safe place for a closet-cased redneck coming from the country who wanted to be himself and it was a home for me. Just being on Capitol Hill wouldn't have done it."[29]

Others were just as eager to advocate for increased athletic activity among gays if for slightly different reasons. Seeing physical activity as an incredibly positive pursuit for the city's gay and lesbian population, the *Seattle Gay News* in 1977 encouraged its readers to "participate openly" in athletic ventures in parks and on softball fields. The paper's endorsement was bound to the use of recreation as a political tool. It was important, the paper continued, to "publicize our athletic energy and outdoor interests to help break down stereotypes." Every swing of the bat, spike of the ball, or powerful stroke in the pool had the potential to normalize gay life and problematize gendered assumptions many had about gay men. The benefits of athletic participation did not end there, however, as Seattle's gay newspaper noted: "hopefully more people will realize the alternatives that exist, or the ones we can create, and that smoke-filled bars are not the only places to look to when we want to be with other gay women and men."[30]

Bars and taverns, at least for the *Seattle Gay News*, were antithetical to positive and healthful habits, as well as non-viable places in which community could be created and sustained. Gay Seattle softball players did not necessarily share that view. For all the ECSA players/coaches with whom I have spoken, Seattle's gay bars in tandem with softball served important roles in the athletes' ability to form friendships and create systems of support. In many ways, the two institutions had a symbiotic relationship.[31] Bruce Caszatt, longtime player-coach with the Elite Batboys of the ECSA, fondly remembers his introduction to gay softball came from within the Elite Tavern. Shortly after his arrival to the city in 1980, Caszatt recalls seeing a sign-up notice above a urinal in the bar. "My god," he remembers thinking, "you can play sports?!" Soon after, Caszatt was on the field as a player and a coach for the Batboys, where he stayed for nearly fifteen years. He acknowledges that the serendipitous exposure in the Tavern's bathroom to the gay softball league was the "biggest reason" he stayed in the city and remains as one if its residents over thirty-five years later.[32]

Fox's experiences are incredibly similar to those of Caszatt's as they speak not only to the comfort and safety of gay space but the important ties that bound bars and softball. Fox's introduction to Seattle was also his "coming-out" moment—the 1989 gay pride weekend. Upon entering the Elite Tavern, Fox saw a promotional flyer for the bar's team, the Batboys. Fox's surprised reaction was like that of Caszatt's at the start of the decade—"I can be gay and play sports too!?" Indeed, he could and did. For over two decades, softball was Fox's "foundation." His life revolved around the sport, its culture, and the men who played it. After working in the bars that sponsored gay teams, Fox defines gay softball and its athletes as a "brotherhood."[33] On one level Fox simply inhabited gay bars and ball fields, but in other ways he claimed and purposefully made space for his own self-preservation and that of his teammates and friends.

It was in the Deluxe, a gay-friendly Seattle restaurant/bar, that Stuart Feil found his way onto the softball diamond. Like Caszatt, Fox, and others, Feil's chance interaction in a gay-friendly establishment with a group of ballplayers from the Elite Tavern made him aware of organized softball in the community and that, in turn, "changed his life," though his path to that point was not direct. "Frankly," Feil admitted with a laugh, "I kept meeting guys [who] were vegetarians and non-drinkers. God, I'm like, somebody has got to drink. Somebody has got to like sports. All homos can't be vegetarians!"[34] For Feil and many of the other men of the ECSA, meeting "these softball guys" via social networks created and sustained in gay bars altered their understandings of themselves as gay men.[35] Gay bars created "refuges" for men when homophobic responses to same-sex attraction left few alternatives to create community. Far from "metaphors for evil," bars, taverns, and saloons spurred lifelong friendships and a common consciousness among the gay men who frequented such spaces.[36] Moreover, gay clubs offered room for a collective passion for the game of softball and strong bonds between men to grow and flourish in Seattle. Feil, in recalling his first day on that practice field in the Queen Anne district, stated: "I'm out having a blast with these guys and I don't even know them at all!"[37] As these ECSA athletes' stories attest, sites, such as gay bars and softball fields, are imbued with power and serve as their anchors to constructions of individual identity and expression, a source of survival, and a sense of belonging.

As athletic participation among members of Seattle's gay community grew during the 1970s and early 1980s, it paralleled gains in visibility and political power by sexual minorities more broadly. Seattle, one observer noted, was a "main theater" of the gay rights movement in the post-Stonewall era.[38] Resistance struggles played out on the pages of Seattle newspapers throughout the era, as gays and lesbians, more than ever, spoke up/out in defense of themselves and their community. Gay liberation triggered more radical activism as leaders asked less and demanded more in terms of civil rights. Police harassment of gay Seattleites in the early 1970s, for example, was met with an orchestrated and a very public response from several organizations, including the predominantly gay Metropolitan Community Church, the Gay Feminist Coalition, the American Civil Liberties Union, and the Gay Liberation Front.[39] By the mid-1970s, calls for employment and housing protections, representation on the police force, and more influence in local politics were made as the gay community expanded its own network of support to include a job center, counseling services, a community center, a library, and a food bank, among other services and agencies.[40] The shift from silence to openly occupying public space and demanding a public voice was swift in the decade-and-a-half following Stonewall. Interestingly, sporting endeavors were sometimes central to the rapidly shifting political landscape of gay life and rights.

Athleticism was used as leverage to ignite political activism and spur social change within the gay community during the 1970s and 1980s. On one level, Seattle's gay community used sports to raise money and awareness about political issues and causes. In other ways, gay athletes, including ECSA ballplayers, sometimes saw themselves as political agents of change and every swing, slide, and sprint advanced causes for sexual minorities. Seattle's sporting contests and endeavors engaged in by gay men and lesbians were both a time for play and politics. The gay athletic community's involvement in two major issues, Initiative 13 (a challenge to legal protections for gay Seattleites) and the AIDS crisis, illustrate sports' relationship to the political.

As the gay community's efforts to win civil rights for themselves grew in momentum and success during the first half of the 1970s, so too did the backlash against those advances. Seattle police officer David Estes was "horrified" at the city's acceptance of gays and lesbians and its support, via local ordinances, of legal protections for sexual minorities in the early to mid-1970s.[41] Estes and fellow police officer Dennis Falk successfully led a signature campaign to place an initiative (Initiative 13) on the November 1978 ballot to repeal citywide employment and housing protections for gays and lesbians. This example of a local offensive against gay rights was part of a national crusade spearheaded by Anita Bryant.[42] Her efforts to repeal local anti-discrimination ordinances within Dade County, Florida, the place in which she lived, were successful, leading to similar actions in other municipalities around the nation. So popular was Bryant that the magazine *Good Housekeeping* in its annual readers' poll named her the "most admired" person in the world for 1977, besting Mother Teresa.[43] Locally, Seattle's Initiative 13 had the support of KIRO television station president Lloyd Cooney, among others, and as a result, many gay rights supporters in city feared the measure's outcome.[44] If politically liberal Seattle could not survive anti-gay efforts, some observers noted, similar ballot initiatives were sure to win in other cities around the country.[45]

Anti-Initiative 13 activists rallied in Seattle, using sports' prominent place in the gay community to do so. In June 1978, just months before the vote, the *Seattle Gay News* announced the "biggest bowling bash ever." Event organizers hoped for 1,000 participants "rolling their balls to strike down" Initiative 13.[46] Subsequently, the paper reported on the success of the "Bowl

Over 13" event with "several hundred" people "crammed" into the venue. The single day's event raised $4,000 for the Anti-Initiative 13 campaign.[47] In October, less than a month before Seattleites went to the polls, gay leaders, once again, used athletics as a mechanism to raise money and the profile of their cause. Nearly 500 people, gay and straight, participated in the "Run Against 13."[48] Recreational physical activity was used, in this instance, to cross boundaries in forging alliances with a broader spectrum of Seattleites in defense of gay rights.

Athletic events were part of a larger strategy by gay leaders to galvanize a community and advance civil rights. Their efforts were successful as voters came out in large numbers to defeat Initiative 13 by a two-to-one margin. The *Seattle Gay News* reported that the victory energized the gay community, proving that "we can win electoral battles."[49] Interestingly, even in the weeks and months *after* the victory, physical activity was used a final time to aid in political battles against injustice. In a "Skate for SCAT" [Seattle Committee Against Thirteen] roller-skating fundraiser, nearly 300 people gathered to roll around the rink to raise money for the campaign debt encumbered by the Anti-Initiative 13 forces.[50] The win at the polls engendered a new and much bolder optimism going forward within the gay community. The following summer, the mayor's office in Seattle released its first-ever Gay Pride Week proclamation, urging "all citizens to recognize and support the successful efforts of our city to make this community one which truly does treat all its citizens with a fair and equal hand."[51] The highest level of city government not only acknowledged gay and lesbian Seattleites but also revealed a level of validation and respect never before extended to sexual minorities. The gay community's sense of itself and its collective power changed a good deal over the course of the 1970s, and sports were a part of that transformation. In slightly different ways, sports' important place in the community offered assistance in combatting the local gay community's next and perhaps its biggest crisis to date.

In January 1982, a *Seattle Gay News*'s story noted that the "cause of 'gay cancer' [was] unclear."[52] Later that same year the first AIDS case was reported in the city over a year after the disease appeared in the United States.[53] Characterized as a "second wave" city, Seattle had the "bittersweet luxury of fearing the plague before it actually arrived."[54] AIDS did appear in Seattle, and two years after the initial case, sixty men had been diagnosed, with fifty-seven of them dying within a few years from the disease's related illnesses. By 2014, over 3,700 men were dead from AIDS in King County, and thousands more were living with HIV-AIDS.[55] "AIDS was everywhere," Feil remembers, "[and] I mean *everywhere*."[56]

The community's response in battling the AIDS crisis was similar to that of the 1970s political battles when fundraisers were aimed at raising awareness and money. Just as they had done in the Initiative 13 battle, sports and physical activity sometimes provided a rather high-profile and powerful path to battle injustice. Long-distance swims and walkathons, among other athletic events, became important ways that the gay community rallied support for itself.[57]

Indeed, the gay community reacted to the crisis out of necessity as they knew more than others the horrific realities of AIDS within their circles. Throughout the 1980s, fear spread as quickly as new infections, with no one far from the illness and death that ravaged the community. It was not until the mid-1990s that new drug therapies proved more successful in preventing almost certain death for those with AIDS.[58] Well over a quarter-century later, ECSA players spoke in quiet, measured tones about their loss, both on collective and very personal levels. Bruce Caszatt's experiences illustrate the unimaginable grief and fear brought on by the disease and its life-altering effects on survivors. In 1990, Caszatt lost his life partner [to AIDS] and became a single father to a six-year-old boy: "It [AIDS] was everywhere—it was all around us."[59]

AIDS reached far into every corner of the gay community in the 1980s when softball fields became both an escape from and constant reminder of its presence.[60] Softball, Nic Bacetich, recalls, provided a "safe haven [and] a place where we could [just] play ball," putting a bit of distance between ECSA athletes and the atrocity unfolding around them. Of course, the game and the spaces on which it was played were not impervious to the disease. Bacetich recounts, "[softball] teams were decimated by deaths. It was a dark time."[61] After a teammate began missing practices and appeared weaker each time he did come to the field, Stuart Feil asked if he had AIDS. Initially reluctant to disclose his AIDS status, Feil's teammate finally did acknowledge that he had the disease. It was at that point Feil remembers that "we were able to rally around him and take him to doctors' appointments [and] make sure everything was ok with him." Unlike the reception Feil's teammate might well have received from those outside of the gay community, their aim was not to "chastise him for it, just support him," adding "because we knew what we were dealing with."[62] The game provided some sense of comfort even for those who were quite ill and dying, including Bacetich's partner, who passed away in 1996:

> My partner, Jim Harper, had a Hickman PICC [Peripherally Inserted Central Catheter] in his chest and still wanted to play in the World Series when we hosted it in 1995. This was 1995, just six months before he died—and he still wanted to play ball even though he had full blown AIDS and had IVs in his chest. He was the pitcher and that's kind of a difficult position anyway and to put yourself in a place of vulnerability while being sick. I wasn't so sure it was the best thing for him to do from a safety standpoint. But he felt so determined to play; you know you had to allow him that opportunity. And he did, he got through that and we had a successful World Series in 1995.[63]

Softball served different meanings for those, including Fox, living with the disease. Fox acknowledged:

> I found out in the early 90s that I had AIDS, so [softball] took on a whole different purpose for me. It gave me a support group [and] it gave me an escape from my own thoughts. The one thing I could always focus on was softball and once I was on the field I was laser focused. So it was a nice escape from what was happening and what I was waiting to happen to me.[64]

Softball also helped Fox and others create and cultivate fellowships with other men. "I think the social part of it was as important as or as satisfying as the sports part of it," said Nic Bacetich of the deep trust that was born out of exchanges on and off the field.[65] The strength of these bonds served them as they weathered the harsh realities of AIDS. Feil noted, "We had this core group of guys covering our backsides," adding, "I don't even know how it is that we are even sitting here talking to you right now. I know I shouldn't be here." Teammates and coaches were considered part of an "extended family" to all the ECSA players. Feil added, "I was very happy to have my extended family. Even though we lost a lot of them."[66]

Softball carried varied meanings for the gay men who played the game in the 1980s and early 1990s. While they shared a keen passion for playing the game and the feelings of kinship formed within athletic spaces, they differ on the extent to which their participation advanced a cause or an agenda—or even if they desired such a thing. For Brian Washburn, gay softball was "never political."[67] In terms of what participation meant to Washburn, little surpasses the visceral reaction of simply being present on a softball field. Some of his most fond memories are as a child, "just practicing." Remembering "the smell of the grass" and his love of "just being out there," Washburn concedes that "if we had to stop play so someone could go to the bathroom and take a leak, it was annoying to me. I wanted to chase that ball!"[68]

For others, however, the game and being athletic, more generally, was political in the sense that it challenged stereotypes of gay men and athleticism. The simple act of being on the softball field as an athlete was a statement, pushing boundaries and preconceived ideas about gay men and masculinity.[69] In the early 1980s, the *Seattle Gay News* was quick to see the political importance of softball's rise among men in the community. "There are groups throughout the country," the paper reported of organized softball, "that are trying to show that gay men have as much claim to the game as any other group."[70]

Softball offered a unique point of resistance for some. Feil recalls that two friends were eager to have him get more politically involved and join them in ACT UP (AIDS Coalition to Unleash Power) demonstrations. Feil believes ACT UP's activism is important but adds, "I think it's a screaming cause. I think quiet conversation goes a lot further. And I think that's what softball does. And so I finally said, 'listen you guys keep doing what you're doing, that's really good, but I'm affecting our rights and stuff like that by going out and rockin' it as an athlete because these people don't know that I'm gay and when I tell them that I'm gay....'"[71] Friend and former teammate Brian Washburn interrupts quickly, adding "he is the best ambassador for the gay community," as straight folks tried to reconcile their assumptions of gay masculinity with Feil's superior athletic skill.[72] "The longer we played ball," Nic Bacetich noted, "the more we broke down barriers."[73]

This process was far from linear, however, as gay men's presence in softball exposed the homophobia that persisted among some Seattleites. When gay teams began playing in the Metro League (a predominately heterosexual league), Nic Bacetich recalls being called a "sissy" as he stepped to the plate in a game in Seattle's Interbay neighborhood. A girlfriend or wife of one of the Metro League players shouted in Bacetich's direction, "don't worry about her—she can't hit the ball—she's a sissy." After hitting a home run at that at bat, Bacetich remembers looking over at the woman and thinking, "now you can explain to your boyfriend or husband how he just got his ass handed to him by a bunch of sissies."[74]

Individual athletic feats were often the ways through which ECSA players challenged narrow and sometimes homophobic attitudes, though gay ballplayers simultaneously understood themselves as part of a collective. There was a unique sense of "solidarity and pride" among gay players, Fox explained. ECSA players had a shared consciousness about their entitlement to take up space in a setting not always believed to be a place in which gay men were welcome. Fox continues, "we knew we were as good as straight ball players. We had proven that by beating them handedly for many years here in the straight leagues in Seattle and straight tournaments throughout the state that we went to." Thus, attempts by some to "negate what we were doing, our abilities, and our humanness," according to Fox, fell flat and were not successful in the face of a resistive strategy employed by ECSA players.[75]

Athletic masculinity was not, however, expressed by gay men in fixed fashion nor steeped in traditional or finite conceptualizations of gender. Rather, ECSA players created a culture in which gender and manhood were expressed in multiple and diverse ways. This, in turn, forced some observers, gay and straight alike, to reconsider what the embodiment of sporting masculinities looked like. In terms of press coverage, ECSA activity was nearly always relegated to the sports pages of the *Seattle Gay News*. However, in 1991, the success of the Elite Batboys in the city's Metro League drew the attention of the *Seattle Times*, Washington's largest newspaper. According to the article's author, the Batboys' "big noise" was the result, in part, of the team's endless preoccupation with cheering, "bright red uniforms, legion[s] of fans, and ring[ing] a cowbell every inning." The uproar was about something else too as players were anxious to prove that "gays can play ball."[76] The Batboys' unique style, superior athleticism, and sporting success gave readers much to consider in expanding definitions of masculinity and quieting stereotypes of gay men.

On occasion, even gay athletes and the community from which they came were forced to reconcile their own preconceived ideas about gender and athleticism with the realities before them. The *Seattle Gay News* conceded in 1981, as organized softball tried to get its start, that the "biggest obstacle" to gay men's softball participation was gay men. While some gay men rejoiced at the opportunity to play softball, others saw athletics as an unwelcome site as the misogyny and homophobia fostered within men's team sporting cultures dissuaded potential participants.[77] Claims from gay men that they could not get involved in softball because they were "lousy" at the sport in high school were "irrelevant," according to the newspaper, as it rallied all men to join a team.[78] The paper encouraged gay Seattleites to move in and take up space on softball fields and in doing so pushed against narrow definitions of athletic manhood.

Working through their own issues of internalized homophobia and the gender contradictions that arose from those perspectives, ECSA players were quick to note one of the ways that gay softball changed their stereotypical views. "I would always say look out for the nelly [effeminate] ones," Parham conceded, "those are the ones that are going to hurt you. They'd come up [to the plate] swishing with the wrist and the hands throwing their hair back from their face."[79] Like Parham, Fox struggled with conventional understandings of how athletes should look and act as his tenure in gay softball began. At first he did not know what to make of the "nelly ass" cheers, finding it all "awkward" and not wanting to participate in them.[80] Fox acknowledged that the "self-hate" he felt as a gay man in a homophobic society came with him onto the field, coloring his perspective on gender and athleticism. Over time, however, he grew more and more at ease with the diverse range of ways gay male athleticism was expressed. He relinquished the "macho" persona he constructed for himself and "let [his] true self come out . . . becoming a better person" and more at peace with his world and sexuality.[81]

Camp behavior was a central way in which gay softball players built and maintained community, as well as disrupted dominant understandings of masculinity. Although gay men do not have "sole title to the estate of camp, they are, in all likelihood, its chief tenants," according to sports studies scholar Brian Pronger.[82] Singing, dancing, dressing in "drag," calling attention to or playing up stereotypical feminine demeanor or referring to each other with female or feminine names characterized camp for ECSA players. Athletic masculinity and the display of camp style were not mutually exclusive as gay softball players' theatrical and flamboyant performances both on and off the field were core to gay softball culture, though this was not without tension. A form of agency for gay male softball players, camp behavior was enabled and supported among ECSA athletes as unique constructions of manhood and masculinity were created within softball spaces.[83] "We were relaxed" Parham explained, "and this was *our* league," in which camp expressions denoted a particular collective consciousness among gay men who took ownership of the public spaces upon which softball was played.[84]

Appearance and stylistic expression were often at the root of camp behavior. Brian Washburn remembers a player whose hair was always "immaculate" even after a diving, tumbling catch. On those rare occasions when the player's hair was out of place, Washburn and others were sure to highlight the moment with a lively cheer about their less-than-perfectly-coiffed teammate for all to hear.[85] Feil recalled an exchange as teammate Donny Moritz walked toward other players and Moritz's partner sitting in the bleachers. Usually, Feil remarked, you could see these two men from a distance "because they would carry [so many] clothes in their bat bags [as if] they were going on a trip."[86] It was hard to miss them. Feil adds, "how many clothes do you need to play softball?"[87]

Feminine modifiers were often employed as part of the fun banter between players. Not meant as an insult, the linguistic shifts instead can be read as challenging notions of conventional manhood.[88] In greeting his partner and the large bat bag he carried, Moritz's partner said, "oh, it's costuma!" Another player quickly responded, "I know you're not talking, wardroba."[89] Camp exchanges such as this, directed at teammates or opposing players, were rarely, if ever, confrontational. The players' unique lexicon and manner of exchange were instead meant to be humorous. They underscored a keen level of trust and camaraderie between and among players.

Drag show fundraisers to benefit ECSA teams and other sports activities became highly anticipated annual events within Seattle's gay community and provided another avenue of camp expression. As "a powerful, blatant, and radical undermining of masculinity," according to Pronger, drag made some ECSA players uncomfortable.[90] Despite being beyond some gay athletes' comfort zones, they fondly recalled their involvement in such activities and the place of drag, more generally, in the community. The need to fundraise to cover the steep cost of players' insurance meant Bruce Caszatt reluctantly "put on a dress and did a show at the Brass [Connection]," collecting over the needed $1,000.[91] From the early 1980s through to the present, funds raised from events, such as "Jocks in Frocks," the "Miss ECSA Pageant," or the "Miss Batboy" Crown, amassed thousands of dollars to offset travel and other expenses.[92] Feil explained the events' popularity: "People love to see an ugly drag queen." "The uglier the better," he added.[93]

Whatever ambivalence Caszatt and the others may have felt at the time dissipated as each seemed to understand camp as a distinct cultural form within Seattle gay softball. Caszatt proudly declared with a laugh, "My best [drag show] finish was first runner-up."[94] Others were just as eager to pay tribute to themselves and teammates' drag performances. Feil extended a compliment to his teammate Nic Bacetich, saying with the right makeup "he looked like Delta Burke!"[95] The public recognition sought by softball athletes for their on-stage activities underscores its value to individuals and the community. Parham's ECSA Hall of Fame induction biography proclaimed, besides his many athletic achievements, he "brought the house down" with his Tina Turner impersonations.[96] Clearly, drag performances were important markers of Parham's overall athletic identity, and something he wished to make known to others. Conceived almost as celebratory practices, these examples of camp highlight a certain pride among gay male athletes in their otherness and the strong connections that created in marginalized spaces.

It is easy, perhaps, to dismiss camp activities among ECSA players and Seattle's gay athletic community during the 1980s and early 1990s as pure frivolity. Conceptualizing camp in this way, however, depoliticizes it as a form of resistance to orthodox understandings of gender.[97] Seattle's gay male Disco Drill Team of the early 1980s made clear that their aims were to enjoy themselves and also to "poke fun at heterosexual/homosexual preconceptions about drill teams," as stated by Victor Wellington Jones of the *Seattle Gay News*.[98] For participants, there was much more at work, for example, in the team's "signature move . . . the disco kick" than simply choreographed moves to music, according to Jones.[99] Relegating camp strictly to parody obscures the deep and powerful associations the activities and exchanges fostered between and among gay men of the league.

The strength of those bonds is quite evident in the cheers that helped to define the Elite Batboys of the ECSA. Song and dance embedded in the cheers were central to the team's performance off the field. No cheer was more significant to team members than the "Batboy Twirl," with Bruce Caszatt noting, it "was one of our favorites." The cheer, Caszatt explained, was performed "whenever someone was down and needed a lift or if someone made a mistake on the ball field and was feeling bad about it." Teammates gathered around the player and cheered as a way of letting them know, "no matter what was going on, we would be there for them and we would always have their back."[100] It seemed, however, that other occasions were reason enough for the "twirl." Fox explained that "Cha Cha" was one of the team's most dedicated fans, bringing chili for anyone who hit a home run. In remembering the cheer, Fox sings, "Cha Cha, Cha Cha, she's our girl, let's give her a Batboy Twirl!"[101] Both Fox and Caszatt finished off the description with their hands in the air, cheering "woo! woo!" followed with laughter over this shared memory.[102] For gay studies scholar Andy Medhurst, camp behavior and expression, including the Batboy Twirl for ECSA players, was one of their "most fearsome weapons" in response to marginalization and oppression while it was simultaneously one of their "most enriching experiences."[103]

The power and depth of gay male friendships formed as part of ECSA involvement is clear in the stories told by former athletes.[104] In the late 1990s, "Terry," a former ECSA athlete and Batboy team member, was dying of AIDS. After being diagnosed, Terry left Seattle and moved back to the Midwest, where he was born and raised, to be close to family because, as former teammate Bruce Caszatt explained, "back then everyone who was sick with AIDS died."[105] Struggling to find a way to comfort his ill and dying friend, Caszatt penned a poem and sent it on to Terry.

Just Twirl

When you just don't understand
and your head begins to swirl.
When your stomach's so upset
that you think you're going to
hurl. When all you can do is lay
in bed all wrapped up in a curl.
When you need a little gem just
remember this little pearl. When
all seems lost—just do the
BATBOY TWIRL
From all around the world
and beyond. Because of you
we are so fond. We'll hear
your twirl. We know that
song. We'll come a running.
It won't take long. For this
poem I know I'm wrong. But
always remember. Even when
we're not there, we're never
really gone.[106]

This intimate, intensely personal communication also speaks to the powerful process in which community was constructed out of the athletes' shared worldview as gay men. Moreover, the expansive ways manhood was understood by athletes is thrown into sharp relief as nurturance was core to gay male friendships fostered within what was simultaneously a very competitive softball setting.

The early period of the ECSA's existence is a small but incredibly valuable piece of Seattle history. ECSA players and coaches with whom I spoke are intensely proud of their achievements on the field. Indeed, their many athletic accomplishments are part of this larger history and certainly warrant our collective attention. Some of the history's richness, however, lies beyond a tally of runs scored and championships won. The ECSA and gay Seattle sports are so important to helping us understand how marginalized groups negotiate systems of oppression. as they carve out spaces in which to live and play gay male athletes of the ECSA offer us a unique perspective on the past that challenges us to consider the meanings attached to athletic masculinity, agency, and community. The result adds dimension and depth to Seattle's rich and complicated past. "We were having fun," commented Parham, "we didn't think we were making history."[107]

CHAPTER FOUR

"Is Seattle in Alaska?"

My Life on the City's Courts and the Centrality of Seattle Basketball in the Creation of Modern Legends

ANTHONY WASHINGTON

I love basketball. I did not start playing organized basketball until I was in the fourth grade, but I had a ball in my hand as young at three years old (I will never forget when my Uncle Thomas blocked my shot on my play hoop). Growing up, my father used to tell me all the time, "Ant [his nickname for me], you don't watch enough basketball. You don't study it." He was both wrong and right—I did watch basketball because he watched basketball, as did every other man in my family, so there was no way around it. He was right because I was not that interested in the game. Do not misunderstand me; I loved Michael Jordan, and my favorite player was Patrick Ewing around 1990. When I was seven years old, two of the players who would be added to my list of favorites, Gary Payton and Shawn Kemp, had just gotten drafted by the Seattle SuperSonics. Within a few years, they would evolve into a legendary duo. But over a short period of time, I fell in love with basketball—a change not only in part facilitated by my admiration for superstars but also by the stardom I experienced.[1]

At first it was lust. I enjoyed the attention that I received and the perks that came with playing Amateur Athletic Union (AAU) basketball—the travel, the cheers—but I was not serious about the game. It took me a while to learn how serious one had to take their craft to be successful. I was what you considered a late bloomer as I did not start receiving attention from colleges until the spring of my junior year in high school. At that time, I had only played one year of varsity, but my six-feet-nine-inch stature and my ability to block a shot made me a viable recruit. I was fortunate to get a scholarship to the University of Washington (UW) for basketball. By the time I got to the "Udub" (as it is called locally), I did love basketball, but I do not think I fully understood how big basketball had and could become for me as I made choices that truly hurt my career. Nor did I appreciate how local superstars from my UW team as well as from my generation, such as Nate Robinson, Will Conroy, Jamal Crawford, Brandon Roy, and so many others, lent to the creation and centrality of Seattle as a basketball supercenter.

Basketball has long been part of Seattle's identity. In 1953, the great forward/center Bob Houbregs led the Washington Huskies to the Final Four, scoring 42 points against Louisiana State in what was his last collegiate game. Although not from here, NBA Hall of Famer Elgin Baylor played college ball at Seattle University. Basketball teams were among the very few professional teams in the city to win championships prior to the Seahawks' 2013 Super Bowl win. The Seattle SuperSonics won the NBA championship in 1979, and the Seattle Storm won the Women's National Basketball Association (WNBA) championship in 2004 and again in 2010. I grew up watching Sonic greats Shawn Kemp and Gary Payton battle against Western Conference foes in the 1990s. Seattle natives have also contributed to Seattle's basketball history. During Game Six of the 1983 NBA Finals, Seattleite Clint Richardson, an O'Dea High School graduate who played college ball at Seattle University, hit a game-winning shot to secure the NBA championship for the Philadelphia 76ers. James Edwards, another Seattle native, graduated from Roosevelt High School and played for UW in the 1970s. He went on to play nineteen seasons in the NBA and won three championships. Edwards was a key contributor on the Detroit Pistons' back-to-back championship teams in 1989 and 1990. Doug Christie, who had a successful NBA career and is known as one of the best perimeter defenders to ever play the game, was a star at Rainier Beach High School. Jason Terry, one of the most decorated players the city has every produced, attended Seattle's Franklin High School before winning a NCAA championship with the University of Arizona in 1997. He went on to be named Pac-10 Player of the Year and earned First Team All-American honors his senior year in 1999. Terry was drafted tenth by the NBA's Atlanta Hawks. At the time, it was the highest a player from Seattle had ever been picked in the NBA draft. That would change over the next few years.[2]

As I look at prep rankings that regularly feature Seattle talent, I think about how far Seattle has come on the national basketball scene. I am proud to say that I was part of a ten-year (1998–2008) period during which Seattle increasingly rose to basketball prominence in a manner not seen since the SuperSonics' 1979 NBA Championship. That decade witnessed eleven first-round NBA draft picks. Three of those players—Jason Terry, Doug Wrenn, and Jamal Crawford—lent particular visibility to the city by the late 1990s. Wrenn is arguably the best high school basketball player ever from the state of Washington. He brought attention to Seattle with his great play in national camps and tournaments. In 1998, Wrenn was the first *Parade* All-American from the city and second from the state of Washington, which undoubtedly got colleges curious about the local talent. He was followed the next year in high school by the ambassador of Seattle basketball, Jamal Crawford—also a *Parade* All-American. Like Wrenn, Crawford was a standout at the national camps and tournaments. During one memorable performance while at the University of Michigan, Crawford put up 27 points against the mighty Duke Blue Devils and their star player at the time, Jason Williams. After playing only seventeen games with Michigan, Crawford would go on to be a lottery pick in the NBA draft. By 2015, Crawford's Seattle-based local summer league was the largest of its kind in the nation. He is still wowing crowds with his ball handling and scoring abilities.

Both Wrenn and Crawford played a tremendous role in my development as a basketball player. Their style of play and mentorship, as well as that of other local notables, were instrumental in my success. I am proud to be able to say that a few years after them, I also played well on the national level and did my part to show that Seattle has talent on the hardwood.

To Be Young, Black, and A Ball Player: My Basketball Origin Story

Playing basketball is not required to be black, but it sure helps. Basketball is a sizeable component of black culture. So, playing hoop was a part of my identity as a black kid because I theoretically had no choice—yes, even in Seattle. I remember when we would travel out-of-state for basketball tournaments and meet other black kids in the lobby from places like Los Angeles. They would ask my teammates and I questions, such as "Where is Seattle, in Alaska?" One question that really got to me was "Are there any black people in Seattle?" The line of inquiry had nothing to do with an ignorance of geography or demographics and everything to do with the fact that these kids were questioning our blackness and, by extension, our ability to play basketball. Although there was no way to prove how black we were, as no such litmus test exists, one thing that we could do was show them that we were just as good, if not better, than them at a sport they valued just as much as we did. It was only after we played them and often beat multiple teams that we would gain their respect. We took further offense to dumb questions about our abilities as related to our hometown because although we did not have the traditional "ghetto" that rivaled the structural inequality and poverty of cities like Chicago, Detroit, or New York, we still experienced institutionalized racism. Seattle provided the perfect landscape for generating ball players. Socioeconomic issues present in the black community due to racial discrimination, together with a lack of respect from players in larger cities, created an insatiable love for the game of basketball among local black youth.

I was born and raised in Seattle. It is a picturesque city, located between two mountains ranges—the Olympics to the west and the Cascades to the east. The beauty of these ranges is highlighted by Mount Rainer, which can be seen on clear days from different viewpoints throughout the city. Lake Washington is on the city's east side and the Puget Sound to its west. Seattle summers are amazing, but the days when grey dominates the sky and rain falls, beating on my window pane, are my favorite days in "The 206."

I love my city. I could not be prouder to be from Seattle. But there is a false sense of racial equality here. I learned from an early age that Seattle has two faces. The first is the beautiful, liberal, and progressive metropolis where anyone can be successful. The other one does not like to reveal itself as it is a face that totally contradicts the other. The socioeconomic disparities present in Seattle show up in education, income disparities, rates of unemployment, and homeownership and are similar to the disparities seen nationally among African Americans and other races.[3] Walking through my old neighborhood trying to find inspiration to write this piece, I began to think about how at one time, socioeconomic issues created a chip on the shoulder of so many black basketball players from inner-city Seattle. Every game against teams from nice, predominantly white neighborhoods was played as an opportunity to demand respect. My Central Area Youth Association (CAYA) AAU teammates made it a point to dominate white teams that had more than us. On the court, possessions and money did not matter.

In 1880, Seattle's black population was just under 200. By the turn of the century, black migrants were arriving in the city to work primarily on ships or trains. In 1882, William Grose, an early black pioneer of Seattle, bought twelve acres of land in Madison Valley from Henry Yesler. Black families began to move into the area and established a community. Over the next seventy years, Madison Valley and the hill up to Twenty-Third Avenue would continue to be the epicenter of Seattle's black community. African Americans only numbered approximately 2,300 by 1930. Their population in Seattle dramatically increased during and after World War II when wartime production would lure African Americans from the South. During much of the twentieth century, Madison Valley and the hill up to Twenty-Third Avenue would continue to be the epicenter of Seattle's black community. The centralization of the black population was born in large part to the existence of racially restrictive covenants placed on deeds that, until the US Supreme Court deemed them unconstitutional in 1948, would prevent African Americans from purchasing residential properties in many portions of the city. In the absence of restrictive covenants, other discriminatory measures such as redlining and blockbusting were used to ensure that many area neighborhoods remained white.[4]

Racial discrimination inadvertently helped to create a tight-knit black community in Seattle's Central District, or "CD" for short. I grew up in the CD in an area located up the street from the epicenter of the neighborhood at Twenty-Third Avenue and Union. My house was on Twentieth Avenue and Union Street. I remember becoming aware of the fact that my neighborhood was in the process of being gentrified during the mid-1990s while I was in middle school. In 1983, the year I was born, the CD was 64 percent black. By the time I started high school in 1998, the CD's black population dropped to 55 percent. The area is projected to be only 10 percent black in the near future. To watch the gentrification and subsequent destruction of that community breaks my heart as African Americans in the area took great pride in their neighborhood. The food, the parks, and the culture that were created, cultivated, and embraced are nearly all a memory now, a relic of a great past. Sadly, the locations of a lot of the memories I had on basketball courts are also no longer there.

My basketball career actually began on the football field. I was in fifth grade, and my parents let me play football for CAYA. During the 1980s and early

1990s, CAYA was an important organization for young black boys growing up in Seattle's CD. The yellow and putrid brown (or, as we called it, "dookie" brown) jerseys became a point of pride for the boys in my neighborhood. Growing up, we could not wait to put them on, but by the time I was involved in the league, they had come to their senses and swapped the brown for blue.

Founded in 1964, CAYA originally focused on youth football for children who resided in the CD. The organization was established to provide education, recreation, and social development activities for youth ages nine to eighteen. Many local college and professional athletes began their football or basketball careers playing for CAYA. My first coaches in CAYA recognized the need for role models in our community. Kevin Davis and Charles Proctor, both of whom have since passed, really invested genuine time in us. Both were educated black men with good jobs. They were family men who spent much of their time paving a path toward success for kids from economically marginalized areas. Proctor worked for Boeing, and Davis was a high-profile attorney. Proctor lived in the CD, and Davis lived in Mt. Baker, a very nice neighborhood just southeast of the CD near Lake Washington. It was extremely important for me to have black men like them in my life because I needed positive black male role models.

I remember going to a local hardware store that sold a little bit of everything on Rainier Avenue. My father and I went there to purchase my football cleats. Then we drove down to the Eastlake neighborhood to get a helmet. We ended up leaving with far more than a helmet as my father felt that I was going to need extra protection out there against kids who were clearly eager to hit. I was not the toughest kid at the time and was extremely uninterested in getting hit. I had to have forearm pads and an Eric Dickerson shoe collar. If I *were* Eric Dickerson and I had the Jheri curl, the glasses, and the running ability to match, I probably would have been fine, but this was my first year playing football, and I got placed on a team with a lot of older kids. Some of the kids were my age, but they were more developed than me. Pee wee football in Seattle determines the team a kid plays on based on weight not age. In my case, I was a fifth-grade kid, but I weighed the same as seventh and eighth graders. This was very unfortunate for me because it meant that I was likely going to be one of the weaker kids on the team.

That season was hell. I wanted to play wide receiver and ended up playing on the offensive line. To make matters worse, everyone made fun of the amount of equipment my dad made me wear. After that, I did not want to play football anymore. It had more to do with not wanting to have to wear the protective gear than anything else. I did not quit, but something happened that changed the course of my life.

I remember being at my grandma's house for dinner. The phone rang, and I answered it. A man, whom I later learned was Kevin Davis, asked for me. As a fifth-grader, I was amazed at the fact that someone called my grandma's house for me. I replied that it was in fact me on the phone, and he wasted no time asking me if I wanted to play basketball for a CAYA AAU basketball team. AAU basketball is different from recreational basketball. Based in the United States, it is a multi-sport organization dedicated to "the promotion and development of amateur sports and physical fitness programs," according to the AAU official website. My parents were a little upset because I immediately said yes prior to asking them and hurried to get one of my parents so that they could talk to Mr. Davis. I remember my dad telling people that Mr. Davis saw me while watching football practice one day and realized that I was tall for my age. That is actually true. I loved basketball, but I had never played on a team before and really had little interest until then of doing so. I ended up being a bench warmer on that team. I played a bit, but I was never a game-changing factor. That would come later.

The team practiced at Sharples Junior High in Seattle's South End. Sharples was an alternative school for the "troublemakers," and the area at the time was considered "bad." I knew this because my grandfather lived a few blocks from the school. Basketball was like a cocoon that gave us temporary safety from the many issues that plagued our community. It was therefore logical that Sharples' courts drew kids from around the area.

There were two white kids, Erik Bond and Graham Slaughter, who played on my first AAU team. They lived on the east side of Lake Washington. There was a stark, socioeconomic difference between the CD and the east side of Lake Washington. One of the white kids' parents had a fifteen-bedroom second home on Green Lake, a man-made lake in north Seattle. When I was young, many white, affluent parents believed that the best basketball was always going to be played in black urban communities by black kids. So, for affluent white kids to be competitive, the parents believed they should grow up playing with and against inner-city black kids. That is how Bond and Slaughter ended up on my AAU team. I think I was better than Slaughter, although he could shoot. Bond, on the other hand, was a very talented player and perhaps better than me at the time. He had older brothers who were playing in college, and his father had also played basketball, which certainly enhanced his skills. His knowledge of the game was accentuated by the fact that he could shoot and was tall.

Despite their talent, there was a clear difference between Bond and Slaughter and the rest of us on the team. For instance, Bond and Slaughter's houses made Davis's large house look like a shack. Until that point, Davis had the nicest house I had ever seen. They never needed help coming up with any of the expenses associated with playing a sport at the AAU level. Bond's father was serious about hoop and so, by extension, was Bond. But he never let it consume him like some of us did—neither he nor Slaughter had to because their circumstances did not require it. The things that I had to worry about never even crossed the minds of Bond and Slaughter. For them, basketball was not a way out of their economic circumstances. Their parents wanted them to be successful and receive athletic scholarships, but if it did not work out, they would be fine. For these kids, playing in the NBA was not nearly as important as it was for those of us in my neighborhood.

Some of my teammates had never been outside of their neighborhood, and if not for basketball, the boundaries of that neighborhood may have encompassed their entire reality. The league, then, would serve a dual purpose of providing a team setting for involved youth and exposing them to people and places they may have never encountered. I played CAYA AAU basketball from fifth through seventh grades, and in that time, we went on trips all over the country. I had been to California for my dad's family reunion. Other than that, I had never been out of the state of Washington. The first trip that we took as a team was to Las Vegas, Nevada, for the Las Vegas Easter Classic. Our biggest rival in the tournament was a team from Compton, California. The team featured a point guard named Kelan Fortune. He was a relentless guard who did not back down from anyone. We, however, had our own point guard who was very much like Fortune—the future NBA player Will Conroy. We ended up taking second place in that tournament.

Following our trip to Las Vegas, we traveled to Florida, where we finished eleventh in nationals. Seattle teams were not supposed to finish that high out of fifty to sixty teams because we were not considered a basketball city, in part due to the small black population. Everywhere we went, we showed that Seattle had talented kids. One of my teammates and good friends, Fred Baisy, really represented what Seattle had to offer during that national competition. He had an unstoppable spin move! I mean, it was pure beauty. He was, unsurprisingly, one of the top basketball players in the city for his age group.

Davis and Proctor coached my fifth and sixth grade teams. After that, a thirty-year-old white man named Tom Johns[5] took over the team with Jay Bond, Erick's dad, as his assistant coach. My dad used to call Johns "a street agent" because he had no ties to any of us kids prior to coaching us. Like William "Worldwide Wes" Wesley, who helped John Calipari land numerous recruits during his time as head coach at Memphis University, Johns helped the UW recruit me and others like Will Conroy and Nate Robinson, both of whom I would play AAU basketball with in high school.

Johns had attended O'Dea High School, a prestigious, all-boy Catholic school located in Seattle just a few blocks from downtown. He had wealthy parents and belonged to a prominent yacht club. I remember staying in the MGM Grand while playing in the Las Vegas tournament after Johns took over the team. Prior to that, we stayed off the Strip in the Sahara, one of the older hotels.

Seattle's Basketball Royalty: Garfield and Rainier Beach High Schools

My parents took me off the AAU team my eighth-grade year. I was upset, but I was not serious enough about basketball to really voice my frustrations. At that point, although I had no plans of playing hoop, I was looking forward to going to Garfield High School, where I would join my older cousin.

In the 1990s, Garfield High School's significance to the CD (which was, at the time, still predominantly black) was on par with the UW's significance to the city of Seattle. Garfield was more than a high school—it was the pride of the neighborhood. Garfield Bulldogs represented black excellence. They were a testament to the best that the state had to offer. I remember wanting to go to Garfield at a very young age. Kids hoped that they went to middle schools that funneled them into "the Field," as they called it. Thankfully, I went to Meany Middle School, which meant that I was a lock to go to Garfield.

I had numerous family members who had attended Garfield. It was a generational thing when uncles and aunties used to ask, "Is Ms. Brown still there?" She was a short black woman with a Marge Simpson-type of hairstyle who taught biology. They would tell stories about how crazy she was in the classroom. The memory of Ms. Brown and others at the school seemed to invoke a kind of nostalgia within my uncles and aunties that made me proud to attend the high school.

Garfield is the most-decorated basketball high school in the state of Washington with fourteen state titles. The only other school that comes close is Rainier Beach, where Nate Robinson played. Garfield's impact on the game of basketball in the city—more importantly its cultural significance to the community in which it is located—is unsurpassed by any high school in the area. When Garfield won, the CD won and *brothas* who bet won as well. Playing hoop in the hood was an extremely big deal. Betting money on games—into the thousands—was a common thing, as was talking "smack" about basketball at local barber shops. I have fond memories of sitting down for haircuts as a child in Preston's Barber Shop, located on Jackson Street between Twenty-Sixth and Twenty-Seventh Avenues, listening to black men of all ages arguing about basketball. It was a staple of my childhood. Although they talked about the NBA, NCAA, and other high schools in the area, when Garfield came up, the room's energy made a palpable upward shift. It was one thing to listen to these men in the barber shop speak about basketball prior to me being on the team, but when I started playing, it was a completely different experience. They began to speak directly to me about *my* basketball skills and what I *should* be doing on the court: "Your tall ass needs to fucking dunk everything. If I was yo' height. . . . Shit."

My basketball career is one big story of nontraditional routes. I had no intention of playing when I first got to high school. I was in the band but chose to skip class and smoke weed all day with my older cousin who was a junior at Garfield at the time. I enjoyed my time with AAU but felt satisfied that my basketball career was done. My life changed a bit as I grew about five inches and went from five feet, eleven inches to around six feet, four inches over the summer after my freshman year. The attention that I received following the growth spurt was uncomfortably noticeable. The head basketball coach, Wayne Floyd, went from not really talking to me to insisting that I play basketball due to my height. Until then, I never lamented the fact that kids can walk around a school for years and go unnoticed by most adults. If the same kid is tall or fast or has some type of amazing ability that is easy to see, he or she is automatically given a certain amount of admiration that will undoubtedly help that kid. At times, I wonder what happens to the kid with some untapped talent that is not related to athletics. Will he or she get noticed by adults in high school?

Coach Floyd's interest was not enough for me to try out for the team. During my first year at Garfield, I saw arguably the best defensive backcourt the city has ever seen when Jerry Petty, Clayton Smith, and "Super Sophs" Roydell Smiley and Ed Roy stepped onto the hardwood. They won the state championship in Seattle's Kingdome against Curtis High School. Curtis featured another CAYA alum, Curtis Allen, who would go on to play college ball at the UW. Garfield did not seem to need any help. Despite that, and although I was a little hesitant, I decided to try out for the basketball team my sophomore year. I was starting to feel like I had no choice after I grew. Additionally, Floyd would not let up about me trying out for the team. Another reason that I tried out is because I wanted to be allowed inside the gym for an exclusive run during school. There was a special gym class that was taught by Mr. Metzger, a white driver's education instructor who loved basketball. It was a 5-on-5 basketball session, and only the best basketball players were allowed. I remember skipping class as a freshman and sophomore, trying to get in, only to be denied by Metzger. Although I did not care about playing for the actual hoop team, basketball was still life—I loved the game. You could be outside the school all day and sell drugs, but there was still a good chance that you could shoot or at the least liked watching the best players do their thing on the court. So, while I was not allowed in the gym during those exclusive sessions, it didn't stop me from watching games through the cracks of the gym's double doors. Some of the most serious games took place in there. I did not want to miss them.

When tryouts arrived, there were sixty boys who wanted to play for the Bulldogs. All of them gathered in the gym to compete for a small number of coveted spots. Those trying out for the team were separated by talent levels, ages, and whether or not the player was on the team the previous season. If you were older or a returning player, you were on the east court. If you were younger or not as good, you were on the west court. All newcomers started on the west court, and if you were good enough, they would bring you over to the other side to see how you played against the older and better players. You had to be one of the best because everyone wanted to play for the Bulldogs. At one point, there were twenty senior ball players who attended Garfield who did not make varsity but were good enough to be starters at any other high school in the city. Nowadays, these guys would have transferred to other schools to play, but to my knowledge, none of the ones who were cut during my time did anything like that.

I had a great tryout and earned a spot on junior varsity (JV) and was, of course, excited. I was back on the court after settling into the notion that my basketball career was actually finished. At times during that season, I ended up on the varsity court.

Jason Jones was an assistant coach for the varsity team, and he was the head coach of the JV team. Unlike Coach Floyd, or legendary Coach Dave Belmonte, who actually coached Floyd at Franklin High School, Jones was a Bulldog himself, and he took great pride in passing on some of the traditions that set Garfield apart from the rest of the state. Jones was easily the toughest coach for whom I have ever played. I remember Jones made the team run in the snow once after he felt like we were not giving our all during a conditioning session. Alex Hatzey, a teammate of mine, was sick at the time and threw up during the practice. Jones showed no mercy. He was a no-holds-barred type of coach. If you did not understand what Garfield was about prior to playing for Jones, there was no way that you would have missed the message after spending time on his team. It was at this point that I started to take basketball a little more seriously.

We had a team room at Garfield. If you were not on varsity, you could not be in that coveted space. I remember peeking my head in there when the door was cracked, waiting for the day that I would be able to step foot in the hallowed varsity team room. The room had purple carpet and pictures on the walls of the great Garfield teams that had won district and state championships in the past. There was nothing but greatness in the team room, and to be in there meant that you had made a commitment to greatness as it was not enough just to strive for it. The only objective was to be great, to win. There were names written in white letters on red tape in the corner of the pictures that featured the best players on the teams. Clint Lomax, Andre Winston, Keith Harrell, and LeNard Jones had their names on the tape. They were just a few of the legends who came out of Garfield. It was not enough for me to just step foot in that room. I wanted to be on that wall. It was a big deal because if you did not win, you were not going to be up there, no matter how many points you scored. In the two years that I played on varsity, we lost to the same team my junior and senior years. Henry Foss High School, located in Tacoma, beat us two years in a row. I still hate looking at the Tacoma Dome as I drive through that city on Interstate 5 because it was the site of our defeat.

There have been many great Garfield teams. From 1980 to 1991 alone, for instance, Garfield won five basketball titles. They remain a basketball power-house in the city. Many of the players went on to play in college and then the NBA. My junior year included two more Division I players: Roydell Smiley, my favorite Bulldog of all time, and Tre Simmons, my cousin. Smiley signed with the University of Southern California, and Simmons signed with the UW after a stint in junior college where he became a scoring legend. Four of the five starters on my senior year team went to Division I colleges. Three of us—Will Conroy, Brandon Roy, and myself—went to UW. Marcellus Kemp (no relation to Shawn Kemp) went to the University of Nevada. At a lot of schools, seven Division I basketball players on one team would easily be the best team in school's history but not at Garfield. The fact that we did not win state my junior and senior years took my team out of any discussion for the best team title. Even if we did win state with all that talent, it would not have necessarily made us the best team Garfield had ever seen.

Although I only played a minute a game during my junior year, I was starting to gain respect among local ball players by playing pickup games at community centers and other gyms around the city, including a great run at Seattle University. Seattle community centers where pickup games occurred played a very important part in keeping a lot of kids out of trouble during the 1990s and early 2000s. The parks and late-night programs founded in the inner cities of Seattle, from the CD to the South End, provided black youth sanctuary. Even though the outside courts were subject to rain and other elements, for some reason, it seemed as if the hoop court was covered by a force field. Those basketball courts kept kids safe, off the streets, and focused on a life of something greater. It did not matter if it rained, snowed, or hailed. The courts seemingly were a guarded space. Drama did, however, take place on the court as I witnessed many fights while at the parks. At a young age, I was scared to fight as most of the people in altercations were grown men or some notable tough, young guy. As I got older, I realized that the fighting was inevitable; sometimes there was just no way around it. Whether you were fighting to get your shoes back or fighting due to someone trying to rough you up on the court, there were reasons to put up fisticuffs. Despite the harsh weather or bellicose atmosphere, the ball courts were where a lot of us went to find peace. We were dealing with all types of scenarios, from drug abuse and physical abuse to neglect and several other issues that were commonplace for many of us who frequented the courts. The weekend late-night programs saved lives, provided meals, and helped countless kids develop into good ball players. I was not always allowed to leave the house in the evening for fear that I would end up dead or in prison. That changed when I showed a genuine interest in hoop and left the house to play in one of the area pickup games, an interest that developed once I made the JV team at Garfield. My parents granted me a little more freedom to be out and about late at night because they knew that, for the most part, the basketball gym was safe place to be. When I made varsity at Garfield, I pretty much came home when I wanted if I was working out.

The competition at these basketball courts was everything. Getting on the court took a while due to the number of people waiting to join pickups, and staying on the court was tough. You tried to come with at least three people so that you had some idea of how others on your team played, thereby ensuring a win and extra time on the court. All the fun that the late-night programs brought, all the work that kids could put in on the court, was truly incredible. The main parks that I frequented varied. As a younger kid, I spent a lot of time at Madrona, Barnett, and Jefferson Parks. As I got older and started going to parks with my cousins and uncles, I started to play all over the city, from Lowell Elementary School in Capitol Hill to Van Asselt Elementary in the southern portion of the city. My favorite places to hoop were Miller Park, Rainier Community Center, Green Lake Park, Othello Park, and the half court hoops at TT Minor near my childhood house on Twentieth Avenue and Union Street.

Of all the courts on which I played, I probably gained the most respect as a ball player at St. Joseph's, a Catholic K-8 private school located on the border of the Capitol Hill neighborhood and the CD. St. Joe's, as we called it, transformed into the training grounds for some of the best players from my generation. Brandon Roy and Martell Webster were two players who frequented St. Joe's. Both went on to be lottery picks in the NBA draft. Without realizing it, the work that I was putting in at St. Joe's and courts throughout the city was preparing me for my second stint on the AAU scene. This time, however, I would play for the legendary Rotary AAU program.

By now, I was taller and extremely eager to play basketball. Following my junior year at Garfield, I had one school, the University of Portland Pilots, sending me letters. They did not offer a scholarship; it was a request for more information about myself as they probably never saw me play and simply heard that I was tall. I was not playing for an AAU team and, therefore did not have access to some of the exposure that helps players court interest from college programs. The local Youth Educational Sports Foundation (YES) began to show interest in me, however. I probably would have played for them if I had not received an unexpected phone call from an old coach. I had not talked to Johns in five years. "Do you want to play basketball," he asked me as soon as I answered the phone. At the time, it did not dawn on me that the only reason he was calling after five years was because he was desperate for a big man and that he had heard that I had grown quite a bit since we last spoke. I was six feet, eight inches tall by this time, and although I was clumsy, I was athletic for my size. I know that Johns took a chance on me, and I will always be thankful for that. He also enabled us to stay at beautiful hotels while we traveled for AAU. But at times I felt that he really could not have cared less about me as a person and was instead interested only in what my height could do for his team, which detracts from a lot of the significance of what he did. He had not checked on me once in those five years since I quit playing AAU ball. I heard that is how he is toward numerous kids whom he used to coach. Johns took in Fred Baisy, for instance, and helped him out while Baisy was in high school. Baisy has not spoken with him in some years now. Johns's actions show that what he was doing for Baisy had everything to do with what Baisy may have been able to give him later if, for instance, he had become a star in football or basketball. Once he saw that Baisy was not going to make it, Johns disappeared.

Johns contacted me at the end of my junior season at Garfield. I had averaged two minutes of playing time and 1.2 points per game. It was somewhat embarrassing. So, when Johns called, I was not thinking about how long it had been since I talked to him; I was just thinking about the fact that I would be able to play. All I wanted to do was play. He told me who was on the team, and I was sold; it did not matter that I was the only actual center on the team. I was going to be reunited with some of my old AAU teammates: James Delgardo, a point guard with lighting fast speed; Baisy, a six-feet-four-inch athletic forward who could guard multiple positions and provide an offensive presence in the paint; Will Conroy (with whom I had also played at Garfield), a hardworking, gritty point guard who went on to be UW's all-time leader in assists; and Gerald Smiley, one of the most talented athletes from Seattle. Smiley was eventually drafted by the Texas Rangers baseball team. I had not yet played with Rodrick and Lodrick Stewart, twins who would prove to be flat-out amazing. They were truly ahead of their time on the basketball court. Reggie Lamar, a strong but undersized big man from Everett, and Nate Robinson, in my opinion, the best athlete ever from the state of Washington, were also on the team. Roydell Smiley, a Garfield player and Seattle basketball legend, joined us for tournament play.

Johns often provided shoes for local players. My father never let me take them, that is until the coach offered me a spot on his team. The shoes, however, were not coming directly from him this time but rather from former SuperSonics Vin Baker and Gary Payton, who sponsored the AAU team and used their Nike endorsement deals to get us the company's footwear. (I still swear by Gary's signature shoe, the GP; it is easily the best shoe that I ever worn on the basketball court).

The SuperSonics also played an enormous role in helping develop the talent in Seattle. Head Coach George Karl did a lot for AAU basketball in Seattle. Superstars Payton and Shawn Kemp were very present in the neighborhood while I was growing up and funded court use and teams throughout the CD and South End of Seattle.

I could not have been more excited for my first game back in AAU. Equipped with my new shoes and spot on a highly visible AAU team, I felt like I was finally getting the opportunity to make a name for myself. I remember walking into California State's Dominguez Hills' gym in Carson, not really knowing what to expect. Games were being played simultaneously on three courts—one main court, which faced north-south, and two on opposite ends of the main court, which faced east-west. Several of the teams in the tournament featured great players who were nationally ranked. At the time, I was not ranked, and the only team that showed any interest in me was the University of Portland. I remember looking into the stands and seeing Kenyon Martin, who was a member of the Cincy Bearcats the year before and was on his way to being drafted by the New Jersey Nets. I felt like I had no choice but to ball out given the present talent. As we were stretching on the side of the bleachers in the corner of the gym, legendary AAU Director Darryl Henning came up to me and explained that I had an opportunity to make a name for myself in Seattle. I took it to heart. At the same time, however, I thought about the fact that I wanted to be known not only in Seattle but also across the country. Our first game was against a team from California. I had 9 blocks and 13 points, falling just shy of a double-double.

The second game is when my story really began. The opposing team shot the ball, and my teammate and I both went for the rebound—both of us at different points of the ball's trajectory. As I was coming, his elbow met my right front tooth. I remember yelling, "my fucking tooth!" and running right off the court and through the double doors into the hallway. I had to have the tooth extracted while I was in Los Angeles. Something happened to me when I lost my tooth; something about me changed. My anxiety on the court disappeared. I had a huge gap in my mouth, but I did not care. It somehow fueled me. I became a player at that moment.

I returned for the next game, which was against the EBO All-Stars—a California team. (Jamaal Williams was on that team. He would later be my teammate at UW.) This time, I had found my basketball acumen. I nearly had a triple-double that game. The next game was the semifinal game against another all-star team. This team was one of the favorites going into the tournament. It featured multiple players who were ranked in the top fifty in the country. Rick Rickert, for instance, a top-ranked power forward, went on to play for the Minnesota Timberwolves. Salim Stoudamire, who ended up being one of the greatest shooters I have ever played against, signed with the University of Arizona—the premier program in the Pac-10 at the time—and then played for the Atlanta Hawks. Isaiah Fox and Dennis Latimore, power forwards who also went on to play for Arizona, were on that AAU team, as was Chris Hernandez. He ended up playing at Stanford University. During that tournament, Nate Robinson would prove that Hernandez was overrated, in my opinion. I ended up with a triple-double and a tournament-record 17 blocks. Robinson chipped in with 36 points, and Roydell was the difference maker in the game as he also scored 36 points, carefully choosing his spots and picking the opposing team apart. We went on to beat that team, a team that was better than us on paper, but I suppose that is why they say "on paper."

We made it to the championship game and faced a team from Flint, Michigan. I will never forget Robert Whaley, a power forward who stood six-feet-nine-inches tall. Although the game was close, the Michigan Mustangs beat us. They were better than us or perhaps just more mature. I will also say that of all the ball players against whom I played in my twenty-year basketball career, the toughest, most consistent players came from Michigan. You talk about a chip—they played like they had boulders embedded into their shoulders.

I remember coming back home to letters from the University of California, Los Angeles, and the University of Kansas. Phone calls came in from Syracuse University, the University of Oregon, and the UW. I was being recruited! I went from receiving a questionnaire from the University of Portland to opening letters and talking to coaches from schools all over the nation! My play even got me an invitation to the Nike All-American Camp. It was an honor and something that I did not take lightly because Smiley was invited the year before me. Former NBA basketball player Luke Ridnour, who also played for CAYA growing up, was the other player invited to camp the year Smiley went. Ridnour used to drive from Blaine, Washington, a small town on the US-Canadian border, to Seattle so he could play with the best competition in the area.

The enormity of being selected for the Nike All-American roster was amplified for me because I was joined by Will Conroy, my high school and CAYA AAU teammate, and Erik Bond, also an AAU teammate. It took me a little longer to become a good player; therefore, making it to the Nike camp solidified the fact that I was on their level. To have three Nike All-Americans from the same grade-school AAU team was monumental at the time. It happens quite frequently now. The camp was full of prep star ball players that I had read about in *Slam* magazines. Never in a million years did I think that I would be in the same gym with them. It might sound crazy, but my favorite part about camp was the fact that they were serving us Hi-C Orange drink, which was and still is the only drink that I get from McDonalds. I also met a lot of star prep players at the camp.

While at the camp, I became good friends with Tyson Chandler, who was the top-ranked high school player in the country at the time. He would bypass college and go straight to the NBA draft and be selected first overall. He gave me the nickname "Tooth" due to my missing tooth. I did not have a chance to get it fixed before the Nike All-American camp. We were drawn to each other and became friends quickly. We were teammates, which was cool for me as I took full advantage of the attention he drew on the offensive end of the court. I dunked every ball he passed to me.

At the end of the first day, everyone was talking about stats and how many points and rebounds they averaged during the high school season. Everyone was throwing out ridiculous numbers, talking about the colleges that they were thinking of attending. I remember how in disbelief Tyson and other players were when I told them that I only scored 1.2 points a game my junior year. I explained that I had a great tournament and thus was invited to the camp. They were really impressed, and it was in that moment that I began to feel like I belonged there. As a result of the tournament, I became a top recruit, someone teams would come and see. I was part of all the talk about Seattle talent.

Although I had the opportunity to go nearly anywhere I wanted to in the country, I chose the UW. I wanted to be part of the team that got the city's beloved "Udub" back to the tournament and put the school on the basketball radar once and for all. Many of my friends and family members always remind me that I could have played with Carmelo Anthony at Syracuse as they were recruiting me at one point. While I was in high school, UW had a few bad seasons, but the team was good my freshman year. I remember Donald Watts led the team to the Sweet Sixteen and came within one shot of getting to the Elite Eight, where they would have faced the North Carolina Tar Heels. Although the Huskies lost to the University of Connecticut, their success that season was stuck in my head.

I am proud to say that I was a part of the resurgence UW saw after hiring Coach Lorenzo Romar in 2002. By my sophomore season (2003–2004), we accomplished things that few Huskies teams had ever accomplished. We beat Arizona State University, which was considered a powerhouse basketball programs. We swept the two-game series against Arizona while they were ranked fourth in the nation. Our biggest win occurred, however, when we ruined Stanford's bid for an undefeated season. We were a team full of Seattle kids: Nate Robinson, Will Conroy, Brandon Roy, Tre Simmons, and me. Perhaps one of the best parts of our storied wins is that Robinson, Conroy, and I had beaten Chris Hernandez from Stanford and Salim Stoudamire from Arizona during the California AAU tournament. Now, we had beaten them on two different levels of play.

We would go on to finish the season winning fifteen out of our last sixteen games, which earned us a trip to the NCAA tournament. We fell to the University of Alabama at Birmingham (UAB) in the first round. I will never forget the excitement we experienced the day before that game. We had a shootaround and after we finished going over the plays and the scouting report, we all took turns doing our best dunks. Despite only playing a short time in the game against UAB, I was able to get a tip dunk at the buzzer, which was featured on the "One Shining Moment" highlight reel shown at the end of the tournament. Even though we lost, the entire tournament experience was one of the best experiences of my life.

I chose weed over my basketball career at UW, a choice that I very much regret. As early as ten years old, I was smoking weed with my cousins and later my friends before we would go to the park or the gym to play basketball. There were times that I would smoke weed before I went to basketball practice at Garfield High School. I grew up not really thinking weed was a problem. It was not until I injured my left foot during my freshman year at the UW that my marijuana use become increasingly problematic. I had too much time on my hands, I was in pain, and I was upset because, as a result of the injury, I lost my starting position. I quickly learned that marijuana was frowned upon, but I did not want to stop engaging in my habit. My reluctance to change in part led to off the court issues with Romar. I had to leave UW as a result after my sophomore year and ended up transferring to Portland State University (PSU), where I began to look at basketball from a different lens. This new perception was due largely to the difference in the quality of scholarships offered at UW and PSU. Athletes were not heralded at PSU quite like they were at UW, and this was reflected in the dorms, the money allotted for education, and myriad other things.

While I enjoyed my professors at PSU, I cannot say the same for the two head coaches for whom I played. One, Ken Bone, happened to be an assistant coach during my time at UW. Bone took the head coaching job at PSU, and it was the worst news that I could have received. We had had issues during my time at UW, and he had not forgotten about it. He made it a point to make my time at PSU very hard.

The year after I transferred, the Huskies would go on to win the Pac-10 Championship. The team was so good they earned a number one seed in the NCAA tournament. Although they lost in the Sweet Sixteen, that team was a testament to Seattle basketball. I felt good because while I did not make it there with them, I was part of that process. I was the first to sign at the UW out of all the Seattle guys on that team, and I was able to help them build a team that would make it to the tournament.

After I left PSU, I had a solid career playing basketball in numerous countries overseas. My career ended due to injuries. Somewhere between my time at PSU and playing basketball overseas, I really started to look at basketball as a detriment. Some began to point out that I would have never gone to school if I did not play basketball, which is very true. The heavy push helped many of us get of the hood and allowed us to play basketball at the collegiate level, but what happens after basketball? What happens to the kids who do not have the opportunity to play after they are eighteen years old? In recent years, AAU basketball has become highly monetized, and the only ones who seem to miss out on the money are the kids. While I have no doubt that they are happy about receiving shoes and going on trips, they are being cheated in many ways.

We have legendary basketball coaches and AAU directors like Darryl Hennings and Andro Bernard who have dedicated years of service and have helped hundreds of kids receive scholarships to go off and play basketball. I have nothing but respect for them, and I am grateful that they allowed me to play for Rotary the one year that I did because that year changed the course of my life. You would not be reading these words if not for that one year. I do, however, harbor a concern that there are few equivalents to Hennings and Bernard's program in economically marginalized communities when it comes to academics. The same energy that was used to help kids get scholarships on the basketball court needs to be duplicated and used for kids in underserved communities to receive scholarships for non-athletic reasons. There are some people who are trying to ensure that athletes are academically driven. Lou Hopson, for instance, co-founded YES, a program designed to ensure that high school athletes are studying and taking the classes necessary to enroll in college. Hopson's program helps to ensure that kids who play sports have more balance between athletics and academics. It helped to produce players such as Brandon Roy and Martell Webster. I have noticed that a lot of my former teammates who now have kids do a great job of balancing school and athletics and I commend them, but there are still kids whom I have worked with who are far too focused on basketball. While I still love basketball, I cringe at times because the same stories of kids getting hurt or in trouble, only to ruin any chances of them making it to college or the professional level, are still commonplace. Despite my concerns, undoubtedly AAU launched the careers of multiple local players who helped to render Seattle relevant on the national and international basketball scene. Seattle basketball has reached a level of popularity that rivals the bigger, more well-known basketball cities like Los Angeles and New York.

Seattle's popularity on the national basketball scene is now at an all-time high. Seattle's Metro League, for instance, is currently one of the premier prep leagues in the country. The significance of Garfield High School's excellence is lessened a bit, however, by the fact that the CD is being rapidly gentrified and many of the working-class African American residents are

Anthony Washington

being displaced. Many of the kids who now attend the school are not driven by the same need to escape their economic circumstances that drove us to success. Nonetheless, Garfield is still ranked nationally on a regular basis and has produced numerous Division I athletes since my time there. At one time, it was a big deal for kids from Seattle to be recognized nationally in the world of basketball. Today, kids from Seattle receiving college scholarships and making it to the NBA is commonplace. I highly doubt any of these kids today have to explain or prove that Seattle isn't in Alaska.

CHAPTER FIVE

"That Splendid Medium of Free Play"

Japanese American Sports in Seattle during the Interwar Years

SHELLEY LEE

One evening in March 1934, George Okada, the president of the Seattle Taiyo Athletic Club, gave an address during the *Courier Broadcast* on radio station KXA. Looking to boost the club's membership and impress upon listeners the importance of physical fitness, he extolled the personal and professional benefits that play and exercise accrued: "The art of physical development is the one form of amusement, which is not only invigorating, but beneficial to mind and body alike. One cannot be a good athlete . . . without being in perfect physical condition, keenly alive mentally, cheerful of spirit, and of high moral character. It is obvious that such training prepares a man to better fulfill whatever career he may undertake."[1]

At the time, such rhetoric touting athletic play as a nurturer of good physical and moral qualities resonated broadly in America. It echoed the sentiments of baseball promoter Albert G. Spalding, who wrote in 1911 that, "the emotional and moral as well as the physical side of a man's nature are brought into play by Base Ball. . . . And there is nothing better calculated than Base Ball to give a growing boy self-poise and self-reliance, confidence, inoffensive and entirely proper aggressiveness, general manliness."[2] The quotation came from a book entitled *America's National Game*, in which

Spalding further intoned, "Base Ball elevates and . . . fits the American character."[3] Seeing the compatibility of profitmaking and patriotism, he channeled baseball's popularity to sell sporting goods while promoting an ideal of the United States as a nation of athletic, confident, and *manly* citizens.

Okada expounded on this view of sports as morally and physically fortifying but for different reasons. He tailored his message around personal improvement and ethnic solidarity for Japanese Americans in Seattle, and he also spoke to the global arena, where US–Asia affairs were rocky due to Japan's aggressive actions in China. Sports, Okada thought, could contribute to a "real good understanding between America and Japan."[4] During the 1930s, goodwill trips to Japan by American professional athletes tried to enact this goal of strengthening US–Japan relations. In 1939, a writer for the *Japanese-American Courier* elaborated: "I always said participation in any clean sport does more towards creating understanding and strong friendship than anything else. If these politicians and so-called statesmen spent less time arguing for more guns and battleships, and put in more effort towards advancement of the international sports competitions, perhaps we wouldn't have to worry so much about wars and misunderstandings."[5]

During the prewar decades, sports filled the time of thousands of Japanese Americans in Seattle as players or spectators, and ruminations about the social and political meanings of athletics preoccupied Japanese American leaders and observers. Impassioned commentary came from people like George Okada, who saw sports as a vehicle to improve Japanese American life in terms of personal development, interracial understanding, and better relations between the United States and Japan. In reality, athletics in the early-twentieth-century United States—from urban playgrounds to professional leagues—were highly segregated, and in the context of internationalism, sports like baseball were subject to the nationalistic claim that they were *American* pastimes. Yet, as evidenced in Okada's remarks, something about sports—perhaps their theoretical color-blindness—sustained the hope that a universal humanity was possible and could overcome the divisions separating people. This belief offered consolation to observers who wished that the United States and Japan could remain friendly despite the troubles in the Pacific, as well as to racial and ethnic minorities long denied opportunities and inclusion in the mainstream society.

This chapter considers how athletics were a flexible terrain on which Seattle's Japanese Americans negotiated racial, ethnic, spatial, and geographic boundaries, examining what they said about sports as well as the varied experiences that athletic participation made possible. A significant portion of the competition Seattle Japanese American athletes faced came from co-ethnics in the countryside, other parts of the American West, Canada, and even Japan. These translocal dimensions of sports illuminate the salience of place and scale in Seattle Japanese Americans' conceptualization of their dualistic identities as Japanese and American. They also show how sports *could* be nationalizing and Americanizing for Seattle's Japanese but in unexpected ways. As a common symbol for international relations and one of few activities that offered Japanese Americans the chance to travel outside the city, sports helped map their expansive outlook on and engagement with the world. Sports were also a site for the early cultivation of a pan-Asian consciousness as competitions against local Filipinos and Chinese played out against the backdrop of Pacific Rim politics.

Through sports Japanese Americans expressed their local and international aspirations, invoking them to reflect on prospects for continued peace in the Pacific, call for friendship between the United States and Japan, and express their hopes for local acceptance. Because in theory, anyone could play, and physical ability—not racial or ethnic background—determined the outcomes, sports could be a space in which to discursively challenge a white-only vision of Americanism and pose in its place an egalitarian, cosmopolitan ideal. Although achieving this ideal in the real world was another matter, and racial segregation in American sports remained largely in place until after World War II, Japanese Americans and other Seattle minorities did have one play space that embodied and emboldened their hopes for a more inclusive society. At Collins Park, the playground closest to most of the city's nonwhites and ethnic minority residents, a veritable multicultural mosaic of young Seattleites emerged by the late 1920s. Hailed as the city's most "cosmopolitan" park, the people who used its facilities and worked there regarded Collins with pride and described it as an exemplar of an enlightened, open, and globally conscious Americanism that drew strength from internationalism and diversity.

Sports and Recreation in Seattle and America

Amidst modernization and crisis in the late nineteenth to early twentieth centuries, sports emerged as a popular form of recreation in the United

States. Americans entered a new era as the pace of industrialization and urbanization accelerated, work lives became more regimented, and foreign immigration diversified a predominantly Anglo Christian population. In this context, members of the growing middle class turned to outdoor recreation and physical play as antidotes to the physical and psychological strains of living in a modernizing, fast-paced world. A generation of experts imbued with the Progressive Era's faith in science and expertise touted the benefits of structured play for children's physical and moral development. Among the leaders of the recreation movement and "gospel of play" were middle-class reformers and specialists working in such organizations as the Young Men's Christian Association (YMCA), the Young Women's Christian Association (YWCA), and the Playground Association of America.[6] The construction of hundreds of resorts in the East and Midwest during the late 1800s enabled (well-heeled) families to partake in the recreation culture in peaceful, natural settings away from the overcrowded cities.

The need for parks where people could play or sit in contemplation became especially pressing in growing cities toward the turn of the twentieth century, including those in the American West. Proponents of the construction of recreational and athletic spaces argued that structured, supervised play was a wholesome alternative to the dangerous vices that lurked in urban settings. In terms of recreational options, Seattleites were blessed by geography. The surrounding lakes and mountains made the Puget Sound area a haven for skiing, hiking, mountain climbing, and boating. Boosters worked hard to promote Seattle as a unique place that offered nature and urbanity, indeed, the best of both worlds, and urban planners worked to develop the city around showcasing these qualities. In 1884, Seattle's first public park was built, and three years later, a Board of Park Commissioners was established to oversee the development of a citywide park system. In 1903, the board hired the Olmsted Brothers firm to design the system, which was envisioned to place every resident within walking distance to a park.[7]

The national recreation movement coincided with a wave of foreign immigration that transformed the America's cities. Concerned about the effects of urban life and the challenges facing new immigrants, Progressive reformers looked to sports and structured play to help facilitate immigrants' acculturation and learning of good values and habits. Groups like the Playground Association of America and YMCA took the lead in arguing for the universal benefits of sports. Because the ability to play required only physical aptitude and understanding of rules, sports appeared to be a unique arena in which cultural barriers were surmounted and understanding across social boundaries prevailed. Furthermore, the spectacle of foreigners from Greece, Poland, or Russia—people seen as barely removed from their premodern, old-world existences—participating in such sports as baseball or basketball signaled the triumph of American values in immigrants' hearts and minds. Although images of immigrants enjoying American sports underscored for many the transformative power of the national culture, the realities of segregation and nativism meant that minorities usually played sports with and against members of their own racial and ethnic groups. That many athletic associations in the United States during the late nineteenth and early twentieth centuries were organized along ethnic or religious lines further reinforced group boundaries rather than blurring them.[8]

Among Seattle's Japanese, sports were Americanizing *and* affirming of ethnic solidarity. Sports coverage filled a quarter to half of the content of Japanese American newspapers, and by the 1930s, the Seattle Japanese American community had one of the largest organized athletic leagues in the city, the Japanese-American Courier League. S. Frank Miyamoto attributed the popularity of sports to the organizational propensity of the community. "The sports activities in the Japanese community were very much better organized than in my white society," he recalled. "In the Japanese community, it was typical that if you played football or played baseball or basketball, very rapidly you would get drawn into some kind of team organization."[9] With such a well-developed structure, sports became an avenue into a rich social life for Japanese Americans. Toshio Ito noted, "In the older days I think the sporting, sports events, and participating in that was one of the major social outlets for the *Nisei*, because so many of the other mainstream activities were closed to the Japanese at that time."[10] Community leaders endorsed sports for the youth as a wholesome alternative to activities they disapproved of, such as drinking alcohol and gambling. Sensitive about public perceptions of their co-ethnics and accusations that they were unassimilable, they extolled athletics for fostering a "clean" image and allowing Japanese people to demonstrate their capacity to become "American" and, thus, to counter the claims of naysayers.

For Japanese in America accustomed to being viewed and treated as outsiders, inclusion in the sports world, whether as spectators, commentators, or participants, created a meaningful sense of belonging and empowerment. Accomplished athletes on all-Japanese teams or in mixed settings were widely admired by their fellow Japanese Americans, and sometimes their accomplishments symbolized triumphs over racism. Organized sports were also integral to the social scene in Nihonmachi as clubs hosted dances and mixers to raise funds and community-wide events were held to celebrate major victories or mark the start and conclusion of a season. As far as the symbolic meanings of athletic competition, ethnic leaders and writers sought to inspire ordinary Japanese Americans by insisting—much as progressive whites did—on the potential for sports to bring different people together in a color-blind spirit to foster understanding and equality. Such rhetoric, lofty as it was, could nonetheless be a source of consolation that sustained Japanese Americans' hopes for overcoming the social and structural barriers that they faced in their daily lives.

Baseball and Ethnic Authority

The establishment of *Issei* baseball clubs around the turn of the twentieth century planted the seeds of a flourishing sports culture in Seattle's Japanese American community. As early as the 1910s, it was a common Sunday afternoon sight in Nihonmachi to find young Japanese men playing on the local diamond before cheering spectators. The earliest athletic organizations for Japanese in Seattle were devoted to baseball, the first being the Nippons Club, formed in 1906. The Nippons were composed of *Issei* men employed as cannery workers, janitors, domestics, and other low-wage workers who found in baseball a welcome diversion.[11] By 1911, there were three *Issei* baseball teams in Seattle: the Mikado, the Seattle Nippons, and the Asahi. Into the 1920s, with the rise of the *Nisei* and aging of the first generation, baseball became more identified with the second generation. For a time, the Japanese Language School provided the only structured outlet for *Nisei* baseball, forming the first *Nisei* baseball team in the city, the Cherries, in 1911. The Seattle Japanese American sports infrastructure grew substantially in 1924 when the Nippon Athletic Club (NAC) was created to defuse tensions between the Asahi and the Mikado and to meet players' and fans' desire for a sports club rather than just individual teams. Shortly afterward, the Taiyo Athletic Club was established, and the two clubs commenced a spirited rivalry that lasted until the outbreak of World War II.

Japanese American baseball fans were passionate about the sport and their favorite teams, and sometimes, rivalries and fanaticism led to worrisome problems like betting and fighting.[12] Another way fans showed their team loyalty was to organize boycotts of businesses run by rival teams' supporters, which occasionally required leaders to intervene and admonish people for their pettiness. At the height of the NAC-Taiyo rivalry, a group of Taiyo fans boycotted stores run by NAC supporters. As they did during the days of the Asahi-Mikado rivalry, community leaders and local journalists were drawn in. "The present N.A.C.-Taiyo feud is a thorn in the side of the Japanese community for real harmony and progress," a columnist wrote in the *Japanese-American Courier* in 1928. "Small as this keen, embittered rivalry is considered by many of the business men of the Japanese center, it bids well to crop into an inflammatory malady that may take years to remedy." The writer then beseeched fans to summon their "intelligent" and "commendable qualities" to overcome this "ill" before it became untenable.[13]

Key figures in the Seattle Japanese American community were instrumental in assuring baseball's popularity, and few were as consequential as Frank Fukuda, known as the "Father of Japanese Baseball in the Pacific Northwest." In 1917, he founded the Asahi Club, located at Tenth and Washington and managed the team for eleven years, during what locals later referred to as Seattle Japanese baseball's "glory days."[14] The *Japanese-American Courier* recounted how Sunday mornings in Nihonmachi frequently found Fukuda "making the rounds" from house to house, rousing boys to come out and play ball. "He early taught the lads through baseball," stated the *Courier*, "the advantages of team work, of quick thinking and of the never-say-die spirit." Interested in his players' holistic development, Fukuda also held weekly Friday meetings devoted to "the art of public speaking, which they gained unconsciously when they stood up in their gatherings to tell their comrades of their ideas."[15] Although parents and fans sometimes found him to be overbearing, they "hate[d] to admit the good that Fukuda accomplished in this city but to him much of the credit should be given for the benefits that their sons received through his training."[16]

A turning point in the history of Seattle Japanese American sports was the formation of the Japanese-American Courier League in 1928.[17] It was the brainchild of newspaper publisher, former Franklin High star football player, and professional boxer James Sakamoto. He envisioned the Courier League as a large independent sports league for all the Japanese athletic teams in the Puget Sound area that would unite participants above the rancorous rivalries of the past.[18] As an organization primarily for the *Nisei*, the Courier League reflected a broader demographic shift in the Japanese American community as well as Sakamoto's view that sports could facilitate *Nisei* acculturation and the generation's role as "bridges of understanding" between the United States and Japan.[19] From 1928 to 1941, the Courier League was the heart and soul of Seattle Japanese baseball. Initially consisting of ten teams, it grew to fourteen within three years, and at its height in the late 1930s, thirty-two teams represented four classes—AA, A, B, C. While Seattle was the league's headquarters, it included teams from other cities and rural towns, such as Kent, Tacoma, Fife, and Auburn, with teams typically formed around churches, neighborhoods, and other athletic clubs.[20] The Taiyo and NAC joined the Courier League in the early 1930s after initially refusing to do so.

Describing the social significance of baseball in Japanese American history, Gail Nomura and Samuel Regalado argue that the sport's bottom-up popularity and community leaders' endorsement strengthened ethnic bonds and identity. And unlike other forms of "American" culture, such as music or dating practices, baseball did not appear to cause generational friction. *Issei* leaders and parents did not worry that *Nisei* were becoming less Japanese or that the older generation's authority was being undermined. Instead, the *Issei* often claimed *they* were more devoted to the sport. Because many first-generation immigrants had been introduced to it in Japan, baseball represented generational continuity rather than discontinuity. In 1928, the *Great Northern Daily News* waxed nostalgic about the "old days" of Japanese baseball in Seattle and chided the *Nisei* for lacking the dedication of their predecessors to the game:

> The Taiyo and NAC do not take their baseball as seriously as the old-timers. The players of years ago ate baseball, slept baseball and talked baseball continually. The present day youngsters may be better ball players but they do not possess that faithful spirit. The ball players of years ago would never think of staying down town shooting pool until eleven or twelve o'clock on Saturday night; they would shudder at even the thoughts of such unholy things.[21]

Baseball and Japanese Networks Across Space

The camaraderie among Japanese Americans cemented by a shared passion for baseball went beyond the limits of Seattle as games also brought together

Jimmie Skamoto. Photograph with handwritten inscription: "To my associate and pal, Elmer Ogawa, with best wishes, Jimmie Sakamoto, April 14, 1928." Also handwritten on photograph: "Presented to the Round Table, January 1949, Elmer Ogawa" Property of University of Washington Libraries, Special Collections Division

Japanese throughout the Northwest, along the West Coast, and on both sides of the Pacific.[22] The Courier League covered the Pacific Northwest and included teams from throughout Washington State and Oregon, and it also regularly sponsored traveling all-star teams to play against co-ethnics in California and British Columbia.[23] Because few other activities offered young Japanese Americans the opportunity to travel to the countryside and across state or international lines, participating in sports leagues opened them to new experiences outside Seattle and Nihonmachi. Moreover, traveling or interacting with visitors from afar reinforced their identities as urban, northwestern, and American.

Japanese Americans in Seattle participated in and helped weave together an enduring and dynamic Pacific Northwest baseball culture. Players from the cities and rural areas of Washington, Oregon, and British Columbia traversed the region each season from April to August in a quest to call themselves the Northwest's best, and annual traditions like the Fourth of July Tournament, the Labor Day International Series, and the crowning of the Courier League champion, solidified the regional sporting culture. Banquets and socials in honor of visiting teams allowed for the creation of new friendships that, in turn, sustained long-distance ties between disparate Japanese American communities. Intraregional sports could, thus, nurture an ethnic consciousness transcending the local community while also heightening Seattle Japanese Americans' sense of themselves as urbanites, particularly facing competitors from rural areas. For instance, fans in Seattle often paid homage to the Wapato Nippons of Central Washington, a team respected for its talented players and domination of the Mount Adams League in Yakima County. The characterization of the Wapato Nippons as "rip-roaring, sun-burned, lean-muscled luminaries," however, underscored how Seattle Japanese Americans viewed their rural counterparts.[24] And in 1935 when teams from White River, Fife, and Portland had taken nearly all the top titles, the *Japanese-American Courier* lamented, "Painfully, the Seattle Japanese community wrote finis to the 1935 baseball season," adding that the season had been "the most disastrous year in local diamond history." The only consolation for "local rooters" was a team from Green Lake's victory over the Wapato Nippons in the annual Northwest Tournament sponsored by the Seattle Japanese Association.[25]

Regarding coast-wide competition, Seattleites expressed interest in a regular baseball series between teams from the Pacific Northwest and California, but a robust West Coast tradition never materialized before World War II. In 1921, the Seattle Asahis battled their brethren in the "Southland" of Central California, and despite the community's excitement over this event, it would be the only such meeting for more than a decade in part because of the logistical and financial costs involved. When a Northwest-California "clash" resumed in 1937, thanks to the fundraising and organization of local sports booster G. K. Nakamura, the *Great Northern Daily News* hailed him as the "Man of the Year."[26] Following this trip, hyped as "the greatest mass baseball movement ever staged in the Northwest," locals raised the possibility of an annual all-star Japanese Northwest-California matchup that would be billed the "Lil' Tokyo World Series."[27] This never came to fruition, as Nakamura's death in 1938 left a void in the local Japanese American baseball booster community, and subsequent games against Californians were sporadic. Nonetheless, interest in a West Coast tradition remained. During a Northwest squad's 1938 trip to the San Francisco Bay Area, the visiting athletes were struck by the California clubs' eagerness to play against them. "Word of Northwest hospitality must be circulating rapidly," said the *Japanese-American Courier,* "for the San Jose Asahi baseball club was pretty hot about coming north for a series. They hope the make the trip next spring."[28]

Finally, Japanese baseball networks also crossed the Pacific. During the heyday of college and professional American baseball world tours in the 1920s and 1930s, lower-profile tours were also occurring among Japanese teams to the United States and Japanese American teams to Japan. According to Riyochi Shibazaki, a "Seattle-Japan baseball connection" dates back to 1905, when Waseda University's team visited the United States to play against college teams.[29] Japanese Americans were very proud to witness this exchange of hospitality between people from their country of origin and their adopted homeland. To show support, the Japanese Club of Seattle presented money and gifts to Waseda during its visit to play against the University of Washington. Inspired and eager to maintain ties with the homeland, *Issei* club managers organized trips to Japan for their players. The Mikado went first in 1914 and then again in 1921 and 1922. During the 1920s, manager Frank Fukuda took his teams several times for what he called "educational tours," and the boys' and girls' divisions of the Taiyo Athletic Club took at least five trips during the 1930s.

By the late 1920s, Seattle's Japanese squads were hosting and even playing against teams from Japan. In 1928, the Kwansei Gakugin, a team of Japanese secondary school students, came to play against a Courier League team.[30] Although they beat the Japanese Americans handily, the Courier players were commended for "[making] it interesting and . . . [showing] their gameness." The game reportedly drew the largest crowd of the season and included "quite a number of Americans."[31] Other highlights of Japan-Seattle baseball included a visit in 1929 by Keio University's team to compete against the NAC and Taiyos and a 1939 meeting between an all-star Courier League team and the Tokio Giants.[32]

Americanism Through Internationalism

These baseball circuits of travel across the Pacific illustrated the internationalization of the sport, a subject that tends to foreground the export of the sport from the United States to other countries as a function of its global influence. Such a view obscures the existence of two-way dynamics and how recipients shaped their relationship to baseball for their own purposes. In the case of Japan, baseball by the late nineteenth century was considered *its* national sport. Many *Issei* in Seattle, thus, had been familiar with it long before they arrived in North America. Americans like Spalding insisted that baseball reflected American values, but Japanese devotees argued that it was compatible with *their* national character, especially the qualities of loyalty, honor, and courage.[33] Additionally, a distinct Japanese style of playing baseball was said to have evolved in which pitching, speed, and bunting were emphasized over American baseball's trademarks of "heavy hitting" and home runs.[34] Sports historian Robert Sinclair argues, "Not only did baseball enhance any sense of national identity among the Japanese people, but the country's excellence in playing the summer game, particularly against American opposition, helped redefine Japan's international image."[35]

If baseball was Americanizing for Seattle's Japanese, it was in ways that also affirmed their ethnic identities and allegiances. To take one example, in American society by the early twentieth century, the Fourth of July holiday had become widely associated with sports events, something immigrant communities came to share in. Among Seattle Japanese Americans, the "Northwest's biggest sporting event" was the annual Fourth of July baseball tournament, which began in 1931 and was sponsored by the junior and senior Japanese Chambers of Commerce and the Japanese Association of North America.[36] By 1935, the tournament included some 250 athletes and

16 teams from all over the Northwest. But it was not simply an imitation of white, middle-America Fourth of July celebrations. The 1935 tournament, for instance, included a *bon odori* in which 300 Japanese "dressed in gay colored kimonos" performed outdoors on Maynard Avenue and then the following day at the Toyo Club. Also, as part of the festivities, the Japanese American Citizens League (JACL) invited local and visiting *Nisei* to a dance at the Faurot Ballroom, where Rosemary Oshio performed a tap dance, Clarence Arai conducted a flag ceremony, and former congressman Ralph Horr gave a "short talk on Americanism."[37] This event, thus, exemplified the multifaceted nature of Japanese American identity and practices during the early twentieth century. Celebrating the holiday in itself signaled assimilation as it involved observing an American holiday, but the substance of the celebration was Japanese *and* American. Carried out as an explicitly Pacific Northwest tradition, it also placed regional identity at the fore.

Becoming American, Against the Canadians

The Fourth of July Tournament was a major community event, bringing together teams from Seattle and the Northwest to determine who was the best in the league while fans and families came out to enjoy the summer weather and festivities. The tournament's popularity led to the organization of another baseball series, also held over a major American holiday weekend. The Labor Day International Series, beginning informally in 1928 and becoming an official annual affair in 1936, further sheds light on the complex and unexpected ways that Japanese in the United States understood and performed their American identities. The team named the AA champion of the Courier League at the end of a season earned the right to play in this series, and the opponent was always the Vancouver Asahis from British Columbia, Canada. The Labor Day International Series was to be the climactic end to each baseball season, bestowing upon the winner the unofficial title of champion of Northwest Japanese baseball. Over the years, such Courier teams as the Fife Nippons, the Seattle Western Giants, and the Auburn Nine faced the Asahis in dramatic, widely attended contests at Sick's Stadium and other venues.

If baseball had an Americanizing effect on Seattle's Japanese, it was most evident when they played against Japanese Canadians during the Labor Day tournament and other occasions over the season. When Japanese

Americans played against white Americans, these games were typically discussed in terms of carrying out friendship on behalf of Japan or the "Japanese people." When they traveled to Japan or hosted teams from Japan, these encounters were framed as meetings of fellow countrymen or educational opportunities to learn more about Japanese culture. However, when they played against Japanese Canadians, they were not meeting authorities on Japanese culture nor learning a different way of playing baseball nor were they encountering a group of racial or cultural "others." The most significant imagined difference here was the *national* one, and the games became contests between Americans and Canadians. Furthermore, on these occasions, the heated rivalries between Japanese American teams in the Northwest took a back seat to a unified and collective determination to beat the Canadians.

As mentioned above, the perennial Canadian team to beat was the mighty Asahi Club from Vancouver. This semiprofessional team was formed in 1914, and between 1919 and 1940, it won five league championships, making it one of the biggest draws in its league and earning the support of Japanese and white fans.[38] That they proved so adept at a Western sport and frequently beat their "*hakujin*" ("white") competitors generated pride among the Japanese in Vancouver, although, as discussed above, they did not necessarily regard baseball as something they had adopted from whites. Their "sportsmanlike attitude, the skill and fervor the Asahis displayed in their game," earned these "nimble Nipponese" the respect of their non-Japanese competitors.[39] Because the Asahis were usually the only Japanese team in their leagues, they rarely faced Japanese competition unless it came from outside the area, most notably south of the border in Washington State. After its first trip to Seattle in 1919, the club's border-crossing excursions became common the following decade. Because of the Asahis' formidable reputation and the large crowds that their games drew, teams from all around the Puget Sound area would eagerly seek to schedule series against them. And although the 150-mile trip between Seattle and Vancouver was much shorter than the journeys to Oregon or California, the added hurdle of having to clear Customs at the border elevated the drama around these series, dubbed international "clashes" and "invasions."[40]

Seattle-Vancouver baseball generated excitement by focusing attention on the international boundary, and it also strengthened ties between the Japanese communities in the respective cities. For the Vancouver athletes, these games were often their only chance to cross the international border and travel along the West Coast. They would furthermore receive the royal treatment from their Seattle hosts with banquets and picnics thrown in their honor. Trips to new towns also afforded experiences off the beaten path, from making new friends to partaking in otherwise taboo activities like watching a burlesque show.[41] The circulation of athletes between teams in Vancouver and Seattle carved out a well-worn route between the two cities. Tom Niichi Matoba was one of these athletes, playing for the original 1914 Vancouver Asahis and later joining the Seattle Asahis, only to rejoin the Vancouver team in time for a tour of Japan. Other Vancouver Asahis played on a part-time basis for Seattle teams on weekends. From 1928 to 1934, Asahi Mickey Maikawa would travel across the border every weekend to play for the Seattle Taiyos. One reason he kept such busy a travel schedule was so he could see his friends in Washington. Shortstop Roy Yamamura was one of the most popular Asahis during the 1920s and 1930s and had also been the only Japanese on the Fraser Café Senior A Team and Arrows. He and Asahi catcher Reggie Yasui were invited to play every weekend for the Seattle Nippons.

The Labor Day International Series got off to a rousing start in 1928 when the Asahis came to Seattle and beat the NAC in what was described as "the best Japanese baseball game played on record in the Northwest."[42] From there, the series became one of the most anticipated and widely attended annual events in Seattle's Japanese community and attracted its share of white spectators.[43] Intensifying community interest, in addition to the series being billed as "international clashes," was the significant time lag—sometimes over a month—between the first game and the subsequent doubleheader. This delay gave sportswriters and fans time to analyze the matchups, to make predictions, and to build anticipation. As far as the games themselves, the Seattle-area teams usually came up short. In the series' thirteen-year run, the Vancouver Asahis won eight times, winning consecutive titles between 1937 and 1941. Most of the time, the Courier teams could not overcome the superior pitching of such Asahis as "Lanky Lag" Nishihara and the batting prowess of such players as "flashy" Reg Yasui.[44]

After the Asahis won its fifth straight title in the International Series in 1941, Budd Fukei, a sportswriter for the *Japanese-American Courier,* bemoaned the embarrassment of the International Series for Seattle's Japanese. He tried to rally them, as Americans, to regroup and reverse their losing record to the Canadians:

Regardless of weather, crowd or publicity, it has been the accepted custom of this town to allow the Class AA champions to absorb a beating from the Vancouver Asahis for the Northwest diamond championship each year. The fans are getting mighty tired of the old act. . . . This thing—the Canadian brothers whipping our pals season in and season out without so much as a thank you—has gone far enough. We Americans must not stand idly by and watch our friends be beaten to helpless hunks of cheese.[45]

For Seattle-area teams to prevail over the Asahis, the rules needed to be changed, thought Fukei. Instead of having the Courier AA champions take on the Canadians, he proposed that the winners of the Fourth of July Tournament play against them. The standing rule, argued Fukei, had resulted in a losing record and the impression that "Americans produce only puny ball clubs."[46] His exasperation and the International Series more generally exemplified how the dynamics of "becoming American" did not always play out in expected ways. As tempting as it might be to characterize Seattle Japanese American baseball as evidence of this community's incorporation into the rituals of Americana, such a view ignores a number of factors. By itself, baseball did not foster an intimate identification with or allegiance to American culture among Japanese Americans, because, more often than not, it brought them into contact with other Japanese—in the United States, Canada, and Japan. For Seattle's Japanese Americans, proximity to the US–Canada border proved to be the most palpable reminder of their American-ness. And in looking at the big picture of the baseball networks, the physical mobility the sport afforded Japanese American athletes brought into focus the salience of place in how the players understood and articulated their identities. When they played against Japanese from Vancouver, they referred to themselves as Americans; when they traveled to California, they identified more with the Northwest, and when they played against rural neighbors, they felt more urban.

The Meanings of Intra-Minority Encounters in Sports

In addition to facilitating encounters and forging bonds among geographically dispersed Japanese, sports afforded opportunities for social interaction across ethnic lines. This interaction was particularly common among children. Longtime Seattle resident Shigeru Osawa remembered playing sandlot baseball at a diamond on Fifth and Main as a child around the turn of the twentieth century. He recalled playing catch with Chinese and Japanese friends on the way to and from school and challenging the Jewish and Italian children who lived nearby on Tenth Avenue.[47] On organized Japanese American teams, some of the notable players were actually non-Japanese. In the early days of the Mikado, for instance, an American Indian pitcher, known only by the nickname "Chief Cadreau," threw several winning games for the team.[48] Finally, on occasion, Japanese American baseball teams would compete against non-Japanese minority teams. In April 1930, the Seattle NAC opened its preseason against the Royal Colored Giants, a local black team. The well-trained NAC "[mixed] hits with squeeze plays" and "proved too much for the colored boys," winning by a score of 9–0.[49] Eight years later, however, the Taiyos lost to the Colored Giants in a game in which the "powerful colored boys toyed with Taiyo, and made Taiyo look helpless indeed by stealing home twice in one morning."[50]

Looking at other sports, the picture becomes even more diverse. A sampling of sports pages in the ethnic press from the 1920s and 1930s reveals a wide spectrum in terms of age and skill level, venues, leagues, and sports. Basketball, bowling, wrestling, golf, football, boxing, and tennis were also part of the Japanese American sporting culture during the early 1900s. In 1928, one of the major basketball victories of the year was the Japanese Girls' triumph over the AME Church Girls, an African American team. Perhaps more than any other sport, boxing placed Japanese American athletes in multiethnic settings. Mixed bills at Seattle's Crystal Pool, with "Nordic, Negro, Filipino and Japanese" boxers drew large crowds.[51] Hal Hoshino, perhaps the most revered Japanese American boxer of the early 1900s, drew much of his fame from his victories over non-Japanese challengers. One of his most celebrated wins was over Filipino American Young Nationalista II from Watsonville, California, in 1938.[52]

Interethnic athletic encounters between Japanese, Filipinos, and Chinese often led participants and observers to reflect upon and at times reconceptualize the boundaries between these communities, occasionally giving expression to a shared "Oriental" consciousness. A spirited bowling rivalry between Japanese and Filipinos during the 1930s was one example. For a time, it dominated the front page of the *Great Northern Daily News,* which recounted such nail-biters as Takeo Yoshijima and Spike Nakamoto facing off against Filipinos Ciso Guzman and Bill Seladang. The relationship between these communities was shaped by economic and social conditions in the United States, in particular class differences between Japanese and Filipinos. In agriculture, Japanese farmers often employed Filipino laborers, and in salmon canning, the groups vied for group advantages in wages and working conditions.[53] Further, a series of sensationalized headlines about Filipino-Japanese courtships resulting in disaster contributed to intercommunity strains.[54]

In the Japanese-Filipino bowling rivalry, described as an "international bowling feud," the power dynamics were reversed as the Filipinos usually dominated.[55] The rivalry reached its climax in late 1934 after Japanese bowlers had lost a series of matches against the Filipino Barber Shop Four. Determined to end the streak, Japanese American bowler Kaz Tamura vowed in late October to stop shaving until a Japanese team beat the Filipino Barbers. Each week in November built up to Sunday matches at Larman's Recreation Center on Maynard, where the Japanese tried to unseat the Filipinos. Before a November 11 match, the *Great Northern Daily News* speculated that, with persistence and luck, the Japanese might prevail: "The Filipino Barber Shop team is itching to scalp the Japanese All-Stars. The Luzon boys are looked upon to take the series on the basis of past performances, but the Nipponese, who have the knack of turning in inspired bowling, may play over their heads to upset the dope."[56]

A packed house at Larman's witnessed the anticipated match between the Barber Shop Four and Japanese All-Stars. Playing for the All-Stars were Hiko Setsuda, Taiji Takayashi, Spike Nakamoto, and "Dr. Nomura, the bowling dentist." Kaz Tamura was, unfortunately, out of town that day. Despite the hype, the Japanese team lost by a score of 1,661–1,422. The following Sunday, a different Japanese team, the Alley Cats, played against the Barber Shop Four in a match promised to be the "top-notch sporting event" of the weekend. This time, Tamura was there, reportedly looking like a "Bolshevik bombthrower."[57] Another full house watched the Japanese team go down in defeat against the Barbers in a three-game match, and this result repeated the following weekend.[58] Japanese had better success in individual matches. Clarence Arai, the "second generation lawyer and unofficial Mayor of Main Street," became so determined to beat a Filipino at bowling that, according to his wife, he would sneak away from home to get extra practice.[59] When he broke a score of 200 and beat Filipino V. Agot, the all-time record holder at Larman, he was hailed as a local hero.

The bowling contests between Japanese and Filipinos illuminate an energetic and multicultural social scene in Jackson Street, a neighborhood that was usually derided as the city's "skid row." They also represent an aspect of the sports culture in Japanese Seattle, in which a bowling match would make front-page news and become a community-rallying event. The rivalry between Japanese and Filipino bowlers additionally demonstrates how such everyday situations became occasions in which to work out and articulate the meanings of race and ethnicity. In the context of bowling matches, Japanese and Filipinos aligned with their ethnonational affiliations, reaffirming their identities as *Japanese* and *Filipinos*. But for Japanese Americans, the events were also opportunities to express an emerging Asian American outlook as defeating a Filipino bowler or team conferred two kinds of gratification—overcoming stronger competitors in the "Manila boys" and claiming victory as the best "Orientals." Winning in an intra-ethnic competition entitled one to claim only being the best among other Japanese, but beating someone from a different Asian community elevated the meaning of the victory. Securing "Oriental" supremacy, moreover, affirmed a nascent pan-Asian consciousness.

Athletic competitions with Japanese and Chinese Americans similarly illustrated the points above as well as the conceptual navigations of scale that Japanese Americans, especially sportswriters, engaged in to explain the significance of the encounters. Japanese and Chinese Americans commonly drew upon international events to understand and to articulate their local, concrete realities and goals. Although Sino-Japanese relations offered useful parallels and meanings to delineate interethnic boundaries in Seattle, events in Asia were remote enough that they did not preclude Japanese Americans' and Chinese Americans' recognition of a common status as "Orientals" in America.[60] Furthermore, Japan's escalating aggressions in China during the 1930s precluded friendship between the two nations, but the buffer of the Pacific Ocean allowed Japanese and Chinese in North America to distance themselves from Asia and foreground the local connections they created through living in the same neighborhoods, attending the same schools, and patronizing each other's businesses. The *Japanese-American Courier* and *Great Northern Daily News* covered the feats of fellow Japanese as well as Chinese athletes, such as local Art Louie, the center for the Chinese Students team and Garfield High School, and Buck Lai, the "wonder boy" third baseman from Hawaii.[61] Lai had played for the semiprofessional

Eastern League in Bridgeport, Connecticut, and his signing by the New York Giants in 1928 was covered in a "Sports Scope" column in the *Courier*.[62] The University of Washington student and budding journalist Bill Hosokawa, who wrote about sports for the *Courier,* provided much of the information about Chinese American athletes. A Seattle native and a 1933 graduate of Garfield High School, Hosokawa, who would go on to have a long career with the *Denver Post* after World War II, grew up in the multiethnic social landscape and sports scene in the city, and he developed admiration for and friendships with the "colorful Celestials from Canton, King Street, and way points."[63]

All-Chinese teams competed in a variety of sports in the Japanese-American Courier League, but they made their greatest impact in basketball.[64] In the late 1920s, with the inauguration of the Courier Basketball League, Chinese teams joined, and by the start of the 1935 season, four Chinese teams, including Young China, the Chinese Students, and the Lotus Troys, applied for entry.[65] Before the Courier formed a basketball league, Chinese American teams were limited to playing in citywide leagues in which they achieved notable success. During the 1929 City League season, for instance, the China Club amassed a seven-game winning streak and led the Class B South Division.[66] As part of the Courier League, which it joined in 1929, the China Club dominated, leading its coach Stanley Louie to boast that his team's record entitled it to the "mythical Oriental Basketball Championship of the Pacific Northwest."[67]

By 1937, the Courier Basketball League comprised forty teams and about 400 players, with the Chinese-Japanese clashes being the highlights of each season.[68] The fact that the Chinese American teams were known to be very strong further fueled the rivalry, and the games, framed as contests to determine the superior "Oriental" team, drew keen interest among local fans.[69] By late 1940, the Japanese American teams, which still made up the majority of the Courier League squads, were simply no match for the Chinese teams at nearly every level from AA to C.[70] Although this situation frustrated the Japanese American players and coaches, they also reveled in the excitement and heightened athleticism that the Chinese brought to the Courier League. Clarence Arai, who managed the Japanese Hi-Stars, praised the Chinese Athletic Club team for its "splendid showing in the Class 'B' City League and . . . clean record against any organized Oriental basketball team in the Northwest for the past four years." Despite his team's struggles against the Chinese Athletic Club, he asserted, "We feel that it is a great honor to meet the Chinese boys even in victory or defeat."[71] Arai's remarks navigated between the strategies of asserting ethnic boundaries and acknowledging a shared status as "Orientals."

Chinese-Japanese athletic match ups outside Seattle and the Northwest also generated interest among Japanese American sportswriters and further developed the sense of interethnic friendship. In 1931, the *Japanese-American Courier* reported on the start of an annual Japanese-Chinese All-Star football game in San Francisco's Kezar Stadium. It "originated several years back when a group of Japanese and Chinese youths decided that the Americanization process necessitated a regular football game."[72] Perhaps to underline that objective, non-Asian coaches participated: Frank Wilton, a former Stanford football player led the Japanese team, and "Smoke" Francis, who had played for the University of California, coached the Chinese team. Despite organizers' emphasis on Americanization, the game saw players falling back on their ethnic affiliations, again demonstrating the constant negotiation between ethnic particularism and common ground that characterized Chinese-Japanese relations during this period: "The quarterbacks call signals in their native languages which make it difficult for the opposition to know what they will do. Special precautions are taken not to permit Chinese students in Japanese Language schools and vice versa."[73] In 1936, the Chinese Students team of Seattle went to California to face several Bay Area Japanese American squads. Covering the story, Chinese American Seattleite Eddie Luke remarked, "In recent years, there have been few athletic relations between Chinese and Japanese in the Bay Region. . . . Perhaps the Student-Y [YMCA] example will bring about a resumption of athletic competition between the two communities."[74]

The "Far East" provided ready analogies for Chinese-Japanese sporting competitions in Seattle. In January 1935, when the China Club beat the Japanese Black Hawks by a score of 21–14 at the Garfield High gym, the *Japanese-American Courier* invoked Sino-Japanese relations, saying the game renewed "basketball hostilities" between the two groups.[75] In 1941, as international tensions were mounting, the *Seattle Post-Intelligencer* published a story about Garfield High School's basketball squad, which included Chinese and Japanese teammates Phil Mar Hung, Bill Yamaguchi, and Al Mar. Although they played on the same team, the newspaper nonetheless likened Garfield basketball to the Sino-Japanese War, saying, "With the

Japanese and Chinese at each others' throats in the Orient, there's also an 'all out' fight being staged right in the high school basketball league."[76]

In addition to bringing drama to the basketball court and generating material for sportswriters, Japanese-Chinese sports in Seattle facilitated and sustained relationships between these ethnic communities. The story of Chinese American Eddie Luke, mentioned above, stands out. In 1936, Luke started guest authoring the *Japanese-American Courier*'s "Hangovers" sports column. By then he was well known to Japanese American sports fans, having distinguished himself in the Japanese-American Courier League playing baseball for the Chinese Students team during the mid-1930s. He helped lead the Chinese Students to a top division berth and in 1937 won the Courier League's Kay Okimoto Most Inspirational Player Award.[77] Substituting for his friend Bill Hosokawa, Luke wrote several "Hangovers" columns, which he devoted to bringing attention to the local Chinese American sports scene, particularly the exploits of the Chinese Students basketball squad. Luke's service as a guest author for the *Courier* was in itself significant and unprecedented as the newspaper was narrowly focused and targeted. His columns also shed light on how he, as a Chinese American, related to Japanese Americans he encountered through athletic participation. He recalled a 1934 Courier League road trip to Wapato in which "the highlight" was "eating a full Japanese meal next to Art Kikuchi's mother without her discovering that I was a son of Cathay. Thank you so much for the meal, Mrs. Kikuchi."[78] Crossing ethnic boundaries to access the social and culinary world of Japanese Americans, Luke's experience was mediated by the fact that he looked like his hosts, indicated by "Mrs. Kikuchi" not realizing he was a "son of Cathay." Chinese-Japanese relations in Seattle were informed by the simultaneous recognition of their differences—signaled by references to food, language, and geography—and their similarities, by way of physical features, use of the term "Oriental," and, on occasion, food. In June 1937, Luke left Seattle for California to pursue acting, and the *Courier* bid him farewell with a tribute: "Perhaps more than any other person, Eddie has been responsible for the friendly relations which exist today in Seattle between the rice-eating descendants of Cathay and Yamato."[79] In connecting Luke's contributions to China-Japan relations, the author imagined interethnic relations playing out along multiple, connected scales. On the broadest level, the "descendants of Cathay and Yamato" surely had their differences, especially at the time the tribute was published, but zooming in, what remained in the picture, and presumably what mattered most, were the "friendly relations . . . in Seattle."

Japanese Americans pivoted between the international arena and local friendships as they understood and discussed their relationships with Chinese Americans. As shown above, framing sporting matches in terms of Sino-Japanese relations elevated the consequence of otherwise ordinary events, and commentators moreover noted that the athletes' lives in America and shared experiences as "Orientals"—particularly among the US-born—fostered a pan-Asian consciousness that transcended interethnic differences. Before a girls' softball game between Chinese and Japanese teams, the *Japanese-American Courier* remarked, "China and Japan may be at war; some meddling crackpots may be trying their darndest to make the Chinese and Japanese in America fight a little war of their own over here, but the second generation Chinese and Japanese girls don't seem to let those things dampen their friendship."[80] As the 1937 basketball season was about to begin, the *Courier* expressed its hope that Chinese teams would return "and have a good time with us again. It is unfortunate that there should be such trouble in the Orient, but I believe that is not going to spoil the friendship that has grown up between the Japanese and the Chinese second generation of this city."[81]

Salvation Through Sports

It is commonly asserted that sports are a neutral and neutralizing terrain where individuals' preconceptions and prejudices take a back seat to the color-blind rules of the game. And with the growing internationalization of sporting culture from the turn of the twentieth century onward—signified, for example, by the revival of the Olympic Games in 1896—the idea that athletic competition was a level playing field bolstered among many people the belief that racial equality and inclusion could be achieved through it. The *Northwest Enterprise,* one of Seattle's black newspapers, invoked this idea in exulting the performance of African American athletes at the 1936 Olympics, with especially high praise for runner Jesse Owens. "The accomplishment of these athletes," stated the *Enterprise,* "will do much toward building up a greater respect for and more kindly feeling toward the Negro race, for in the end, fair and just treatment must be accorded a people who are consistently loyal, fair, and just to their country and its cause."[82]

Japanese Americans voiced similar hopes, and among individual athletes, none inspired greater hopes than professional boxer Hal Hoshino. A featherweight from Pendleton, Oregon, who moved to Seattle in 1935, Hoshino fought nationally during the late 1930s and became a hero to co-ethnics, winning the Seattle Golden Gloves title in 1937.[83] After he defeated two white opponents in 1938, the *Japanese-American Courier* declared that this was also a victory for racial progress: "If Hal Hoshino had knocked out those two white boys in any other place except the boxing ring, the 'indignant' whites would have mobbed the 'Jap' who insulted the white people. But . . . he used his punches in the ring and at once, the white people acclaimed him as the champion to represent the whole Northwest in the featherweight division."[84] Hoshino's accomplishments would not have generated such interest had they not been achieved in mixed-race settings. The writer seemed particularly gratified that Hoshino beat white competitors in the inherently violent, hypermasculine sport of boxing. In racialized communities in the United States, this attitude was not uncommon. Historian Linda España-Maram has found similar dynamics among Filipino American boxing fans in Los Angeles who viewed co-ethnic boxers' wins against whites as symbolic collective victories.[85] In Seattle, Japanese Americans were aware that their African American neighbors likewise attributed great significance to the triumphs of their boxing heroes, indicated, for instance, when the *Great Northern Daily News* said Hoshino was to Japanese Americans what Joe Louis was to "the colored colony on Jackson Street."[86]

Japanese Americans concerned about their own communities, their status in the United States, and the state of US–Japan affairs turned to sports to articulate their hopes. As shown earlier, with respect to Pacific relations, writers expressed how encounters between the United States and Japan in the sporting arena could help to foster goodwill crucial for maintaining a peaceful, harmonious Pacific world. Ruminating on exchanges between college teams, which by the 1920s were taking place on a regular basis, a 1928 editorial in the *Japanese-American Courier* stated:

> In the creation of goodwill and mutual respect nothing has ever succeeded to a greater extent than athletics. Facile diplomatists with their silvery tongued orations and superficial announcements of idle declarations of friendship have at all times fallen short and failed of achieving the object. . . . Athletics have often given expression to a spirit of good sportsmanship through actual demonstrations. To the ordinary sport fan nothing strikes a

more respectful and sympathetic chord than demonstrations that bespeak of sportsmanly conduct and action. Where diplomacy failed clean sportsmanship has succeeded.[87]

The concerns of international and interracial understanding were linked, so the hopes Japanese Americans placed on sportsmanship and play transcended US-Japan diplomacy; as minorities in America, they also looked to sports to foster improved race relations. In summer 1939, following a softball game between the visiting Togo All-Stars from Japan and the white East Madison YMCA team, in which the All-Stars lost 6–2, a writer for the *Japanese-American Courier* insisted that the game's significance was not in who won or lost but that "Americans" (presumably referring to white Americans) witnessed the good sportsmanship of Japanese people. The writer hoped the feelings generated at this meeting would, in turn, improve white Seattleites' perception of their Japanese neighbors. "That All-Star gang did more than just play a softball game. I'm willing to bet my last nickel that some of the Americans who watched the game went home feeling might friendly towards the Japanese," stated the writer. "Some of these first-generation who are howling so much about 'Japanese-American friendship' ought to look into this sport angle of creating good-will."[88]

In a column titled "Democracy in Action" in the *Japanese- American Courier, Nisei* writer James Shinkai invoked the idea of sports as a vehicle for building relationships across ethnic and national boundaries and focused his remarks on domestic race relations. He singled out Seattle high school athletes, such as Dick Itami, the captain of Cleveland High's football team; Homer Harris, the black All-City football player from Garfield; and Roy Nakagawa, the All-City guard from Franklin. To Shinkai, this assemblage of accomplished minority athletes demonstrated that sports were the "most democratic institution in America" and the one field "where they do not care whether your ancestors came over on the Mayflower or in the steerage of the Miike Maru."[89] Referencing the Japanese ship that made the first regular steamship run between Japan and Seattle in 1896, Shinkai inserted Japan and Japanese people into the saga of immigrant America, which usually revolved around trans-Atlantic migration and such icons as Ellis Island, Plymouth Rock, and the *Mayflower*. In 1932, a writer for the *Courier* elaborated on the connections between sportsmanship, interracial understanding, and Japanese belonging in Seattle, observing, "Many American fans attend the games played by Japanese baseball teams" and "are surprised at their speed, their clever headwork and their good sportsmanship."[90] Instead of describing the most recent visit of a team from Japan to the United States, however, the article discussed the history of Japanese American baseball. It described, for instance, how during the summer of 1915, a group of white American mill workers went to see the Selleck Yamatos of rural Washington play, out of "idle curiosity and were amazed to see the Yamatos with Mizutani, Bert Kochi and Sano as the backbone of the team set back a visiting team from Seattle."[91]

Other columns ruminated on how sports lifted the blinders of racial prejudice to free individuals from deeply entrenched preconceptions. Playing sports gave young Japanese in Seattle a glimpse at a world in which race did not determine outcomes. As a writer for the *Japanese-American Courier* reflected:

> One thing I like about this sport circle is that no one is left out of it just because his face is not white. People may talk about 'Boycott the Jap,' 'lynch the niggers,' 'drive out the Filipinos' . . . but, let one 'Jap' 'Nigger' or 'P.I.' excel in any branch of the sport and he is at once accepted by the white people. Nobody says 'He can't fight in this ring because he is a "Nigger,"' nor do they say 'You can't play on this football team because you're a Jap.'[92]

Such sentiments, naïve as they may be, highlighted the idealistic hopes that Japanese Americans, along with other minorities, held to transcend the racialized barriers that limited their life prospects and fortunes in America. As a popular pastime that was also an amenable vessel for communicating a variety of ideas, hopes, and dreams, sports mattered to Japanese Americans in deeply complex and meaningful ways.

Collins Fieldhouse

Participation in athletics enabled Japanese Americans to cross social and geographic boundaries and, in turn, clarify their local identities and positions. Playing and watching sports also entailed an explicit awareness space, and if there was a single location in Seattle where the interracial, spatial, and ideological dimensions of sports converged for Japanese Americans, it was at Collins Park. Regarding issues of space, this chapter has focused on how Japanese Americans crossed, transcended, and redefined it, but playing sports, of course, also entails a concrete engagement with urban spaces. One cannot play baseball without a diamond, basketball without a court, or football without a field. This spatiality is a crucial part of the story of Japanese American sports in Seattle because a specific locale within the city—Collins Park—became a prime object of the community's cosmopolitan imaginary and its claims to local belonging. Collins's history exemplifies how ordinary people inscribed cosmopolitanism onto physical space and the interplay of real and imagined space in the construction of community in Jackson Street.

Located on Washington and Sixteenth, Collins Park was several blocks east of Jackson Street's center, but it was the main park that Jackson Street residents used. Consisting of a playfield and field house, Collins by the 1920s was well known as the city park with the most diverse users, becoming a social center and safe alternative to the streets. It was also the closest city park to Nihonmachi and one of the few open spaces where Japanese American youths could play sports. Collins also offered afterschool programs with singing, free play, handcrafts, parties, and athletics. The field house schedule for the week of September 27, 1929, gives an idea of a typical week at Collins and its multiracial crowd: Monday, three Japanese teams; Tuesday, the Twenty-Third Avenue team and Bankers team; Wednesday, the Black Manufacturers Union Pacific; Thursday, three Chinese teams; Friday, the Washington Bakeries and City Light. The Italian Society was on the waiting list.[93] In 1931, a park employee who worked with children there observed, "No spot in the city holds more imaginary tragedies more truly interesting incidents or more courses for joy ... than the plot of ground and its frequenters, located at 16th and Washington." It was, in her opinion, the embodiment of the American melting pot, a meeting ground for the people of the world: "All nationalities, faces and creeds meet as individuals on a common level here through that splendid medium known as free play or recreation of some type."[94]

Collins's diversity elicited feel-good sentiments, but it also made it a highly contested space, and the minorities who used Collins were not always treated with the equanimity to match the utopian rhetoric about it. For example, a Japanese high school student who had immigrated to Seattle in 1919 wrote about an experience he had there. "My two friends were playing tenis [sic] at the Colins [sic] Field," he said. "A Jewish boy was passing by ... and ... said to one of my friends that we could not play there, for that court was for only those who could be naturalized, or Americans. I know that

Jewish boy, for he was one of my classmates at school and graduated from our school first honor student."[95]

Collins employees helped construct the park as a cosmopolitan space within Seattle. Many of the first workers had been recruited from the YMCA, and over the years, the organization would provide much of the vision and direction for programs at Collins. Employees often commented on the striking diversity of children who played there and enrolled in recreation and education programs. In 1930, Alice M. Lopp, an employee who held the title of "play leader," remarked:

> The children who attend the field house are ... very appreciative of all that is done for them and are very responsive to the field house activities. Although there is a minimum amount of quarrelsomeness among the children, most of them are learning the rules of good sportsmanship. They get along with each other admirably well for such a cosmopolitan group which includes Spanish and Turkish Jews, Japanese, Negroes and representatives of many other nationalities. It is a group which is different from any in any other parts of the city.[96]

Others expressed similar appreciation for and pride in the park's unique diversity. Nobuko Yamaguchi, another Collins worker, stated in 1930, "I was surprised at the many nationalities represented on the playfield. Japanese, Chinese, Negro, Italian, and different sects of Jews as well as the white people. I don't say Americans because they are all Americans regardless of race. ... The district is so cosmopolitan and so crowded that many types of environment is [sic] shown."[97] Another employee remarked that in sports competitions or "that splendid medium known as free play," children of all "nationalities, faces and creeds" met as individuals on an equal level.[98]

Around 1920, the city started a basketball league in which Collins's teams attracted attention for their diverse crews and skillful playing. Field houses in Seattle organized teams of various levels to compete in interdistrict tournaments, and thousands of youth in over one hundred teams for men and women from ten recreation centers participated. At Collins, the basketball squads included black, Jewish, Chinese, Japanese, and Filipino players, many of whom were recruited from nearby Garfield, Franklin, and Broadway High Schools. In 1936, sixty-eight Japanese played for Collins teams.[99] They were once described as the "cosmopolitan Collins casaba crew" and a United

Nations basketball team.[100] Teams from Collins, which included such play-ers as the Okamotos, Al Mar, and Al Wong, dominated much of inter-field house basketball in the 1930s and 1940s. They were especially successful in the annual Northwest Basketball Tournament, which had begun in 1930 and was sponsored by the *Seattle Post-Intelligencer,* the Park Board, and the Seattle Inter-League Council.

After World War II, Collins remained a force in local basketball, and descriptions of its multiethnic teams continued to draw parallels to the international arena. In 1946 and 1947, it won interleague council titles and advanced to the Northwest AAU Basketball Championships. Widely cele-brated for his success, Gene Boyd, the coach at Collins, was also noted for working with "the melting pot of youngsters at Collins Fieldhouse in the Central Area from 1938 to 1951. There were Chinese, Negroes, Japanese, Filipinos, Greeks, Jews—you name it and Gene could produce one, and all held him in high esteem."[101] Boyd came to Collins after coaching in the Green Lake District because, as he explained, he wished to help youths of lesser means and opportunities to become better citizens. As before the war, the multiethnic makeup of its teams remained one of Collins's most striking characteristics, something commentators could not resist remarking on. "Collins Fieldhouse looks like a juvenile edition of the United Nations," said Phil Taylor of the *Seattle Times,* "but in this case one world means a friendly basketball game, not a subject for debate."[102]

Conclusion

Before the wartime removal of Japanese from the city, one of the last orga-nized events that Seattle Japanese Americans held took place at Collins Fieldhouse. In January 1942, the city Park Board agreed to allow the JACL's Emergency Defense Council to hold a Red Cross Relief Fund dance there. Seeking to show their loyalty to the United States and support for the war against Japan, many of the city's Japanese Americans threw their lot with the nation that would eventually oversee their removal and incarceration. Shortly after the fundraiser, James Sakamoto wrote a letter to Ben Evans thanking him for the use of the field house and for the Park Board's support of the community during this uncertain time.[103] Once the site of a dynamic multiethnic play community and the symbol of cosmopolitan dreams, with the war, Collins would be transformed into a fortress of US nationalism from which the people of Japanese ancestry who had been so integral to its distinct character would soon be displaced.

Also with the US entry into World War II, the celebration of sports as a pastime that brought together peoples and nations in a spirit of friendship, at least where Japanese and Japan were concerned, abruptly dissolved. In an atmosphere of belligerent nationalism, Americans reclaimed baseball as their sport and repudiated any claims that Japan made over it. According to sports historian Richard Crepeau, "The fact that the attack on the United States came from Japan was especially galling to many connected with the national pastime."[104] Building on the anti-Japanese baseball propaganda, the popular magazine the *Sporting News* derided Japanese baseball players as second-rate hitters who "lacked the genuine fortitude that made baseball America's national pastime."[105] No longer regarded as a medium for fostering international friendship, baseball was rearticulated during the war as the exclusive domain of the United States. This attitude was especially jarring for Japanese Americans for whom baseball and other Western sports had been part of the fabric of their identities and routines for decades. Although they continued to form teams and to play sports in the internment camps, athletic participation took on much different meanings in the context of wartime incarceration. Whereas sports were once avenues that broadened Japanese Americans' social and geographic horizons and highlighted their relationships to space in ways that validated their claims to local belonging, during the war, in a breathtaking turnaround, athletics became ways to endure social isolation and physical confinement.

CHAPTER SIX

Seattle's Rat City Roller Derby

Making Strides and Pushing Boundaries

JAMIE BARNHORST

With legs like Jell-O and a heart resembling a pounding sledgehammer, I stepped onto the blue sport court tiles covering the warehouse floor of the Rat's Nest and skated my first warm-up lap. After four full seasons playing with a fun and supportive Division III Tacoma League, I decided it was now or never. I needed to see if I had what it took to skate with one of the top leagues in the world: Seattle's Rat City Roller Derby (RCRD). With internationally recognized skaters like Missile America, Carmen Getsome, and Luna Negra, Rat City felt like the big leagues, and after a grueling tryout, I somehow received the seemingly impossible invitation to join. I thought back to several years prior, when I shuffled into KeyArena, an event venue for celebrity acts like Radiohead and Justin Timberlake, along with thousands of other fans, to witness the RCRD home team championship bout firsthand. I remembered sitting with overpriced nachos in hand and a grin plastered across my face, being minutes away from seeing roller derby's most accomplished skaters tear it up on the track. The lights dimmed, the Jumbotron projected clips of the season's biggest hits, and music blared over the loudspeakers. Then, a sea of tough women and gender nonconforming skaters on eight wheels—some donning full-sleeve tattoos and face paint—rolled out to a crowd of mesmerized fans. Now, I was no longer a spectator but a participant in full gear, waiting for my moment to compete shoulder to shoulder with the skaters who had captured my interest, my passion. I was about to be on that track—me, the girl who did not make her eighth-grade basketball team, spent her teenage years frequenting punk shows, and devoted most of her twenties to studying sociology in local coffee shops.

As an adult woman rapidly approaching thirty, I was finally an athlete. I was a Rat City skater, a member of an organization with a short but storied history in the city and the nation at large.

The Seattle roller derby league emerged soon after Lilly "Hurricane Lilly" Warner returned from Austin's 2003 South by Southwest music festival, where Warner first learned of roller derby's 2001 revival. Warner, along with friends Rahel "Rae's Hell" Cook and Katie "Dixie Dragstrip" Merrell, grew determined to build a league in their own city. They placed an advertisement in the free local paper called the *Stranger,* and within a short time, they had acquired forty new league members and a business license. The RCRD league, including its four distinct teams, was officially established in 2004. The league quickly drew the attention of locals with its public debut the following year. In 2006, RCRD was invited to host a tournament at Seattle's Bumbershoot festival, one of the largest and most popular festivals in North America. The invitation clearly demonstrated the increased visibility of RCRD as it lent credibility to the burgeoning league. In 2007, a documentary about RCRD, entitled *Blood on the Flat Track: The Rise of the Rat City Rollergirls,* premiered at the Seattle International Film Festival. The league gained national recognition in 2010 when it was featured on *Top Chef—Seattle.* Eddie Vedder of Pearl Jam fame sported a RCRD hat in a 2013 video interview with Judd Apatow, once again placing the league in national spotlight. On January 18, 2014, the Seattle City Council established Rat City Roller Derby Day. Rat City skaters and officials have since further facilitated their increased popularity through a variety of engagements with their local communities, including, for instance, supporting the Queen Anne Helpline, the Down Syndrome Community of Puget Sound, and the Special Olympics. Seattle's Rat City Rollergirls—renamed Rat City Roller Derby in 2017—has remained a household name since they joined the modern roller derby movement shortly after the sport's resurgence. Seattle established the first flat track league in the Pacific Northwest and served as one of the thirty founding leagues of the Women's Flat Track Derby Association (WFTDA). RCRD remains Seattle's premier league. It is a league that continues to move beyond the boundaries of race and gender as it works to be an inclusive, equitable alliance that forces participants and spectators alike to erase notions of "othering" on and off the track.[1]

The Advent of Roller Derby

Understanding the uniqueness and importance of roller derby in Seattle requires an examination of the sport's broader historical context in the nation. One of the few team sports to originate in North America, roller derby has been on a distinct and fascinating journey since its 1935 debut. Roller derby was the brainchild of Leo Seltzer, an entertainment business-man from Portland, Oregon. During the Depression, members of the roller derby industry had to get creative in order to attract paying fans; they also had to promise countless hours of entertainment, ensuring an extended distraction from the treacherous reality of the time. Moviegoers frequented theaters, and though Seltzer owned three successful theaters in Portland, he felt he could offer customers more, believing that live productions offered bigger and better possibilities. The most popular live events at that time were of the marathon variety—dancing, bicycling, and walking. Seltzer got a taste of nationwide success when he ran an innovative and lucrative walkathon series across the United States. The series was broadcasted live on the radio and included different forms of entertainment each night—weddings, ice sitting contests, ladies' nights—in order to attract in-person spectators and returning customers. Once his walkathons ran their course, Seltzer imme-diately sought out new ideas. He first conceived of roller derby as an event similar to a skating marathon hosted at Madison Square Garden in 1885 with one very important difference: His version would feature both men and women. At that time, roller skating was a popular pastime for young adults, and the vast majority of Americans had at least tried skating at some point in their lives. He was convinced he could draw large crowds, including a female demographic. Though Seltzer's idea received ridicule from his associates, his first roller derby event—called the Transcontinental Roller Derby—was held at the Chicago Coliseum in the summer of 1935 and had approximately 20,000 audience members in attendance. Fans enthusiastically watched coed teams skate an impressive total of 57,000 laps, or roughly the distance across the continental United States; with this, the sport of roller derby was born. [2]

Seltzer committed to making roller derby a complete success. Prioritizing the audience experience and ticket sales, Seltzer was ever quick to alter the rules of the game as long as it incited cheers from spectators. One major shift was transforming roller derby into a full-contact sport. After some prompt-ing by the famous New York sportswriter Damon Runyan and discovering that falls and big hits drew huge reactions from crowds, Seltzer decided to incorporate these collisions into regular game play in 1938. For added speed and thrill, he also chose to offer the sport on a banked track with a 45° degree angle. In addition, Seltzer figured out how he could control the audience's perception of the sport's growth; he made it seem as though there were a variety of roller derby teams competing all around the country when, in reality, Seltzer just created a "home team" and an "away team" within the Transcontinental Roller Derby. The "home team" always took on the name of the city they were visiting, and the "away team" was supposedly made up of skaters from a rival city. Even at the peak of its popularity—during the early years of its stint on television—there were only six teams: New York Chiefs, Brooklyn Red Devils, Jersey Jolters, Philadelphia Panthers, Chicago Westerners, and Washington (D.C.) Jets. While roller derby had a solid run for decades, selling 55,000 tickets for a National Roller Derby League five-day World Series in 1949, the sport eventually morphed into more of a spectacle than anything, in which rivalries were played up between the skaters who were dubbed heroes and villains; this is how roller derby grew into something resembling modern-day pro wrestling, where hair pulling, tripping, and brawling were par for the course. With an emphasis on entertainment and performance, roller derby went down a very unique path than other mainstream sports. [3]

While Seltzer prioritized the entertainment piece, it is important to note that he took the sport seriously—he selected skaters who were both athletes and performers, and he required that they adhere to a strict set of rules. For instance, skaters were required to train for long hours, prohibited from drinking alcohol, and prevented from fraternizing with those outside of roller derby; this last rule actually resulted in a number of married couples and even children within the Transcontinental Roller Derby. Of course, Seltzer was able to turn even this into a benefit, showcasing the children of roller derby skaters in what he called "the Diaper Derby"—mini speed competitions during the breaks in the adult action. Seltzer essentially had complete control over skaters' actions in hopes of producing high-quality athletes, and they each willingly agreed to his rules since they were given food, shelter, monetary compensation, and medical care at a time when work was scarce. They were also given the opportunity to travel. In fact, they were often treated like celebrities, capturing the attention of local newspapers and fans on the streets. The arrangement was mutually beneficial: Seltzer had committed and talented athletes, and skaters had job security and community.[4]

Women have always played a key role in roller derby's success. Hoping to capture the attention of female fans, a demographic traditionally underrepresented at athletic events, Seltzer had recruited both female and male athletes to participate in the sport from the very beginning. He also ensured that discounted tickets were made available at places like fabric shops and grocery stores, which were easily accessible to women. As a result of these efforts, female fans consistently comprised over 50 percent of the fan base. With its inclusion of varied types of women as its athletes and fans, roller derby has always challenged traditional notions of "sports" and "femininity." While many of the female athletes were traditionally beautiful, Seltzer intentionally featured female athletes of a variety of shapes, sizes, and ages, arguing that female fans would prefer to see "real people" compete rather than just those who resemble models or movie stars. Consequently, a woman like Josephine "Ma" Bogash, a housewife in her forties, was able to become a roller derby star. Female fans loved that they could see themselves in Ma, and they were enamored with the fact that she skated alongside her eighteen-year-old son, Billy Bogash. While fans were admittedly sucked in by the personal stories of the skaters, roller derby also championed the athleticism and aggressiveness of the female athletes, encouraging sportswriters and fans alike to focus on more than just gossip and looks. One journalist wrote, "the guy who called the gals 'the weaker sex' would soon change his mind if he were to take a peek at the femmes competing in the Transcontinental Roller Derby now at the Civic Auditorium." Further, roller derby provided female skaters the opportunity to play a sport for equal pay and recognition, which was unheard of at that time.[5]

With the focus on creating high-quality entertainment for fans, Leo Selzter—and his son Jerry, who ended up inheriting the family business— jumped on talent when it presented itself. When a great skater named Darlene Anderson, an African American woman from Pasadena, California, tried out for roller derby in 1958, she was quickly signed by the Brooklyn Red Devils. Anderson became a huge star within roller derby and a pioneer for other African American women who would soon enter the ranks of the young sport. Nineteen years old at the time, Anderson was named Rookie of the Year for the 1958 season. Black male skaters were recruited to participate in roller derby before Anderson, just shortly after Jackie Robinson broke into Major League Baseball in 1947. The integration of athletes of color into the sport was rather smooth for skaters and management: "Myself being black I don't think ever mattered to anyone," Anderson recalled. "I was respected, treated by all skaters on an equal level, and I don't ever remember once that black was an issue. . . . We were family. We were not color. I truly believe this," she insisted. What distinguished roller derby from some other professional sports at that time was the fact that its athletes, trainers, announcers, and officials ate, lived, and traveled together; everyone in the sport became part of a tight-knit family. This was reflected in the skaters' decision to rebel in the early 1960s. When they discovered that they were slated to play at a southern arena with mandatory segregated seating, they confronted management as a united front. Consequently, they were never scheduled to play at a segregated venue again. Living and playing by their own set of rules, the roller derby community was unafraid to challenge the norms of the time. [6]

Roller derby's popularity peaked around 1950, and after approximately twenty years of far-too-regular television play, it faded into nonexistence. Attempts to repackage it in the eighties and nineties were complete failures with outrageous additions like a live alligator pit and a Wall of Death. Then, in 2000, something shifted. Daniel Eduardo "Devil Dan" Policarpo traveled to Austin, Texas, with the idea to build an alternative local women's league from scratch. He canvassed Sixth Avenue, an area known for its plethora of rock venues and bars, and by 2001, he had recruited a solid base of women interested in participating. After huge fundraising efforts, Devil Dan blew through all the money—supposedly on drugs—and fled town. He left the group of Austin women with nothing but their bonds to each other and an idealistic notion of what roller derby could become. Even with that setback, they were able to establish the first modern roller derby league, called Bad Girl Good Woman Productions (BGGW), in 2001. After a year-and-a-half of logistics, rules development, and training, they put on their first public bout; approximately 350 people showed up to this event. The next bout brought in double the fans. With its alternative attitude, pinup-inspired look, and carnival-like atmosphere, modern roller derby offered a fan experience unlike any other sport—in many ways, it was the antithesis of traditional sports. Within no time, roller derby was embraced by the locals and became an underground sensation in the self-proclaimed "weird" city of Austin.[7]

Soon after BGGW's popularity grew, a significant number of its skaters began to express concerns about its structure. The organization was established as a for-profit league with a small number of "She-E-Os" in control

"Two women's league roller derby skaters leap over two who have fallen." 10 March 1950. Al Aumuller, *World-Telegram* staff photographer. Library of Congress Prints and Photographs Division, *New York World-Telegram and the Sun* Newspaper Photograph Collection. http://hdl.loc.gov/loc.pnp/cph.3c33382

of all the decisions and earnings. Since each skater dedicated a significant amount of time and energy to the operating efforts of BGGW not to mention their own personal finances in the form of monthly dues, many skaters called for an equal distribution of ownership and benefits. Unlike the Seltzer era, the skaters themselves actively shaped the look and feel of this version of the sport. And for most participating, roller derby was not about making money; it was about maintaining and promoting a sport they grew to love. When the She-E-Os refused to give up power, the league broke into two factions. BGGW retained fifteen of its league members, invested in a slanted vintage banked track, rebranded themselves as Texas Roller Derby (TXRD) Lonestar Rollergirls, and recruited a new set of skaters. The sixty-five women who left formed a new skater-owned-and-operated flat track league called the Texas Rollergirls, who played a large role in developing the international governing body of modern flat track roller derby—the WFTDA. The association's philosophy is "by the skaters, for the skaters." Each WFTDA league offers their skaters a vote, a voice in the decision-making process, and equal ownership of their league's business. These remain essential features of modern roller derby. [8]

With limited materials needed for the flat track version of the sport and the opportunity to participate in this unique expression of female empowerment, cities across the nation began establishing their own roller derby leagues. Like the old versions of roller derby, women were key players in this full-contact sport, showcasing female strength and aggression. But unlike those iterations, modern roller derby did not care whether someone was an athlete or a performer. This new version trained people at all levels; women who had never played traditional sports were encouraged to strap on skates and join the movement. Not only were women given an opportunity to be in the spotlight, but they also got a chance to run the show. They were in full control of the rules of the game and operations of the league.

By the second decade of the twenty-first century, flat track roller derby became bigger than anyone could have imagined. Egypt, Japan, the Czech Republic, Mexico, the United Arab Emirates, and Iceland are just some of many countries that have established leagues. In 2011, the first Roller Derby World Cup tournament was launched. Roller derby continues to be embraced by women across the globe and is quickly gaining popularity among youth and men. It currently boasts approximately 2,000 amateur leagues, including men's, women's, coed, and junior. With over forty-five leagues in Washington State alone, the trajectory of the sport in Seattle is no exception. [9]

"Rat City"

An amateur Seattle sports league, Seattle's RCRD, which includes a variety of teams, is owned and operated by its skaters, a model adopted by the vast majority of modern flat track derby leagues. There is a team for new skaters and transfers called the Rat Lab. Skaters in the Rat Lab train with the league and skate against newer teams around Washington State; some of these skaters will earn the chance to advance their derby careers by getting drafted to one of the four home teams—Derby Liberation Front, Grave Danger, Sockit Wenches, and Throttle Rockets. These teams primarily skate against each other at the Rat's Nest, the league's practice space and event venue currently located just north of Seattle in the city of Shoreline. Many of the best skaters from the four home teams, plus a growing subset of skaters who skate solely for the all-star program, make up RCRD's two travel teams—the Rat City All-Stars (A team) and the Rain of Terror (B team). The Rat City All-Stars, the team that represents the league internationally, competes against other all-star teams for its WFTDA ranking. By February 2018, the Rat City All-Stars were ranked sixteenth in the world, securing a top spot among the more than 300 WFTDA member leagues.[10]

The RCRD name pays homage to White Center, a neighborhood just south of Seattle, which was nicknamed "Rat City" in the 1940s. The origin of White Center's "Rat City" nickname is the subject of debate. Some believe it is directly linked to the roller rink, whose patrons were often called "rink rats." Others claim it is an acronym for Restricted Alcohol Territory. Some link it to the military recruitment and training (RAT) center that existed during World War II. Still others assume it is because of a former rat problem. Regardless, the "Rat City" name is owned by White Center with pride, and it is perfect for roller derby: it's "a little bit edgy, a little bit tough, and rough around the edges." The area houses Southgate Roller Rink—the league's initial practice space and event venue. Southgate has played a central role in the history of White Center since its opening in 1937, serving as a popular hangout for youth and an unofficial United Service Organization (USO) for the soldier and sailors during World War II.[11]

The Seattle roller derby league's name has received criticism in recent years, but not for the "Rat City" part. In 2017, just thirteen years after its inception, the league officially changed its name from Rat City Rollergirls to Rat City Roller Derby. Many other leagues have also chosen to ditch terms like "girls," "dolls," and "dames," in favor of language that represents inclusivity and athleticism. For instance, the Philadelphia league formerly known as the Philly Roller Girls rebranded themselves as Philly Roller Derby in 2015, and the Boston Derby Dames are now known as Boston Roller Derby. One reason for these changes is that the WFTDA updated its policies to be more gender-inclusive, welcoming nonbinary and trans athletes to the sport, and leagues want their names to reflect this shift. Additionally, leagues function as a result of the hard work of coaches, referees, non-skating officials, and volunteers; they include more than just their skaters. Further, many skaters want to refocus the attention to the athleticism required to play roller derby rather than the gender of those participating in the sport. With its commitment to female empowerment, the queer community, and athletics, RCRD made the decision to update its name to reflect the values of both the local league and the sport as a whole. [12]

As a top league, RCRD's All-Star A team is recognized nationally and internationally. Interestingly, RCRD's home teams—rather than the All-Star teams—have been best known and supported among locals and have consistently generated the majority of revenue for the sports league. It should be noted that ticket sales have historically covered just a portion of the total costs. The league has raised additional funds in order to sustain itself, requiring skaters to pay monthly dues and volunteer at least ten hours each month; league costs include rent and maintenance of the practice space, advertisements for upcoming events, and merchandise production, to name just a few. During the 2010 season, when RCRD was at its height of popularity, home teams consistently had impressive tickets sales, drawing crowds of more than 4,000 people to each of their bouts. In fact, RCRD broke the national record for the largest roller derby crowd that year with an attendance of over 6,000 people at their home team championship bout. At that time, RCRD had the right combination of visibility, talent, and space. Not only did the league invest quite a bit in marketing its home team bouts, with cable TV ads, posters, billboards, and bus advertisements, but the popularity of the 2009 derby-focused film *Whip It*, starring Ellen Page and Drew Barrymore, also brought in swarms of new fans. Furthermore, at that time, RCRD bouts were regularly held at a large event venue in Seattle Center called KeyArena—the home of the Women's National Basketball Association's Seattle Storm and former National Basketball Association's Seattle SuperSonics. While RCRD still plays select bouts at KeyArena, it began to scale its operations back by the second decade of the twenty-first century due to the oversaturation of roller derby and slower—yet more strategic—game play. The RCRD's home teams are still generating solid turnouts and ticket sales in order to help sustain the skater-owned-and-operated Seattle league. [13]

The Rules of Play

While many have heard of its revival, few actually know what the sport of roller derby entails. Modern flat track roller derby incorporates some of the basics from earlier versions though a lot has been altered over the years. It is a full-contact competitive sport that is played on roller skates; there are no predetermined rivalries or outcomes, and rules are strictly enforced by referees and non-skating officials. Mouth guards, elbow pads, helmets, wrist guards, and knee pads are required for all skaters. The sport is played on an oval track that is painted or taped onto a flat surface—typically concrete, sport court, or hardwood. Games are called bouts, and they include two thirty-minute periods. Within each period, there are a series of shifts called jams, which last a maximum of two minutes each. While there are a growing number of coed and men's leagues, the majority of flat track roller derby bouts feature women's leagues.

There are no balls or additional objects added; the skaters themselves are the primary focus of the sport. While a team may include up to twenty skaters, only fourteen are rostered for a bout. These are the skaters who will rotate in and out after each jam. When no one is in the penalty box, teams will field five skaters at a time: one jammer and four blockers. Jammers are the only skaters who can score points for their team; they are easily identifiable because they wear a starred helmet cover and start behind all the other skaters, who make up the pack. Jammers score points by legally passing the hips of the opposing blockers. The first time they skate through the pack of blockers, no points are awarded. This pass simply determines who the 'lead jammer' is. Lead jammer status is awarded to the first jammer who gets through the pack legally. This skater is the only one who can "call off," or stop, a jam before the full two minutes elapse; the lead jammer can call off the jam at any point by repeatedly tapping her hips.

Blockers have two main purposes: prevent the opposing jammer from scoring points and help their jammer get through the pack. One of the four blockers is a pivot—designated by a striped helmet cover—and they have a unique role on the track. If the jammer passes the starred helmet cover to the pivot and the pivot puts it on top of the striped helmet cover, then the pivot may act as the jammer for the remainder of the jam. All skaters, including jammers, may initiate a block by using their torso, upper arms, and legs above mid-thigh. Tripping, elbowing, clotheslining, back blocking, and fighting are not allowed—they lead to thirty-second trips to the penalty box or even expulsions, depending on the egregiousness of the act. And because penalties hurt a team's chances of winning, they are rarely intentionally committed. The team that earns the most points by the conclusion of the second period wins the bout.[14]

A tension exists between retaining the kitschy and fun parts of derby and treating the sport like the serious athletic endeavor it has become over time. Even though the Austin women who first resurrected roller derby spent long hours training, even dedicating early weekend mornings to practicing their skating skills, they placed a much greater emphasis on roller derby's look and attitude at that time. The women who were responsible for the revival—donning tattoos, dyed hair, and an alternative sense of fashion—did not resemble other women in athletics. They created teams like the Holy Rollers, who dressed as naughty Catholic schoolgirls, and the Rhinestone Cowgirls, who sported sexy cowgirl attire. The teams were divided based on the bars the skaters frequented, skaters were encouraged to choose unique derby names like Betty Rage and Lunatic, fishnet stockings and short skirts were regular additions to uniforms, and rock 'n roll bands were invited to entertain fans during halftime shows. This first iteration of modern roller derby also included a penalty wheel. When referees caught skaters breaking a rule, they would require skaters to spin the wheel, which resulted in something as ordinary as a loss of three points to something as outrageous as a visit to "Spank Alley"—where select members of the audience were asked to spank the rear of the penalized skaters. Fans and skaters alike embraced the do-it-yourself (DIY) punk rock attitude and circus-like atmosphere that roller derby offered.[15]

While roller derby retains many of the historical elements that make it different from traditional sports, there is now a much greater emphasis on the skill and athleticism required to play. Instead of dividing up teams based on drinking establishments, as in the early days of the sport's revival, skaters are now typically drafted onto teams after an intensive training process. In fact, some skaters start at less competitive leagues in order to gain experience before transferring to more competitive leagues. Derby names are no longer embraced by all skaters. Some leagues—Denver Roller Derby, for example—now encourage each of their skaters to go by their real names on and off the track. This is quickly turning into a more common practice among many all-star skaters around the world. Further, uniforms have become more about comfort and fit rather than fashion though many skaters still add their own unique twist to their look. It should be noted that it far less common to see racy clothing like garter belts during game play. Of course, fans may still catch skaters pushing the envelope in less competitive contexts, such as expo games or home team bouts. For instance, RCRD hosts an annual expo bout called "Home Teams for the Holidays," where skaters may paste facial hair under their noses to resemble nutcrackers or don fishnet stockings to pay homage to the leg lamp from *A Christmas Story*. This is the exception, no longer the norm. Roller derby is truly a sport like no other, and it continues to evolve rapidly.

Inclusivity in Seattle

As a sport that is owned and operated by the skaters themselves, modern roller derby puts equity and inclusion at the forefront—welcoming people of all body shapes, ages, sexual orientations, genders, and racial and ethnic backgrounds. For instance, one of the best-known northwest pickup teams is "Overbeaters Anonymous." They are a conglomeration of plus-size women from leagues in Seattle and its surrounding areas. They described themselves as follows: "We are fat and we play roller derby really well without apologizing for either." They regularly post articles, videos, and images on their social media to encourage their skaters and fans to recognize the strength and beauty of their bodies regardless of size. They have a huge contingent of fans, and their merchandise can be spotted across the Pacific Northwest. Their emphasis on acceptance and empowerment is replicated by just about every other roller derby skater and league in the world. [16]

Roller derby in Seattle also proudly includes athletes from a variety of age groups. On the older end, there is a large community of skaters, officials, coaches, and fans over the age of forty—many of whom are parents or grandparents. A Seattle skater named Hot Flash started a "Derby over 40" website. The US over-forty group alone has over 5,500 members. On the younger end, there are children rushing to join the sport when they are still in elementary school. Seattle's own Derby Brats, one of the first junior leagues established in the US, offers four divisions to female skaters ranging in age from eight to seventeen years old. The Seattle Derby Brats' travel team, the Galaxy Girls, was ranked second in the world in 2017 in the Junior Roller Derby Association's (JRDA) all-female division. For young boys and gender nonconforming youth, there is the Southside Revolution coed team. At any age, skaters can find a space for individual growth, community, and empowerment within the sport of roller derby. [17]

The LGBTQIA+ presence has been strong in roller derby ever since its revival. Established in 2005, the Vagine Regime is the most well-known international collective of roller derby skaters from different sexual and gender identities; they currently have more than twenty chapters and teams

Ashley "Tia Wrecks" Dailide of RCRD discusses body size in an interview with photographer David Jaewon Oh: "I feel like I've reached to the point where I can find my voice and derby helped me with that. It's hard to describe but in life, you feel like you are slightly off track but then it suddenly clicks and you feel centered into the place. That kind of happened with me in derby. Part of it is I've realized that the warrior inside of me found the place and also, I was being respected for things I've always been shunned for. Like being a bigger girl because especially in my family, it was a constant battle since I was four years old. But (being big) has become an asset all of sudden which is really cool. It went from 'oh, you need to be thinner' to 'oh, I want to be stronger' so that was really good shift. Also, finding that group of people you can click with is really important. I've gained a lot more confidence and allowed me to center myself little more."

worldwide. Not only does the Vagine Regime serve as an avenue to connect the queer roller derby community and its allies, but it also promotes social justice through its events, fundraisers, merchandise, and social media posts. A documentary called *In the Turn*, which premiered at the Seattle Gay and Lesbian Film Festival in 2014, captures stories of skaters who find acceptance and connection through roller derby—including the filmmaker, who came out as a lesbian after discovering the Vagine Regime, and a ten-year-old transgender girl who had been excluded from sports until she was invited to participate in a junior roller derby camp in Los Angeles, California. Roller derby has become much more than a sport to many of its skaters and fans; it serves as a safe haven for members of the LGBTQIA+ community. [18]

Roller derby has forged new territory with its gender-inclusive policies. Since 2011, the WFTDA has welcomed gender nonconforming skaters. While the 2011 policy was the most progressive set by any sport at that time, it has since been revised to be more expansive; the original gender-inclusive policy referenced skaters' hormone levels, which excluded those who had not undergone hormone therapy. The updated 2015 policy allows transgender women, intersex women, and gender-expansive athletes to compete within the WFTDA. It should be noted that the Men's Roller Derby Association (MRDA) is even more open to membership than the WFTDA, allowing all genders to participate. According to their non-discrimination policy, "the MRDA does not and will not differentiate between members who identify male and those who identify as nonbinary gender (including but not limited to genderqueer, transmasculine, transfeminine, and agender) and does not and will not set minimum standards of masculinity for its membership or interfere with the privacy of its members for the purposes of charter eligibility." With this flexibility, a number of athletes who skate for the WFTDA also skate with the MRDA; for instance, several of Seattle's Rat City skaters also play with the Puget Sound Outcasts. Roller derby proudly welcomes skaters of all gender identities into its fold. [19]

Over time, the sport has made notable progress in recruiting and retaining skaters of color as well. For instance, the Black Roller Derby Network was created in 2011 for black skaters, officials, and volunteers. According to its founder, Scarbie Doll, the Network was established in order to create a space in which the black roller derby community can candidly share their experiences—both good and bad—in the sport. Now there are over 500 members internationally, and they are proactively reaching out to new

Gráinne Hunter of RCRD discusses junior roller derby and finding acceptance in an interview with photographer David Jaewon Oh: "When I was little, I thought I was a little different than everyone else. I almost pretended as if I was having crushes on boys. As I started playing derby in middle school, I realized, 'oh, I don't think I like boys. I'm pretty sure I like girls.' I guess, in a way, derby helped me to find out about myself. But because derby being so open to everything that I didn't even have to realize that it was helping me subconsciously or [to be] accepted. I remember telling my teammates that, 'I think I'm gay but I am not sure' and that was even before I came out to my parents. Playing derby gave me new friendships that made me feel close enough to tell them about myself."

Photo of the author, Jamie "Ethel Vermin" Barnhorst, by David Jaewon Oh

members. Through the establishment of supportive networks and in-person meetups, roller derby has made great strides toward becoming a welcoming place for skaters of all racial and ethnic backgrounds.[20]

Over the past century, roller derby has cycled through countless iterations. From the beginning, it included female athletes of varying ages and body types, disrupting traditional notions of femininity. While segregation was still the norm in some parts of the United States, men and women of color lived, trained, and played with their white counterparts, without question. Because modern roller derby was built from the ground up—a system in which skaters continue to be responsible for running and maintaining the sport in collaboration with officials and volunteers—its current form has broken entirely new ground. There are leagues in all parts of the world, and each is owned and operated by the very athletes who participate. Men, women, and those who identify outside of the gender binary—of all ages, sexual orientations, races, and ethnicities—have a place to thrive, compete, contribute, and develop community. Its predecessors laid a strong foundation, and modern roller derby in the city of Seattle is leading the pack on how to be an inclusive and empowering sport for all. Throughout the history of the sport in the nation at large, and particularly in Seattle, there has been one strong constant: roller derby has never been afraid to push boundaries and challenge the status quo.

CHAPTER SEVEN

Ultimate

Seattle's Greatest Export

ELLIOT TROTTER

Chances are, if you live in Seattle, you are already familiar with Ultimate. Your friend probably convinced you to join a fall league. Or maybe you have been to a game featuring one the city's two semiprofessional men's teams. Perhaps you caught an exhibition game of Seattle's nationally competitive women's club team, Seattle Riot. If your son or daughter has not played Ultimate in elementary, middle, or high school, you likely know a kid who has played. At the very least, you have walked by a park where two teams wearing brightly colored jerseys throw a 175-gram piece of plastic around in the quiet drizzle. What you may not know is that Seattle is home to numerous Ultimate Club Championship teams in multiple divisions. Seattle is the world's benchmark for developing youth players and is home to many businesses, individuals, and organizations known worldwide for their contributions to Ultimate.

For the uninitiated, Ultimate is easy to understand. Two teams of seven move a plastic disc up and down the field, trying to throw it to a teammate in the opposing end zone, much like American football. However, in contrast to football, players cannot run with the disc; they must stop and set a pivot foot once they have received it. But just like any sport, there are many nuances and strategies to the game.

After college, I became rapidly fascinated by the sport of Ultimate and one thing was clear—Seattle was Ultimate's mecca. I grew up in the northern suburbs of Chicago where discs were an uncommon sight other than a casual toss at the park. Though I had some exposure at summer camp, those

---

There is some debate in the field as to whether "Ultimate" should be capitalized or not in reference to the sport. The author of this chapter chose to capitalize.

of us from the Midwest in the 1990s were far more interested in the Chicago Bulls who were on their way to a second *three-peat*. Michael Jordan was everyone's hero, and I remember humid summer nights laying up a pink-and-green, kid's-sized basketball into the white backboard of the hoop on our garage, trying to "be like Mike." Similar to many kids of my generation, I would visualize myself as one of the Bulls, dribbling past Shawn Kemp and the Seattle SuperSonics, doing an awesome spin move and making the championship's winning shot. (I was actually a fan of Kemp and the Sonics when they faced the Bulls in the National Basketball Association (NBA) finals of 1996. My support landed me in a swimming pool courtesy of my father when Seattle beat Chicago in Game Four of the finals. I still have not forgiven him for ruining my collection of Tamagotchis and Giga Pets).[1]

Ultimate was not a common sight in my part of the world until I was exposed to the significance of it my senior year of high school by a physics teacher, Kunal Pujara. A track athlete at the time, I first played Ultimate when friends invited me to join them in a game. Pujara had played Ultimate at Rutgers (1988–1991) and Duke University (1991–1993) and shared his experience with us, offering insight into playing "serious" Ultimate. I was quickly hooked. I loved being able to run full speed for an object that floated through the air; it certainly beat running around the track oval. During that first encounter with Ultimate, I was also exposed to some of the unique elements of the sport like Spirit of the Game (SOTG)—a guiding principle that, simply stated, is about self-officiating and mutual respect for your opponent. This ideological element of Ultimate further secured my interest in the game.

Ultimate's beginning draws back to the mass production and rise in popularity of the Frisbee in the late 1950s by the Wham-O Corporation. Although simple games of catch became a staple of college quads in the 1960s, it was only a matter of time before myriad associated games were invented (some by Wham-O themselves, but most by fans of the new toy), such as disc golf, GUTS (a Frisbee game similar to dodgeball), freestyle, and Ultimate. Ultimate's well-documented origin story harkens back to when a young Joel Silver (today a well-known film producer in Hollywood) encountered a version of the game at summer camp during the later portion of the 1960s. Soon after, at Columbia High School in Maplewood, New Jersey, Silver and a group of friends drafted the first official rules of Ultimate, a game initially viewed as somewhat of an "anti-sport"—one that, in part out of necessity and perhaps as a hippie-inspired notion, included a rule set based in self-officiation and mutual respect known today as SOTG. While the debate over whether to officiate through SOTG or referees rages on (the United States' semiprofessional league utilizes referees), this concept has aided the rise of Ultimate in both Seattle and worldwide and has become the centerpiece of many organizations focused on social good.[2]

Today, Ultimate is played regularly by over seven million people in eighty countries. It has an international governing body and world championship competitions on grass and beach in alternating cities. Since 2001, Ultimate has been included in the World Games. The International Olympic Committee recognized Ultimate as a sport in 2015, and the sport has since been rumored to be in consideration for inclusion in future Olympics Games. In the United States, Ultimate is played competitively at universities, in recreational leagues, in two semiprofessional men's leagues, and at the club and youth level in regional, state, and national competitions. At the youth level, Ultimate is emerging as a popular alternative to impact sports like American football and has found a foothold in Seattle, which has established itself as a flagship for the sport at all levels.[3]

Seattle, the Hub

By the time I had moved to Seattle in 2009, I was flying around the country with Cultimate, a tournament-organizing business based out of Seattle. Though I had strengthened my appreciation for the sport in college, playing at regional tournaments sanctioned by USA Ultimate, the sport's governing body in the United States, I was now being exposed to the wider and wilder world of the sport—the stories, the dynasties. I would also play a role in telling the sport's story. In 2012, I founded Ultimate's first major online media resource, *Skyd Magazine*. Two years later, I co-founded RISE UP, an educational video-on-demand platform and international clinic facilitators. I would shortly thereafter travel the globe, producing Ultimate's first documentary web series, *Ultimate Globe Trotter*.

It soon dawned on me that Seattle was far more important to the sport than I had realized. In Seattle, we had Sockeye, Riot, and Shazam—historic club teams that had won multiple national championships early in the twenty-first century. There was Five Ultimate, an Ultimate apparel company, which today has become one of the most recognizable brands for the sport around the world. We had multiple tournaments and leagues in which to participate, which were run by a burgeoning local governing body, Disc

Northwest (DiscNW). There were opportunities to coach middle school, high school, and even elementary school teams and actually be compensated. As the sport exploded in the United States, Seattle became home to multiple semiprofessional teams and became internationally renowned for developing youth players. It sent its leaders and players overseas to coach at clinics and camps around the world. It became a key voice for gender equity and diversity through youth programs like All Girl Everything (AGE UP) and Girls Ultimate Movement (GUM). Furthermore, Seattle influenced national-governing bodies to make changes to their programming.[4]

"In other cities, I might have gotten excited to see a stranger wearing Ultimate attire or carrying a frisbee," noted Seattle Riot's Dominique Fontenette. "In Seattle, it's a normal thing. As popular as our sport is in the major cities that I've lived (New York, Boston, LA, Portland, San Francisco), none quite match the popularity of Ultimate in Seattle." What makes Seattle so special? How is it that a rainy, culturally alternative place like Seattle became the mecca for the sport and a city that has affected and influenced the sport worldwide? Having seen the sport all over the nation and the world, there is truly no other place like Seattle for the sport of Ultimate. A keystone in the sport's historical growth, bolstered by progressive values that complement its alternative nature, Seattle's position in the sport is perhaps no mystery. But the progressive attitude was not the only factor contributing to its growth in the city. As explained by many of its proponents and historians, Ultimate blossomed in Seattle for reasons ranging from geography to field access. [5]

"Seattle has a few things going for it," explained Tyler Kinley, a former member of Seattle's men's club team Sockeye. "First, geographically, lots of players are within a close-enough proximity to create a massive population of players." In Tyler's mind, that proximity is key to the development of Seattle Ultimate. While other communities are more spread out by distance or commute time, Seattle Ultimate is benefitted by opportunities to interact regularly. Miranda Roth, former star of the women's club team Seattle Riot, highlights a mindset of Seattleites that applies itself well to the counterculture "anti-sport" originally envisioned by Joel Silver and friends: "Ultimate fits very well into the psyche and sociology of the average Seattleite, so it makes sense that Ultimate has taken hold there: relaxed but competitive, outdoors but organized and fun for all." Kinley's teammate and revered coaching mind Ben Wiggins concurs with Roth and points to Seattle's climate and the ability to play year-round as an advantage over other communities like Boston or Chicago: "Seattle has done well economically, and this makes it marginally easier for devoted players to move and stay here (rather than having to leave their club teams to find jobs elsewhere)." Kinley, who has since moved home to Michigan, recognized a difference immediately. "In Michigan, I have trouble finding people as invested in the game as I am," he explained. "In Seattle, I found my interest in the sport was not only normal, but I could even do more, think more, train more, play more," Kinley insisted.[6]

"When I was coming up in Ultimate, one of the former USA Ultimate executive directors had the Denny's test," recalled Matthew "Skip" Sewell, my boss at Cultimate. They would know that Ultimate had made it if "after walking into any Denny's [restaurant] and proclaiming 'I play Ultimate,' 50 percent of the people would know what they're talking about. I'd say that Seattle has achieved that," Sewell proudly noted. In addition to playing for Seattle's club team Sockeye, Sewell played a critical role in the history of the sport. A self-taught designer and web developer (among other skills), Sewell founded Cultimate in 2005, the sport's first major tournament-organizing company, which closed its doors in 2012. Cultimate developed and managed college and club tournaments across the United States. As a result of owning numerous critical competition events, Cultimate could affect perception and direction of the sport, sometimes putting serious pressure on decisions made by USA Ultimate. Sewell also helped develop one of the foremost professional leagues in the United States, Major League Ultimate (MLU). For Sewell, a self-proclaimed "recovering Ultimate addict," moving to and headquartering his business in Seattle seemed logical.[7]

Simply put, Ultimate is taken seriously in the city. These factors have contributed to robust playing opportunities in Seattle. "There are niches for everyone within the community," said Gwen Ambler, a legendary club champion with Seattle Riot and San Francisco Fury. "Whether you are an avid Goaltimate [Ultimate variation] player who meets up at weekly pickup, a youth player who plays wherever you can, a retired player who stays involved by coaching, or one of the top athletes in the game, there are others like you to connect with and enjoy the sport together," she insisted. Wiggins highlighted in detail just how special playing opportunities are in Seattle:

There are legitimate E-leagues for dozens of teams of players who want a playing experience and are not ready for the A-league, or B or C or D. That's pretty incredible for a sport that barely exists in many larger cities. You can also play one tournament per month all year without ever leaving the city, and that's a lot more than most players ever play.[8]

The Seattle Scene

When you are a young and ambitious Ultimate player in any city, the teams you look up to are the club mainstays. They are well known throughout the city's Ultimate scene and, in Seattle's case, on the national and international stage. These teams, like Seattle Riot, have and continue to inspire and attract talent to the city.

After a core of women from a team known as Women on the Verge retired, a new women's team was born in 1999, named after the infamous World Trade Organization protests: Seattle Riot. By 2004, Riot had won their first US National title, and they repeated in 2005. Since then, they have placed in the top three at US Nationals ten times and won two World Championships—in Honolulu in 2002 and in Lecco, Italy, in 2014 over their archrivals, San Francisco's Fury. Today, the familiar Riot logo of the space needle engulfed in flames is worn proudly by young boys and girls throughout the city.

Miranda Roth was one of those talented players who was a household name by the time she graduated Carleton College in 2004, winning the Callahan Award (college Ultimate's MVP), and a club championship in that same year. After a couple years in Atlanta playing for the club team Ozone, she took her talents west and found a distinct competitive atmosphere. "When I first moved to Seattle, there was a highly competitive nature to the teams—that we played to win and enjoyed seeing other teams crumble beneath our feet," maintained Roth.[9]

The year 2004 proved to be quite successful for Seattle teams with Shazam winning the mixed championship and Seattle Sockeye winning their first men's title. Though Sockeye had existed since the early nineties, with three consecutive second-place finishes from 1995 to1997, they saw their first title in 2004. This Sockeye team, much like Riot, capitalized on an influx of young players who had grown up playing Ultimate in the Emerald City. Sockeye won their second and third titles back-to-back in 2006 and 2007, battling with rivals from the north, Vancouver's Furious George. "The Northwest Regional was the crucible," recalled ex-Sockeye player, Sewell.

"We used to call the Northwest Regional tournament 'Mini-Nationals' as, from 2002–2008, every national champion came from that region. Not only did you have the best competition close at hand, but you faced them four to six times a season. It forced innovation in strategy, training techniques, etc." This crucible, Sewell insisted, helped build a reputation for Seattle as one of the most competitive cities for Ultimate in the world. As ex-Sockeye player Chase Sparling-Beckley noted, "Sockeye's success with the horizontal stack, an offensive strategy utilized by Furious in Vancouver, influenced offensives to implement it for years to come."[10]

As a young player moving to Seattle in 2008, Tyler Kinley instantly recognized this aura around Seattle Ultimate. "Both Sockeye and Riot had a mystique about them," insisted Kinley. Sockeye had just won their third national championship in four years as they entered their 2008 season. "They were one of the rare teams that had a website, had some of the biggest athletes, but also were clearly very invested in the fun side of it all, and seemed to enjoy their success in a way that really encapsulated the way I'd most want to win," she added. As evidenced by Sockeye's use of Furious's horizontal stack, Miranda Roth saw Seattle as being a competitive community that has always accepted ideas from outside. Kinley saw the accumulation of knowledge as a big factor: "Much of Seattle's success can be attributed to having so many leaders stay and develop and pass along their knowledge." "When youth teams are coached by ex-world champions, when elite teams have decades old systems in place for team management and logistic facilitation, when youth programs are so well established that school systems need no convincing that they should exist," he continued. Kinley acknowledged that "these things are what really set Seattle apart. And, this kind of deep, established community only attracts more people who are similarly obsessed."[11]

Looking back on her time in the city with Riot, Roth observed the almost obsessive nature of Seattle Ultimate club players: "I do think a negative is that Ultimate players in Seattle are often one-track minds. We ate, breathed and slept Riot and Sockeye, to the detriment of other facets of life (work, school, relationships, etc.). People in Seattle tend not to have as much of a 'real life'—especially in their 20s—as those playing Ultimate in other cities." Though Seattle has not seen a national title since 2007, it remains a consistent contender in all club divisions. [12]

For those less obsessed with competition and simply seeking fun, there is Potlatch—an annual coed tournament held on the Fourth of July weekend at Sixty Acres Park in Redmond, just fifteen miles northeast of Seattle. Teams composed of over 2,000 high-level club and recreational players from across North America and often overseas attend each year in a celebration of the sport and its community. Since its founding in 1989, Potlatch has become known for its teams clad in ridiculous costumes, its promotion of gifting "spirit" prizes to opponents, a salmon dinner, and excessive evening celebrations. While interviewing tournament directors, I was asked by them to remind my audience that alcohol is not permitted at the fields. "Potlatch is one of the reasons our organization was created," insisted former DiscNW executive director William "Bunny" Bartram.[13]

A Community of Giving Back: Youth Ultimate in Seattle

Perhaps more notable than Potlatch is a youth tournament organized by DiscNW, Spring Reign, held an hour north of Seattle in Burlington. In 2016, Spring Reign saw ninety-six elementary to high school-aged, coed youth teams from upwards of twenty American states and Canadian provinces compete in what is resoundingly the largest youth Ultimate tournament in the world. Much like Potlatch, Spring Reign is more about the players than the competition. "We try to make it a celebration of the community," asserted Bartram. "We try to promote spirit and fun," he averred. DiscNW provides teams with miniature disc spirit awards to share with other teams as gifts to promote community.[14]

Though there are more kids playing single-gender leagues in Seattle and in the United States, Youth Ultimate in Seattle began with a coed focus. To DiscNW organizers, it seemed natural for Spring Reign to continue as a coed tournament as well. "It's tradition," maintained Bartram: "We still think there's value in coed sports. There are different opportunities with coed."[15]

Indeed, the pride of Seattle Ultimate has to be its opportunities for youth. From summer camps to elementary school leagues, there is no other place in the world that has done for Youth Ultimate what Seattle has. Talking to the many players in the city, it is clear why that is. Based in Chicago, Coach Arnoush "Java" Javaherian has been working to develop Youth Ultimate in the Windy City. He runs CUT, a popular Youth Ultimate summer camp in multiple locations around the US. Javaherian sees Seattle as the golden standard. "Seattle is the standard on which all cities model their Youth Ultimate leagues," said Javaherian. "How did Seattle do it? That is how we will do it. They are the model as their Youth Ultimate world has grown considerably," he continued. "Seattle has really set the bar for Youth Ultimate," noted Riot's Ambler. And she is correct on multiple accounts. As Ambler points out, Seattle's girls' Under-19 Youth Club Championship team was undefeated from 2005 until 2017, winning seventy-six straight games. Ambler insists, "our USA junior world championship teams are often full of boys and girls from Seattle; and Seattle coaches like Shannon O'Malley and Alyssa Weatherford have helped to set coaching curriculum for USA Ultimate." "We are deeper and more organized in Youth Ultimate than any city in the world," Sockeye's Wiggins echoed. "Worldwide, cities with a high school program are on the forefront," he continued. "In Seattle, there are entire elementary school leagues."[16]

O'Malley was an awkward, sweatpants-wearing eleven-year-old when they first encountered Ultimate in gym class at Eckstein Middle School in 1999. "I remember watching the in-class demo game and being intrigued, then finding a lot of success with my throwing accuracy as I chucked a disc at a line on the wall," O'Malley recalled. "And when we finally played, I loved it! I remember bringing the paper to my dad at dinner for sign-ups, he had no idea what I was talking about." O'Malley's father eventually agreed to let Shannon play. The player continued on with the sport through high school at Seattle's Nathan Hale and with the youth club program More Horizontal (MoHo). In 2010, O'Malley won the Callahan Award at the University of Washington and went on to play with Seattle Riot for many years. For O'Malley, after years of playing T-ball with the boys, the Ultimate community they found at Eckstein gave a kid who had not yet found a place in which they fit a feeling of welcome. "The Ultimate team immediately brought me in," O'Malley explained. "They made no judgements on who I was, willingly taught me the game, and gave me friends that I still have today," they proclaimed.[17]

It was perhaps that community O'Malley found that helped inspire the nascent player to start coaching as a sophomore in high school. O'Malley was asked by a high school coach to help at Eckstein and was soon asked to help coach another youth team with future Riot player Molly Suver. "I really loved working with the kids; they were totally goofy and silly yet very respectful and wanted to learn more about the game," remembered O'Malley. A desire to engage in community service lent heavily to O'Malley's sustained interest in the sport:

This feeling of spreading my passion and helping kids enjoy it equally made me fall in love with coaching. I think already at this point, I realized the importance of giving back to the community. I knew it was still a growing sport, and I knew all my coaches up until that point were volunteers. I was part of helping get the Nathan Hale program to be more legit and knew our coaches were putting in a ton of unpaid time and energy for us. It was a contagious feeling to give back to the community. I haven't stopped coaching since that point."[18]

With Riot teammates Alyssa Weatherford and Sarah Griffith, O'Malley went on to organize the youth club organization Seven Hills Ultimate. Seven Hills has roots in a similar organization known as the Seattle Fryz, which was organized by Ultimate parent Randy Lim. According to O'Malley, Seven Hills is committed to working with youth players on both their on-field skill and off-field character. O'Malley wanted "a program that has representations from as many different schools and communities as possible." "It could have the potential to bring the Seattle youth community even closer together and I truly hope it does," insisted O'Malley.[19]

Such sentiments of giving back are prevalent throughout the city. Everyone from high-level club players to college and high school athletes seek out and find opportunities to coach. Sockeye stalwart and Cultimate founder Matthew Sewell noted Seattle's uniqueness in elite players giving back: "There is no other place in the world where it is expected that, if you are an elite Ultimate player, that you are giving back," said Sewell. "Coaching or volunteering. In most places in the world it's enough just to play Ultimate and hold down the rest of your life."[20]

"Leadership of both Sockeye and Riot, at least since 2001, has placed a high priority on community service," argued Chris Page, DiscNW board member and Sockeye captain from 2001–2003. "[Sockeye] arranged to provide volunteer instructors for beginner middle school coaches from among our players in exchange for DiscNW finding us practice field space," he noted. [21]

In addition to there being so much demand for coaches, O'Malley highlighted possible reasons why players in the city insist on giving back. "I think so many players choose to coach in Seattle for similar reasons that I started coaching," O'Malley explained. O'Malley maintained: "They grew up with players volunteering for them and had role models who demonstrated how you give back to the game. You almost feel a need to do it because people did it for you. You also love the game and want people to love the game like you do. You want them to have the incredible experiences you had. You want them to grow as much as you grew." [22]

Khalif El-Salaam grew up in Seattle and benefitted from many of these top coaches in the area. "My idols, the people I looked up to, would coach me at tournaments and at summer camps," El-Salaam recalled. "The fact they would look out for me and instill their knowledge showed that they believed in me." he insisted. El-Salaam—a star player for the University of Washington, the USA Mixed National Team, and Seattle's Major League Ultimate MLU franchise, the Rainmakers—further highlights Ultimate's sense of giving back as unique even to other sports like the NBA. "In other sports, as you get bigger, more famous, you start to disconnect from where you came from," argued El-Salaam. He highlights the philanthropic nature of many Ultimate players: "Elite men's, women's and mixed players, they are all consistently watching kids, giving advice, coaching. They are there and influencing the upcoming generations. You don't get that in other sports." [23]

Though organizations like O'Malley's Seven Hills give those hooked youth players an opportunity to sharpen their skills, perhaps the most critical component of youth opportunities in Seattle has been DiscNW. Established in 1995, it is the largest local Ultimate organizing body in the nation. By 2016, it was serving over 6,000 players annually and had the nation's largest operating budget, as well as the highest number of full-time staff and many seasonal coaches and volunteers. In the city, all recreational leagues, youth camps, and clinics are run through DiscNW. The organization's work rewarded Seattle with the most youth players in the world and the appreciation of organizers all over the world (many of whom have contacted DiscNW or even traveled to Seattle to better understand how to develop the sport). "Being supported by DiscNW is a huge advantage, because they can help to keep coaches networked and keep quality high both on and off the field," explained Wiggins. "Innovations like combined high school training teams, coaching development, individual and team youth camps, and connections between teams and trainers," he argued, "are all things that have been started or developed here in new ways." [24]

Ambler also highlights DiscNW and Seattle Ultimate's focus on investing in underserved communities as groundbreaking. "DiscNW's willingness to cover stipends for public school coaches has helped Ultimate expand out of private schools and into neighborhoods that are not the same demographics as the prep school college players who found Ultimate," Ambler explained. "Other Ultimate communities across the US have been asking how to reach more diverse populations with Ultimate," she noted, "and Seattle is leading the way."[25]

Seattle Ultimate Gives Back

Perhaps as an embodiment of Ultimate's ethos of SOTG, combined with Seattle's willingness to give back, this desire to reach diverse and under-served populations has led to the development of many philanthropic and social justice focused organizations in Seattle. "Especially in the last fifteen years, Seattle has become known for its effort towards SOTG at all levels (especially at the highest club levels)," insisted Ambler, "but even more importantly for prioritizing the Ultimate experience for women, youth, and people of color."[26]

Despite the growth of over 13,000 youth players in the United States from 2007 to 2013, only 3,000 of them were girls. Seattle resident and club player with Seattle Underground Heather Ann Brauer sought to address that by establishing a task force and brainstorming ways to change the landscape. Backed by USA Ultimate, this led to the establishment of Girls Ultimate Movement (GUM) which focuses on creating opportunities for youth and high-school-aged girls to participate in Ultimate. "Clinics have been run from Maine to Texas to Seattle," asserted Brauer. "Requests for information on GUM have come from Ireland to Jordan to India to Mexico and beyond. We've always been about dreaming big for GUM—and the sky is really the limit!" she affirmed. Brauer described Seattle's impact on GUM as "huge." Seattle has run the largest GUM clinics and brought in 100 participants in a GUM clinic with Seattle Underground (women's club) for girls under the age of sixteen. [27]

All Girl Everything (AGE UP), founded by players and coaches Hana Kawaii and Sam Terry in 2010, started several programs for youth living in South Seattle that focus on healthy friendships/relationships, understanding race and class, overcoming fear, and developing positive body image. It uses Ultimate to teach and bring its groups together. Youth Ultimate Project (YUP) uses Ultimate in a similar fashion as both AGE UP and GUM. After a class trip to Phnom Penh in the spring of 2010, a group of the Northwest

School students grew exceptionally fond of the Cambodian way of life. But they were struck by challenges that Cambodian youth face every day. Shortly after, they started YUP with the help of Rodwell Kov, a Cambodian native and math teacher at the Northwest School. Since its inception, YUP founders have traveled to Cambodia yearly and run student-led camps with the mission of providing a positive outlet to underserved communities through Ultimate.[28]

The work done by these organizations through the sport has made a serious impact in the city, according to O'Malley. "I think Ultimate has become a social justice community because the community is built on being accepting of all players," O'Malley maintained. "We should be inviting everyone in because our sport is growing, unique, and has a backbone value of respecting/trusting others," O'Malley averred. "Our values," the Ultimate enthusiast continued, "if transferred to the real world, could change how people interact in the world. This idea, I think, is why people are motivated to see change and to use our community as the mechanism." [29]

The Olympic Windjammers and Seattle Ultimate Origins

If one looks at the history of Ultimate's inception in Seattle, it is easy to see where the thread of giving back begins. Mary Lowry was extremely modest when I interviewed her about her incredible impact on the development of Ultimate in Seattle. "If it wasn't me, someone else would have done it," she remarked. Many well-known coaches and leaders in the city can trace their involvement in the sport to Lowry and others like her. Lowry first moved to Seattle in 1978 to attend college at the University of Washington. She saw an advertisement taped to a garbage can on campus for some pickup Ultimate at Green Lake Park and decided to attend. Most people ignored that advertisement. In 1978, most people were not looking at garbage bins for Ultimate games. But Lowry was already familiar with Ultimate, having played at the University of South Florida before transferring to UW. Just a year prior, Lowry had attended the annual Apple Blossom Festival in Tampa, Florida, and first saw the dance and acrobatic-inspired freestyle disc at an event-sponsored performance. Often this was how the freestyle was promoted in the 1970s—at events and through a national series funded by Wham-O. This series hit a pinnacle at the 1975 World Frisbee Championships, which took place in the Rose Bowl. If you were a freestyler, you participated in all sorts of disc disciplines like double disc court, GUTS, and Ultimate. By the time Lowry found herself in Seattle, she was hooked on any activity involving a disc. [30]

At Green Lake Park, Lowry met Jeff Jorgenson and a group of freestyle and disc sport fanatics called the Olympic Windjammers. The Windjammers had been riding the wave of freestyle's growth in America. Introduced to freestyle two years prior, Jorgenson was at the Rose Bowl in 1975 for the second-ever World Frisbee Championships. It was the first year that Ultimate was introduced into the competition. With the help of a local disc jockey, Jorgenson hustled to get a freestyle halftime show at a SuperSonics game that same year and began doing a variety of shows at school assemblies and clinics. [31]

"In '77 and '78 we started getting traction as a club," Jorgenson contended. "Ivy League schools had Ultimate players coming out to work at Boeing. In March of '78 we had our first organized game against a team from Eugene," he recalled. Among those early recruits was Bill Nye of "The Science Guy" fame. Jorgenson declared that, "Bill helped solidify some practice techniques and structure. He was an integral part of moving the Windjammers along." [32]

By the early 1980s, Lowry and other Seattle women wanted to start a women's team (with the Ultimate Players Association, now USA Ultimate, just initiating a women's division in 1981). This team became the Bad Apples, then the Predators, and eventually Women on the Verge—a predecessor to Seattle Riot that won three world championships from 1995–1999. [33]

Asked about why Ultimate started to spread in Seattle, Lowry noted: "Seattle has a lot of smart and athletic people. It's strategically a fun game and creates a sense of community. It draws the type of people who like to be outside and think outside of the box." "We started having to turn people away from our practices," recalled Jorgenson. "People would see us at Green Lake and ask to join, but we were too intense. But we didn't want to turn them away. We wanted them to play," he insisted. [34]

The Puget Sound Ultimate League, the predecessor to DiscNW, was founded in 1984 by Windjammer Mark Friedman. The league offered an alternative to the more serious Windjammer practices and helped provide further opportunity to grow the sport. By the early 1980s, Lowry landed a job at Seattle Country Day School (SCDS) and began teaching Ultimate as an elective. "I moved to Seattle because it's a beautiful place," admitted Lowry.

She believed it would be an ideal place to start a camp where children could hike and play Ultimate after school. Lowry's Seattle dream soon became reality at SCDS, where it led to an unexpected encounter that would spur the growth of Seattle Ultimate. [35]

Shortly after she began at SCDS, Lowry saw Joe Bisignano out of her classroom window. With him were a bunch of students playing with discs walking back to New Option Middle School after playing Ultimate at Queen Anne Park. Until then, Lowry had not found opportunities for her kids to play other schools. She asked Bisignano if his kids wanted to play. They started playing at Rogers Park. Lowry soon decided that if she had six groups playing, she could bring them together at Magnuson Park, the Windjammers' practice space, on weekends. Lowry did everything she could think of to get more teams on board. She sent out packets to teachers and school directors with rules, basic strategies, and information on how to throw, along with any literature she found about Ultimate. It was very hit or miss, but soon she had enough teams to join at Magnuson. [36]

On weekends, Lowry and Jorgenson would go out to the fields and monitor the youth games, then they would play their own. Bisignano started helping to schedule youth games and teams started to come in from Bainbridge Island. Then, in 1987, Lowry, Jorgenson, and Bisignano started the popular youth tournament Spring Reign. By 1995, Joey Grey (one of Lowry's teammates from Women on the Verge) founded DiscNW, which provided that crucial formal backbone for Youth Ultimate in the city.

Mike Mullen, a coach at the Northwest School, turned to DiscNW to help establish Seattle Youth Ultimate Camps, which exposed hundreds of elementary school kids to the sport. Mullen recalls the partnership: "We worked with DiscNW for insurance and built the camps into not only a great experience for campers and a way to pay coaches a good stipend for their work, but also a way to make a significant amount of money for DiscNW to help fund programs that struggled to cover costs." "One of the main early lessons we learned," he declared, "was to charge more and give away a lot of financial aid instead of charging the minimum: In this way we could ensure that we only got campers who wanted to be at camp instead of being the cheapest option for childcare." Even today, Seattle Youth Ultimate Camps continue to connect hundreds of kids with Ultimate. [37]

Lowry and Gray also took advantage of a partnership with the city of Seattle when a family education levy was passed that included middle school athletics. This funding of fields and stipends for public school coaches helped to establish a coed middle school league during the fall in which fifteen middle schools participated (the largest club participation numbers for any sport in Seattle at the time).

In the late 1990s, Bisignano also helped to establish youth club opportunities for those Ultimate-impassioned kids. He created MoHo, which with the coaching help of Lowry and Jorgenson led to a National Youth Ultimate championship in 2000 (Seattle's first youth title). Many of those original MoHo players are familiar names to those in the Ultimate world: Alex Nord, Sam CK, Jeremy Cram, Jimmy Chu, Chase Sparling-Beckley. This group went on to lead Seattle Sockeye to their first club championships just five years later. Britt Atack, a former Sockeye player notes the specific importance of MoHo: "Ben Wiggins, Miranda Roth, and others continued that tutelage of youth on MoHo, lighting a fire among athletic and motivated high school players." "The bonds and friendships forged across the city among kids from all different schools were one of the most awesome outcomes of MoHo that continues today as the youth movement has expanded," he added. [38]

The work by Lowry, Jorgenson, and Bisignano, among others, set the foundation for Ultimate to develop in the city. By early 2000s, Seattle had an entire economy of organizations, funding, passionate coaches, and talented club teams. Seattle had built its perpetual motion machine that would churn out passionate talented youth players to fuel its future. Even today, many Ultimate cities are still working to catch up to the infrastructure Seattle has in place.

At its core, Seattle Ultimate was about giving back. "We created these opportunities for the kids because they wanted to play," proclaimed Lowry. They had a group of middle-school-aged youth who wanted to play in high school, which placed pressure on local high schools to create additional opportunities. "It is really the organizing and building of opportunities that I am [proudest] of," recalled Mullen. He recognized that his involvement was both produced by and produced a charitable engagement with the sport:

> I believe that I did for a generation or two of Youth Ultimate players what other youth sports organizers did for me as a youth soccer, basketball, baseball player. I'm also very, very proud of all of our young players who have gone on to organize many of their own great opportunities for young athletes in Ultimate and other sports, not only locally but also internationally with things such as the Youth Ultimate Project in Cambodia.

Students like Shannon O'Malley and Khalif el-Salaam would continue to give back to the community they loved by coaching for free. "They loved Ultimate," recalled Lowry. "It gets in your blood, and you can't shake it."[39]

This Seattle success in coaching and at the club level has even extended itself overseas. Amidst their national championship success, Sockeye's Chase Sparling-Beckley traveled to Colombia to compete in the World Games in 2006. There he met Mauricio Moore, a young leader for the developing sport in Colombia. This exchange led to a realization that Seattle could influence developing Ultimate countries. Three years later, Sockeye and Riot traveled to Colombia to compete and to run clinics during Torneo Eterna Primavera (TEP), a tournament in Medellin.[40]

Sockeye and Riot coaching corps was born, and over the next several years, players from both teams traveled all over South America, Mexico, the Philippines, Russia, Germany, and Ireland to coach and lead clinics and camps. "Seattle players and coaches strive to be ambassadors to the sport," insisted Riot's Kate Kingery. Ultimate players "travel around the world to play, coach and share their love of the game." "This endless devotion and passion for the sport from top players and coaches helps to keep Seattle out in front of the curve as Ultimate grows around the country and the world," Kingery affirmed. Multiple international players have come to Seattle to learn and try out for club teams. "People looked at Sockeye—your not-so-typical athletes," confessed Sockeye's Sewell, "they realized we could teach them something about Ultimate."[41]

Chase Sparling-Beckley saw practice styles and drills as having a major lasting impact on international teams. "We tend to train and practice at a much higher level than other countries," explained Sparling-Beckley.[42] He argued that several countries began to train differently as a result of the influence of American players who traveled abroad.

The Business of Ultimate

Riot's Gwen Ambler looks to other sources as the drive for exporting Seattle Ultimate internationally over the past several years: the rise of Ultimate media. Worldwide audiences were consuming Ultimate media from Seattle. *Skyd Magazine* and RISE UP were exceptional resources for producing and sustaining international Ultimate communities, for instance, and the connection to Seattle further demonstrated that by the early twenty-first century, the city was a space with incomparable Ultimate experience.

I like to tell people that when I founded *Skyd Magazine*, players and teams did not even have Twitter accounts. As Tyler Kinley noted, Sockeye was one of the few teams with a website. Most Ultimate players and fans were getting their news from a now-defunct forum known as Rec.Sport.Disc. That changed in 2010 when a group of Ultimate players from the University of Puget Sound decided to create a modern media resource for the sport—one that covered tournaments, provided analysis, and more. The idea stemmed from working with Skip Sewell and running tournaments around America with his Seattle-based business, Cultimate. In part, Cultimate was one of the reasons I moved to Seattle.

In its formative years, *Skyd* would publish tournament previews and editorial submissions. Soon we started seeking sponsors and went to cover tournaments in person, providing additional analysis. As the first successful media of its kind, *Skyd* quickly established itself as a valued voice of the sport's community and a world-renowned brand. Over the years, *Skyd* has evolved to focus less on coverage and now serves more as an outlet for editorial storytelling and event video production. In its short history, *Skyd* has flown its banner and provided video-streaming coverage of games at many world championship events.

Seattle is no stranger to the sprouting of Ultimate-focused organizations. In 2006, Sewell created Cultimate, the world's first tournament-organizing business for Ultimate. It sought to establish a higher quality of events and a more formalized and competitive schedule for college and club. Sewell saw Seattle as a welcoming place for running a business in the Ultimate industry. "Seattle Ultimate took itself seriously," Sewell acknowledged. It was a situation that allowed him the latitude and support to try to make a career out of Ultimate: "It wasn't insane to think that you can try to build a series of tournaments that would help midwife Ultimate into more popular culture."[43]

Sewell left Seattle for Oakland after Cultimate formally closed its doors in 2010. Although Cultimate no longer exists, Sewell's impact on how tournaments are run remained evident. After Cultimate closed, Sewell still saw Seattle as a critical component and testing ground for his latest project: USA Goaltimate—a governing body and organizer for its namesake disc sport variation founded in 2017. Goaltimate is most akin to half court basketball and features a goal structure that players must pass the disc through in order to score a goal.[44]

Like Sewell, Ben Wiggins and Andy Lovseth were Ultimate nerds. Lovseth grew up in Seattle, surrounded by Ultimate. Wiggins won the

Callahan Award as a college player at the University of Oregon and went on to win national championships with Sockeye in 2004, 2006, and 2007. Together they coached DIRT (the A team) at Western Washington University in Bellingham, Washington, and developed an online Ultimate journal called *The Huddle*. Beginning in 2007, *The Huddle* released issues on a monthly basis that included articles authored by the top players in the sport on everything from strategy to community and USA Ultimate policy. Though by 2011 *The Huddle* was releasing its last issue, it heavily influenced *Skyd's* creation and is still referenced by players today.

It is impossible to talk about Seattle Ultimate without discussing the literal and figurative fabric of Seattle's Ultimate world, Five Ultimate. In 2006, five siblings—Zahlen, Rohre, Vehro, Xthen, and Qxhna Titcomb—established Five Ultimate, the quintessential Ultimate business. An apparel company known for its stretchy, colorful shorts and iconic fuzzy hats, Five emerged as an industry leader by connecting with Ultimate's irreverent attitude. Four of the five siblings had attended SCDS, where they were coached in Ultimate and freestyling by Mary Lowry. The siblings, all five of whom were Ultimate and freestyle prodigies, adored being a part of the Ultimate culture and decided to build a company that filled a void for quality gear while giving back to the community. Five Ultimate quickly became well known for its presence at tournaments, often decorating its tournament sales booth with thrift shop couches and other Dadaist accoutrements they would find at local thrift shops. Five Ultimate partnered with Sewell and Cultimate's catalog of events in the late 2000s, which helped grow the brand within the national college community.[45]

Rohre Titcomb acknowledges the important role Seattle played in Five's growth: "I think as important as any reason was the fact that we, as owners, we know this community so well," admitted Titcomb. "We grew up in it," she added, and "understand all the different things that make it thrive and make it unique. This means we get great support and we're able to provide great support in return. As the community changes and as we grow, we're also able to stay in touch and adapt accordingly. If Seattle weren't at our fingertips, that would be so much harder to do." Five Ultimate's influence extends far beyond the city of its inception. The owners have made outreach and giving back to the Ultimate community a pillar of their business, often supporting local tournaments and businesses like *Skyd* and international events from Israel to Africa with discounted or free apparel.[46]

In 2014, Qxhna Titcomb, the youngest of the five siblings, developed the

All-Star Tour—a national tour that showcases a team of college women all-stars competing against the top club women's teams in the country. Inspired by the NexGen Tour, a similar tour that featured the All-Star's male counterparts and solidified a platform of stadium competition for Ultimate, the All-Star Tour promotes their mission of showcasing women's Ultimate and increasing media coverage devoted to female athletes in a variety of ways. Like the NexGen Tour games, the All-Star Tour events have become something of a community gala, bringing together players and fans from all age groups. The All-Star Tour has streamed games, uploaded highlights to YouTube, and even produced a full-length documentary on the project in 2016 entitled *All-Star Ultimate Tour: The Documentary*, produced by Qxhna Titcomb and directed by Alex Axworthy.[47]

Film has not just been used as a medium for storytelling in Seattle—it's also used as an education platform for the sport. In 2013, Ben Wiggins sent an email to a handful of movers and shakers in the Seattle area, describing an idea he had for a new Ultimate business. Wiggins revealed his plan to create a video series that communicated Ultimate strategy and knowledge. Andy Lovseth, Mario O'Brien, and I heeded the call and initiated the creation of RISE UP Ultimate—Ultimate's first instructional video series. Our first concept video shoot took place at the University of Washington shortly after that initial email conversation. That concept was presented to the Ultimate community in a crowdfunding video that raised nearly $18,000 of seed funding. The production of several seasons followed, and RISE UP quickly made its mark as a critical platform for educating players around the world about the finer mechanics and strategies of playing the sport.[48]

A year after *Skyd* had partnered with a tournament in Amsterdam called Windmill, Mario and I developed a critical partnership with the organizers to run clinics and produce an additional season on the grounds of the 2014 event. Many of the same Sockeye coaches who had traveled to Russia, Germany, and Colombia joined to coach, and the clinics were an exhausting but resounding success. Windmill helped shape O'Brien's vision for RISE UP as it moved to run more clinics around the world in Korea, the Philippines, Mexico, Colombia, and beyond. O'Brien's team programming has since provided the standard for many of the sport's world governing bodies.

Sewell once stated something that has guided me for many years and has, in large part, validated my Ultimate filmmaking endeavors. In Seattle, he insists, one can devote oneself to the sport of Ultimate and not seem . . .

well . . . misguided. For players in Seattle, Ultimate is a way of life and I, too, have been inspired by those who have let this truth become reality. After many years of watching Sockeye and Riot players travel the world to coach and play Ultimate, I got my first taste of it in 2012, traveling to cover the world championships in Sakai, Japan, thanks to a Five Ultimate sponsorship. I created a series of short documentaries on the US men's and women's team, which were some of the first narrative video storytelling the sport had seen. After connecting with the RISE UP crew at Windmill in Amsterdam in 2013, I joined a fellow *Skyd* founder, Liam Rosen, on a trip to Queretaro to play with Malaki, a team he had met previously while on vacation in Mexico[49]

Malaki was training to compete at their national championship that November, and inspired by my recent Ultimate experiences overseas, I asked if I could join him. On a whim, I decided to secure a sponsorship to produce a thirty-minute documentary on the team and my experience with them as they tried to overthrow the reigning champions, Fenix. This piece and my time with Malaki only strengthened my resolve to not only tell the stories I had been sharing on *Skyd* in a video format but also to experience those stories firsthand and share in the culture of these places and teams.

My original plan for *Ultimate Globe Trotter* was ambitious. There were about fifteen or twenty countries on my list spanning from India to Australia. My plan was to join the best teams in the world and compete with them at the world's greatest tournaments while telling their stories and the stories of their countries. So, on the recommendation of Ben Wiggins, I traveled to Boracay Island in the Philippines and met the Boracay Dragons. This initial two-month journey took me to Auckland and Melbourne as well, followed a year later by trips to Copenhagen and Italy (piggybacking on *Skyd's* video production of the world championships there). To date, I have produced seven well-regarded episodes of *Ultimate Globe Trotter (UGT)*, featuring teams from all over the globe, including Vancouver's Furious George. Though *Skyd* may have made the biggest impact in Ultimate, *UGT* remains one of my proudest projects.[50]

Seattle Ultimate's Future

With a robust and developing youth scene, Seattle seems primed to continue to be considered the mecca for Ultimate. Though as Seattle continues to change, establishing itself as one of the United States' fastest growing cities, perhaps the sport will continue to transform as well. In some ways, Ultimate's culture has already started to change in the city. For instance, Mary Lowry mentions that she hears about kids turning away from Ultimate because it has become too competitive and mainstream in the city. As Seattle and Ultimate grow, both may shed their alternative roots in favor of more mainstream principles.

In 2013, MLU established itself in Seattle with the Seattle Rainmakers. MLU is a semiprofessional men's league that does not rely on self-officiating: Games are refereed and played as single-game stadium matchups as opposed to the established weekend-long tournaments typical in Club Ultimate. I was excited to be selected to the Rainmakers in their first season in Seattle. The thrill of playing in a stadium packed with fans, being paid a small stipend (with expenses like travel, practice fields, and uniforms covered), and signing autographs after games is a special feeling. But the pro leagues have been criticized by members of the Ultimate community around the world for their single-gender and officiated focus. Indeed, many vocal opponents have been from Seattle, which has been represented by many organizations focusing on the tenet of SOTG and gender inclusivity.[51] More recently, a number of players have boycotted pro Ultimate, citing a failure to provide gender-equitable opportunities.[52]

Founded in 2012, the American Ultimate Disc League (AUDL) established its roots in Seattle with a team called the Raptors in 2014. This made Seattle one of a handful of cities featuring two professional men's teams. In 2015, Five Ultimate's Titcomb siblings took over the Raptors, renaming them the Cascades. The newly formed team made an effort to promote female athletes by featuring banners of Seattle Riot players and the All-Star Tour at their events. While initially the top talent in the city and across the nation were represented by their MLU team, the AUDL poached the best players to its ranks. After MLU suspended operations at the end of 2016, the AUDL became Ultimate's sole pro league.[53]

While the professional leagues have not quite succeeded in reaching major attendance levels at games, some matches have seen over 2,000 fans in the seats, often lined with young players who are coached by the athletes on the field. "The explosion of youth in the last decade has built a whole new community of motivated, and often powerful, parents in the city and they are seeing the value of Ultimate for their kids," argued Chase Sparling-Beckley.[54]

He sees the signs of Seattle's continued position as a keystone for Ultimate

Ultimate   Credit: Wiki Commons

all over the city. "I think a great example of this is the number of city fields that are starting to be marked with Ultimate lines," says Sparling-Beckley, pointing out Magnuson Park's permanently lined turf fields—a result of lobbying by DiscNW and community members. "Amazing non-profits are getting involved and are forwarding both playing and funding opportunities in parts of Seattle that historically do not have as large of a political voice or economic base," Sparling-Beckley notes.[55]

Ultimate may always be considered alternative by the mainstream sports world, but for the Seattle community, it is something more. It is an outlet to achieve social change and inspire young athletes, an opportunity to give back and showcase one's talents, a chance to follow your dreams and travel the world. The obsession that the Seattle Ultimate community shares has inspired the world, and it will continue to do so for many years to come.

CHAPTER EIGHT

Helene Madison,
Aquatics Queen

Seattle's First Sport Hero

MAUREEN M. SMITH

In 1932, Seattle swimmer Helene Madison won three gold medals at the
Summer Olympic Games in Los Angeles. Madison's achievement made
her only the second American woman to win three medals at one Olympic
Games, repeating swimmer Ethelda Bleibtrey's unprecedented 1920 feat (an
accomplishment that would not be matched again until 1960 when track
athlete Wilma Rudolph and swimmer Chris von Saltza both won three
gold medals in Rome). This chapter examines Madison's aquatics career
as a young swimmer from Seattle, which culminated in her 1932 Olympic
performances. Madison's aquatic successes and the city's embrace of her
throughout her swimming career highlight the unique relationship between
the city and its citizen and reveal Seattle in the late 1920s and early 1930s to
be a city engaged in the promotion of a female athlete as a sporting hero.

Even before the turn of the twentieth century, swimming was considered an appropriate activity for girls and women. Though they had limited
opportunities for sports participation, swimming offered them a sporting activity deemed feminine and suitable for their gender. With the sport
offered to women in the Olympic Games in 1912, American girls and women
soon began to populate swim clubs across the United States. The Amateur
Athletic Union (AAU) offered championship swim meets for both female
and male swimmers. Louis deBreda Handley, a 1904 Olympian in water polo
and swimming, coached the New York Women's Swimming Association
(NYWSA), home of the sport's greatest performers by the 1920 Olympic

Games. Considered the father of women's swimming in the United States, deBreda Handley was the head coach of the women's swimming team at the 1924 Olympic Games. He also authored several books about swimming, which contributed to the growth and popularity of the sport. The success of American female swimmers like Ethelda Bleibtry, Gertude Ederle, Martha Norelius, and Aileen Riggin also contributed to the sport's increasing visibility with Ederle's swim across the English Channel in 1926 resulting in national coverage.[1]

Meanwhile, Seattle was the first major American city to elect a woman to serve as mayor when Bertha Knight Landes won the mayoral race against the incumbent candidate in 1926. Initially elected to the previously all-male city government in 1922, she was voted to lead the city council as its president two years later. As a woman in politics during this time period, Landes "navigated popular beliefs about the corruption of politics and purity of women by campaigning on a platform of municipal housekeeping. Early female candidates maintained that women's entrance into elected office would purify politics and rid it of corruption," according to scholar Tiffany Lewis.[2] Landes's two-year stint as mayor from 1926 to 1928 has been characterized as "two turbulent years of 'petticoat rule.'"[3] Landes's mayoral stint was challenging for many Seattle residents and Americans as they grappled with the roles of women in politics and the public sphere. Lewis writes:

> The polluted nature of politics countered the beliefs about the very nature of women, making it difficult for women to enter public office. In the mythically masculine West, women faced even more barriers to entering office.... Thus, Western women had to compete with the mythic constructions about their role in the West to portray themselves as independent political actors.[4]

Seattle in the 1920s was considered part of the American West, though in stark contrast to the cultured metropolis of Los Angeles. Some have argued that Landes's loss to Frank Edwards in 1928 was a result of her reform efforts and pressure on police to conduct liquor raids; others have argued it was "sex prejudice."[5] In the decade preceding Madison's entrance into competitive swimming, Seattle residents most certainly experienced some shift in how they perceived the role of women in public space, whether politics or sports.

It is within this context of the 1920s that Helene Madison, the only child of Charles and Cecelia Madison, began swimming in Seattle's Green Lake. Swimmers would dive off a floating platform into the lake to start each race. Early stories of Madison reveal that she was afraid to dive into the lake and instead would jump in and then swim furiously to make up the distance lost by her unconventional entry. Eventually, a coach helped her to dive into the lake and her performances improved. Details of these early races before Madison was in her teens were not reported in the newspaper, though they later became part of her legend.[6]

Madison began swimming with coach Ray Daughters at the Crystal Swimming Club in August 1928. Daughters started coaching in 1915, served in World War I, and was named the head coach at the Crystal Swimming Club in 1924. He was reported to have seen Madison swim in Green Lake and encouraged her to train with him at the Crystal Pool. The duo found early success with Madison setting a state record in the women's 100-yard freestyle within eight months.[7] Her achievement led the local *Seattle Times* to speculate that swim records would be challenged whenever Madison was in the pool. By the summer of 1929, Madison's reputation was that of a "swimming ace," and Seattle was already basking in their "local girl" and her early successes.[8] In a July 1929 dual meet against Portland's Multnomah Athletic Club, Madison broke the Pacific Coast record in the 100-yard freestyle.[9] A few weeks later, the Crystal Swimming Club hosted an exhibition with Madison attempting to break her own record in the 100-yard freestyle and the Pacific Coast record in the 100-meter freestyle. Monies earned at the exhibition were used to help fund Madison's travel to the Women's National Junior Tournament in Detroit, Michigan.[10]

The city had high hopes for Madison's first national outing but also conceded that her youth could stand in the way. Believing she was capable of winning the title in her specialty, the 100-yard freestyle, the *Seattle Times* confessed, "Helene is just a youngster. So far from home and lacking in experience that would carry her through, she may get 'buck fever' and fail to do her best."[11] Madison became the national junior champion in the 100-yard freestyle in her first national indoor championship meet. Upon her return to Seattle, the sixteen-year-old Madison, the new junior champion, was considered the city's "greatest swimmer," according to a local journalist who offered no comment in regard to her gender expect for noting her "unpretentious bathing suit of faded pink." In an exhibition where she swam in front of the "largest swimming audience ever gathered in Seattle," she just barely beat the country's senior champion in the 100-yard freestyle. One reporter suggested Madison was "close to national and world-wide recognition."[12] In her first full year of competition, Madison emerged in the pages of the *Seattle Times* as the city's aquatic star with even greater expectations for the year ahead.

1930: Madison Emerges on the National Stage

Several themes materialized in 1930 that would be consistent through Madison's swimming career, most notably amateurism, youth, and the support of Madison by her hometown. Seattle journalists frequently wrote about Madison in their sports pages in ways that lauded her successes. At the start of 1930, Alex Shults, writing about Madison's upcoming competition at the Pacific Coast Indoor Swimming Championships in the *Seattle Times*, proclaimed to his readers, "More worlds to conquer loom ahead for Helene Madison, the young Seattle natator who last summer climaxed a brilliant first year in competition by capturing the national junior 100-yard free style swim."[13] Moreover, organizers fostered rivalries between Madison and her opponents by setting up exhibition races, in this case, against world record holder Josephine McKim of the Los Angeles Athletic Club (LAAC). This rivalry with McKim cast the two swimmers as "a clash of the tropics against the breath of the North, of youth against budding womanhood, of silky smoothness against rippling power," Shults vividly noted. McKim, the proclaimed "queen of the swimming world," was facing "a young pretender from the Northwest," he continued.[14] Madison soundly defeated McKim, setting a new world record in the 220-yard swim.[15]

Leading up to the national indoor championship meet in Miami, amateurism was a topic of frequent discussion largely as a result of the costs of travel to the national meet. Madison could not pay for her travel, the travel of her mother as her chaperone, and the cost of her coach's travel—nor could the Crystal Swimming Club. Ideas to fundraise on her behalf were determined to violate amateur standards, and as a result, Madison swam unattached, so she could accept travel support from the WAC and the Seattle Chamber of Commerce, leading to her split from the Crystal Pool.

Madison became a national name in swimming at the championships in Miami in March 1930. On her way to Miami, she stopped in New Orleans for an exhibition meet, which one newspaper suggested was her "first real taste of big time swimming."[16] If New Orleans offered her first real taste, Miami was a banquet. Winning three national titles, Madison dismantled records almost every time she entered the pool. Winning the 100-yard freestyle for her first title, she also set a new world record in the 100-meter freestyle.[17] The next day, Madison shattered the 220-yard freestyle record.[18] In her final event of the championship meet, she handily won the 500-yard freestyle and in the process established new records at the 200 yard, 220 yard, 300 yard, 400 yard, 440 yard, and the 500-yard marks.[19] Madison, McKim, and Eleanor Holm of New York collectively combined to establish ten new world records at the Miami championships, four of which Madison set. Additionally, she set six American records.[20] Reflecting upon Madison's performance, Shults, writing for the *Seattle Times*, suggested that "a new pedestal" stood in Seattle's "imaginary hall of fame" for its local sporting heroes.[21]

Madison's Seattle roots set her apart from the other top swimmers who hailed from large cities with storied swim clubs, such as the LAAC and the NYWSA. Peter Salvus, in observing her outsider status, celebrated Madison and her Pacific Northwest origins at the championships in Miami. He wrote:

> The New York quartet, in the most up-to-date of swimming paraphernalia, including gaudy beach robes and shows to match, were introduced to the assemblage and took their bow in a coolly receptive manner which champions can attain. The last to be introduced was a tall, thin girl, who didn't possess the flowing beach robes nor the brilliant sandals of the New Yorkers. She strode rather awkwardly to the platform and looked quite out of place with the faded green wool bathing suit that covered her racing suit. She was Helene Madison and the thunderous applause that greeted the then unknown Seattle swimmer caused her no little embarrassment.[22]

Salvus heralded Madison and saw her swimming successes as a symbol of Seattle and the city's recognition among the country's bigger and more well-known cities.

Madison's hometown saw her victories as an opportunity to celebrate their citizen and immediately began making plans to welcome the "swimming marvel" back to the Pacific Northwest. Within days, the Seattle Chamber of Commerce and the WAC engaged in discussions related to how to honor the new champion. Hailed as a "civic asset," Madison's victories provided a new opportunity for the city to, as one reporter claimed, express "their vast pride in her brilliant achievements."[23] Reminding readers that previous American swimming champions such as Albina Osipowich and Gertrude Ederle were celebrated with hometown tributes and celebrations, the reporter added, "Seattle should do no less for Helene Madison."[24] In fact, the young swimmer was "oblivious of the furor she has created in Seattle where her achievements have won the hearts of every sports follower," the reporter continued. She was "on her way home to the greatest fete ever accorded a 16-year-old athlete."[25]

Seattle Times writer George Varnell lamented, "Seattle will not be allowed to show its appreciation for Helene Madison for her marvelous swimming in a material way. Helene will be welcomed back to Seattle with her package of world's championships and records under her arm, but acclaim and applause will be the only way this city will be able to show the great young girl swimmer its appreciation."[26] Within a week of her victories, a letter was issued by T. Morris Dunne, secretary-treasurer of the Pacific Northwest Association of the AAU., stating that the city could, in fact, bestow Madison with a watch as a gift for her accomplishments. A trust fund to help support her future travel would be allowable, according to the letter, but a scholarship for future studies at the University of Washington was impermissible.[27] Dunne's ruling was cause of celebration for the people of Seattle who wanted to celebrate their young champion in tangible ways. Madison, celebrated as a world champion swimmer, was to be welcomed home with "as triumphant an athletic tour as any representative of this city ever staged," and was set to be "the recipient of a gift from her admiring townspeople," noted a local reporter.[28]

Part of the post-championship festivities included a swimming exhibition on April 4. Sponsored by the Crystal Swimming Club and the *Seattle Times*, Madison was scheduled to swim in three races, including "against an outstanding male swimmer to show her prowess," argued a reporter for the *Seattle Times*. The AAU-sanctioned event would allow 12,000 Seattle citizens to see Madison swim, the "most outstanding event ever presented to swimming fans," the reporter added.[29] Her first appearance in Seattle no longer representing the Crystal Swimming Club, Madison's unattached status (but link to the WAC) raised many questions and the AAU was at the center. The Crystal Swimming Club was considered "poor as the proverbial church mouse," and when Madison traveled to Miami, the swim club could not afford to support her travel, Shults commented. He continued: "Everyone knows that swimming isn't a game that offers much financial returns to backers."[30] The Crystal Swimming Club's inability to support Madison financially led to an arrangement between the WAC and the Seattle Chamber of Commerce and resulted in Madison leaving the Crystal Swimming Club for WAC, though she would need to swim unattached for one year due to AAU rules. By moving to the WAC, Madison would be able to train year-round (the Crystal Pool closed every winter).[31] The move to WAC was also hoped to preempt any advances from other cities' swim clubs toward Madison. Varnell, in his defense of Seattle and Madison's residency in the city, claimed, "All things being equal, Helene Madison, a Seattle girl, would rather compete under the colors of the Washington A.C. of this city than any other organization in the country. The business of the Washington Athletic Club (WAC) and of Seattle is to see that all things are made equal for the young champion."[32]

Varnell again lamented Seattle's inability to celebrate the teenage Madison with appropriate gifts but acknowledged that her amateur status was worth saving. He explained:

> An automobile, a diamond ring, a scholarship! None of these things would be worth to this wonderful girl swimmer what her amateur status will mean to her in 1932 when she has the opportunity to be the leading United States entry in the swimming events. Miss Madison should have a long and merito-rious career ahead of her as a swimming champion. What a disaster it would have been to have killed this career, almost in its inception, by kindness! Especially kindness from her own people and friends.[33]

In any case, Madison was being celebrated as the "greatest woman swimmer in the world today despite the fact that she is still in her teens." The *Seattle Times* said the "young Lincoln High School miss whose swimming accom-plishments created a sensation all over the country" merited a homecoming worthy of her accomplishments.[34] Madison's location in Seattle was central to the city's celebration of her victories. Her national titles represented their emergence on the national stage in her sport but also more broadly brought recognition to the city. Described as "a woman and a national champion whose name has fired the swimming circles of the world; whose feats have shattered national and world's records, and whose performances have placed her on a pedestal of achievement never equaled in the history of Seattle sportdom," Madison, at sixteen years old, was bringing national attention to her hometown in ways no other athlete had done before. [35] Daughters claimed, "Northwest swimmers, given the opportunity for competition, rate with the best of the world."[36] Madison had put the city on the map—and the city was intent on thanking Madison.

In an interview with Madison's mother, printed the day before the home-coming parade on the front page of the *Seattle Times*, Mrs. Madison said of her daughter's talent, "it did not come all at once. She has been working for this for a long time and winning her honors one by one. This is a logical development. It shows what youth can do." Explaining that both she and her husband had swam as children, she told readers that she let Helene "do the things she wanted to do, and she has turned naturally to athletics."[37] Madison's mother, in thinking about how she would support her daughter's swimming, said she would "fit in her plans now" and "not interfere with her diet nor her play."[38] Acknowledging her daughter's interest in art, Mrs. Madison also explained, "If motion picture offers are made her, she will consider only those which do not interfere with her amateur standing." Mrs. Madison was also cautious about anything that might hinder her daughter's plans in swimming, such as romance, commenting, "She is too young and she has serious work ahead. She has boy friends [sic], of course, and older admirers, and she's not entirely indifferent herself, but I think her swimming and her art will keep her busy. And the Olympic games are ahead."[39]

The welcome home festivities were slated to begin on Friday, March 26, with a parade and community banquet at the Civic Auditorium and culminated with the swimming exhibition on April 4. Madison's plane from Portland arrived in the middle of Friday afternoon, and her parade commenced from the airfields continuing through the downtown district. The swimmer was met at Boeing Airfield by the city's mayor, Frank Edwards, other local politicians, and over 5,000 locals, a number that would quadruple along the parade route and in the downtown district. Along the parade route, the fans "cheered and clamored" for Madison, who waved in response to those who celebrated "fair play and keen sport and the gameness and skill of youth."[40] The next morning's newspaper tried to quell some of the celebration on the front page, stating "Helene Madison is deserving of all praise. Hers was a most notable achievement in the world of sport, and Seattle is justified in doing her unstinted honor. Just the same," the newspaper continued, "exaggeration during moments of enthusiasm can be pushed too far." The daily continued in response to one of the previous day's speaker's claim that Madison had "brought more renown to Seattle than any other individual" that such a statement "seems to be stretching it just a tiny bit."[41]

Coverage of the April 4 splash party and exhibition at the Crystal Swimming Club received considerable press attention. In the days prior, the Seattle Times reported that 1,000 tickets had already been sold.[42] Fans were excited to see her attempt to break Josephine McKim's record in the 300-yard freestyle, and the meet was being sanctioned by the AAU, meaning any record established would count in the eyes of the AAU.[43] The day before the event, the Seattle Times made clear the connection between Madison and her hometown, suggesting "Seattle has drifted along half-heartedly in supporting water events for the past fifteen years. Now Helene has awakened the city aquatically."[44] Daughters believed Madison could break the record, 300-yards, nine lengths of the pool, as did the newly crowned national champion, who it was suggested had not allowed fame to spoil her.[45] On the night of April 4, 1,350 fans packed the Crystal Pool to witness Madison's new world record in the 300-yard freestyle, with a time of 3 minutes, 41.6 seconds. With Madison's record-breaking performance, Salvus paired the city and its swimmer, proclaiming to his readers, "Seattle had proved beyond a doubt to her home folks that she is a true champion. She proved it conclusively to Eastern skeptics. She was faithful to the loyal fans at home."[46]

In the summer of 1930, the national outdoor championships were held in Long Beach, California. It was the greatest stage since Madison's coming-out at the indoor championships, and she was slated to swim in four events: the 100-yard freestyle, the 440-yard freestyle, the 880-yard freestyle, and the mile swim. According to Daughters, heading into the competition, he didn't think Madison had a favorite event. He opined, "The race she is going into is the race at which she is best, and I feel that she can make as great a showing at one distance as another. Personally, I am not claiming championships for this young miss, but I will predict that she will be at her best in ability and condition, and if she is beaten at any of her distances it will be because some girl is just a naturally faster swimmer than Helene."[47] Daughters, as a result of Madison's move to the WAC, resigned from his position at the Crystal Pool and was hired by the WAC, bringing Madison and two other swimmers, Dawn "Babe" Gilson and Sven Anderson.[48]

Madison headed to Long Beach, California, with her mother and coach Ray Daughters to compete in the outdoor championships.[49] McKim was seen as her greatest challenge, and it was unclear how she would fare against her rival.[50] In the first rounds of both the 100-yard freestyle and the mile, Madison set two world records, earning her spots in both finals.[51] Over the course of the championships, Madison won four titles in the four events she entered.[52]

After her performances in Long Beach, a repeat of her multiple victories at the indoor championship in March, the celebration of Madison was in contrast to the parade and week-long festivities upon her return from Miami. Instead, the city paid close attention to the advances made by other swim clubs, most notably Los Angeles, that attempted to woo Madison to their warmer climes. Varnell, anxious about rumors that Madison's mother preferred the warmth of Los Angeles, told his readers, "Down Los Angeles way they persist in trying to take Helene Madison away from Seattle. And if the power of suggestion is worth a lick, they are giving it all the rope it will take, for almost every day for a week some kind of suggestion or offer has come out of Los Angeles relative to Helene wearing the colors of the southern city or one of its athletic institutions."[53] Varnell had a tone of relief when he concluded, "No immediate change is contemplated by the Madisons that will cause a change of affiliations from Seattle to Los Angeles. For which, of course, we are all grateful."[54] Additional offers came that put Madison in the unenviable position of turning down a $10,000 offer to swim professionally.[55] An offer of such a large amount of money was cause for concern as $10,000 was, contended Shults, "more money than the average girl can earn in years and years of hard work, and then oblivion, for professional swimmers do not long hold the spotlight."[56]

In the days that followed the championships in Long Beach, Seattle played host to a swimming exhibition that included top swimmers from the prestigious NYWSA, home club of Eleanor Holm and formerly Gertrude Ederle.[57] The exhibition marked Madison's last swimming appearance in Seattle for the year. Madison was recognized as the world record holder in the following distances in freestyle: 100 yards, 200 yards, 200 meters, 300 yards, 300 meters, 440 yards, 500 yards, 880 yards, and one mile. She held ten of sixteen recognized world records.[58] She set two new world records at the Far Western Swimming Championships hosted by San Francisco's Fleishhacker Pool in September.[59]

To close out her banner year, Madison finished in fourth place in the voting for the 1930 Sullivan Award, an award for the nation's top amateur athlete who "by his performances and his example and influence as an amateur and a man, has done most during the year to advance the cause of sportsmanship."[60] The award, in its inaugural year, went to golfer Bobby Jones, who had won all four major golf championships in 1930, tallying 1,625 total votes. Receiving 375 votes, Madison finished behind tennis star Helen Wills Moody, who garnered 666 votes.[61]

1931: Preparing for the Olympic Games

The start of the indoor swim season saw Madison breaking yet another record, this time the world records in the 440-yard freestyle and the 400-

meter freestyle.[62] Within the week, it was reported that Madison had turned down another lucrative offer to swim in exhibitions and become a professional. The tandem offers of $10,000 from Bert Mezins of New York and $7,500 from an Australian group were not enough to entice Madison to rescind her amateur status. Her father said she was not ready, adding "when Helene enters the Olympic Games, and if she is successful there will be plenty of time then to think of any offers to swim for money." He later added, "She doesn't want to do it now. The Amateur Athletic Union has been wonderful to her. We all realize—Mrs. Madison, Helene and myself—that a career of professional swimming would be short-lived. For the money and after the fine treatment from the AAU, amateur sport followers and the host of friends and acquaintances Helene has made, it is not worth it."[63]

Madison's spring schedule was hindered in part due to illness, but in April, Madison and her WAC teammates departed for New York and the indoor championships, where she hoped to defend her titles.[64] The four-swimmer delegation, their largest ever, planned to take the train to New York, swimming at exhibitions along the way, and on their return trip would participate in swim exhibitions throughout Canada.[65] In a Minneapolis exhibition, Madison bettered her mark in the 50-yard freestyle. The team then headed to Chicago, where she broke Gertrude Ederle's record in the 220-yard freestyle. At their last exhibition in Buffalo, Madison set a new mark in the 100-meters, though the record was not recognized because it was set in a non-regulation length pool.[66] At the championships, Madison defended her titles from the previous year in the 100-yard, 220-yard, and 500-yard freestyle, along with the 400-yard relay, accounting for 18 individual points in the meet.[67] Salvus told his *Seattle Times* readers, "Four national titles! Enough of their accomplishments, which have blazoned their names across the newspaper pages of the world. Seattle's homage is due them. The WAC will receive them. Old folk, young folk, real Seattle folk should turn out to welcome them. . . . Let Seattle welcome them as the champions they are."[68] Martha Norelius, Olympic gold medalist at the 1924 and 1928 Olympic Games, offered her assessments of Madison, saying, "One thing is certain, and that is that sensational 17-year-old Seattle girl, Helene Madison, who has broken about every amateur record I ever made, will be called upon to carry the bulk of the United States' labors in the Olympics."[69] In Norelius's opinion, Madison, the "Pacific Coast mermaid marvel," was "not just a shooting star," had rather "established herself as supreme conqueror of all other free-style amateur swimmers," and would "remain peerless for some time to come."[70] The month of May was a celebration of Madison and her teammates with Madison's record-breaking streak showing no sign of decline. At the Pacific Northwest Tournament, Madison, on her seventh attempt, finally lowered her own world record in the 220-yard freestyle. Salvus proclaimed, "This business of breaking world swimming records—especially when a person has clipped and shattered them beyond human effort—gets to be quite a job." At this point, the young swimmer was the world record holder in thirteen world records (out of sixteen).[71]

Madison's summer schedule included the national outdoor championships in New York in July to be followed by a trip to Paris the next month. Plans for the championships took an unexpected twist when the AAU failed to fund Madison's travel party. The *Seattle Times* reported, "The greatest woman swimmer of all time, who has made dollar after dollar for the Amateur Athletic Union, may not defend her national outdoor swimming titles won at Long Beach, Cal., last year because that same A.A.U. trimmed by more than half expense money allowed the mermaid."[72] The previous summer, the AAU had provided Madison with $700 in travel funds, but those funds were cut to $300 in 1931 for the trip to New York. It was reported that Madison's father would not let her travel without being accompanied by her mother.[73] Madison left for New York with her mother and Coach Daughters in tow, paying for her chaperones and hoping to offset the costs with exhibition swims in New York. Within days, the AAU reimbursed Madison an additional $300 that had been set aside for a chaperone from LAAC who ended up not travelling.[74] Madison defended her titles in the 100-meter, 440-yard, and mile freestyle races, setting world records, and even swimming exhibitions during the championships just to break additional records.[75] As an individual swimmer, Madison scored 20 points, enough for third place in the meet, behind the LAAC and NYWSA.[76]

After the championships in July, Madison stayed busy swimming in exhibitions and continuing to break world records. After an exhibition swim in a fifty-yard pool in Spokane, Madison came home to Seattle to celebrate what Varnell termed "her exceptional feats" in New York.[77] Late in August, Madison swam in an exhibition at Lake Washington in Seattle in support of Laundry Workers' Local 24 with the proceeds going to the "union's relief fund for sick and unemployed members," noted one reporter.[78] At the Far Western Swimming Championships in San Francisco, Madison took four minutes off the 1500-meter freestyle record, as well as lowering the record in the 700-yard swim.[79]

As the year closed out, Seattle and Madison looked ahead to 1932 and the Olympic Games, presumably her last hurrah. Salvus predicted:

> Helene, next spring, will start her final season as an amateur and turn pro. That is not definite, as far as any announcement from herself, her family or her coach are concerned, but 1933 will see a new amateur women's free style champion. The same tinkle of gold and greenbacks that drew Bill Tilden, Bobby Jones, 'Red' Grange and a host of others from the amateur division, will attract Helene. She will compete for the United States in the Olympic Games, carrying the colors against the best of the world's natators. She then will retire as an amateur, capitalizing on the fame she has compiled three years of competition. She will be approaching 21 years of age, reaching the pinnacle of her swimming prowess.[80]

By the year's end, she had fifty-one of sixty-two recognized American records. She held every freestyle record in the world.[81] There was talk of her winning the prestigious Sullivan Award for what one reporter described as her "unprecedented performance as a swimmer."[82] Salvus saved his greatest compliments for Madison, telling his readers, "Were Helene a prize fighter or football player—how we do talk!—she would be characterized as the 'killer' type. Relentlessly she mows down opposition. Hers is not the nature to ease off and let someone else gain an advantage."[83] Varnell, Salvus's colleague at the *Seattle Times*, also predicted Madison's success for the upcoming year, stating, "Certainly Helene has established herself head and shoulders above any American girl swimmer at every distance from 100 yards to the mile. The Seattle miss who holds all but one of the official world's records, does not appear to be in any danger of having her reign terminated by an American during the coming Olympiad."[84] Seattle was disappointed when Barney Berlinger won the award for the year's top amateur athlete, expressing disbelief and dissecting the voting process as well as comparing Berlinger's performances to Madison's victories. Varnell asked, "Just what did Berlinger do during the 1931 season to be acclaimed the outstanding athlete of the year? Answer—nothing." Noting that Berlinger had beaten Madison in the voting, 424 to 422, he then recognized Berlinger as being a "credit to sports. He is a fine, upstanding sportsman." However, Varnell noted, the award is not only for just good sportsmanship but also performance and sportsmanship. The reporter felt the results were "just another Amateur Athletic Union joke." He explained, "politics would probably be the better word," noting that East Coast voters did not vote for Madison because of their regional bias. He went on to further explain Madison's merits, stating unequivocally:

> During the year of 1931 Helene Madison wrote swimming history. She added record after record to her list until she held virtually every United States mark from the sprint to the mile. She annexed world's marks. She did more than any woman swimmer ever did in competition. Would that not ordinarily have been ranked as an outstanding athletic performance? Fifty-five Amateur Athletic Union marks are Helene's and 16 world's records find the name of the Seattle mermaid written behind them. Can anyone conversant with the amateur athletic situations; anyone knowing what it means for one young girl to turn in as many wonderful performances as that, miss fire on who ranks with Helen Wills Moody as America's greatest woman athlete?

Varnell added that Berlinger had failed to win even one event at the IC4A Track and Field Meet or the National AAU Track and Field Championships. Berlinger's failure in comparison to Madison's record-breaking year, in Varnell's defense of his hometown swimmer, "only adds strength to the statement that the James E. Sullivan medal award is a great big joke. It means nothing unless the politics which without question have to do with the naming of its holder, are eliminated."[85]

Madison and the 1932 Olympic Games

At the opening the Crystal Pool in March, the crowd chanted "One tonight and nine to go," apparently referencing the number of times the local swimmer had left to swim in Seattle before the Olympic Games. "Seattle's most famous athlete" was continuing to break records almost every time she competed, and the spring season was viewed as critical to her Olympic success.[86] In examining Madison's record-breaking performances, Varnell tallied that in less than three years of competition, the swimmer had cut 899 seconds off 56 national records and 272 seconds off 16 world records. He crowed, in celebrating the accomplishments of one of his most favorite subjects, "without any question, the most terrific beating that has ever been given in athletic history to old Daddy Time by a single individual has been meted out by Helene Madison, the Seattle miss who holds swimming records innumerable and who wears the colors of the Washington Athletic Club." Varnell concluded, "American records are one thing. World's records are another. There are none faster, yet Helene Madison, the Seattle and WAC mermaid, holds all the recognized free-style world's marks in existence. Think of that and marvel."[87] At the same time, Madison's fame and success brought attention to her WAC teammates and Coach Daughters, who often tried to argue that his team was more than just one swimmer. But Shults, of the *Seattle Times*, wasn't having it. He responded to Daughters's claim with the retort, "as long as Helene Madison smashes world's records with such reckless abandon, how can you get excited over just ordinary stars? She's simply turned the swimming world topsy-turvy."[88]

The national indoor championships were hosted by the LAAC in April. On the way to Los Angeles, the five member WAC team swam at the Pacific Coast Championships in San Francisco. There was some speculation that the WAC team might be able to win the women's title, led by Madison in the 100-yard freestyle, 220-yard freestyle, and 300-yard freestyle, along with anchoring the relay.[89] While Madison held up her end of the bargain, the team fell short, finishing tied for second place with New York, with both teams losing to the host LAAC team. Madison, in defending her titles, was lauded by Zimmerman as "this daughter of the Northwest," and the second-place finish was reason to celebrate.[90] The next big meet was the Northwest Olympic Trials hosted in Portland, Oregon, in June and then the Olympic Trials in Jones Beach, New York, in July.[91] "Peerless Helene," as one observer described her, was ready for the trials.[92]

The *Seattle Times* claimed that Madison "toyed with her field" in winning the 400-meter semifinal and later the final, suggesting her "supremacy was never threatened."[93] With over 35,000 spectators at the Olympic Trials, Madison ably swam to earn a spot on the Olympic team in three events (the maximum number of events for female swimmers): the 100-meter freestyle, 400-meter freestyle, and the 400-meter relay.[94]

In the weeks leading up to the Olympic Games, it was predicted that Madison would win the Olympic sprints. There was one small glitch that loomed in the form of jealous Olympic coaches who were preparing another American swimmer to challenge Madison. It was suspected that these coaches were bothered by Daughters's continued training of his WAC swimmer, and as a result, the Olympic coaches put their efforts into San Francisco swimmer Eleanor Seville.[95] Los Angeles provided the backdrop for the Olympic Games, with Hollywood actors and actresses appearing at events and Olympic athletes being photographed with the celebrities.

In the preliminary heats of the 100-meter freestyle, Madison and Seville traded records, with Madison setting one record, only to have Seville, characterized by one journalist as "the swimmer . . . primed to defeat her," break it in the following heat.[96] In the semis, both swimmers qualified for the finals of the 100-meter freestyle while Madison "paddled comfortably" to win her semifinal.[97] Madison won the 100-meter freestyle in an Olympic record, with Holland's Willy Den Ouden finishing second, and Seville ending up in third place. Madison raced to the finish, sprinting at the end to grasp the record and beat the younger Den Ouden.[98] Footage of the 100-meter freestyle finals was shown in American movie houses, including clips of "Helene and her swimming pals in Hollywood. They created a sensation even in Hollywood."[99] With one Olympic medal to her name, Madison's parents admitted that their daughter planned to retire after the Games. Her father told a reporter, "She's fed up herself with all of it. . . . I don't think she has the same zest for racing that she used to have. She's hit her peak. She's won her titles, won all the records practically, and now it's time she did something else. What else? Well, there's time enough for that after the games." He admitted that amateur swimming was "quite a business" and followed that he'd "like to see her get something out of it."[100] Madison did not comment on her plans but did express her gratitude to the city of Seattle, saying:

> Tell the people in Seattle how happy I am. Tell them all how glad I am that I was able to win an Olympic championship for them after they made it possible for me to come to this meet. I feel now that I have in a measure compensated them for their generosity. Gosh, I am tingling all over! I cannot realize that I have won an Olympic championship for Seattle and the Washington Athletic Club.

With two events remaining, Madison continued, "Tell Seattle that I am that happy and that I will do everything I can to repeat in the 400 meters and try to bring back a second championship to the city that made it possible for me to be here."[101] In front of 8,000 spectators, Madison won her initial heat of the 400-meter freestyle, advancing to the semifinals, which she also won, this time in front of 10,000 fans, advancing to the finals. After the semifinals, there was a report that Madison had signed a movie contract effective after the Games, ending her amateur swimming career.[102] Madison won the 400-meter freestyle race, "true to expectations," and was deemed the "outstanding star of all the men and women entered in the swimming competition." Madison was the only "double winner," though she actually won three events, the 100-meter freestyle, the 400-meter freestyle, and the 400-meter relay.[103] Just as in 1931, there were predictions that Madison's performances would perhaps result in her winning the Sullivan Award.[104]

The talk of Madison's retirement continued throughout the Games, with Daughters contributing his thoughts. He assumed she might try a movie career, concluding that the Olympic Games were "the climax" of Madison's swimming career. He even suggested that she would be unable to "again reach the peak" and believed she would face a terrific "let-down" and have a difficult time to "muster the ambition or interest to make any more records." He predicted that eventually another swimmer would come along and break Madison's records, though perhaps that would take some time.[105] Daughters thought that his protégé deserved a vacation for all her hard work and accomplishments, then he concluded, "I suppose she must think of serious things."[106]

Newspapers from across the state of Washington celebrated the Pacific Northwest native, sharing in her victory. The *Aberdeen World* wrote, "She is the only athlete from this state to win and should be acclaimed accordingly."[107] In the *Bremerton News*, "Miss Madison's triumph is all the more pleasing in view of the fact that in victory she is the same modest, unassuming person."[108] The *Enumclaw Herald* offered, "if she retires, the sports world will miss one of its most modest and popular champions."[109] The *Yakima Herald* noted that "for three or four years, Helene has kept her name on the sport page."[110]

As they did in 1930, when Madison first emerged on the national aquatic scene, the city of Seattle planned to celebrate their hometown heroine with welcome home celebrations. An official reception committee was formed, including some of the city's politicians, who hoped to boost their status by being connected to the Olympic champion. Varnell added, "Behind this committee will be thousands of Seattle citizens eager to show the Olympic champion that her swimming accomplishments have been appreciated." Madison would be "accorded a welcome that will equal anything ever given a daughter or son of Seattle."[111] The festivities included a naval escort for a parade route along Second Avenue to Pike to Fifth Avenue and finishing at the Olympic Hotel. Madison was named Fleet Week Queen and was set to preside over the International Ball held in the Civic Auditorium and then make an appearance at a boxing benefit at the city's arena. Three tons of confetti were ordered, and "every available inch of ticker tape in Seattle will be added to this supply to furnish the makings of a first-class storm of paper."[112] Accompanying Madison in addition to the naval escort were Mayor John Dore, her coach Ray Daughters, and the reception committee. The committee was intent on besting the 1930 reception Madison received. Varnell explained:

> That the peerless Helene Madison may be accorded a regal welcome Friday when she returns to Seattle from her triple triumph scored recently in the women's events of the Olympic Games, Seattle reception committee is preparing to outdo the reception that even Lindbergh received here. And when Miss Madison drops from the skies Friday in a plane of the United Airlines at Boeing Field she will literally drop into a coach of royalty in the form of a Buick automobile which will be Seattle's gift of appreciation to the lass who has made athletic history for this city.[113]

Charles Moriarty, chairman of the reception committee, explained, "The committee plans to outdo anything Seattle has ever done previously in the welcoming line. Helene is entitled to our best and our best will excel anything done to date. We want Seattle citizenry to take part in the ceremonies for after all Helene belongs to all of us."[114] John Dore, mayor of Seattle, made a proclamation, encouraging all of Seattle to celebrate their daughter. His proclamation read:

> Seattle on Friday greets a world champion. She has done more to make Seattle favorably known in recent years than any person. We should give her a Seattle welcome and express our appreciation as she returns for a brief stay. Therefore, as mayor of Seattle, I call upon the citizenry to lay aside their duties at 4 p.m. Friday, August 26, to greet Helene Madison. I also respectfully request all those who desire to participate in Seattle's gift to Helene to deposit their contributions at The Seattle Times, The Seattle Star, The Seattle-Post Intelligencer or at the Washington Athletic Club. Let us make it an hour of glory for the Seattle maid who has brought honor to our city.[115]

Dore's support for Madison was noteworthy as it signified the city's celebration of its most famous resident and confirmed their status as a first-class city. The parade, with almost ninety floats, "far exceeded the expectations" of Dore and the organizing committee. One reporter commented, "Helene rules not only as queen of the waves but as queen of pulchritude as well."[116] At the naval ball that evening, Madison, the event's main attraction, was welcomed with cheering from what another reporter described as the swimmer's "townspeople and her country's defenders on the seas."[117] "Dignity, just for the moment, forgotten," the reporter opined.[118]

Finally, after three years and much speculation about her future, Madison swam in an exhibition at Seattle's Playland at Bitter Lake for which she received financial compensation, officially ending her amateur career. The day before the Playland exhibition, Madison explained that she had "entered my last race in amateur competition and will leave the field for good and all." Recognizing that her "ambitions were realized" when she medaled at the Olympic Games, she suggested that she had "nothing else to look forward to." She confessed that the "grind has been a hard one, a tremendous task" and that she was "glad to give it over to other girls." She finished with, "My exact plans I am not at liberty to divulge, but I have given my affairs into the hands of Mr. Kahn and will return to Hollywood in a few days, at which time I will know more about my plans. Yes, it is possible that I will enter the cinema world, but until that is final I can say no more. But it is definite that I am through with swimming as a pastime."[119] At the swimming exhibitions, Dore served as the city's representative in presenting Madison with a Buick paid for by citizens of Seattle.[120] With the bestowing of the automobile on Madison, Dore celebrated the generosity of his city's residents, telling the crowd, "So much has been said about Miss Madison's great achievements, but this is the finest tribute of all. When so many people, in times like these, will dig down and pay for such a fitting gift it is praise indeed."[121]

More accolades poured in from across the state, again making it clear that Madison's sporting accomplishments brought great pride to the Pacific Northwest. The *Aberdeen World* noted that "Helene Madison was the one State of Washington athlete to win greatly."[122] According to the *Bellingham Herald*, "no single star received more public attention than the Pacific Northwest's great swimming champion."[123] After the parade and city celebrations, the *Bremerton News* suggested that "it seems right that this young star should reap some benefit," and the *Shelton Journal* claimed "the state is pleased that one of its girls has bettered the best in all the world."[124] The *Hoquiam Washingtonian* believed that Madison would "seek to capitalize the renown that has come to her," and the *Everett Herald* "comments approvingly on 'woman's place in athletics.'"[125]

Madison signed a contract with Mack Sennett in November 1932 to appear in a two-reel comedy titled *Help! Help! Helene!* Sennett had "developed more screen candidates than anyone in Movieland," exclaimed a local reporter.[126] Her Hollywood career seemed promising with manager Ivan Kahn at the helm. However, it became clear after the release of her film debut that Madison's time in Hollywood would be temporary.[127] While there was some talk of Madison winning the coveted Sullivan Award, instead it was awarded to James Bausch, the gold medalist in the decathlon at the 1932 Olympic Games. Varnell, writing for the *Seattle Times*, had given up all hope of his hometown heroine ever winning the top prize for amateur athletes and still lamented her not winning the year prior.[128]

Madison's foray into the film business did not last long. While she taught some swim lessons in Southern California, an assessment of her screen career was offered as "not so hotsy totsy these days" by one observer. As a result, Madison entered into several swimming exhibitions and races (some against men) in Chicago.[129] It appeared that her parents supported her return to the pool with her mother commenting, "Helene is a swimmer, not a movie actress, and that's where her future lies." [130] Her short-lived movie career, deemed a flop when even movie theaters in Seattle "shunned the pie-slinging effort," allowed for her return to "swimming in earnest."[131]

In September 1935, Madison entered the nursing program at Virginia Mason Hospital.[132] A year later, the US sent a squad of Olympians to Berlin for the 1936 Olympic Games, recalling Madison's stellar performance just four years earlier. The *Seattle Times* reminisced, providing readers with a short synopsis of the swimmer's retirement, sharing:

> Everyone knows the story of the things that happened to Helene Madison after the 1932 Olympic Games—how, only 19 years old and perched on a giddy pedestal of fame, she decided that she might her fortune in motion pictures; how she believed the stories of those who signed her to make a picture, and how her hopes faded. How then she taught swimming on a quick slide into oblivion which so many famous people have known. And how, with the courage and common sense which so few people whose heads have been turned by fame ever recapture, she decided to forget swimming. To earn money she sold hot dogs last summer at the same Seattle beach

where she learned to swim, and then she began her training for nursing at Virginia Mason Hospital.[133]

It later became public knowledge that her hot dog stint came as a result of the Parks and Recreation Department denying her the chance to teach swimming lessons, a job reserved for men. The city that had once celebrated their female swimming heroine was unwilling to extend the courtesy of a teaching position in her sport. Madison also reminisced, telling the newspaper, "I wanted to be with them. I knew I could still swim as fast as ever. I began remembering how it felt to stand in the stadium four years ago and see the flag going up and know that after all my years of working I'd won for the United States. I wanted to be with them." [134] However, she also knew that her new focus was on becoming a nurse and even admitted to hoping to become a doctor one day, concluding "but that's so far in my future that I don't let myself worry about it."[135]

Madison's marriage to Luther C. McIver, a forty-five-year-old power company executive at Puget Sound Power & Light Company, garnered front-page coverage in the *Seattle Times*. McIver had been a patient under Madison's care at Virginia Mason in January 1937, and their marriage only three months later came as a surprise to her parents. It also led to her dismissal from the nursing program at Virginia Mason, consistent with the time period.[136] Throughout the 1940s and 1950s, Madison would routinely appear in the sports pages of the *Seattle Times*, usually as a result of her swim records being broken.[137] Other times it was related to her own daughter, Helene Jr., who was reported to start swimming at age five. It was noted, at that time, that Madison the elder was devoting "her time to her family, her garden and her sketching."[138] Madison began coaching the Helene Madison Swimming Club in 1946 and two years later was hired to coach the Moore Hotel swim team.[139] A decade later, Madison was still coaching at the Moore Pool but also had her own Helene Madison School of Swimming.[140] Coaching allowed Madison to put her swimming acumen to work, and she sometimes spoke of how the sport had evolved since her participation as an athlete. She remembered, almost twenty-five years after her retirement from swimming at age nineteen, "I don't think I had hit my peak when I quit. But that was after the 1932 Olympics, and those were depression days. I had to go to work." It was one of the few times Madison admitted to the need to earn money in her post-swimming career. In discussing the trend of teenage swimmers, Madison offered, "competitive swimming is not a thing you can do in your idle moments. It takes time and a lot of work to keep in condition. It isn't very long before a young girl's thoughts begin to turn to something besides jumping into a tank of water. That's probably why a new crop of youngsters seems to take over each Olympic year."[141]

In December 1968, news of Madison's declining health appeared in the *Seattle Times* with Madison entering Virginia Mason Hospital to have surgery for cancer of the throat.[142] Days later, the WAC decided to name their swimming pool in Madison's honor.[143] When Madison finally succumbed to cancer and diabetes in 1970, she was only fifty-seven years old. Her obituary reminded Seattle citizens of their once-famous daughter, who once held every world record in the freestyle between 100 yards and the mile. She died in relative poverty with her gold medals housed at the WAC.[144] Two years later, Seattle honored Madison when they dedicated a newly constructed swimming pool, at a cost of $660,684, which the mayor viewed as strengthening the city's efforts to be among the most livable cities in the United States. Hans Thompson, director of the city's Parks and Recreation Department, told the crowd, "It is fitting that this pool, representing the epitome of modern construction is named for Helene Madison. The young lady was the epitome of swimming 40 years ago."[145] Her obituary noted her attendance at Lincoln High School, her three Olympic gold medals, and her short-lived movie career along with her recent 1966 induction into the National Swimming Hall of Fame.[146] It did not mention additional honors and accomplishments, such as being named one of the top ten greatest swimmers in the first half of the twentieth century or her induction as one of the first inductees into the State Athletic Hall of Fame in 1960. Nor did it mention her two parades, the first in 1930 and the second after her triple-gold-medal performance at the 1932 Olympic Games.[147]

Helene Madison, once the "female Johnny Weismuller," was Seattle's first sporting hero, winning national Amateur Athletic Union titles, leading to her 1930 welcome home parade. The city bestowed the same celebratory honor for Madison two years later when she returned home with three Olympic gold medals.[148] Madison's victories over swimmers from Los Angeles and New York put Seattle on the nation's sporting map. Despite her successes in the swimming pool and her city's embrace of those successes, her gender still prevented her from landing a position as a swimming instructor with the Parks and Recreation Department, a snub that was only made public years later. Madison feared losing as a swimmer, though she rarely felt the sting of defeat. She once commented, "I had come out of nowhere, from out in the Indian country is what they thought in Los Angeles and New York. And I always felt that someday there would be a little nobody from out of Podunk who would show up in the far lane and beat me. I just knew it."[149] It never happened.

CHAPTER NINE

More Than Just an Athlete

Race, Identity, and the Seattle Seahawks

SHAFINA KHAKI

On November 18, 1990, future National Football League (NFL) Hall of Fame quarterback and Seattle Seahawks player Warren Moon found himself being escorted out of the Cleveland Stadium. Moon was surrounded by security assigned to protect him from one of many death threats he would receive during his football career. It was the former University of Washington (UW) Huskies' thirty-fourth birthday, and on this day, like many, Moon would walk on and off the field as much more than just an athlete. During a home game the following month, his nine-year-old son, Joshua, overheard a man in the stands exclaim about Moon, "I can't believe they gave that nigger $14.3 million." Despite the hateful jeering and death threats from the crowd, Moon did not speak publicly about the incidents at the time. Instead, he chose to persevere on the field, largely because he knew the success of future black quarterbacks hinged greatly on his ability to demonstrate that black quarterbacks could be triumphant. There were very few of them in the NFL during the time due in large part to long-standing, racist notions that they were not intelligent enough to lead an offense. Moon also faced the additional challenge of not succumbing to the potentially crippling emotional impact associated with the racism he faced in his position as a leader of the team. Both his awareness of the racism he would face during his football career as well as his efforts to counter it would begin when he started his career as a quarterback for the UW Huskies and would follow him throughout his tenure in the NFL.[1]

In May 2014, Seattle Seahawks' outspoken cornerback, Richard Sherman, candidly disclosed to a journalist, "There's a lot of racism still alive and still active.... We have to actively push it out." The remarks came months after

Sherman's sharp commentary related to a game-winning tipped pass in a playoff game against the San Francisco 49ers. During a postgame interview after he prevented Michael Crabtree from completing the pass, Sherman proudly proclaimed that he was "the best corner in the game." He then unabashedly called Crabtree "mediocre." The incident subjected Sherman to countless charges from sportswriters and others that he was a "thug." Sherman, a graduate of Stanford University, believed his dreadlocks and race prompted the label, one that he argued was tantamount to being called "the N-word." The May press conference was not the first time Sherman had confronted controversial topics. He raised similar concerns in multiple press conferences following the January 2014 incident. More importantly, it would not be his last time addressing the uncomfortable complexities of race and racism in America. In February 2015, Sherman wrote a piece published by *Sports Illustrated*, asserting what it means to be an athlete of color: "They want to hear us speak, but only if we're saying something they want to hear. . . . We understand, though, what it is to grow up as a black man in America." Over the years, Sherman has had a platform on which to speak about the racial slurs and discrimination often directed at black athletes, as well as the paradox they face in a society that lauds professional football players yet has historically discriminated against them because of their race. This discrimination has in myriad ways left them to face a double consciousness that often informs their actions as a seemingly contradictory figure.[2]

Collectively, the incidents involving Moon and Sherman both foreshadow and reflect the complex existence of many African American Seattle Seahawks who have felt marginalized or targeted because of their race, and who have responded in disparate ways to reconcile the double consciousness to which they have been subjected in society. The stories of Moon and Sherman are merely two examples of many in which race often overshadowed the athletic skills, victories, and defeats of professional African American football players and demonstrates how their racial identity was integral to their identity as a professional athlete. In a nation where racial discrimination has a historical continuum of oppression and control, arguably affecting all aspects of life, football has never simply been just a game. This means that racialized public scrutiny, violence, inequality, and everything in between would often define the terms of play for African American professional football players. In turn, the varied and broad actions taken by these players to counter the racism they experienced were often made possible by the visibility they enjoined as a prominent athlete. Moon's and Sherman's actions sit on a continuum of Seattle Seahawks who were subjected to and addressed racial discrimination during their football careers, players who sought to reconcile their dual identity as a celebrated football player and admonished man of color through the platform provided by professional play. While this is a story about the Seattle Seahawks, their stories are not unique. Focusing on the experiences of local players enables people to more fully gauge how black players across time and space would use their platforms as professional athletes to push back against the historically oppressive boundaries of race in America.

Double Consciousness

Famed intellectual, social pundit, and political activist William Edward Burkhardt (W.E.B.) Du Bois first introduced his theory of double consciousness in an *Atlantic* magazine article published in 1897. He would then explain the theory at length in his 1903 collection of essays *The Souls of Black Folk*. Du Bois examines the multifaceted identity many Africans Americans face, an identity divided by various social layers. He explores the "two-ness" of being "an American, a Negro; two souls, two thoughts, two unreconciled strivings; two warring ideals in one dark body." DuBois targets the psychosocial divisions within American society, shining a light on the struggles of being a black person in America, a person who should receive all of the benefits and protections inherit in being a citizen of a democratic country yet a person continuously subjected to racial discrimination. The concept of double consciousness is used in this chapter to examine the dual identity of being a professional athlete and an African American.[3]

Male African American athletes have often lived and continue to live a double consciousness. They are forced to confront on a daily basis what it means to be black in a society where racial othering is still prevalent, yet they theoretically exist as a lionized professional athlete who is typically allotted a status that affords one special treatment. They are left to muddle through the complexities of a dual, frequently "warring" existence while determining how to reconcile their varied identities. Through various accounts, it will be made clear that while not all athletes share identical perspectives on or experiences with racism, the double consciousness of African American professional football players have often been reconciled in various manners.

Carl Eller (Seahawks—1979)

"With movements like Black Lives Matter, there's some recognition of what it was like [in the 1960s]. That's a great burden and weight [as an athlete], and that is not a responsibility we should take lightly," acknowledged NFL Hall of Fame defensive end Carl Eller. Arguably one of the greatest defensive players in NFL history, Eller believes that athletes are given a unique platform to speak out on such issues and, as a result, effect change.[4]

Growing up in an era where racism was a dominant factor in societal arrangements, Eller was no stranger to racial injustice. Born in Winston-Salem, North Carolina, on January 25, 1942, and raised in the area, Eller experienced life in a society in which *de jure* and *de facto* segregation dictated nearly every aspect of African Americans' existence. Winton-Salem was a city where ordinances, custom, and law enforcement agents upheld and reinforced the separation of blacks and whites through legal and extralegal means.[5]

Eller's father died when he was young, and as a result, he began lashing out in anger at school. His high school principal recommended that he release his anger on the football field. Eller followed his advice. Football provided Eller with an arena to use what he would call his "God-given skills," and in doing so, Eller began to set greater goals for himself after high school due in part to the encouragement of his high school football coaches, Ben Warren and Warren Oldham. He enrolled in the Army National Guard in the late 1960s in order to begin his NFL career without the specter of the Vietnam draft. He had to be excused on occasion from NFL practices to fulfill his obligations with the National Guard. [6]

Eller played only the 1979 season for the Seattle Seahawks before ending his NFL career, which began with the Vikings in 1964. The Seahawks organization was only three years old when Eller took the field. Eller, who had already played in four Super Bowls with the Vikings, played sixteen games during that single season with Seahawks. He amassed three sacks during his short tenure with Seattle and was integral to the Seahawks' early success.[7]

Eller's experiences as an African American man and NFL football player in the 1960s and 1970s illustrates the double consciousness he faced. He was forced to walk on and off the field recognizing that being a black athlete set him apart. Arguably one of the greatest players in the NFL, Eller used his platform to give back to his community. During the last several years of his

NFL career, Eller battled an addiction to cocaine. He eventually sought help then worked with the NFL to develop policies regarding substance abuse. In the 1980s, Eller operated a rehabilitation clinic that provided outpatient care to hundreds of substance abusers for nearly ten years. Eller also involved himself in the league in ways that allowed him to help players in varied ways. For instance, Eller auctioned some of his personal memorabilia and donated the money raised to nonprofit organizations. Additionally, he worked for years to ensure that retired NFL players received increased pensions, tuition compensation, and better healthcare benefits. Eller played sixteen NFL games at the age of thirty-seven for the Seattle Seahawks before retiring. But in doing so, he left behind a legacy that reached far beyond the game of football.[8]

Eller's goals would be met both personally and professionally. In 2004, he was honored with induction into the Pro Football Hall of Fame. During his Hall of Fame enshrinement speech, Eller responded to his own question about what he could do with this great honor. His words recognized that his position, his fame, and his career as a professional athlete did not separate him from his blackness. He was forced to walk on and off the field as more than just an athlete. He was given a platform, he stated in his speech, that would be used to "help young African American males to participate fully in this society." Eller would use his platform to promote a message to black youth that they could head toward "the great universities and colleges of our nation, not to the prisons and jail cells."[9]

Years after his enshrinement, Eller spoke to ESPN about a trip made back to his hometown in the summer of 2014. He visited a house where his grandmother worked as a maid in the 1950s. Eller recalled how when he was a young boy, he would go through the back door to spend time with her as blacks were not allowed to enter through the front door. Upon his visit that summer, the current occupants of the home invited the famous football player into their home. Eller froze at the front steps: "emotionally I could not [comprehend] going through the front door because that was denied to me. I would not have gone through that front door in my youth." The story illustrates much about the lingering impact of discrimination and the double consciousness faced by Eller. It also reveals the progress that had been made since he was a youth in North Carolina. Eller relayed the story to young people in the Minneapolis-St. Paul area two years later: "Where I am today, it's a different life when I go back to Winston-Salem. . . . I can do things I could not do there when I was a youth. There has been some advancement." [10]

Kenny Easley (Seahawks—1981–1987)

On April 28, 1981, Kenny Easley was selected by the Seattle Seahawks in the first round of the NFL Draft. A safety from the University of California, Los Angeles, (UCLA) Easley would be voted NFL Defensive Player of the Year in 1984. The five-time Pro Bowler and recipient of All-Pro titles three of those five years accumulated 32 interceptions in 89 NFL games. Easley, an intimidating defensive force during his seven seasons with the Seahawks, gained the title of "The Enforcer," and his career highlights and abilities earned him recognition not only in Seattle but also throughout the nation. Almost thirty years prior to Richard Sherman bringing the noise to Seattle, Easley was setting the bar high for defensive players in the league. [11]

Yet, like his predecessor Carl Eller, Easley's experiences in life were deeply marred by racial discrimination. Easley admits that growing up in the 1960s and 1970s was not easy. Born in Chesapeake, Virginia, on January 15, 1959, he was raised in nearby South Norfolk, a segregated society that was just beginning to feel the impact of the modern Civil Rights Movement when he entered elementary school. While schools in the area were starting to integrate, Easley remembers there were two local parks, Cascade Park for white children and another park, which was given the name "Black Cascade Park" by African Americans. Unlike white football stars Ed Beard and Steve Delong, who spent their youth enjoying Cascade Park, Easley and his friends would be forced to travel a few blocks north to their "Black Cascade Park." This was just one challenging aspect of Easley's life in the Jim Crow South. He described his childhood in South Norfolk to the *Virginian-Pilot*, a local newspaper in his home state: "I got tired of the racism, of going into a white store and being followed around, of being called names. Some people used the n-word. To me, that meant they had no respect for me as a human being." He went on to share that he remembered the racial slurs and the rocks that were thrown at him as he walked home from football practice in a white neighborhood. As a high school football star, he would see people cheering him on at the Friday night football games, "but Monday through Thursday they would be chasing me home." So, it goes without question that when offers from across the nation came knocking at his door, he chose a college far from South Norfolk. Easley went on to become a three-time All-American safety at UCLA, earning a degree in political science. Easley was selected in the first round, fourth overall, out of UCLA by the Seahawks, and his seven-year career would prove to be highly influential for Seattle.[12]

Easley's final season with the Seattle Seahawks would hold significant meaning not only for Easley but for the NFL at large. The 1987 season brought both a division between Seattle Seahawks players Kenny Easley and Steve Largent and an NFL strike. While many factors contributed to the end of Easley's professional football career, primarily his kidney ailment, he believed that his involvement in the players' strike caused an ugly disenchantment with the Seattle Seahawks organization. The platform that Easley gained as both a professional athlete and the player representative allowed him in some ways to reconcile the double consciousness he felt as an idolized football player in a society burdened by a history of racial discrimination. As the Seattle representative for the NFL Players Association (NFLPA), he was able to use his visibility and influence to lend his voice to those concerned players who felt marginalized by the league's owners, many of whom were African American. But the strike was about securing rights and increased salaries for all players, regardless of race, and Easley risked much to champion the cause of his colleagues. Although the strike was short-lived, ending just a few weeks after it started, some argue that the actions of the NFLPA eventually led to the free agency and salary cap system that exists today. [13]

This was not the first strike the NFL had experienced, but it led to replacement players and tensions among a divided Seattle team. Easley represented Seattle for the NFLPA and encouraged his teammates to walk off the field in support of the strike. Largent, by contrast, was not in favor of participating in the strike. He and four other Seattle players participated in what became known as the three "replacement player games," in which the positions of those players who were on strike were played by replacement players. While the strike led to controversy across the nation, there was a perception described by a journalist for the *Seattle Times* that the aftermath of that strike "long lingered (in Seattle) . . . because of the differing views of their two stars—[the Seahawks] were more divided than many other teams."[14]

Easley and Largent's differences extended beyond the strike and the game of football. Largent was the image of the all-American, blond-haired, blue-eyed football player from Oklahoma, whereas Easley faced discrimination because of his race. Largent came from a poor background and understood that football would allow him to attend college. He had accepted a scholarship from the University of Tulsa. Easley had faced racism throughout his life, which informed his decision to leave Virginia. He stated that the reason he had opted to head 3,000 miles from home and play for UCLA was to "to get as far away from here [South Norfolk] as possible."[15]

Easley and Largent would become legends in the NFL—both players would have their jerseys honored and retired in Seattle, and both would be inducted into the Pro Football Hall of Fame. Years later, the tension between players would come to an end with a friendship between the players rekindled. "I think it's fair to say that when Steve and I were teammates, we weren't the best of friends," noted Easley after the event. "Because I was the player rep, and when we went into those strikes, there were some things that happened with certain players crossing the picket line that made it untenable for me and other people," he added. During the halftime ceremony on October 1, 2017, that celebrated the retirement of Easley and Largent's jerseys, Easley insisted, "It's really terrific to be here tonight to see my number retired alongside Steve Largent, my teammate."[16]

During his Hall of Fame speech in 2017, Easley expressed his pleasure in watching athletes bring light to the racial injustices they see in the United States. Easley insisted, "we've got to stand up as a country, as black Americans, and fight the good fight to protect our youth and our American constitutional right not to die while driving or walking the streets black in America. It has to stop." In an interview with *Seattle Times* columnist Jerry Large, in response to learning that social media comments stated that the induction ceremony was not the right place for Easley to deliver a message on race, Easley queried, "What's the sense of having a platform, if you're not going to step out on it?"[17]

Warren Moon (Seahawks—1997–1998)

One of the most influential players in the league, Warren Moon made his mark as the first African American quarterback for the Seattle Seahawks in 1997. Recognized in 1989 as NFL Man of the Year and as Pro Bowl Player of the Year in 1997, Moon's career highlights are endless. He played seventeen seasons in the NFL and was selected nine times to play for the Pro Bowl. With 291 touchdowns and over 49,000 passing yards, Moon's NFL successes, which culminated in his induction into the Hall of Fame on August 5, 2006, came after he won five Grey Cup championship titles in the Canadian Football League (CFL). Yet his story cannot be defined by statistics and titles alone. His successes and journey to stardom carried implications that extended far beyond the gridiron. Moon's story embodies the true meaning of perseverance, while it demonstrates the double consciousness African American athletes have been forced to face. In an era when racial tension and discrimination was highly visible, Moon struggled with the hardships that came with being an athlete of color and his experience serves as a prime example of the struggles many African American football players have been forced to confront.[18]

Born November 18, 1956, in Los Angeles, Moon was raised by his mother alongside his six sisters after his father passed away from complications related to alcoholism. Moon was only seven years old. As a result, he grew up faster than most because he felt it was his responsibility to take on the role of the "man of the house." While his mother continued her education and worked two shifts to provide for the family, Moon focused his attention on staying out of trouble. He played multiple sports growing up, but basketball was his avowed favorite. He started playing Pop Warner Association in Baldwin Hills community football at the age of ten. When he reached high school, due to the family's financial situation, Moon was forced to pick one sport and work a part-time job in order to cover the cost. With a passion for the game and an arm that could throw a football "harder and faster than anyone he knew," Moon chose to play quarterback and focused on football during his high school. His senior year in high school, Moon took his team to the city playoffs and was recognized as Los Angeles' All-City Quarterback.[19]

While Moon's dream was to play in the Rose Bowl, he recognized at an early age that he was living in an era when being black meant facing obstacles and limitations in all aspects of life, including football. As a youth in Los Angeles, he witnessed firsthand the 1965 Watts Uprising that took place in his hometown; Moon recalls walking past national guardsmen who held machine guns while posted along streets in his hometown following the uprising. He watched on television the aftermath of the assassinations of African American civil rights activists Medgar Evers, Malcolm X, and Dr. Martin Luther King in 1963, 1965, and 1968, respectively. Moon understood that he lived in a difficult time, and he was well aware that people of color, specifically African Americans, faced great adversity. While many would consider 1973, the year Moon graduated from high school, as falling outside the parameters of the modern Civil Rights Movement, the fight for justice and equality was far from complete, and the world of football was no exception. By 1973, only four black quarterbacks had started for the NFL in its more than fifty-year history: Frederick Douglas "Fritz" Pollard (1920), Marlin Briscoe (1968), James Harris (1969), and Joe Gilliam (1973). Most NFL teams refused to allow African Americans to be quarterback and frequently attempted to make those few who played the position in college switch to wide receivers in the NFL. With the exception of Historically Black Colleges and Universities, college football programs followed the discriminatory actions of professional teams and typically refused to allow African Americans to play the quarterback position.[20]

While disappointed, it did not come as a surprise to Moon that colleges refused to recruit him as a quarterback. Moon's rejection from schools to play quarterback resulted from long-standing racist notions that cast black men as devoid of the leadership skills and intelligence required for certain positions. During the better part of the twentieth century, "in football, the 'thinking' positions down the middle—quarterback, center, [inside] linebacker—were the ones that we weren't allowed to play," Moon lamented. Major colleges that approached Moon wanted him to change his position, which he declined to do. Instead, he opted to attend West Los Angeles Junior College, where he would be able to play quarterback.[21]

During his time in junior college, Moon broke multiple records and was named All-State champion, allowing him to be placed in the spotlight once again. As a result, he began to get recruited by various colleges, including the UW. Coach Don James believed in Moon and invited him to come to Seattle to be the team's starting quarterback. "He saw something in me that a lot of other people didn't see," Moon insisted about James. Moon signed on as the university's first African American quarterback.[22]

He struggled his first year on the team. The Huskies did not do well, and as quarterback, he took the blame from Seattle fans. The criticism Moon received was relentless and often racially charged. Decades following his tenure at UW, he vividly remembered being "booed" while running onto the field. Some fans would hurl racial slurs at him. He recalled the time as having been exceptionally challenging. Moon was required to act as if it did not bother him when internally it was "killing me," he insisted. Moon understood that if he reacted with a similar level of hate, his failure to remain composed could be used as fodder for those who sought to argue that African Americans could not handle the responsibilities associated with being the leader of a team. He represented not simply himself but all African Americans who would desire to play the position of quarterback.[23]

The following seasons, the UW football team began to play better, and Moon's turning point arose when UW played at the University of Southern California (USC) in a 1977 game. After Moon ran for a 71-yard touchdown, UW beat USC 21–10. The stadium erupted in cheers as Moon led his team to victory. It was in this moment that Moon felt total gratification, and he has described this win as the one that rendered all the hardships, the work, and the dedication completely worthwhile. More so, he had proven that as quarterback he could lead a team that was considered the underdog of college football to the Rose Bowl. During the previous month, USC was ranked number one in the nation. Two weeks after the Huskies' win, USC defeated UCLA and ensured UW's spot in the Rose Bowl, which takes place in Pasadena, California, against the University of Michigan. Despite Moon's stellar performance, the unjust treatment and discrimination Moon had endured was far from over, and his experiences surrounding the 1978 bowl game would provide strong reminders of what it meant to be an African American football player.[24]

There is a long-held tradition that the quarterbacks of both Rose Bowl teams pose together for a picture with Mickey Mouse at Disneyland. Michigan's quarterback refused to take this picture with Moon as the stigma associated with a black quarterback was at the time still strong. Nonetheless, Moon insisted that his experience at the Rose Bowl was one of the most exhilarating moments in his career. He remembered coming out of the tunnel, holding hands with his fellow teammates, and becoming very emotional as he reflected on the hard work and sacrifices that brought him to that field. The UW defeated Michigan 27–20, and Moon was named the Rose Bowl MVP. He secured a monumental moment in his career—a moment he would remember not only for his victory but also for his ability to walk on and off the gridiron as more than just an athlete. Moon had proven something about African Americans that was far greater than an on-field performance. "After college, there just wasn't a good feeling about me going to the National Football League by the things that I was hearing," Moon lamented.[25]

Despite his Rose Bowl championship and MVP title, NFL teams were not interested in signing him as a quarterback: "I was not really invited to the pro football combine. I had no coaches come out and give me individual workouts. It was just pretty much a foregone conclusion that quarterback was not in my future in the National Football League, but changing positions was." While he received draft offers if willing to change his position to wide receiver, no NFL team would take him on as a quarterback. By stark contrast, the CFL "came along and gave me that opportunity" to play quarterback in Canada, Moon mentioned thankfully during his Hall of Fame enshrinement speech. Moon played six seasons with the Edmonton Eskimos and "didn't hear anything racial" while he lived in Canada. He added: "The Canadian people were so refreshing, so supportive of me. I had six of the greatest years of my life up there with those guys. I will never regret making that decision." As a result of his success, Moon began to receive offers from the NFL to play as quarterback and made the decision to leave Canada to finally pursue his dream of playing in the NFL. His original hope was to play for the Seattle Seahawks, but the Houston Oilers offered him a larger contract. Houston wanted to change the culture of the game by fielding an African American quarterback. Moon and his family moved to the South, and while things started off slow, Moon brought his team to the playoffs eight years in a row. Moon became the highest-paid player in the game. His time with Houston was far from easy, however, and Moon experienced a lot of racism in Texas. His children would be sitting in the stands watching Moon play football while hearing people chant racial slurs and demonstrate explicit racism toward their father. His children at a young age had to be told why people treated their father differently from white players, and they had to be told what it meant to be black in America. It was a challenge, to say the least, for Moon to not only experience racism on his own but also to watch his children go through it as they were placed in the spotlight of what it meant to have their father be a black quarterback[26].

Racism was not just centered in a specific place or region. Moon was playing football in a time when inequality and discrimination were still a dominant social force throughout the United States. When Moon was escorted off the Cleveland Browns' field surrounded by security due to a death threat in 1990, he had just played one of the best games in his career, and someone in the stadium had threatened to kill him. At thirty-four, he was "a relic by professional standards," according to his own admission. Nonetheless, his performance was outstanding: "The Browns couldn't keep pace," he boasted, "as I completed twenty-four of thirty-two passes for 322 yards and a career-high five touchdowns." It was during moments such as this that Moon realized he was not just playing the game of football. He believed that he was playing for his race, and he recognized in that moment as he had during many others that his success mattered. Moon was regularly told by fans of color to "represent [us]." He took on this burden with a lot of pride but always wondered what it would have been like for himself and future African American quarterbacks had he not performed well or kept his composure in racially charged situations. [27]

In 1997, Moon signed with the Seattle Seahawks. He was approached by Seattle during the previous decade before he signed with Houston. The decision to join Houston's team was an agonizing one for Moon: "Seattle was my home, and everywhere I went people pleaded with me to sign with the Seahawks." Despite the pleadings, Seattle fans would have to wait thirteen seasons for their UW quarterback to come home. [28]

Moon's journey to stardom came as no easy task, but while he experienced extreme racial discrimination, he broke down many barriers and paved the way for the increased appearance and success of black quarterbacks in the NFL. In 2014, when Seattle Seahawks quarterback Russell Wilson led his team to Super Bowl victory, he become the second African American quarterback to ever win a Super Bowl. Doug Williams had led the Washington Redskins to victory in Super Bowl XXII. As President Obama stated, "The best part about [Wilson being the second to win] is nobody commented on it, which tells you the progress we've made, although we've got more progress to make." The journey that has led to this progression came with great challenges and hardships; it came at the expense of athletes of color being forced to walk on and off the field as being more than just an athlete. [29]

The Modern Seattle Seahawks

On September 22, 2016, Seattle Seahawks' cornerback Richard Sherman made headlines across the nation when his words struck a powerful chord in the hearts of many Americans. Sherman had never held back from speaking on the controversial issue of race, and this day would not be the exception. He was addressing the deaths of Terence Clutcher and Keith Lamont Scott, two black men who were killed by police officers during the previous month. At his weekly press conference, Sherman refused to answer journalists' questions about football and instead offered an assessment of the killings:

I think you have players that are trying to take a stand and trying to be aware of social issues and try to make a stand and increase people's awareness and put a spotlight on it, and they're being ignored. Whether they're tak- ing a knee or whether they're locking arms, they're trying to bring people together and unite them for a cause. I think the last couple days, a couple more guys have gotten shot and killed in the middle of the street. More videos have come out of guys getting killed, and I think people are still missing the point. The reason these guys are kneeling, the reason we're locking arms is to bring people together, to make people aware that this is not right. It's not right for people to get killed in the street.[30]

After a white nationalist rally that took place in Charlottesville, Virginia, the following August and ended with the killing of twenty-three-year-old counterprotester Heather Heyer, Seahawks defensive end Michael Bennett added his name to the list of his outspoken African American teammates. "I can't stand right now. I'm not going to be standing until I see the equality and freedom," he exclaimed to television reporters.[31] Bennett made headlines in December 2017 when he was held at gunpoint then handcuffed by Las Vegas police after gunshot noises forced him, along with a crowd on the city's Strip, to run for safety. He claimed that "Las Vegas police officers singled me out and pointed their guns at me for doing nothing more than simply being a black man in the wrong place at the wrong time." The outspoken defensive end who grew up in Texas explained that the horrific events in Charlottesville reminded him of the 1998 murder of James Byrd in Jasper, Texas, by three white men. Byrd was dragged to his death from the back of a pickup truck in the rural town that had been known for its deep-rooted racism and Ku Klux Klan activity. He then pointed out that President Donald Trump hesitated to condemn the actions of the Charlottesville protestors: "I grew up around that, listening and remembering those things, and thinking about Charlottesville brought back those memories, it actually brought tears to my eyes to see people fighting and having hate for somebody because of their color. I couldn't believe it took [Trump] forty-eight hours to respond. I thought he would have responded within seconds. And when he came on, I thought he should have handled it just as fast as when he's tweeting about Russia or something." After San Francisco 49er Colin Kaepernick's took a knee during the national anthem in protest of racialized police brutality and racial inequality, Trump called for "son of a bitch players" to be fired from the NFL if they opted to follow Kaepernick's lead. Sherman admitted that he too found it "very interesting" that Trump saw players silently "protesting the injustice and bigotry and racism that [have] plagued our great country for so long" as "radicals," while "it took him a while to even condemn [white supremacists]."[32]

During a September 2017 press conference, Bennett revealed his thoughts about what would be required to combat racial discrimination:

> It would take a white player to really get things changed. Because when somebody from the other side understands and they step up and they speak up about it . . . it would change the whole conversation. Because when you bring somebody who doesn't have to be a part of [the] conversation making himself vulnerable in front of it, I think when that happens, things will really take a jump.[33]

Seahawks wide receiver Doug Baldwin, in support of Bennett and the protests, insisted:

> I think we take for granted the fact that in our country we have freedom of speech. "We should be proud of individuals who feel strongly about certain topics and certain situations that are happening in our country, and are willing to put themselves out and be vulnerable about it. Mike has done that.[34]

The following month, the entire Seattle Seahawk team elected to stay in their locker room during the anthem in a unified effort to support those who were protesting racial injustice and inequality. Baldwin then explained the significance of the Seahawks concerted protests:

> The reason I thought it would be a unifying opportunity was because you had individuals speaking specifically to injustice and inequality, but then now you have somebody saying 'I don't want to hear your protest, I don't want to hear your grievances,' which is a First Amendment right. If an American can't air their grievances to the republic for which it stands, where can they air their grievances? And when you have the President of our country basically saying 'I don't want to hear your protests, I don't want to hear your grievances' then I think that is where we have the challenge . . .
> . . . yeah he did detract from the actual point of inequality and injustice, but at the same time, it's giving us an opportunity to unify.[35]

Seahawks Quarterback Russell Wilson, who often is not as outspoken regarding issues of race as some of his teammates, acknowledged, "We wanted to do something as a team. We're such a tight-knit group. . . . We wanted to figure out, how can we do something as a whole team collective effort to show that the injustice in America needs to be fixed?"[36] Head Seahawks Coach Pete Carroll noted that this was not the first time players advocated for change: "This is just the next time, but it is a very significant time."[37]

Conclusion

Discrimination and racism continue to be overwhelming influences on and off the field. While black athletes have often struggled with a double consciousness, many have taken advantage of a platform made possible through their celebrity and visibility to empower themselves and their communities— to speak out against racism, inequality, and social injustice. Yet each voice is different. Carl Eller spoke out in disagreement with NFL players protesting during the national anthem. When his coach at the Minnesota Vikings, Bud Grant, had his team practice standing at attention for the national anthem, Eller was the one he chose to model the stance. Eller noted in defense of his convictions, "In sports, it's the only place we hear the anthem, they don't play it at concerts. They don't play it at movie theaters. They don't play it at church. Sports is the only place you show allegiance to the anthem. It's important for sports to maintain that tradition."[38] One of the oldest former players of the Seattle Seahawks, Eller values tradition, but he also holds a different ideology on how black athletes should do so. He publicly stated that though he disagreed with Kaepernick's protest, he applauded Kaepernick's desire to make his voice heard. On the other hand, Kenny Easley insisted that if he still played football, he would take a knee. "Oh, certainly, certainly if that's what was going to bring attention to the issues that are problematic for America, then yes! I would do it," Easley said to a crowd at the Northwest African American Museum in Seattle. Warren Moon discussed his own thoughts on the NFL player protests ignited by Kaepernick, specifically the Seahawks' decision to stay in the locker room during the national anthem. He stated that he did not necessarily agree with protesting during the national anthem, but he did believe that the team unifying to use their platform to address issues of racial injustice was important. He "love[d] the show of solidarity" and believed that the attention garnered by the protests conducted during the national anthem would help to facilitate what should happen to address the issues at the center of the protests.[39]

In an interview conducted for this chapter, cornerback Michael Tyson, who was drafted by the Seattle Seahawks in 2017, insisted, "we must let struggle inspire us." In March 2018, he was driving to practice at the Virginia Mason Athletic Complex when a white woman followed him to the entrance gate and rolled down her car window. She shouted, "get off your knees, stand up for the flag, we pay your taxes so get your ass up." Tyson had participated in protests during the season that included taking a knee during the national anthem. While Tyson is no stranger to racism and the hate-filled acts that people of color often face, this was an eye-opening experience for him. He realized that because he is a black athlete in the NFL, many expect him to only care about the game of football. Some "people disregard the fact that athletes have their own thoughts, beliefs, and values that go far beyond the game," Tyson stated, "we are forced to carry ourselves a certain way, and we are shamed for showing our personality." He realized that standing on a platform where his voice can be heard can facilitate change. He feels a sense of division and wants to just focus on the game he loves, yet the current nature of our society forces him to constantly recognize that he is both a high-profile athlete and a black man.[40]

Defining the freedom struggle comes as no easy task, and though there were monumental individuals who sought to address and eradicate racial injustice across the country, insurgency came from many angles. The work of activist groups, varying media outlets, strong leaders, legal triumphs, student activism, and interracial cooperation can never be undermined. But one component that should not be overlooked is the dramatic influence the intersection of race and sports has and continues to play in bringing about racial justice in the United States. The actions of various Seattle Seahawks players since the team's inception make it clear that the topic of racism among NFL players has been one that holds great significance. While the personal journeys and experiences of Seahawks—from Carl Eller and Kenny Easley to Warren Moon, Richard Sherman, Michael Bennett, Michael Tyson and others—are varied, the visibility afforded them as players in the NFL has served as a foundation for making a difference. The intersection of sports and race matters because of this—it has always mattered because of this—and the manner in which certain players have utilized the visibility afforded by their lionized status pushes society to think about football as far more than just a game.

CHAPTER TEN

The First American Hockey Town

Seattle's Place in the Margins of Hockey History

CHRISTINE S. MAGGIO

If you were to ask someone which American city was home to the first American hockey team to win the Stanley Cup, you would likely hear suggestions such as Boston, New York, and Chicago, as these cities host famous National Hockey League (NHL) franchises. A more seasoned hockey fan might guess Detroit, whose reputation as "Hockeytown" is so firmly set that the nickname is emblazoned at center ice in the arena where Detroit's Red Wings play. That the first American Stanley Cup winners hailed from Seattle might come as a surprise to most. After all, this is a city that has never had a team in the modern NHL (though that could likely change). Despite the modern lack of a professional team in the city, early leagues built a reputation during the early days of professional hockey in Seattle. The region has been home to minor league teams, and most recently in 2016, Seattle hockey fans proved their passion for the sport in a bid to bring an NHL expansion team to the city. The NHL seemed to take notice of the 33,000 people willing to put down a minimum of $500 per seat toward season tickets when in 2018 the city was again awarded a hockey team. Nonetheless, Seattle is still generally not seen as a hockey town. Snow in Seattle is a rarity, let alone the freezing over of ponds that are needed for outdoor play on natural rinks, so the climate certainly does not lend any wintry weight to the city's bid for hockey fame. Just as Seattle is disregarded as a hockey city, so too are some of the communities that have made an impact on hockey in Seattle— from the women's hockey players who helped to make history to the local Salish-speaking tribes whose art and culture have inspired team branding.

The city as a whole from its early-twentieth-century Stanley Cup victory to the contributions of historically marginalized groups is central to the history of hockey in the United States. On the eve of a new era for hockey in the city and in view of the largely unknown contributions of Seattleites to the cultural development of the sport, this chapter seeks to reflect on the achievements and history of the sport in Seattle. [1]

Lord Stanley's Trophy:
The Early Days of Seattle Hockey

There are many self-proclaimed hockey purists who believe that the sport should only be played where ice occurs naturally during the winter. Much to the vexation of those purists, hockey's origins as an organized sport in Seattle did not begin until the advent of indoor ice arenas as Seattle winters are not particularly frigid. The original Seattle Arena, built in 1915, was located at the corner of Fifth Avenue and University Street, where the International Business Machines (IBM) building stands today. It was, at the time it was built, a state-of-the-art facility that allowed for the artificial creation of ice. From 1915 to 1924, the building served as the home of the Seattle Metropolitans before its conversion into a parking garage and its demolition in the 1960s. The Metropolitans were a part of the Pacific Coast Hockey Association (PCHA), which had been dreamed up by the Patrick brothers, Lester and Frank, logging heirs and hockey enthusiasts who had moved from Montreal to Vancouver with the hope of starting a league on the West Coast. The PCHA started in 1911 but expanded to Seattle for the 1915–1916 season, poaching four players from the roster of the 1914 Stanley Cup champion Toronto Blueshirts of the National Hockey Association (NHA) in order to fill the bench with proven competitive players.[2]

While the Metropolitans only managed to break even in their first season, they would finish at the top of the PCHA the following year with a record of 16-8, which earned them the right to challenge the Montreal Canadiens of the NHA for the Stanley Cup. Unlike the present format of the Stanley Cup championships, which is solely within the NHL, in the early days of professional hockey, the trophy was first a challenge cup and later, in the days of the PCHA and NHA, was decided in a manner similar to baseball's World Series, where the champions of each league played one another for the right to the Stanley Cup. In a 1917 best-of-five series, the Metropolitans won three games to the Canadiens' sole victory, which they took in the first game with a score of 8–4. Seattle, however, won the second game with an astounding 6–1 score, the third game 4–1, and ultimately secured the Stanley Cup on March 26 with a dominant score of 9-1 against the Canadiens.[3]

Naturally, when a team succeeds, there is bound to be a movement among the youth of an area to participate in the sport of their heroes. Female athletes in Seattle were no exception; they pushed the boundaries of gendered play in an era when athletic engagement among women was often considered in contrast to strict notions of femininity. The Junior Metettes, a girls' hockey team in Seattle, became champions of girls' hockey in the city, hosting regular fundraising events to promote the sport in addition to playing fierce games themselves. A journalist for the *Seattle Times* observed:

> Girls are not afraid of anything nowadays, it seems. They do practically all
> a boy does in the way of sports; their endurance seems to be equal, if not
> greater, and with determination and enthusiasm, the boys will have to look
> to their laurels if they are to keep ahead.... They play such an exciting game
> that even the men enjoy witnessing it, claiming 'They never had more fun
> in their lives.' Little things like cuts, bleeding noses, and lips, and loosened
> teeth, don't count at all when a game is on.[4]

For all the progressive talk about equality, the championship game was reported on not in the sports section but in the society pages alongside an advertisement for "New Millinery for Easter." Regardless, it is astounding that a youth team, let alone a girls' team, would get a full-page treatment such as the Metettes did in 1917.[5]

The Metropolitans, meanwhile, would come close to the Stanley Cup two more times but on both occasions failed to close out the series. The 1919 Stanley Cup Final, in which they again faced the Montreal Canadiens, was tied at two wins apiece and one draw when the series was cancelled by health officials due to the Spanish flu pandemic. Many of the Canadiens' players and their team manager fell ill. The illness ultimately claimed the life of Joe Hall, a defenseman for the Canadiens, who died in a Seattle hospital of pneumonia as a complication of the Spanish flu. Newspapers at the time noted:

> MacDonald and Couture [of the Canadiens] were the first to come down
> with the disease but they were soon followed by Hall, Manager Kennedy,
> Lalonde and Berlanquette. From the start, Hall's illness took the most

serious turn and his temperature was at a dangerous point for almost a week. No doubt his strenuous exertions in the first four games of the series had much to do towards the weakening of his condition.[6]

A few of the Seattle players fell ill as well, but the Canadiens certainly had the worst of it. The series as a whole, even not counting the eventually fatal flu outbreak, seemed ill-fated: five Mets were seriously injured, as was Corbeau of the Canadiens, and two games went to overtime, which in a time with few substitute players meant exhaustion all around. This series has the dubious distinction of being the only time so far that the Stanley Cup championship series has been initiated but not completed. Though the Stanley Cup was never awarded, the series is commemorated with an engraving on the cup listing the names of both teams along with the phrase "Series Not Completed." With any luck, it will remain the only time that such a misfortune takes place.[7]

The next year, the Metropolitans reached the finals once again, facing the Ottawa Senators in the 1920 Stanley Cup Finals. They took the series to five games, but a definitive 6–1 win by Ottawa in the fifth game meant missing out on the championship once again. This would mark the last time that the Metropolitans had a chance to play for the Stanley Cup. Unfortunately, the years to come would prove to be difficult ones for the PCHA, though they would also contain an interesting element that has been relegated to the footnotes of hockey history.

In 1921, determined to capitalize on hockey's increasing popularity, the PCHA started a women's hockey team in each city that they had an extant hockey fan base. Seattle, of course, qualified as a market for the expansion team given the enthusiasm surrounding the Metropolitans. The PCHA decided to have the women's teams compete against one another in a tournament played during intermissions of the men's game. Thus, the Vancouver Amazons, the Victoria Kewpies, and the Seattle Vamps came to play in what might be considered the first women's hockey league, though women's hockey tournaments had taken place previously. While the Seattle Vamps do not bear the same kind of storied history that the Metropolitans do, with only five games on record, their presence as a women's hockey team at such an early point in hockey's history is worth noting. Unfortunately, records on the women's team are difficult to find. The Vamps' season ended with three losses, a tie, and no wins, putting them in last place. The only recorded victory for the Seattle Vamps was in an exhibition match against the women's hockey club at the University of British Columbia, in which star forward Jerry Reed scored three goals and goaltender Mildren Terran kept all shots she faced at bay for a final score of 3–0.

Despite the progressive nature of the team's existence, the Seattle Vamps were not immune from the sexist inclinations of many reporters at the time. During the Vamps trip to Vancouver and Victoria, the *Vancouver Sun* repeatedly referred to the team as the "Seattle Sweeties," though the reasons for this are lost to time given the scant historical records available. Was it intended as a denigration of the team or of the women's sport in general, or was it simply a misidentification on the part of the reporter assigned to cover the games? While there can be a strong case made for the first two possibilities, the third seems like a stretch—after all, this reporter attended a minimum of three games: in Vancouver against the Amazons, in Victoria against the Kewpies, and against the University of British Columbia. It is also possible that the same reporter had attended the games in Seattle, though these would come later. Even in the Vamps' victory against the University of British Columbia, the reporter referred to the Seattle team as the Sweeties. Given this repetition, it is far more likely that the name was intended to belittle the Seattle team or women's hockey more generally than a simple error on the part of the reporter. [8]

Seattle's press covered these games very lightly when they were covered at all. While there was coverage for the Seattle Vamps' first game, a loss against the Vancouver Amazons, no further coverage was offered for the ladies' team until the series came to Seattle. This meant that the Vamps' sole victory at the University of British Columbia was not acknowledged by local press.[9]

Whether it was because women's hockey was treated as a novelty that failed to catch on or simply a symptom of the financial ailments of the PCHA, official support for the women's teams folded after their sole season. If the Seattle Vamps continued play beyond 1921, they did so as an independent entity, and what little coverage they got in the newspapers vanished without even a notice that the team was folding.

The men's team did not long survive the ladies' team, as the Metropolitans ceased to exist after the 1923–24 season due to financial trouble. The Seattle Arena was subsequently converted into a parking garage. This would also be the death knell for the PCHA itself, as the remaining teams located in

Victoria and Vancouver were sold to the up-and-coming Western Canada Hockey League.[10]

1928–1985: An Era in Flux

After four years without professional hockey in Seattle, the Patrick family would take another swing at a professional hockey league with the establishment of Pacific Coast Hockey League (PCHL) in 1928. It was similar to but legally distinct from the PCHA, of which the Metropolitans had been a part. The PCHL consisted of four teams, including one in Seattle. The Seattle Eskimos were founded by former Seattle Metropolitans manager Pete Muldoon, marking the first in a recurring trend of Native culture-"inspired" names. Unfortunately, much of the motivation behind the branding of these early teams has been lost to history. Muldoon was the driving force behind getting a hockey team back in Seattle, so he most likely had a hand in naming the team. While his reasons may be lost to us, an exploration of the history behind the term may shed more light on the reasons for the team's name.[11]

The tribes commonly referred to colloquially as "Eskimos" are not local to the Seattle area; the term, which many consider derogatory, loosely groups together disparate tribes that live in the region closest to the North Pole. The word has a fraught history, with many seeing it as a highly offensive term; generally, Inuit is preferred by the native peoples of Eastern Canada while Alaskan Natives will still use Eskimo, owing to the fact that the local Yupik languages do not have the word *Inuit*. It is possible that Seattle as a port of departure for those who wished to travel to Alaska, especially during the Klondike Gold Rush of the 1890s, maintained an image of connection to the native people of that area. Whatever the reasons for the name, the team folded in 1931 as they had struggled to sell tickets, something that affected the whole league given the economic instability of the Great Depression. [12]

During the Depression, with professional teams failing to function as a financially viable option, many companies and factories had their own recreational teams that played one another. One such team was the Langendorf Royalettes, a company female hockey team from the Langendorf Bakery in Seattle, which had a fierce rivalry with the Octonek Knitting Company's Octonek Amazons.[13] Without professional sports to attend, sports fans were willing to support recreational teams like the Royalettes, evidenced by the spaces chosen to host the events, including, for instance, the Civic

Ice Arena, which could seat 5,000 spectators. Oddly enough, the Octonek Knitting Company had a connection to hockey in the region that predated their recreational team as they were the company that designed and produced the uniforms for the Eskimos. Perhaps some of the Amazons had a direct hand in producing the uniforms for the Eskimos and had dreams themselves of one day being able to have spectators admire their play. With a lack of professional hockey during the Depression, they would be able to fulfill that dream.[14]

In a trend that would repeat throughout Seattle's hockey history, the city did not have to wait very long to see professional hockey's return. Only five years after the Eskimos folded, the Seattle Seahawks would get their start. While today we think of the Seahawks as a football team, the original Seahawks were a hockey team. Founded in 1936, the Seahawks were originally part of the short-lived North West Hockey League (NWHL), which after three seasons was folded into the second incarnation of the PCHL. In their eight seasons of play between the two leagues, the Seahawks had a record of 144 wins, 138 losses, and 39 ties. After the 1940 season the team was sold and renamed to become the Seattle Olympics, named for the nearby Olympic Peninsula and Olympic Mountains. The Olympics played only for a single season due to the fact that in 1941 the league folded as a result of the onset of World War II. While the United States would not enter the conflict until the end of that year, many players in the league were Canadians, whose country had declared war in September 1939. With the war effort requiring the aid of able-bodied young men, sports took a back seat to patriotism and so ended the first Seahawks franchise in Seattle, though the name had already been different for a full season. The National Football League's Seattle Seahawks would not play their first season until 1976, a full thirty-five years after the hockey franchise of the same team went out of business.[15]

In 1944, as World War II was drawing to a close, the third and final incarnation of the PCHL came into being, this time founded not by the Patrick brothers but by Hockey Hall of Famer Al Leader. Seattle's PCHL team went through a few name changes during this period, known first as the Ironmen from 1944–52. When the team moved from the PCHL to the Western Hockey League (WHL), they then became the Bombers, a name they would hold until 1955, before playing as the Americans from 1955–58. All three names bore the patriotic spirit of the period; the Ironmen represented the shipbuilding industry of the region, the Bombers represented aviation, and the Americans denoted tautology. Finally, in 1958, the team changed hands again, this time to an ownership group headed by Vince Abbey, a man who was born and raised in Seattle. Marvin Burke, who was named as the new team president, said at the time, "There was nothing wrong with the old name, Americans, but we wanted a label which would better connote the Puget Sound area. Also, we wanted to have a completely new operation— new name, new owners, everything new except Coach Keith Allen."[16] An alternative team name, the Jets, had been proposed but was ultimately discarded in favor of the Seattle Totems. The Jets name would have been an excellent nod to the Seattle area's contributions to aeronautics and would have also reflected the Puget Sound region, but the proposal to use a Native American-inspired name was the one that resonated with the team's owners.

The Seattle Totems emerged during an era in which local Native people were fighting for the fishing rights they had been granted in past treaties with the government. While the movement gained mainstream recognition in the 1960s, with high-profile celebrities such as Marlon Brando participating in protests alongside tribal demonstrators, it seems to show a strange lack of empathy that a team would clad itself in a name and imagery that reflects Native culture and yet not work to advance the needs of the community they purported to revere. Whether the team's name or logo reflected a community that was undergoing a struggle that ultimately resulted in violence did not seem to be a matter of concern to the ownership or management of the Seattle Totems. If anyone affiliated with the team participated in or voiced support for the protests that would come to be known as the Fish Wars, no record of this has been made readily available. In all the material found regarding the Seattle Totems, only the business of hockey was reflected. [17]

The Seattle Totems were fairly successful, due in part to a legendary player whose value has not been recognized by the hockey community as a whole. Guyle Fielder spent fifteen seasons in Seattle through three team names, starting as a Bomber in 1953 through the Americans' reign and for the first twelve seasons of the Seattle Totems. His stay in Seattle was historic. He was the first professional hockey player in any league to surpass 100 points in a single season, a feat he accomplished four times. His ability to score points—not only to score goals but also to set up goals for his teammates as the primary assist on goals—was unsurpassed in the WHL. He is part of an extremely small group of professional hockey players to have over 2,000 career points—a feat only Jaromir Jagr, Gordie Howe, Mark Messier, and Wayne Gretzky have also accomplished. Though the Hockey Hall of Fame is intended to reflect the sport and not a single league, players without a history of success in the NHL are often left off the inductee roll. Such is the case with Fielder, who had a number of tryouts and brief stays with NHL teams, most notably with the Detroit Red Wings in 1957. Unfortunately, he played only six games with the Red Wings, and though he appeared on the first line alongside Gordie Howe and Jim Wilson, he never meshed with the team or tallied a single goal or assist. Ultimately, he requested to be sent back to Seattle, where he would continue to play until 1969. Though Fielder has artifacts on display at the Hockey Hall of Fame Museum, he is not an inductee in the Hall of Fame itself in spite of being, in the words of former WHL president Bill McFarland, "sort of Gretzky before Gretzky." His prowess as a hockey player has not been enshrined in hockey legend in the same way his peers on the record sheet have been.[18]

Fielder's story reflects that of hockey history in Seattle in general. For as much as Fielder's skill cannot be denied, the fact that he never made an impact in the NHL means that he is stuck on the margins of hockey history, looking in but largely absent from the dominant narrative. Similarly, despite Seattle's credentials as being home to the first American Stanley Cup winners and regardless of the fact that Seattle has never gone more than five years without a professional hockey team of some kind, it is still not thought of as a true hockey town, owing to the fact that it has never been home to an NHL team. Recognition by the NHL is the path to legitimacy and a place in the popular history of hockey, otherwise any accomplishments are dismissed as not being a part of anything serious.

During the early 1970s, however, there was enough competition in the world of major league hockey that joining the NHL was not quite the foregone conclusion to the question of legitimacy that it is today. The World Hockey Association (WHA) was a competing major league that poached talent and fans from the NHL. The teams of the WHL and the NHL came to an agreement in 1972, which became known as the "White Paper." In short, the NHL agreed to offer at least half of the number of expansion franchises awarded after the 1974–75 season to WHL cities. NHL franchises were awarded to both Denver and Seattle, which meant that with two markets leaving to join the NHL, the WHL would be folding. Unfortunately, though a franchise was awarded to Vince Abbey, one of the owners of the Totems, he had difficulty in getting the necessary funds together to pay the franchise fees and move forward with an NHL team. Though he fought in the courts for more than a decade against what he saw as a violation of antitrust laws, ultimately the prospects of an NHL franchise fizzled out.[19]

The WHL is a professional hockey league, yet they are what is known as a major junior league, in which the players are paid for playing the sport but are considered too young to play in leagues in which the majority of players are adults. Players in the WHL are age sixteen through twenty, though teams have a limit of three twenty-year-olds on their roster. This allows young players to cultivate their talents in an environment with players at a similar stage of development rather than having them play in the adult major or minor leagues and risking injury in play with much larger adults. There are rare exceptions to the minimum age requirement in which a fifteen-year-old may be allowed to play, though to date only five such exceptions have been made across all three major junior hockey leagues, and none of these were in the WHL. When the team first came to town, however, the minimum age was only fourteen, though the rules would change to raise the minimum age to sixteen in the 1980s.[20]

Seattle, as before, was never very long without a hockey team. In 1977, the Kamloops Chiefs of the WHL relocated to Seattle and renamed themselves the Seattle Breakers, taking up residency at the Seattle Coliseum where the Totems had played. In 1985, the Breakers became the Thunderbirds, again drawing inspiration for both the name and the team's logo from local tribal history [21].

A Bid and a Betrayal

After Vince Abbey's failed bid to turn the awarded NHL franchise from paper to a reality, there was a long stretch where it appeared that the Thunderbirds would be the sole professional hockey option available for the Seattle area. The team was always a large draw to the Seattle Coliseum, however, and between the NBA's Seattle SuperSonics and the WHL's Thunderbirds, business at the Seattle Center was brisk. Despite the fact that the building was aging poorly, the time seemed ripe for another try at an NHL expansion to Seattle.

In 1990, the NHL announced that they were accepting bids for expansion teams, and given Seattle's long history with the sport, the city seemed a natural fit for a potential franchise. A few separate potential ownership groups formed with the intent of entering a bid, but these eventually coalesced into a single bid headed by Bill Ackerley, the son of the owner of the Seattle SuperSonics, Barry Ackerley. The Ackerley family had plans to build a new arena with luxury suites, and the bid for an NHL team was supposedly a part of that plan. The money and sports management experience offered by the Ackerley family was a draw for the other groups, and with their desire to build a new arena, it was a reasonable assumption that it was in the family's best interests to bring an NHL expansion to Seattle. [22]

At an NHL Board of Governors meeting held in Florida in December 1990, Bill Ackerley unexpectedly withdrew his bid, leaving the remaining members of the group attempting to present the group's proposal in his stead.[23] A second group, which reportedly included Chris Larson—an executive at Microsoft, along with former Seattle Totems star and attorney Bill MacFarland—were unfortunately unable to secure a franchise, owing in large part to the expansion fees required.[24] However, the high cost of these expansion fees would have been affordable if the Ackerley family had allowed the group a portion of the revenues from the sales of luxury suites. Asked immediately after the meeting in Florida about Ackerley's sudden withdrawal, Bill MacFarland admitted:

> What Ackerley said about our bid not being 'viable' bothered me since he knew it was based on a lease from the Ackerleys in which they would not allow us to have revenues the league required. . . . I understand why we couldn't get them. But I didn't think they were right to say we didn't have a viable group. They [the Ackerley family] have to finance the building, so we [MacFarland and Larson] wanted to pay less for the franchise.[25]

Given that the Ackerley family was invested in having a new arena built, it seemed strange that they would back out at the eleventh hour. Initial reports given at the time of the meeting made it sound as if these were two entirely separate bids that had no cooperation between them. The story, however, grew even more sordid as additional details emerged, for it came to light that Ackerley had initially encouraged Larson and MacFarland to join him as a part of a single bid rather than bidding as separate groups. He then betrayed them and abandoned them to face the Board of Governors as a hamstrung group with no control over an unfavorable potential lease, going so far as to even sneak out of the hotel where the meeting was being held.

> At that point, according to MacFarland, Ackerley asked his 'allies' if he could address NHL officials by himself before the group as a whole met league officials. 'It seemed a little weird,' said MacFarland, 'but what the heck. We said, "No problem."' When Ackerley confronted NHL owners, he formally withdrew the application while MacFarland and Larson waited in the other room, oblivious to what Ackerley had done. Ackerley never did—at least adequately—explain his odd action. He simply departed the hotel via a side door and flew back to Seattle without a word to MacFarland or Larson.[26]

Though no clear explanation has ever been given by the Ackerley family for why the bid was withdrawn in such a bizarre manner, the evidence seems to point to a desire by the Ackerley family to control any possible NHL bid in the city of Seattle as the hockey team would have to share an arena with the Ackerley-owned SuperSonics. While the Ackerleys' proposed new arena never came to fruition, a renovation of the Seattle Coliseum, which was home to the SuperSonics, would be approved by the city council in 1993 and completed in 1995. The approval came with the promise of a long-term lease of the venue by the SuperSonics. The result of these renovations would be a beautiful 17,000-seat venue for basketball, which would seat only 13,000 for hockey—a number far below the minimum required for an NHL franchise. The new venue also included an ice surface that was off-center and oddly sized. Ultimately, by controlling the fate of an NHL bid, the Ackerleys ensured that they would never have to share their space with an NHL team. Given that their proposal for a new arena was approved in conjunction with the "bid" for an NHL team, it is possible that the proposed space was simply a feint designed to encourage the city to sign off on renovations to the aging Coliseum. [27]

Hockey in the Sound Today and Onward

The name of the Seattle Totems has not been forgotten; a local junior hockey program plays as the Seattle Junior Totems. Though there is no organizational relationship between the old Totems and the new Junior Totems, who were founded in 2005 as the Kent Crusaders before changing names and moving rinks, the logo and name are clearly intended to carry on the legacy of the old WHL franchise. Current NHL player T.J. Oshie played for the Junior Totems organization while growing up in Mountlake Terrace, just north of Seattle. Oshie's family is originally from Minnesota, and they are members of the Ojibwe tribe. Representation of Native American and First Nation people in the NHL is still scant with the resource *Native Hockey* listing only 8 out of 936 active players as being registered tribe members. With a potential role model like Oshie, the NHL could do quite a bit of work to promote hockey among the Native people in the Puget Sound area and in the country at large. [28]

The legacy of the Vamps and women's hockey in Seattle continues to this day as well, though the city lacks a professional women's team. The Western Washington Female Hockey Association, which plays as the Washington Wild, is a competitive hockey club with programs for girls under the age of nineteen that was founded after girls-only programs at the local boys' hockey leagues ended.[29] They provide Tier II adolescent teams that attend the Hockey Youth Nationals in their respective age groups. Adult women have the Seattle Women's Hockey Club, which competes in local tournaments but primarily serves as a recreational league. Perhaps if the NHL expands to Seattle, we will see an expansion team from one of the two professional women's leagues that operate in North America, the Canadian Women's Hockey League (CWHL) and the National Women's Hockey League (NWHL). Both leagues have teams that are closely affiliated with and in some cases owned by NHL teams. The NWHL is currently only located on the East Coast, but the CWHL has a team as far west as Calgary, Alberta and an additional two teams located in China. An expansion team for the CWHL in Seattle would make a great deal of sense as a bridge between Calgary and China.

The Thunderbirds continue to play in Kent, about thirty minutes outside of Seattle, and by all outward appearances seem to be a healthy and thriving team. After fan complaints about the aging infrastructure at the Seattle Coliseum (now known as the KeyArena), the team relocated to a new arena in Kent, though they are still known as the Seattle Thunderbirds. While the team does not play in Seattle proper any longer, Seattle hockey's legacy lives on through them to this day. In 2017, they won the Western Hockey League Championships for the first time in the club's history after losing in the finals the previous year. The team became a major draw for the WHL, who saw enough appetite for hockey in the region to add a second team located just north of Seattle in the city of Everett. The Everett Silvertips franchise was awarded in 2001 and played their first season from 2003–2004. Today, a fierce rivalry exists between the Silvertips and the Thunderbirds, or the Tips and the Birds, as they are sometimes known among fans. Though there is certainly some overlap of the fan bases, there are more-than-enough hockey fans in the region to fill both ShoWare Arena in Kent and Xfinity Arena in Everett. [30]

Where the future of major league hockey in Seattle lies is a question that had been in significant flux in recent history. In June 2015, NHL Commissioner Gary Bettman said just prior to a Board of Governors meeting that, "in Seattle's case, the arena situation still seems to have some uncertainty. But perhaps the process will bring some certainty to the arena situation. Nobody has the arena act together yet in Seattle."[31] At the time, there was a proposal to build a new arena in the SoDo (South of Downtown) Seattle neighborhood, near CenturyLink Field and Safeco Field, where the Seattle Seahawks, Sounders, and Mariners play. While the group hoping to build that arena had a Memorandum of Understanding with the city council, they were stuck in a holding pattern and unable to proceed. Other arenas were proposed in nearby Tukwila and Bellevue, though these never went much further than the proposal stage. The possibility of renovating the Seattle Coliseum, which had been built in the 1960s, up to modern standards was estimated to be a nine-figure investment, a stiff bill for taxpayers to get something other than a brand-new facility.[32]

However, the long uncertainty was finally settled. In 2017, the city of Seattle came to an agreement with the Oak View Group (OVG) to renovate KeyArena at the Seattle Center—the venue that was once called the Coliseum and former home to both the Thunderbirds and Totems—to bring it up to modern standards using private funding rather than taxpayer dollars.[33] Based on that agreement, the NHL accepted an initial bid for an expansion team and granted the city a team in 2018. Local hockey historian Jeff Obermeyer knew that an NHL team could succeed in the area, given the current model of how NHL teams do business:

> The NHL lacks the mega television deals of the other three major leagues, so its teams are heavily reliant on ticket sales for their financial success. Is Seattle ready to consistently support a professional hockey team? I certainly

think so. With the Thunderbirds and Silvertips both successful, and Tacoma having a history with minor and junior league teams, there is a wide market of fans who would certainly come to the city for games. Certainly the success of a new team will play a role in attendance, especially after the honeymoon period is over, but the sports culture in Seattle, combined with the ever-growing youth hockey community, should keep the seats filled.[34]

The season ticket deposit drive held on March 1st, 2018, which had to be capped at 33,000 sales, certainly seemed to indicate that he was correct in this assessment and was perhaps the green light the NHL. The ticket deposit drive for the Las Vegas Golden Knights, the last franchise awarded by the NHL, took six weeks to collect their 10,000 target deposits. Seattle's ticket drive reached that figure in just twelve minutes.[35]

Seattle, while it was the first American city to have a team drink from Lord Stanley's Cup, may finally be considered a serious hockey city now that it once again has an NHL team. As with Guyle Fielder's exclusion from the Hockey Hall of Fame, Seattle was kept out of contention for any kind of hockey honors until the NHL's 2018 decision. Despite the expanse of time between the existence of professional hockey teams in Seattle, it nonetheless forever has a place in the history of hockey thanks to the 1917 Metropolitans' Stanley Cup victory.

If Seattle is to be recognized as a hockey city, hopefully it will do so by embracing its own nontraditional history of identity rather than clinging to the narrow but sadly historically accurate definition of hockey as a sport that centers white, heterosexual, cisgender males. With the city's hockey history, its roots to early women's hockey, and connections to local tribal communities, perhaps the best way to move forward as a hockey destination is to embrace in a more holistic fashion communities that are often marginalized by both hockey culture and society as a whole. Perhaps a partnership, more than mere cultural appropriation, but a true partnership complete with youth programs serving local tribes could lead to a more diverse and therefore strengthened hockey community. The next great Seattle hockey player could be from a local community with the deepest roots to the land. While young Canadian women and young American women from more traditional hockey states (Minnesota, Wisconsin, Massachusetts, and New York, for example) are already making strides to elevate the women's game to a competitive level with men's hockey, players from nontraditional hockey markets are still considered a novelty. The 2018 Winter Olympics saw the United States women's hockey team bring home the gold medal for the first time since 1998, and the women's professional NWHL and CWHL are giving women an option to continue playing after college beyond mere recreational leagues. The Washington Wild could be home to the next generation of young women who will help bring the women's game to a level of parity (or, at the very least, proximity) with the NHL. At a free event on March 10, 2018, hosted by the Wild to encourage local girls to try out the game of hockey, more than fifty girls between the ages of four and fourteen got their first taste of the game. Although the scholarly thing to do here is to leave all personal narrative aside, I must note that I was personally in attendance as well, as a volunteer helping girls onto the ice and passing around pucks. The enthusiasm and delight of the next generation of local women for the game of hockey was electric, and there is an exciting future ahead for the women's game in the area. With an NHL expansion franchise in Seattle finally a reality once again, the area seems poised to embrace its history not only as hockey champions of the world but as a city at the forefront of progress.

Notes

Introduction

1. Charles R. Cross, *Room Full of Mirrors: A Biography of Jimi Hendrix* (New York: Hyperion, 2005), "Author's Note."

2. John Vidale, "One year ago, Seattle Seahawks 12th Man Earthquake," Pacific Northwest Seismic Network, accessed January 3, 2019, https://pnsn.org/blog/2011/12/31/one-year-ago-seattle-seahawks-12th-man-earthquake; Joshua Mayers, "Looking Back at the 'Beast Quake' Run on its Three-Year Anniversary," *Seattle Times*, January 8, 2014.

3. Lenny Wilkens, interview with Terry Anne Scott, Medina, Washington, January 14, 2017.

4. Ashley Steward, "June 1, 1979: Seattle SuperSonics Win the NBA Title," *The Daily Herald* (Everett, Washington), May 30, 2013, accessed June 26, 2018, https://www.herald net.com/news/june-1–1979-seattle-supersonics-win-nba-title.

5. Ben Eagle, "Richard Sherman Calls Out Michael Crabtree in All-Time Postgame Interview," *Sports Illustrated*, January 19, 2014.

6. Eagle, "Richard Sherman"; Kyle Wagner, "The Word 'Thug' Was Uttered 625 Times on TV on Monday. That's A Lot," *Deadspin*, January 21, 2014, accessed January 2, 2018, https://deadspin.com/the-word-thug-was-uttered-625-times-on-tv-yesterday-1506098319.

7. Cindy Boren, "Richard Sherman Frustrated by Reaction, Equates 'Thug' with Racial Slur," *The Washington Post,* January 23, 2014.

8. Ryan Wilson, "Richard Sherman: 'Thug' Is Accepted Way of Calling Someone N-word," CBS Sports, January 22, 2014, accessed December 20, 2017, https://www .cbssports.com/nfl/news/richard-sherman-thug-is-accepted-way-of-calling-someone -n-word.

9. Larry Stone, "Sherman: 'I'm the Furthest Thing from a Thug,'" *Seattle Times*, January 23, 2014; "Seahawks Fans Tell CBS4'S Stan Bush Richard Sherman Is No 'Thug,'" CBS4, accessed December 31, 2017, http://denver.cbslocal.com/2014/01/23/seahawks -fans-tell-cbs4s-stan-bush-richard-sherman-is-no-thug.

10. Michael J. Socolow, "Six Minutes in Berlin," *Slate*, July 23, 2012, accessed January 3, 2019, http://www.slate.com/articles/sports/fivering_circus/2012/07/_1936_olympics _rowing_the_greatest_underdog_nazi_defeating_american_olympic_victory_you _ve_never_heard_of_.html.

11. James Daniel Brown, *Boys in the Boat: Nine Americans and Their Epic Quest for Gold at the 1936 Berlin Olympics* (New York: Penguin Books, 2013).

12. Steven Goff, "Soccer Is Different in Seattle. You'll See Why in COPA America Quarterfinals," *Washington Post,* June 15, 2016.

13. Goff, "Soccer Is Different."

14. The Greater Seattle Soccer League, "A Short History of the GSSL," TeamSideline,

accessed January 2, 2019, https://www.teamsideline.com/Assets/767/GSSL%20brochure
.pdf; Grant Wahl, "Streakless in Seattle: A Long History of Choking Ends with a Title for
MLS's Darlings," *Sports Illustrated*, December 19, 2016; Joe Smith, "West Seattle Soccer—
The Early Years," West Seattle Soccer Club, accessed January 2, 2019, http://www.west
seattlesoccer.org/WSSC_History; "Hope Solo," Team USA, accessed January 2, 2019,
https://www.teamusa.org/us-soccer/athletes/Hope-Solo; See also Hope Solo, *Solo:
A Memoir of Hope* (New York: HarperCollins, 2012); Nicholas Mendola, "U.S. Players in
the 2017–18 Premier League," NBC Sports, accessed January 2, 2019, https://soccer.nbc
sports.com/2018/05/15/how-did-u-s-players-fare-in-the-2017–18-premier-league-season.

15. Frederick James Grant, *History of Seattle, Washington: With Illustrations and
Biographical Sketches* (New York: American Publishing and Engraving, 1891), see preface.

16. Gene Balk, "114,000 More People: Seattle Now Decade's Fastest-Growing Big City
in All of U.S.," *Seattle Times*, May 24, 2018

Chapter 1

This chapter was previously published in Chris Donnelly, *Baseball's Greatest Series:
Yankees, Mariners, and the 1995 Matchup That Changed History* (Piscataway, NJ: Rutgers
University Press, 2010).

1. David Wilma, "From Cranks to Fans: Seattle's Long Love Affair with Baseball,"
HistoryLink.org, July 10, 2001, 1; Kenneth Hogan, *The 1969 Seattle Pilots: Major League
Baseball's One-Year Team* (Jefferson, NC: McFarland, 2007), p. 10.

2. Hogan, *The 1969 Seattle Pilots*, pp. 11–12, 154. Russ Dille, "Play Ball! A Slide Show
History of Early Baseball in Washington," HistoryLink.org, January 1, 2003, p. 8.

3. Russ Dille, "Play Ball! A Slide Show History of Early Baseball in Washington,"
HistoryLink.org, January 1, 2003, p. 8.

4. Hogan, *The 1969 Seattle Pilots*, p. 15.

5. John Reeves, "Seattle Angels," Seattle Mariners Dugout, 2000, geocities.com
/colosseum/field.

6. Jim Bouton, *Ball Four* (New York, NY: Wiley, 1970), p. 15.

7. Bouton, *Ball Four*, p. 15.

8. Philip Lowry, *Green Cathedrals* (Reading, MA: Addison Wesley, 1993), p. 217.

9. Hy Zimmerman, "Finley Asks for Kindly Approach to Expansion," *Seattle
Times*, January 16, 1976.

10. Lowry, *Green Cathedrals*, p. 217.

11. Wilma, "From Cranks to Fans," p. 3.

12. Bouton, *Ball Four*, p. 103.

13. Hogan, *The 1969 Seattle Pilots*, p. 128.

14. "Expected Shift of Pilots: High Hopes to a Disaster," *Seattle Post-Intelligencer*,
March 16, 1970.

15. Hogan, *The 1969 Seattle Pilots*, p. 128.

16. "Wanna 'Play Ball' with the Pilots?" *Seattle Post-Intelligencer*, March 1, 1970.

17. Lenny Anderson, "Seattle Could Still Lose Pilots, P-I Writer Says," *Seattle Post-
Intelligencer*, March 8, 1970; Larry McCarten, "It's Off to Milwaukee for Pilots," *Seattle
Post-Intelligencer*, April 1, 1970.

18. Slade Gorton, interview by Chris Donnelly, November 7, 2007.

19. Dick Rockne, "A.L. 'Doctored' Resolution," *Seattle Times*, January 22, 1976.

20. Art Thiel, *Out of Left Field: How the Mariners Made Baseball Fly in Seattle* (Seattle: Sasquatch Books, 2003), 13.

21. J. Michael Kenyon, "57,000 Cheer Mariners," *Seattle Post-Intelligencer*, April 7, 1977.

22. Thiel, *Out of Left Field*, p. 14.

23. "1977 Seattle Mariners Statistics," Baseballreference.com, https://www.baseball -reference.com/teams/SEA/1977.shtml.

24. Dick Rockne, "The Way It Was," *Seattle Times*, March 26, 1997, F8.

25. Gordon Wittenmyer, "The Gory Years," *Seattle Times*, October 6, 1995, E3.

26. Thiel, *Out of Left Field*, p. 272.

27. Randy Adamack, interview by Chris Donnelly, November 9, 2007.

28. Byron Rosen, *Washington Post*, July 15, 1977, D3.

29. "Pitching Improbables," *Seattle Post-Intelligencer*, May 12, 2006, C2.

30. Wittenmyer, "The Gory Years," E3.

31. Thiel, *Out of Left Field*, p. 7.

32. Kirby Arnold, *Tales from the Seattle Dugout* (Champaign, IL: Sports Publishing, 2007), p. 19.

33. Barry Horstman, "Field of Play: New Owner of the Padres Liked Trip around Bases on Way to Business Success," *Los Angeles Times*, April 12, 1987, Metro pt. 2, p. 1.

34. United Press International, January 8, 1981.

35. George Argyros, telephone interview by Chris Donnelly, March 5, 2008.

36. "A.L. Owners Approve Two Sales," *New York Times*, January 30, 1981, A20.

37. Horstman, "Field of Play," 1; Arthur Lingle, "George Argyros: Sportsman, Developer, Philanthropist," *Orange County Business Journal* 10, no. 8, April 27, 1987, p. 12.

38. "Orioles' Pitching, Royals' Hitting Are the Key Factors; Eastern Division," *New York Times*, April 5, 1981, sec. 5, p. 10.

39. Argyros, interview.

40. "1981 Seattle Mariners Statistics," Baseballreference.com, https://www.baseball -reference.com/teams/SEA/1981.shtml.

41. Thiel, *Out of Left Field*, p. 5.

42. Arnold, *Tales*, p. 65.

43. Maury Wills and Mike Celizic, *On the Run: The Never Dull and Often Shocking Life of Maury Wills* (New York: Carroll & Graf, 1991), p. 126.

44. Arnold, *Tales*, p. 65.

45. Thiel, *Out of Left Field*, p. 6.

46. Wills and Celizic, *On the Run*, p. 126.

47. Thiel, *Out of Left Field*, p. 7.

48. "1981 Seattle Mariners Statistics," Baseballreference.com, https://www.baseball -reference.com/teams/SEA/1981.shtml.

49. Jim Street, "Hindsight on a Funny Anniversary," MLB.com, May 8, 2003; "1982 Seattle Mariners Statistics," Baseballreference.com, reference.

50. Thiel, *Out of Left Field*, p. 7.

51. United Press International, June 26, 1983.

52. Wittenmyer, "The Gory Years," E3.

53. G. S. Khalsa, United Press International, June 25, 1983.

54. Jim Cour, "BBA: Mariners-Williams," Associated Press, May 9, 1986.

55. *Los Angeles Times*, July 11, 1985, part 3, p. 16.

56. "1986 Seattle Mariners Statistics," Baseballreference.com, https://www.baseball-reference.com/teams/SEA/1986.shtml; "1986 Boston Red Sox Statistics," Baseball reference.com, https://www.baseball-reference.com/teams/BOS/1986.shtml.

57. Cour, "BBA."

58. Brian Mottaz, United Press International, May 9, 1986.

59. Jim Cour, Associated Press, May 16, 1988.

60. Dennis Anstine, United Press International, June 6, 1988.

61. Bob Slocum, "Williams' Exit Repeats Old Pattern," *San Diego Union-Tribune*, June 7, 1988, C5.

62. Michael Emmerich, *100 Things Mariners Fans Should Know & Do Before They Die*, (Chicago: Triumph Books LLC, 2015), p. 208.

63. "Mariners, Astros Hire Managers," *Washington Post*, November 8, 1988.

64. Arnold, *Tales*, p. 53.

65. Argyros, interview.

66. Thiel, *Out of Left Field*, p. 16.

67. Ken Phelps, telephone interview by Chris Donnelly, May 27, 2007.

68. Arnold, *Tales*, p. 53.

69. Phil Bradley, telephone interview by Chris Donnelly, November 15, 2007.

70. "Pitching Improbables," C2.

71. Thiel, *Out of Left Field*, p. 16.

72. "Baseball," *Washington Post*, March 27, 1987, D2.

73. Dennis Georgatos, Associated Press, March 26, 1987.

74. Thiel, *Out of Left Field*, p. 17.

75. Dave Distel, "San Diego Sportscene: Next Time, Argyros May Just Send Flowers," *Los Angeles Times*, April 22, 1987, part 3, p. 1.

76. Distel, "San Diego Sportscene," p. 1.

77. Jim Street, "Indianapolis Ownership for M's," *Sporting News*, September 4, 1989, p. 16.

78. George Armstrong, interview by Chris Donnelly, November 8, 2007.

79. Larry LaRue, "Kingdome, Like Mariners, May Get a Facelift," *Los Angeles Times*, November 12, 1989, C4.

80. LaRue, "Kingdome," p. 4.

81. Arnold, *Tales*, p. 89.

82. Thiel, *Out of Left Field*, pp. 18, 49.

83. Thiel, *Out of Left Field*, pp. 18, 49.

84. Herman Sarkowsky, telephone interview by Chris Donnelly, October 29, 2007.

85. Gorton, interview.

86. Gorton, interview.

87. Gorton, interview.

88. Thiel, *Out of Left Field*, p. 50.

89. Howard Lincoln, telephone interview by Chris Donnelly, 2007.

90. Gorton, interview.

91. Thiel, *Out of Left Field*, p. 51.

92. Lincoln, interview.

93. John Ellis, interview by Chris Donnelly, November 8, 2007.

94. Norm Rice, telephone interview by Chris Donnelly, November 7, 2007.

95. Thiel, *Out of Left Field*, p. 66.

96. Lincoln, interview.

97. Thiel, *Out of Left Field*, p. 73.

98. Lincoln, interview.

99. Lincoln, interview.

100. Ellis, interview; Chuck Armstrong, telephone interview by Chris Donnelly, 2007.

101. Thiel, *Out of Left Field*, p. 88.

102. Lou Piniella, telephone interview by Chris Donnelly, February 23, 2007.

103. Piniella, interview.

104. Ellis, interview.

105. Piniella, interview.

106. Ellis, interview.

107. Jay Buhner, interview by Chris Donnelly, 2007.

108. Chris Bosio, telephone interview by Chris Donnelly, October 5, 2007.

109. Thiel, *Out of Left Field*, p. 79.

110. Bosio, interview.

111. Rick Griffin, interview by Chris Donnelly, November 8, 2007.

112. Thiel, *Out of Left Field*, p. 80,

113. Griffin, interview.

114. Ronald Blum, Associated Press, June 3, 1987.

115. Mike Cameron, telephone interview by Chris Donnelly, February 12, 2008.

116. Thiel, *Out of Left Field*, p. 25.

117. Chuck Armstrong, interview.

118. Chuck Armstrong, interview.

119. Chuck Armstrong, interview.

120. Ibid.

121. Bosio, interview.

122. Darren Bragg, telephone interview by Chris Donnelly, February 12, 2008.

Chapter 2

1. Ashley Steward, "June 1, 1979: Seattle SuperSonics Win the NBA Title," *The Daily Herald* (Everett, Washington), May 30, 2013, accessed June 26, 2018, https://www.herald net.com/news/june-1-1979-seattle-supersonics-win-nba-title; Randy Wilkens, telephone interview by Terry Anne Scott, July 10, 2018; Kiro 7 News archival televised footage of SuperSonics victory, June 2, 1979.

2. Randy Wilkens, interview; Gil Lyons, "Long, Lean Years Now History for Lenny," *Seattle Times*, June 2, 1979; "Seattle 'Prepped' for SuperSonics' Victory Parade," *Seattle Times*, June 7, 1979; "Students Took 'History' Lesson in the Streets," *Seattle Times*, June 5, 1979.

3. Gus Williams, telephone interview by Terry Anne Scott, July 17, 2018; "Police Found Parade Crowd Well-behaved," *Seattle Times*, June 5, 1979; Kiro 7 News report, televised, June 4, 1979; Lenny Wilkens, interview by Terry Anne Scott, Clyde Hill, Washington, January 14, 2017.

4. Williams, interview, 2018; Lenny Wilkens, interview by Terry Anne Scott, Bellevue, Washington, June 2017.

5. Lenny Wilkens, interview, January 14, 2017; Gary Smith, "He Has Overcome: The

Key to Lenny Wilkens, Soon to Pass Red Auerbach as the NBA's Winningest Coach, Lies Deep in His Past," *Sports Illustrated*, December 5, 1994; Lenny Wilkens with Terry Pluto, *Unguarded: My Forty Years Surviving in the NBA* (New York: Simon & Schuster: 2000).

6. Randy Wilkens, interview; Williams, interview; Gil Lyons, "'Never Give Up': Sonics Followed Wilkens' Playbook Instructions to the End," *Seattle Times*, May 22, 1978; Smith, "He Has Overcome"; Marilyn Wilkens, telephone interview by Terry Anne Scott, October 17, 2018.

7. Lenny Wilkens, interview by Terry Anne Scott, Bellevue, Washington, June 2018; Patti Payne, "Basketball Legend Lenny Wilkens Draws Starts to Upcoming Event," *Puget Sound Business Journal*, 2013; Dr. Ben Danielson, interview by Terry Anne Scott, June 4, 2018; Vicki-Ann Downing, "Champion at Life: Basketball Star Lenny Wilkens '60," Providence College, October 20, 2016, https://news.providence.edu/champion-at-life-lenny-wilkens-60.

8. Lenny Wilkens, interview, January 14, 2017.

9. Lenny Wilkens, interview, January 14, 2017.

10. Lenny Wilkens, interview, January 14, 2017; Wilkens and Pluto, *Unguarded*, pp. 18, 29.

11. Wilkens and Pluto, *Unguarded*, pp. 18, 29.

12. Lenny Wilkens, interview, January 14, 2017; Wilkens and Pluto, *Unguarded*, p. 14.

13. Lenny Wilkens, interview, June 2017 and June 2018; Matias Echanove, "Bed-Stuy on the Move: Demographic Trends & Economic Development in the Heart of Brooklyn" (master's thesis, Columbia University, 2003); Tricia Lee Riley, interview by Terry Anne Scott, Brooklyn, New York, July 31, 2018.

14. Lenny Wilkens, interview, June 2018.

15. Wilkens and Pluto, *Unguarded*, p. 14; Lenny Wilkens, interview, June 2018.

16. Wilkens and Pluto, *Unguarded*, p. 11.

17. Lenny Wilkens, interview, January 14, 2017; Wilkens and Pluto, *Unguarded*, p. 27; Downing, "Champion at Life."

18. Lenny Wilkens, interview, January 14, 2017.

19. Lenny Wilkens, interview, January 14, 2017; Wilkens and Pluto, *Unguarded*, p. 38; Mike Waters, *Legends of Syracuse Basketball* (Champaign, IL: Sports Publishing: 2004).

20. Lenny Wilkens, interview, June 2018 and June 2017; Wilkens and Pluto, *Unguarded*, pp. 39, 42–43; Downing, "Champion at Life"; "Providence College Athletic Hall of Fame," program, May 14, 1972, Providence College Manuscripts Division, Providence, Rhode Island.

21. Downing, "Champion at Life"; Lenny Wilkens, interview, June 2017; "New Release," Providence College Office of Public Information, Providence, Rhode Island, May 1980, Wilkens File.

22. Wilkens and Pluto, *Unguarded*, pp. 60, 64; Lenny Wilkens, interview, June 2017;

23. Lenny Wilkens, interview, June 2017 and June 2018; Wilkens and Pluto, *Unguarded*, p. 92.

24. Wilkens and Pluto, *Unguarded*, p. 94; Lenny Wilkens, interview, June 2018 and June 2017; Colin Gordon, *Mapping Decline: St. Louis and the Fate of the American City* (Philadelphia: University of Pennsylvania, 2008), p. 43; Rev. Dr. Paul Smith, interview by Terry Anne Scott, Clarksville, Maryland, March 2018.

25. Lenny Wilkens, interview, June 2017 and June 3, 2018; Wilkens and Pluto, *Unguarded*, pp. 102–103; Percell Johnson, interview by Terry Anne Scott, Bellevue, Washington, June 2018.

26. Lenny Wilkens, interview, June 3, 2018; Randy Wilkens, interview.

27. Randy Wilkens, interview; Frank Deford, "The Sonic Boom in Seattle," *Sports Illustrated*, October 9, 1967.

28. Dennis McLellan, "Sam Schulman, 93; Original Owner of the Seattle SuperSonics Who Changed NBA's Draft Policy," *Los Angeles Times*, June 14, 2003; Slick Watts and Frank Hughes, *Slick Watts's Tales from the Seattle SuperSonics* (Champaign, IL: Sports Publishing, 2005), p. 109; Dave Fisher, "Sam Schulman—The Key to the Merger," *Life* magazine, April 23, 1971.

29. Fisher, "Sam Schulman—The Key to the Merger,"; Frank P. Jozsa, *The National Basketball Association: Business, Organization and Strategy* (New Jersey: World Scientific, 2011), p. 26; Gregory Peters, *The Man of La Manga* (Xlibris Corporation), p. 229.

30. Gil Lyons, "Remember the Beginning? Sonic Start Was Disastrous," *Seattle Times*, June 7, 1979; Wilkens and Pluto, *Unguarded*, pp. 126–127, 129, 134.

31. "Sam Schulman, 93, Team Owner Who Defied N.B.A. Draft Rules," *New York Times*, June 16, 2003; McLennan, "Sam Schulman, 93"; Lenny Wilkens, interview, June 2017.

32. Ozzie Roberts, "Annual Pro Basketball Roundup: Players Profit from War Between the Leagues," *Ebony Magazine*, January 1974; Wilkens and Pluto, *Unguarded*, pp. 136, 139; Aram Goudsouzian, *King of the Court: Bill Russell and the Basketball Revolution* (Berkeley: University of California Press, 2010), p. 324; "Sonics Coaching History," *Seattle Times*, October 28, 2007; Deford, "The Sonic Boom in Seattle."

33. Goudsouzian, *King of the Court*, pp. 251, 253, 324-325 ; "Sonics Discharge Nissalke as Coach; Assistant Promoted," *Seattle Times*, January 11, 1973; Wilkens and Pluto, *Unguarded*, p. 153; Mike Gastineau, Steve Rudman, and Art Thiel, *The Great Book of Seattle Sports Lists* (Philadelphia: Running Press, 2009), p. 442; "Bianchi Quits as Coach of Seattle N.B.A. Team," *New York Times*, July 12, 1969; Roberts, "Annual Pro Basketball Roundup."

34. "Sonics Discharge Nissalke as Coach; Assistant Promoted," *Seattle Times*, January 11, 1973.

35. George Plimpton, "Sportsman of the Year: Bill Russell," *Sports Illustrated*, December 23, 1968; "19th Hole: The Readers Take Over," *Sports Illustrated*, August 18, 1969; Murray R. Nelson, *Bill Russell: A Biography* (Westport, Connecticut: Greenwood Press, 2005), pp. 24, 36; "Farewell to a Basketball Legend Red Auerbach: 1917–2006," NBA Encyclopedia, accessed June 26, 2018, http://www.nba.com/encyclopedia/auerbach_tribute.html; Goudsouzian, *King of the Court*, p. 68.

36. Bill Russell, *Second Wind: The Memoirs of an Opinionated Man*, (New York: Random Hours, 1979), pp. 254–255.

37. Russell, pp. 254–255; Goudsouzian, *King of the Court*, pp. 251, 253; Donald "Slick" Watts, interview by Terry Anne Scott, Seattle, Washington, June 2018.

38. Russell, p. 256; Lenny Wilkens, interview, June 2018.

39. Nate LeBoutillier, *The Story of Seattle Supersonics* (Creative Education, 2007); "Bob Hopkins," Louisiana *Sports* Hall of Fame, accessed August 2, 2018, www.lasportshall.com/?inductees=bob-hopkins; "Russell Leaves Sonics After 4 Years of Helm," *The New York Times*, May 5, 1977.

40. Watts, interview; Donald Hunt, "Former HBCU Basketball Legend Bob Hopkins Dies at Age 80," *Philadelphia Tribune*, May 28, 2015; Russell, pp. 158–159.

41. Wilkens and Pluto, *Unguarded*, p. 153; Ron Thomas, *They Cleared the Way: The NBA's Black Pioneers* (Lincoln: University of Nebraska Press, 2002), p. 219.

42. Wilkens and Pluto, *Unguarded*, pp. 154–155.

43. Wilkens and Pluto, *Unguarded*, p. 156; Jeff Pearlman, "SuperSonics Center Marvin Webster May 22, 1978," *Sports Illustrated*, May 5, 1997; Richard Goldstein, "Marvin Webster, Basketball's Human Eraser, Dies at 56," *New York Times*, April 8, 2009.

44. Sam Goldaper, "Paul Silas: Spirit of the Sonics," *New York Times*, May 22, 1978; Wilkens and Pluto, *Unguarded*, pp. 156, 159

45. John Papanek, "Add Super to the Sonics," *Sports Illustrated*, January 9, 1978; Wilkens and Pluto, *Unguarded*, pp. 161–163; Lenny Wilkens, interview by Terry Anne Scott, Bellevue, Washington, June 4, 2018.

46. Greg Heberlein, "Sonics Name Wilkens Coach," *The Seattle Times*, November 30, 1977; Lenny Wilkens, interview, June 2018; Goldaper, "Paul Silas"; Papanek, "Add Super"; Wilkens and Pluto, *Unguarded*, p. 165; Greg Heberlein , "Quick-change Sam Returns to Lenny," *Seattle Times,* December 1, 1977.

47. Lenny Wilkens, interview, June 4, 2018; Greg Heberlein, "Bottom Line: 'You Got to Win': Team Was in Mental Rut, Hoppy Admits," *Seattle Times*, December 1, 1977; "NBA Box Scores," *Washington Post*, November 28, 1977.

48. Watts and Hughes, *Slick Watts's Tales*, p. 112; Lenny Wilkens, interview, June 2018.

49. Lenny Wilkens, interview, June 4, 2018; Wilkens and Pluto, *Unguarded*, pp. 164–165; Papanek, "Add Super"; Heberlein, "Bottom Line."

50. Lenny Wilkens, interview, June 4, 2018; see Nate LeBoutillier, *Seattle Supersonics (The NBA: A History of Hoops)*, (Creative Entertainment, 2006); Wilkens and Pluto, *Unguarded*, p. 167; "1976-77 Seattle SuperSonics Roster and Stats," Basketballreference.com, https://www.basketball-reference.com/teams/SEA/1977.html; Williams, interview; "Former Celtics Guard Johnson Dies Suddenly at 52," February 23, 2007, accessed August 8, 2018, http://www.espn.com/nba/news/story?id=2775430; Lenny Wilkens, interview, June 2018.

51. Randy Wilkens, interview; Sam Goldaper, "Stylish Backcourtmen Put Sonics on the Road to N.B.A. Glory," *New York Times*, June 3, 1979; Papanek, "Add Super"; LeBoutillier, *The Story of the Seattle Supersonics*, p. 17.

52. The emphasis on *the* before University of Southern California belongs to Williams. During my interview with him for this chapter, Williams was living in South Carolina. He said that when he mentioned he went to "USC," people in the state assumed that he was referring to the University of South Carolina. His desire to differentiate between his beloved alma mater and the latter university prompted the distinction.

53. Williams, interview; Goldaper, "Stylish Backcourtmen."

54. Williams, interview; Wilkens and Pluto, *Unguarded*, p. 170; "High on Cable," *Sports Illustrated*, August 17, 1981.

55. "Blazers Stay Alive, Rout Sonics, 113–89," *New York Times*, May 1, 1978; Wilkens and Pluto, *Unguarded*, p. 171.

56. Lyons, "'Never Give Up;'" Jack Broom, "With a Sigh, Fans Say: 'Next Year,'" *Seattle Times*, June 8, 1979; Jack Broom and Jerry E. Carson, "Thousands Line SuperSonic Heroes' Parade," *Seattle Times*, June 8 1979; Pearlman, "Supersonics Center Marvin Webster"; Wilkens and Pluto, *Unguarded*, pp. 172, 174.

57. Jack Broom and Jerry E. Carson, "Thousands Line SuperSonic Heroes' Parade."

58. Jack Broom and Jerry E. Carson, "Thousands Line SuperSonic Heroes' Parade."

59. Watts, interview; Greg Heberlein, "Wilkens Sees No Fan Upheaval over Trade," *Seattle Times*, January 5, 1978.

60. Greg Heberlein, "Sonics Get Denver's LeGarde," *Seattle Times*, June 9, 1971; Wilkens and Pluto, *Unguarded*, p. 177; Jeff Pearlman, "SuperSonics Center Marvin Webster."

61. Wilkens and Pluto, *Unguarded*, pp. 174, 184; Williams, interview; John Papanek, "It Was Seattle, Handily," *Sports Illustrated*, June 11, 1979.

62. Lenny Wilkens, interview, June 2018; cite article; Kiro 7 News televised footage of SuperSonics victory, June 2, 1979; Don Duncan, "Sonic Strut: A Jam Session Extraordinaire," *Seattle Seahawks*, June 5, 1979.

Chapter 3

I am grateful to Nic Bacetich, Bruce Caszett, Stuart Feil, Ron Fox, Fred Parham, and Brian Washburn whose generosity made this chapter possible.

1. Stuart Feil, interview by Rita Liberti, Seattle, Washington, June 17, 2016.

2. The Emerald City Softball Association (hereafter ECSA) was organized in 1980. For more information on the organization, see "ECSA," Emerald City Softball Association, accessed September 17, 2016, http://www.emeraldcitysoftball.org/.

3. Fred Parham, phone interview with Rita Liberti, September 9, 2016.

4. Other US cities were host to organized gay softball before Seattle. For example, San Francisco, Los Angeles, Milwaukee, and New York City appear to be the earliest to organize softball within gay communities. On San Francisco's league history, circa 1976, see Teddy Luther, "One of First Gay Sports Leagues in Nation Offers Competition, Inclusion," *San Francisco Examiner*, June 22, 2016, accessed September 18, 2016, http://www.sfexaminer.com/first-gay-softball-league-nation-offers-competition-inclusion/. The Los Angeles organization formed in 1978. See "History of GLASA," The Greater Los Angeles Softball Association, accessed September 18, 2016, http://www.glasasoftball.org /about/. The Saturday Softball League (SSBL) of Milwaukee formed in 1977. See "History of SSBL," Saturday Softball League Milwaukee, accessed September 18, 2016, http:// www.ssblmilwaukee.com/pages/ssblhistory. New York City's league began in 1976, see "History," Big Apple Softball League, accessed September 18, 2016, http://www.bigapple softball.com/about/history/.

5. Brian Pronger, "Homosexuality and Sport: Who's Winning," in *Masculinities, Gender Relations, and Sport*, eds. Michael A. Messner and Don Sabo (Thousand Oaks, CA: Sage, 2000), p. 223. Seattle's gay community rallied around softball and quickly established not only the ECSA but also larger events that featured the sport. The Cascade Cup, an annual softball tournament in Seattle beginning in 1981, attracted teams from across the US and Canadian West. "Out of Town Softballers to Join SGAA Cascade Cup Tournament," *Seattle Gay News* [hereafter *SGN*], May 22, 1981, p. 9.

6. According to the North American Gay Amateur Athletic Alliance (NAGAAA) website, the first gay softball World Series took place in 1977. In 1979 representatives from New York City, Milwaukee, San Francisco, Los Angeles and Toronto, Canada, joined, as the inaugural cities, to form NAGAAA. See "Donate to the Archives," NAGAAA Softball, accessed September 10, 2016, http://www.nagaaasoftball.org/archives/.

7. Andrew D. Linden and Lindsay Parks Pieper, "The Gay Games: Then and Now," Sport in American History, accessed September 8, 2016, https://ussporthistory.com/2014 /08/21/the-gay-games-then-and-now/. For an overall history of the Gay Games, see Caroline Symons, *The Gay Games: A History* (London: Routledge, 2010).

8. Pronger, "Homosexuality and Sport," p. 223.

9. David Carter, *Stonewall: The Riots that Sparked the Gay Revolution* (New York: St. Martin's, 2004), p. 8.

10. Thomas J. Linneman, *Weathering Change: Gay and Lesbians, Christian Conservatives, and Everyday Hostilities* (NY: New York University Press, 2003). For a good discussion about perceptions of Seattle as a progressive city and the realities of racial injustice, see Quintard Taylor, *The Forging of a Black Community: Seattle's Central District from 1870 through the Civil Rights Era* (Seattle: University of Washington Press, 1994), pp. 3–13.

11. Don Paulson with Roger Simpson, *An Evening in the Garden of Allah: A Gay Cabaret in Seattle* (New York: Columbia University Press, 1996), p. 3.

12. John Wilson and Marshall Wilson, "Tavern Operators Describe 'Payoffs,'" *Seattle Times*, January 16, 1967, p. 4. For a comprehensive historical account of Seattle's police pay-off system in the first seven decades of the twentieth century, see Christopher T. Bayley, *Seattle Justice: The Rise and Fall of the Police Payoff System in Seattle* (Seattle: Sasquatch Books, 2015). Bayley suggests that the illicit police activity was centered on the city's early gay bars but not specific to them. A Federal Bureau of Investigation review in 1966 led to an internal reorganization of the department, which in turn resulted in the end of the pay-off system by the late 1960s. A number of police officers, local officials, and others through the early 1970s were charged with various crimes as a result of their involvement in the elaborate system.

13. John Wilson, "Tolerant Reputation: Seattle Homosexual Problem Reported to be 'Out of Hand,'" *Seattle Times*, September 21, 1966, p. 48.

14. Wilson, "Tolerant Reputation."

15. Paul Henderson, "Seattle's Homosexuals Ask: 'Understand; Don't Generalize,'" *Seattle Times*, December 9, 1969, p. 60.

16. Dudley Clendinen and Adam Nagourney, *Out for Good: The Struggle to Build a Gay Rights Movement in America* (New York: Simon & Schuster, 1999), p. 12.

17. Marjorie Jones, "Editor Cites Progress of Gay People in Seattle," *Seattle Times*, April 4, 1976, A4.

18. Dean Katz, "GAY SEATTLE: A Large and Diverse Population is No Longer Quite so Hidden," *Seattle Times*, January 29, 1984, F1.

19. Rick Anderson, "Seattle Has Variety—Even a Transvestites' Potluck," *Seattle Times*, March 14, 1982, C1.

20. William Duvall, "Leisure and Lifestyles Among Gay Men: An Exploratory Essay," *International Review of Modern Sociology* 9, no. 2 (1979), p.185.

21. Michael Brown, "Working Political Geography Through Social Movement Theory: The Case of Gay and Lesbian Seattle," in *The Sage Handbook of Political Geography*, eds. Kevin R Cox, et al. (London: Sage, 2008), p. 294.

22. "Gay Hiking Club," *SGN*, June 1976, p. 7.

23. Bill Parkins, "Bowling," *SGN*, November 1976, p. 11.

24. Stephen Wells, "In Spite of the Weather Opportunities for Gettin' [sic] Outdoors," *SGN*, April 1977, p. 9.

25. Robin Evans, "Sunday Morning Bowling Has Become Traditional," *SGN*, May 22, 1981, p. 1.

26. The *SGN* reported on athletic activity in Seattle throughout this period. The newspaper established a dedicated sports section in 1981.

27. Karen Frank, "SGAA's Expo Full of Fun," *SGN*, September 15, 1981, p. 1. Seattle Mayor Charles Royer was on hand to open the Expo, an indication of the gay community's increasing visibility and power.

28. Frank, "SGAA's Expo," p. 8.

29. Ron Fox, interview with Rita Liberti, Seattle, Washington, June 16, 2016. By the early 1980s the center of Seattle's gay life had moved from Pioneer Square to the city's Capitol Hill neighborhood.

30. Wells, "In Spite of the Weather," pp. 8–9.

31. Allan Bérubé, *Coming Out Under Fire: A History of Gay Men and Women in World War II* (Chapel Hill: University of North Carolina Press, 2010), 271; Brown, "Working Political Geography Trough Social Movement Theory," p. 294.

32. Bruce Caszatt, interview with Rita Liberti, Seattle, Washington, June 16, 2016.

33. Fox, interview.

34. Feil, interview.

35. Feil, interview.

36. Gary L. Atkins, *Gay Seattle: Stories of Exile and Belonging* (Seattle: University of Washington Press, 2003), p. 55.

37. Feil, interview.

38. Clendinen and Nagourney, *Out for Good,* p. 14.

39. John Bell, "Homosexuals Charge Harassment," *Seattle Times,* December 6, 1972, E18; "Gay Liberation Leader Calls Arrest Police Harassment," *Seattle Times,* October 19, 1973, B5.

40. Gay resistance, as well as a more visible gay public presence across Seattle, grew throughout the 1970s. Gay Pride events appear to have gotten started as early as 1974. Beginning in 1975 gay leaders in the community sent a request to Seattle's mayor to issue an official Gay Pride Week proclamation. Mayor Uhlman did not that year nor the next but did in 1977. The act was not well received by all Seattleites. Gay visibility and power continued to rise, and by 1978, more than 4,000 people marched in the city's Gay Pride Parade. On gay rights in Seattle in the 1970s, see "Open Letter to Mayor Uhlman," *SGN,* June 1976, p. 3; Charles Dunsire, Debra Dragovich, and Jim Arnold, "4,000 Gays March in Seattle," *SGN,* July 7, 1978, p. 1. On the gay community's effort to access more civic power, see Joan Wolverton, "Gay Community Wants Police Representation," *Seattle Times,* May 20, 1975, B2; Karen West, "Gays: 'We're Your Neighbor, Colleague, Kid,'" *Seattle Post Intelligencer,* December 14, 1975, D2; Patricia Foote, "Gay Nominees Included on Commission Slate," *Seattle Times,* May 18, 1976, D1; Atkins, *Gay Seattle,* p. 168.

41. Lillian Faderman, *The Gay Revolution: The Story of the Struggle* (New York: Simon & Schuster, 2015), p. 384.

42. Amy L. Stone, *Gay Rights at the Ballot Box* (Minneapolis: University of Minnesota Press, 2012), pp. 13–15; Walter Frank, *Law and the Gay Rights Story: The Long Search for Equal Justice in a Divided Democracy* (New Brunswick, NJ: Rutgers University Press, 2014), pp. 51–53.

43. "Anita Bryant on Most 'Admired' List," *Seattle Times,* December 13, 1977, E1.

44. Seattle's television stations battled over the issue. Lloyd Cooney, president of KIRO-TV, aired a four-part television editorial in defense of Initiative 13. Alice Blanchard of KSTW-TV also ran a several part series as a "welcome contrast" to Cooney's telecasts. John Voorhees, "Channel 11 Plans Gay Report," *Seattle Times,* June 24, 1977, A11. For more on this TV-news debate, see Susan Paynter, "KIRO Wires on Fire Over Gay Editorials," *Seattle Post Intelligencer,* May 18, 1977, B3; "Pickets Protest KIRO Attack on Gay Rights," *Seattle Post Intelligencer,* May 20, 1977, A8.

45. Faderman, *The Gay Revolution,* p. 384.

46. "Bowl Against 13!" *SGN,* June 23, 1978, p. 8.

47. "Bowling Over 13," *SGN*, August 4, 1978, p. 9.

48. "Turn it Around Seattle," *SGN*, October 13, 1978, 5; Sandy Rae, "Run Against 13," *SGN*, October 13, 1978, p. 5.

49. "Thank You, Seattle," *SGN*, November 10, 1978, p. 2.

50. "Skate for SCAT," *SGN*, January 19, 1979, p. 14.

51. "Mayor Signs Proclamation for Gay Pride Week," *SGN*, June 8, 1979, p. 1.

52. "Cause of 'Gay Cancer' Unclear," *SGN*, January 1–14, 1982, p. 1

53. Warren King, "Deadly Disease That Mainly Affects Gay Men Surfaces in Seattle," *Seattle Times*, November 12, 1982, A1.

54. Atkins, *Gay Seattle*, p. 295.

55. Atkins, *Gay Seattle*, p. 295, p. 311. Susan Buskin, Michael Hanrahan, and Tom Jaenicke, eds., "HIV/AIDS 2015 Epidemiology Report: Washington State—Seattle and King County," King County, accessed September 1, 2016, https://www.kingcounty.gov /depts/health/communicable-diseases/hiv-std/patients/~/media/depts/health /communicable-diseases/documents/hivstd/2015-hiv-aids-epidemiology-annual -report.ashx.

56. Feil, interview.

57. "Cops vs. Gays: 3rd Annual 'Jocks in Dresses' Ball Game," *SGN*, March 29, 1985, p. 8; Chuck Martin, "Fundraising Swim to Benefit PWAs [Person With AIDS]," *SGN*, June 24, 1988, 15; Atkins, *Gay Seattle*, p. 338.

58. "HIV and AIDS—United States, 1981–2000," Centers for Disease Control and Prevention, accessed June 30, 2016, https://www.cdc.gov/mmwr/preview/mmwrhtml /mm5021a2.htm.

59. Caszatt, interview.

60. Jay Paul, Robert B. Hays, and Thomas J. Coates, "The Impact of the HIV Epidemic on U.S. Gay Male Communities," in *Lesbian, Gay, and Bisexual Identities Over the Lifespan: Psychological Perspectives*, ed. Anthony R. D'Augeli and Charlotte J. Patterson (New York: Oxford University Press, 1994), pp. 347–397.

61. Nic Bacetich, interview with Rita Liberti, Seattle, Washington, June 17, 2016.

62. Feil, interview.

63. Bacetich, interview.

64. Fox, interview.

65. Bacetich, interview.

66. Feil, interview.

67. Brian Washburn, interview with Rita Liberti, Seattle, Washington, June 17, 2016.

68. Washburn, interview.

69. Michael A. Messner and Donald F. Sabo, *Sex, Violence and Power in Sports: Rethinking Masculinity* (Berkeley, CA: Crossing Press, 1994), p. 119.

70. "Backlots, Baseball, and Beer," *SGN*, February 26-March 11, 1982, p. 3.

71. Feil, interview.

72. Washburn, interview.

73. Fox, interview.

74. Fox, interview. Based on my conversations with ECSA ballplayers, whose involvement with the league stretched well over two decades, encounters with homophobic fans and players were rare, but they did occur. At the 1994 World Series in Nashville, Tennessee, for example, Ron Fox remembers that participating teams needed a police escort as they entered the softball complex, given the threats made against the athletes and the mere presence of a gay athletic event in the city.

75. Fox, interview.

76. Hugo Kugiya, "Batboys Making Big Noise," *Seattle Times*, July 4, 1991, D1.

77. Michael A. Messner, *Sport and Culture: Taking the Field: Women, Men, and Sports* (Minneapolis: University of Minnesota Press, 2002), 30, 35; Perry Deane Young, *Lesbians and Gays and Sports* (New York: Chelsea House, 1995), p. 13.

78. "Gay Athletic Association Thrives: Join a Softball Team," *SGN*, April 24, 1981, p. 17. The article states that the Seattle Athletic Association got its start in March 1980. It seems there were a handful of gay athletic organizations in Seattle throughout the early 1980s, and this certainly underscores the burgeoning interest in sport within the community.

79. Parham, interview.

80. Ron Fox, phone interview with author, September 13, 2016. On the issue of troubling orthodox understandings of masculinity in gay sporting culture, see Varda Burstyn, *The Rites of Men: Manhood, Politics, and the Culture of Sport* (Toronto: University of Toronto, 1999), p. 217.

81. Fox, interview.

82. Brian Pronger, *The Arena of Masculinity: Sports, Homosexuality, and the Meaning of Sex* (New York: St. Martin's Press, 1990), p. 227.

83. Nigel Jarvis, "Ten Men Out: Gay Sporting Masculinities in Softball," in *Sport, Sexualities, and Queer/Theory*, ed. Jayne Caudwell (New York: Routledge, 2006), pp. 62–75.

84. Parham, interview.

85. Washburn, interview.

86. Feil, interview.

87. Feil, interview.

88. Pronger, , *The Arena of Masculinity: Sports, Homosexuality, and the Meaning of Sex*, p. 226.

89. Feil, interview.

90. Pronger, , *The Arena of Masculinity: Sports, Homosexuality, and the Meaning of Sex*, pp. 221–222. Also see Allan Bérubé, *Coming Out Under Fire* (Chapel Hill: University of North Carolina Press, 2010), p. 86.

91. Caszatt, interview.

92. On the Miss ECSA Pageant and the Miss Batboy contest: Fox, interview. See also: "Jocks in Frocks," *SGN*, June 27, 1986, pp. 16–17; "Sunday Softball Social," *SGN*, March 22, 1985, p. 8; "Annual Jocks in Dresses Game Will be Held June 15," *SGN*, June 7, 1985, p. 7. Athletes in drag fundraisers were a popular way to raise money beyond the ECSA. In an effort to provide financial support to Seattle's 1982 Gay Games, team organizers used drag events. See "Jocks Go Drag for Gay Games," *SGN*, July 16, 1982, p. 6; Leonard (Lenny) Larson, "Athletic Supporter," *SGN*, September 10–23, 1982, p. 5.

93. Feil, interview.

94. Caszatt, interview.

95. Feil, interview.

96. "Inductee Bios–Fred Parham," Emerald City Softball Association, accessed September 10, 2016, http://www.emeraldcitysoftball.org/pages/HOF.

97. Richard Dyer, "It's Being So Camp As Keeps Us Going," in *Camp: Queer Aesthetics and the Performing Subject: A Reader*, ed. Fabio Cleto (Ann Arbor: The University of Michigan Press, 1999), pp. 110–116.

98. Victor Wellington Jones, "Disco Drill Team Exposed," *SGN*, March 12–25, 1982, p. 9. The local gay press touted the Disco Drill Team and the cheering squad, the

Tuggettes [named for the Tugs softball team], as part of the reason why gay softball spectators had so much fun at games. See; "Backlots, Baseball, and Beer," p. 3.

99. Jones, p. 9.

100. Bruce Caszatt, email correspondence with author, August 30, 2016.

101. Fox, interview.

102. Fox, interview; Caszatt, interview.

103. Andy Medhurst, "Camp," in *Lesbian and Gay Studies: A Critical Introduction*, eds. Andy Medhurst and Sally R. Munt (London: Cassell, 1997), p. 275.

104. Peter Nardi, *Gay Men's Friendships: Invincible Communities* (Chicago: The University of Chicago Press, 1999).

105. Caszatt, email correspondence.

106. Caszatt, email correspondence.

107. Parham, interview.

Chapter 4

1. The opinions expressed in this chapter are those of the author and not necessarily of the editors of this volume.

2. "Bob Houbregs, Basketball Hall of Fame Member, Dies at 82," *New York Times*, May 30, 2014.

3. Francesca Murman and Alice Park, "Understanding King County Racial Inequities: King County Racial Disparity Data," United Way of King County, November 2015.

4. See Quintard Taylor, *The Forging of a Black Community* (Seattle: University of Washington, 1994); Center for the Study of the Pacific Northwest, "Lesson Twenty-One: African Americans in the Modern Northwest," University of Washington, accessed July 9, 2018, http://www.washington.edu/uwired/outreach/cspn/Website/Classroom%20 Materials/Pacific%20Northwest%20History/Lessons/Lesson%2021/21.html; George Tamblyn, "Grose, William (1835–1898)," Black Past, accessed January 11, 2019, https:// blackpast.org/aaw/grose-william-1835–1898.

5. The name of this person has been changed for this essay.

Chapter 5

This chapter was previously published in Shelley Lee, *Claiming the Oriental Gateway: Prewar Seattle and Japanese America* (Philadelphia: Temple University Press, 2012).

1. George Okada, "Taiyo Teaches High Principles," *Japanese-American Courier*, March 17, 1934.

2. Albert G. Spalding, *America's National Game: Historic Facts Concerning the Beginning, Evolution, Development and Popularity of Base Ball* (Lincoln: University of Nebraska Press, 1992), p. 533.

3. Spalding, *America's National Game*, p. 533.

4. Okada, "Taiyo Teaches High Principles."

5. "Nice Going Gals," *Japanese-American Courier*, July 22, 1939.

6. Peter Levine, *A. G. Spalding and the Rise of Baseball: The Promise of American Sport* (New York: Oxford University Press, 1985), chap. 6; Janet A. Northam and Jack W.

Berryman, "Sport and Urban Boosterism in the Pacific Northwest: Seattle's Alaska-Yukon-Pacific Exposition, 1909," *Journal of the West* 17, no. 3 (1978): 53–60; S. W. Pope, *Patriotic Games: Sporting Traditions in the American Imagination, 1876–1926* (New York: Oxford University Press, 1997).

7. Matthew Klingle, *Emerald City: An Environmental History of Seattle* (New Haven, CT: Yale University Press, 2007), chap. 4.; on the promotion of Seattle as a recreation city, see Janet Northam Russell and Jack W. Berryman, "Parks, Boulevards, and Outdoor Recreation: The Promotion of Seattle as an Ideal Residential City and Summer Resort, 1890–1910," *Journal of the West* 26, no. 1 (1987): 5–17.

8. On Jewish American athletes, Peter Levine has shown that playing Western sports reinforced the ethnic component of personal and community identity. Peter Levine, *Ellis Island to Ebbet's Field: Sport and the American-Jewish Experience* (New York: Oxford University Press, 1992).

9. Frank Miyamoto, interview with Stephen Fugita, February 26, 1998, Densho Visual History Collection, Densho.

10. Toshio Ito, interview with Alice Ito, May 21, 1998, Densho Visual History Collection, Densho.

11. Ito, interview.

12. Mayumi Tsutakawa, "Memories of Nisei Sports Clubs," *Journal of the International District* 3, no. 7 (1976): 1.

13. "A Warning," *Japanese-American Courier*, January 28, 1928.

14. "Sport Scope: A Public Benefactor," *Japanese-American Courier*, March 3, 1928. Also see Gail M. Nomura, "Beyond the Playing Field: The Significance of Pre-World War II Japanese American Baseball in the Yakima Valley," in *Bearing Dreams, Shaping Visions: Asian Pacific American Perspectives*, edited by Linda A. Revilla, Gail M. Nomura, Shawn Wong, and Shirley Hune (Pullman, WA: Washington State University Press, 1993), p. 31; Samuel O. Regalado, "'Play Ball!': Baseball and Seattle's Japanese-American Courier League, 1928-1941," *The Pacific Northwest Quarterly*, Vol. 87, No. 1, Sports History (Winter, 1995/1996), pp. 29–37.

15. "Sport Scope: A Public Benefactor."

16. "Sport Scope: A Public Benefactor."

17. The most thorough treatment of Japanese American baseball in the Courier League can be found in Regalado, "'Play Ball!'"

18. "A Warning."

19. Yuji Ichioka, "A Study in Dualism: James Yoshinori Sakamoto and the *Japanese-American Courier*, 1928–1942," *Amerasia* 13, no. 2 (1986–1987): 49–81.

20. "Sport Scope," *Japanese-American Courier*, January 2, 1928. The Courier League also sponsored other sports, such as basketball and football, and by the 1940–1941 season, it comprised 500 athletes and fifty-five teams in all sports.

21. "Sport Scope: A Public Benefactor."

22. Regalado, "'Play Ball!'"

23. "Coast-wide . . ." *Japanese-American Courier*, February 26, 1938.

24. Quoted in Regalado, "'Play Ball!'" 34.

25. Bill Hosokawa, "Curtain Falls on Most Disastrous Baseball Season; Will Try New Strategy Next Year," *Japanese-American Courier*, September 28, 1935.

26. Budd Fukei, "Budd's Banter," *Great Northern Daily News*, January 1, 1938.

27. "Lil' Tokyo Series to Be Held Next Year," *Great Northern Daily News*, October 5, 1937.

28. "Hangovers," *Japanese-American Courier*, September 24, 1938.

29. Ryoichi Shibazaki, "Seattle and the Japanese-United States Baseball Connection, 1905–1926" (master's thesis, University of Washington, 1981), 7.

30. "Kwansei's Championship Caliber," *Japanese-American Courier*, July 28, 1928.

31. "Kwansei's Championship Caliber."

32. "Keio Sportsmanship," *Japanese-American Courier*, June 9, 1929; "Wapato Team Has Strong Lineup; Set to Meet Tokio Pros," *Japanese-American Courier*, April 27, 1935.

33. Richard C. Crepeau, "Pearl Harbor: A Failure of Baseball?" *Journal of Popular Culture* 15, no. 4 (1982): 67. Also see Regalado, "Sport and Community in California's Japanese American 'Yamato Colony,' 1930–1945," 132; and on the compatibility of Japanese values and baseball, see Robert J. Sinclair, "Baseball's Rising Sun: American Interwar Baseball Diplomacy and Japan," *Canadian Journal of History of Sport* 16, no. 2 (1985): 46.

34. "Sports Scope," *Japanese-American Courier*, December 25, 1928.

35. Sinclair, "Baseball's Rising Sun," 47.

36. "Sport Slants," *Great Northern Daily News*, July 3, 1935. According to Samuel Regalado, this tournament was also sponsored by the Courier League. Regalado, "'Play Ball!'"

37. "Intermission Numbers Set for League Event," *Great Northern Daily News*, July 3, 1935.

38. Pat Adachi, *Asahi: A Legend in Baseball* (Etobicoke, Ontario, Canada: Asahi Baseball Organization, 1992), p. 53.

39. Adachi, *Asahi*, p. 53.

40. "Same Old Story: Vancouver Asahi Tossers Defeat Fife Nippon, 10–5," *Great Northern Daily News*, July 24, 1939; "Giants Set for Canadians," *Great Northern Daily News*, August 21, 1940.

41. "Nippons Are Ready for Vancouver Clash; Close Battle Expected," *Great Northern Daily News*, August 10, 1935.

42. "Vancouver Asahis Shut Out Nippons in Close Contest," *Japanese-American Courier*, September 28, 1928.

43. Adachi, *Asahi*, p. 125.

44. "Vancouver Asahis Take Doubleheader, Series from Taiyo," *Japanese-American Courier*, September 8, 1934.

45. Budd Fukei, "Budd's Banter," *Great Northern Daily News*, July 8, 1941.

46. Fukei, "Budd's Banter," July 8, 1941.

47. Tsutakawa, "Memories of Nisei Sports Clubs."

48. George Ishihara, "We Oldsters," *Great Northern Daily News*, January 1, 1938.

49. "N.A.C. Wins Tilts 9–0 over Royal Colored Giants," *Japanese-American Courier*, April 12, 1930.

50. "Canadians . . ." *Japanese-American Courier*, July 30, 1938.

51. "Four Races Seen in Mixed Bouts on Fight Card at Crystal Pool," *Northwest Enterprise*, March 5, 1931.

52. "Harold Hoshino Scores Technical Knockout Win over Nationalista," *Great Northern Daily News*, November 16, 1938.

53. Eiichiro Azuma, "Racial Struggle, Immigrant Nationalism, and Ethnic Identity: Japanese and Filipinos in the California Delta, 1930–1941," *Pacific Historical Review* 67 (May 1998): 163–199; Chris Friday, *Organizing Asian American Labor: The Pacific Coast Canned-Salmon Industry, 1870–1942* (Philadelphia: Temple University Press, 1994), 130–131.

54. "Beware of Romance with Filipinos," *Great Northern Daily News*, August 8, 1940.

55. "Arai Bowls Self into Big League Company with 200; Match On," *Great Northern Daily News*, January 5, 1935.

56. "Barber Shop Team Favored to Win over Japanese All-Stars," *Great Northern Daily News*, November 10, 1934.

57. "Filipino Barber Four Give New Trimming to Japanese Bowlers," *Great Northern Daily News*, November 27, 1934.

58. "Filipino Barber Four Beat Japanese Pinmen," *Great Northern Daily News*, November 19, 1934.

59. "Arai Bowls Self into Big League Company."

60. Chris Friday, "Recasting Identities: American-Born Chinese and Nisei in the Era of the Pacific War," in *Power and Place in the North American West*, ed. Richard White and John M. Findlay (Seattle: University of Washington Press, 1999), p. 145.

61. "Hangovers," *Japanese-American Courier*, February 13, 1937.

62. "Sport Scope: Buck Lai, Wonder Boy," *Japanese-American Courier*, February 11, 1928. For more on the Hawaiian team that Lai played for, see "Chinese Tour Revives Memories," *Japanese-American Courier*, April 27, 1925.

63. "Hangovers," *Japanese-American Courier*, January 24, 1937.

64. On Chinese American basketball, see Kathleen Yep, *Outside the Paint: When Basketball Ruled at the Chinese Playground* (Philadelphia: Temple University Press, 2009).

65. "Hangovers," *Japanese-American Courier*, November 16, 1935.

66. "Seven Straight Won by Chinese," *Japanese-American Courier*, February 2, 1929.

67. "China Club to Meet Hi-Stars," *Japanese-American Courier*, March 16, 1929.

68. "Lil' Tokyo Series to Be Held Next Year."

69. "China Club to Meet Hi-Stars."

70. "Sports Dusts," *Great Northern Daily News*, November 25, 1940.

71. "Oriental Hoopers Will Clash Tonight," *Japanese-American Courier*, March 3, 1929.

72. "Comedy Marks First Oriental Grid Meet," *Japanese-American Courier*, October 31, 1931.

73. "Comedy Marks."

74. Eddie Luke, "Hangovers," *Japanese-American Courier*, November 28, 1936.

75. "China Club Downs Black Hawks 21–14," *Great Northern Daily News*, January 10, 1935.

76. "Nisei and Chinese Play Together for Victory Says P-I Writer," *Great Northern Daily News*, February 4, 1941.

77. "Hangovers," *Japanese-American Courier*, September 24, 1938.

78. Luke, "Hangovers," November 28, 1936.

79. "Hangovers," *Japanese-American Courier*, June 19, 1937.

80. "Nice Going Gals," *Japanese-American Courier*, July 22, 1939.

81. "No Color Line," *Japanese-American Courier*, November 20, 1937.

82. Editorial, "Sportsmanship and Loyalty," *Northwest Enterprise*, August 14, 1936.

83. Of the 41 bouts for which results are known, his record is 36 wins, 3 losses, and 2 draws. Because 29 of these victories were by knockout, Hoshino became known as the Japanese Sandman or Homicide Hal and a hero to the *Nisei* of the Pacific Coast. Joseph R. Svinth, "Harold Hoshino, the Japanese Sandman," *Journal of Combative Sport*, June 2002, available at http://ejmas.com/jcs/jcsframe.htm (accessed August 8, 2007).

84. *Japanese-American Courier*, November 20, 1938.

85. Linda España-Maram, *Creating Masculinity in Los Angeles's Little Manila: Working-Class Filipinos and Popular Culture, 1920s–1950s* (New York: Columbia University Press, 2006), 81, 94.

86. Bud Fukei, "Budd's Banter," *Great Northern Daily News,* January 18, 1941.

87. "Sport Scope," *Japanese-American Courier,* January 21, 1928.

88. "Hangovers," *Japanese-American Courier,* August 19, 1939.

89. James Shinkai, "Sport Scope: Democracy in Action," *Japanese-American Courier,* December 23, 1933.

90. "Japanese Nines Promotes Respect among Fandom," *Japanese-American Courier,* January 14, 1932.

91. "Japanese Nines Promotes."

92. "No Color Line."

93. Memo, September 27, 1929, Ben Evans Recreation Program Collection [hereafter Evans Collection], Box 5, Folder 5, Seattle Municipal Archives [hereafter SMA]; Pearl Powell, Playfield Report, Summer 1931, Evans Collection, Box 41, Folder 14, SMA.

94. Pearl Powell, Playfield Report, Summer 1931, Evans Collection, Box 41, Folder 14, SMA.

95. "Biography of H. S. Boy," Survey of Race Relations, Box 27, Folder 151, SMA.

96. Alice M. Lopp, "Report of the Activities Carried On at the Collins Field House," October 1932–April 1933, Evans Collection, Box 5, Folder 6, SMA.

97. Nobuko Yamaguchi, Playground Report to Ben Evans, 1930, Evans Collection, Box 41, Folder 14, SMA.

98. Pearl Powell, Playfield Report, Summer 1931, Evans Collection, Box 41, Folder 14, SMA.

99. "68 Japanese Play for Collins Fives," *Japanese-American Courier,* November 21, 1936.

100. *Seattle Post-Intelligencer,* February 28, 1949; "2 Collins Teams Win to Take Leadership," *Japanese-American Courier,* December 26, 1931.

101. "Vince O'Keefe: And Now, Time Off for Just Fishin,'" *Seattle Times,* January 21, 1972.

102. Phil Taylor, "Collins Kids—One World: Boyd's Cagers Form United Nations," *Seattle Times,* January 27, 1948.

103. Letter from James Sakamoto to Don Evans, January 13, 1942, Evans Collection, Box 5, Folder 6, SMA.

104. Crepeau, "Pearl Harbor," p. 72.

105. Crepeau, "Pearl Harbor," p. 72.

Chapter 6

1. "About Us: Founders Club," Rat City Roller Derby, accessed March 25, 2018, http://ratcityrollergirls.com/about-us/founders-club; "About Us: A Brief History," Rat City Roller Derby, accessed March 25, 2018, http://ratcityrollergirls.com/about-us/a-brief-history; Glenn Drosendahl, "Rat City Rollergirls," HistoryLink.org, December 7, 2013, accessed March 25, 2018, http://www.historylink.org/File/10664; Aja Pecknold, "SIFF: Rat City Rollergirls on Film!," *Seattle Weekly,* June 12, 2007, accessed March 18, 2018, http://archive.seattleweekly.com/2007-06-13/film/siff-rat-city-rollergirls-on-film; Allecia Vermillion, "Top Chef Seattle Episode 8: Jalapeno Business," *SeattleMet,* December 27, 2012, accessed March 18, 2018, https://www.seattlemet.com/articles/2012

/12/27/top-chef-seattle-episode-8-jalapeno-business; Ann Powers, "Watch: Pearl Jam In Conversation with Judd Apatow," *NPR Music,* October 8, 2013, accessed March 18, 2018, http://www.npr.org/2013/10/08/225471645/watch-pearl-jam-in-conversation-with-judd -apatow; "Seattle City Council Proclaims Rat City Rollergirl Day at City Hall!," Rat City Roller Derby, accessed March 18, 2018, http://ratcityrollergirls.com/news/seattle-city -council-proclaims-rat-city-rollergirl-day-at-city-hall; "Show Us Your Cans: Canned Food Drive with Rat City Rollergirls," Rat City Roller Derby, accessed March 18, 2018, http:// ratcityrollergirls.com/news/show-us-your-cans-canned-food-drive-with-rat-city -rollergirls; Tom Ellis, "2012 Down Syndrome Community of Puget Sound Buddy Walk," Tom Ellis Photography, accessed March 18, 2018, http://www.tomellisphoto.com/blog /2012-down-syndrome-society-buddy-walk; "Sockit Wenches Revving to Steal Rat City Championship from Undefeated Grave Danger," Rat City Roller Derby, accessed March 18, 2018, http://ratcityrollergirls.com/news/sockit-wenches-revving-to-steal -rat-city-championships-from-undefeated-grave-danger

2. Keith Coppage, *Roller Derby to Rollerjam: The Authorized Story of an Unauthorized Sport* (Oxford, Mississippi: Squarebooks Inc., 1999), pp. 2–3; Jennifer Barbee and Alex Cohen, *Down and Derby: The Insider's Guide to Roller Derby* (New York: Soft Skull Press, 2010), pp. 11–13; Catherine Mabe, *Roller Derby: The History and All-Girl Revival of the Greatest Sport on Wheels* (Denver: Speck Press, 2007), p. 23.

3. Barbee and Cohen, *Roller Derby to Rollerjam,* pp. 14–17; Mabe, *Roller Derby,* p. 39.

4. Coppage, *Roller Derby to Rollerjam,* pp. 6, 35.

5. Coppage, *Roller Derby to Rollerjam,* p 10.

6. Coppage, *Roller Derby to Rollerjam,* pp. 50–52; Jason Lewis, "Darlene Anderson Broke Roller Derby Color Barrier in 1958," *Los Angeles Sentinel,* January 20, 2011, https:// lasentinel.net/darlene-anderson-broke-roller-derby-color-barrier-in-1958.html, accessed March 13, 2018.

7. Barbee and Cohen, *Down and Derby,* pp. 32–43.

8. Barbee and Cohen, pp. 44–47; "Welcome to Roller Derby!," Women's Flat Track Derby Association, accessed March 25, 2018, https://wftda.com/new-fans.

9. "WFTDA Leagues," Women's Flat Track Derby Association, accessed March 23, 2018, https://wftda.com/wftda-leagues/#; "2011 RDWC," Roller Derby World Cup, accessed March 19, 2018, https://rollerderbyworldcup.com/2011-rdwc; "List of Roller Derby Leagues," Derby Listing, accessed March 23, 2018, http://derbylisting.com/dl /grid.

10. "Rankings: February 28, 2018," Women's Flat Track Derby Association, accessed March 20, 2018, https://wftda.com/rankings-february-28–2018; "About Us: The Rat's Nest," Rat City Roller Derby, accessed March 20, 2018, http://ratcityrollergirls.com /about-us/the-rats-nest.

11. Drosendahl, "Rat City Rollergirls;" "The Hood," White Center, accessed May 24, 2018, http://visitwhitecenter.com/the-hood; Ron Richardson, "White Center–Thumbnail History," *HistoryLink.org,* July 23, 2008, accessed March 20, 2018, http://www.historylink .org/File/8616.

12. Brooklyn Defiance, "What's in a Name?," Derby Central, February 11, 2015, accessed March 20, 2018, http://www.derbycentral.net/2015/02/whats-name; "About Us: A Brief History," Rat City Roller Derby, accessed March 20, 2018, http://ratcityrollergirls.com /about-us/a-brief-history.

13. Hurt Reynolds, "Rat City Breaks Modern Attendance Record," June 7, 2010, Derby

News Network, accessed March 21, 2018, http://www.derbynews.net/2010/06/07/rat_city_breaks_modern_attendance_record.

14. "The Rules of Flat Track Roller Derby," Women's Flat Track Derby Association, accessed March 21, 2018, https://rules.wftda.com.

15. Zach Dundas, *The Renegade Sportsman: Drunken Runners, Bike Polo Superstars, Roller Derby Rebels, Killer Birds, and Other Uncommon Thrills on the Wild Frontier of Sports.* (New York: Riverhead Books, 2010), p. 194; Barbee and Cohen, *Down and Derby*, p. 38.

16. Overbeaters Anonymous, "About," Facebook, accessed March 21, 2018, https://www.facebook.com/pg/OverbeatersAnonymous/about/?ref=page_internal.

17. "Roller Derby over 40," Facebook, accessed March 22, 2018, https://www.facebook.com/groups/derbyover40; Seattle Derby Brats, accessed March 22, 2018, http://www.seattlederbybrats.com; Derby Over 40, accessed March 22, 2018, http://www.derbyover40.us.

18. In the Turn, December 11, 2019, https://www.imdb.com/title/tt3796388/.

19. Jane McManus, "Transgender Athletes Find Community, Support in Roller Derby," *ESPN W*, November 12, 2015, accessed March 23, 2018, http://www.espn.com/espnw/athletes-life/article/14110104/transgender-athletes-find-community-support-roller-derby; "WFTDA Gender Statement," Women's Flat Track Derby Association, September 30, 2016, accessed March 23, 2018, https://wftda.com/wftda-gender-statement; "MRDA Non-Discrimination Policy," Men's Roller Derby Association, accessed March 23, 2018, https://mrda.org/resources/mrda-non-discrimination-policy.

20. Scarbie Doll,, "Roller Derby and Diversity," Derby Central, March 31, 2015, accessed March 23, 2018, http://www.derbycentral.net/2015/03/roller-derby-and-diversity.

Chapter 7

1. Tamagotchi and Giga Pets were handheld digital pets popular with children in the late 1990s.

2. Disc golf, GUTS, and freestyle are other disc-related games. Disc golf is essentially golf with specialized discs, GUTS is a competition in which players hurl a soft disc at each other in hopes of getting it past a line of opponents. Freestyle is more of a competitive dance using the disc as a focal accessory; Pasquale Anthony Leonardo and Adam Zagoria. *Ultimate: The First Four Decades* (Los Altos, CA: Ultimate History, 2005). Jerome Pohlen, *Oddball Michigan: A Guide to 450 Really Strange Places* (Chicago: Chicago Review Press, 2014), p. 5.

3. "About Ultimate," USA Ultimate, December 1, 2015, accessed October 20, 2016, https://www.usaultimate.org/about.

4. "USA Ultimate Strategic Plan," USA Ultimate, January 1, 2013, accessed March 18, 2017, https://www.usaultimate.org/strategic_plan.

5. "USA Ultimate Strategic Plan"; Dominique Fontenette, interview by Elliot Trotter, Seattle, Washington, October 8, 2016.

6. Fontenette, interview.

7. Fontenette, interview; Matthew "Skip" Sewell, interview by Elliot Trotter, Seattle, Washington, October 26, 2016.

8. Gwen Ambler, interview with Elliot Trotter, Seattle, Washington, *Ultimate History* (October 26, 2016); Ben Wiggins, interview with Elliot Trotter, Seattle, Washington, October 17, 2016.

9. Miranda Roth, interview with Elliot Trotter, Seattle, Washington, October 10, 2016

10. Chase Sparling-Beckley, interview with Elliot Trotter, Seattle, Washington, October 18, 2016.

11. Sparling-Beckley, interview; Tyler Kinley, interview with Elliot Trotter, Seattle, Washington, October 18, 2016.

12. Roth, interview.

13. William Bartram, interview with Elliot Trotter, Seattle, Washington, September 13, 2016.

14. Bartram, interview.

15. Bartram, interview.

16. Arnoush Javaherian, interview with Elliot Trotter, Seattle, Washington, October 9, 2016; Ambler, interview; Shannon O'Malley, interview with Elliot Trotter, Seattle, Washington, October 18, 2016.

17. Ambler, interview.

18. Ambler, interview.

19. Ambler, interview.

20. Sewell, interview.

21. Chris Page, interview with Elliot Trotter, October 27, 2016.

22. O'Malley, interview.

23. Khalif El-Salaam, interview with Elliot Trotter, November 23, 2016.

24. Ben Wiggins, interview.

25. Ambler, interview.

26. Ambler, interview.

27. Heather Ann Brauer, interview with Elliot Trotter, November 29, 2016.

28. "About," AGE UP, accessed April 24, 2018, http://www.allgirleverything.org; "History," Youth Ultimate Project, accessed April 24, 2018, http://www.youthultimate project.org/our-history; Laurie Ann Thompson, *Be a Changemaker: How to Start Something that Matters* (New York: Simon Pulse, 2014), pp. 102–103.

29. O'Malley, interview.

30. Mary Lowry, interview with Elliot Trotter, October 26, 2016.

31. Jeff Jorgenson, interview with Elliot Trotter, November 6, 2016.

32. Jorgenson, interview.

33. Leonardo and Zagoria, *Ultimate: The First Four Decades*, Appendix B.

34. Jorgenson, interview; Lowry, interview.

35. Lowry, interview.

36. Lowry, interview.

37. Mike Mullen, interview with Elliot Trotter, November 16, 2016.

38. Britt Atack, interview with Elliot Trotter. October 26, 2016.

39. Mullen, interview; Lowry, interview.

40. Christian Jennewein, "Ultimate going strong in Colombia," Ultimate Central, accessed April 25, 2018, https://ultimatecentral.com/en_us/p/ultimate-going-strong-in-colombia.

41. Kate Kingery, interview with Elliot Trotter, October 22, 2016; Sewell, interview.

42. Sparling-Beckely, interview.

43. Sewell, interview.

44. Sewell, interview.

45. Sewell, interview; Rohre Titcomb, interview with Elliot Trotter, October 24, 2016.

46. Connor Radnovich, "Quirky Family Company Catches on with Ultimate Players," *Seattle Times*, August 2, 2012.

47. "About," All-Star Ultimate Tour, accessed March 16, 2018, online video, http://www.allstarultimatetour.com/about; *All-Star Ultimate Tour: The Documentary*, directed by Alex Axworthy (2016; Seattle, All-Star Ultimate Tour).

48. Ambler, interview.

49. *El Nivel, El Grande*. Directed by Gil Mcintire Elliot Trotter. Performed by Liam Rosen, Victor Torruco, Elliot Trotter, 2014.

50. "Ultimate GT," "Episode 1: Boracay Dragons," YouTube video, posted on June 2, 2014; "Episode 2: Auckland Magon," YouTube video, posted on October 17, 2014; "Episode 3: Melbourne Heads of State," YouTube video, posted on February 5, 2015; "Episode 4: Copenhagen Ragnorak," YouTube video, posted on October 8, 2015; "Episode 5: World Championships of Beach Ultimate," YouTube video, posted on January 11, 2016; "Episode 6: Vancouver Furious George," YouTube video, posted on January 26, 2017.

51. Ben Van Heuvelen, "What Do We Stand For?" *Skyd Magazine*, March 11, 2013, accessed June 15, 2016, http://skydmagazine.com/2013/03/what-do-we-stand-for.

52. Charlie Eisenhood and Nathan Jesson, "This Was Ultimate: The Story Of Major League Ultimate," Ultiworld, March 2, 2017, accessed March 3, 2017, https://ultiworld .com/2017/03/02/ultimate-story-major-league-ultimate/; Organizers of the AUDL Boycott, "Statement from the Organizers of the AUDL Boycott," *Skyd Magazine*, December 13, 2017, accessed March 25, 2018. http://skydmagazine.com/2017/12 /statement-organizers-audl-boycott

53. "About Us," Seattle Cascades, accessed April 29, 2018, http://www.seattlecascades .com/about-us.

54. Sparling-Beckley, interview.

55. Sparling-Beckley, interview.

Chapter 8

1. For more on women's swimming in the 1920s, see Lisa Bier, *Fighting the Current: The Rise of American Women's Swimming, 1870–1926* (Jefferson, NC: McFarland & Company, Inc., Publishers, 2011).

2. Tiffany Lewis, "Municipal Housekeeping in the American West: Bertha Knight Landes's Entrance into Politics," *Rhetoric and Public Affairs 14*. no.3 (2011): p. 467. For more on Seattle during this time period, see Sandra Haarsager, *Bertha Knight Landes of Seattle: Big-City Mayor* (Norman: University of Oklahoma Press, 1994); Richard C. Berner, *Seattle 1900–1920: From Boomtown, Urban Turbulence, to Restoration* (Seattle: Charles Press, 1991). Landes was certainly qualified for leadership, as she had held the position of president in the following organizations: Women's Century Club, Seattle Federated Women's Clubs, Coterie Club, University Heights PTA, Washington State League of Women Voters, YWCA, and the American Federation of Soroptimist Clubs. She also founded the Women's City Club.

3. Doris H. Pieroth, "Bertha Knight Landes: The Woman Who Was Mayor," *The Pacific Northwest Quarterly 75*, no. 3 (July 1984): 117.

4. Tiffany Lewis, "Municipal Housekeeping," p. 466.

5. Pieroth, "Bertha Knight Landes," p. 123. Lewis notes that the Edwards campaign focused on Landes's gender. See Lewis, "Municipal Housekeeping," p. 483.

6. Don Duncan, "Seattle's Mark Spitz of 1932," *Seattle Times Magazine*, May 13, 1973, p. 5; Don Duncan, "Green Lake: A Place for Fun," *Seattle Times*, April 19, 1980, A10.

7. Alex Shults, "Credit Him; Ray Daughters Starts Seattle Girl to Fame," *Seattle Times*, January 20, 1930, 16; Peter Salvus, "Diving Events Fancy Ones in Swim Tourney," *Seattle Times*, April 17, 1929. At that meet, Madison won the 50-yard freestyle, 100-yard freestyle, and 100-yard backstroke.

8. "Swim Records May Fall in Dual Meet Tuesday," *Seattle Sunday Times*, June 2, 1929; "Crystal Club Swimmers Go to Portland," *Seattle Times*, July 9, 1929.

9. Peter Salvus, "Helene Madison Again Smashes Record; Seattle's Best Girl Natator Double Winner," *Seattle Times*, July 11, 1929.

10. "Girl Swimmer Seeks Records," *Seattle Times*, July 23, 1929.

11. "Swimming Invasion Seeks Honors for Seattle," *Seattle Times*, July 30, 1929. In this article, it also discusses how Madison achieved the record time as a result of swimming in a smaller pool and having to do five turns. In Detroit, there would only be two turns, which would make it more difficult to break her own record.

12. Peter Salvus, "Helene Madison Nearly Defeats Senior Champion," *Seattle Times*, August 29, 1929. Also see "Match Race Up to Swim Team Stars," *Seattle Times*, August 25, 1929, 24; "Water Show Will Offer Six Events," *Seattle Times*, August 26, 1929; "Miss Madison Will Race Eastern Star," *Seattle Times*, August 27, 1929, 19; "Swim Champ Here Tonight in Exhibition," *Seattle Times*, August 28, 1929, 23.

13. Alex Shults, "Helene Madison Will Race World's Champion," *Seattle Times*, January 16, 1930, 22.

14. "Showing Friday: National Swimming Champion Against Green Lake's Best Girl Champion; Take Your Pick!" January 26, 1930, *Seattle Times*, 21; "Seattle Girl Will Battle Two Champs," *Seattle Times*, January 30, 1930, 20.

15. "Helene Madison, Seattle Girl Swimmer, Coast's Best, and Southerners Who Bow Before Her Speed," February 5, 1930, *Seattle Times*; "Helene Can 'Break Sixty' Say Critics," February 9, 1930, *Seattle Times*.

16. "Seattle Girl Will Swim at New Orleans," *Seattle Times*, February 28, 1930, 30.

17. "Helene Is After New Marks in Swim Tourney Tomorrow," March 12, 1930, *Seattle Times*; "Helene Madison Captures National Title," March 13, 1930, *Seattle Times*, 26; "Helene After More Records," March 14, 1930, *Seattle Times*, 29; "Helene Madison Creates New 100-Meter Record in Swim at Miami Beach," March 15, 1930, *Seattle Times*.

18. "Madison Colors Flash Again at Miami Tourney," March 16, 1930, *Seattle Times*.

19. "Helene Sets Six Records in One Swim," March 19, 1930, *Seattle Times*.

20. "Helene Ends Big Week With Fourth Mark," *Seattle Times*, March 18, 1930.

21. Alex Shults, "Seattle Sports Heroes Are Pushed Into Background By Young Swimmer's Feats," March 16, 1930, *Seattle Times*.

22. Peter Salvus, "Embarrassed, Yes; but She Could Swim! Helene Coming Home to Real Reception," *Seattle Times*, March 25, 1930.

23. "Give Glad Welcome to Helene Madison," *Seattle Times*, March 18, 1930.

24. "Give Glad Welcome."

25. "Helene Homeward Bound! Fandom Awaits Big Show," *Seattle Times*, March 24, 1930.

26. George M. Varnell, "Gift Fund Endangers Helene's Amateur Standing; Secretary of A.A.U. Places Ban on Token," *Seattle Times*, March 21, 1930.

27. "Gift Watch is Permissible; Fund May Be Used to Send Helene to Meets, Is Ruling," *Seattle Times*, March 24, 1930; "Dunne Clears Way for Gift to Girl Swimming Champ," *Seattle Times*, March 24, 1930.

28. "Dunne Clears Way."

29. "Helene Will Swim Here on April 4," *Seattle Times*, March 20, 1930.

30. Alex Shults, "Helene Will Swim Here April 4; Transfer From Crystal Club Explained," *Seattle Times*, March 23, 1930.

31. Shults, "Helene Will Swim Here." Also see George Varnell, "East Seeking Helene! Let's Keep Her in Seattle! This City Must First See That Trainer Sticks," *Seattle Times*, March 18, 1930.

32. Varnell, "East Seeking Helene!".

33. George M. Varnell, "Protecting Girl's Future Motive of P.N.A. Question About Scholarship, Gifts," *Seattle Times*, March 25, 1930.

34. "City to Welcome Helene Tomorrow; Young Mermaid Will Arrive at 2:30 by Plane," *Seattle Times*, March 26, 1930; "Helene Madison Glad to Get Home; Feted by City," *Seattle Times*, March 28, 1930.

35. Peter Salvus, "She Went Away, Just a Rather Young Girl; But Helene Came Home, a Famous Woman," *Seattle Times*, March 28, 1930.

36. Ray Daughters, "Helene's Tutor Sets Out To Tell Why He Likes To Swim Why He Teaches," *Seattle Times*, March 31, 1930. This comment came from Daughters's initial entry in a series on swimming that extended over several weeks. For example, see Ray E. Daughters, "Tricks Add Speed in Swimming Races; Arms 'Thrown' to Increase Momentum," *Seattle Times*, April 20, 1930.

37. "Helene's Mother Will Aid in Aquatic and Art Career," *Seattle Times*, March 26, 1930.

38. "Helene's Mother Will Aid."

39. "Helene's Mother Will Aid"; In this article, it is noted that Helene's father owns a cleaning business on East Roy Street and that the family resides on North 76th Street.

40. "Helene Madison Glad to Get Home; Feted by City," *Seattle Times*, March 28, 1930.

41. "Right Now!," March 28, 1930, *Seattle Times*.

42. Peter Salvus, "Sellout for Helene's Show Certain; Reservations Almost 1000 for National Event," *Seattle Times*, April 1, 1930.

43. Peter Salvus, "Helene's Meet Sanctioned by A.A.U.; Try at Aquatic Mark Approved by Sport Body," *Seattle Times*, April 2, 1930.

44. "Our Helene's Show Will be Big Sell-out," *Seattle Times*, April 3, 1930.

45. "300-Yard Mark in Danger; Helene Swims Tonight; Crowded Pool to Greet Girl History Maker," *Seattle Times*, April 4, 1930; Marian Badcon, "Fame Didn't Hurt Helene; Still Young," *Seattle Times*, March 28, 1930.

46. Peter Salvus, "Helene's Swim is Success; Two Records Tumble; Crystal Pool Beams Quiver as Marks Set," *Seattle Times*, April 5, 1930.

47. Varnell, "Times Dope Forecast Proves Accurate; Simpson and Tolan to Race Williams; Helene Madison Seeking More Laurels," *Seattle Times*, June 8, 1930.

48. Peter Salvus, "Ray Daughters Signs to Boss W.A.C. Mermen," *Seattle Times*, June 15, 1930. It would probably be more accurate to state that Daughters followed Madison, but Salvus used the phrase "three swimmers will follow," giving the coach some credit for Madison's move.

49. "Helene Leaves for More Fame at Long Beach," *Seattle Times*, June 23, 1930.

50. "Helene to Leave Tomorrow for Title Meet; Seattle's Great Swimmer Begins New Record Drive," *Seattle Times*, June 22, 1930.

51. Paul Zimmerman, "Quarter Mile Record for Helene Today's Promise; Mermaid Sets Two Marks in Opening Race," *Seattle Times*, July 4, 1930; "Helene Assaults New Mark

in Swim Test Today; Only 17 Years Old But She Beats 'Em All; Half-Mile Set for Local Ace at Long Beach," *Seattle Times*, July 6, 1930.

52. Paul Zimmerman, "Helene Tops World; Sets Mark in Half Mile Swim; Seattle Girl's Aquatic Feats Feature Meet," *Seattle Times*, July 7, 1930.

53. George M. Varnell, "South Wants Helene! Grid Gospel Will be Spread at Olympiad," *Seattle Times*, July 13, 1930.

54. Varnell, "South Wants Helene!"

55. "Helene Refuses $10,000 Offer," *Seattle Times*, July 8, 1930.

56. Alex Shults, "It Isn't News, But Helene Has Hard Problem; Many Youths Have Faced It; Ruth Gets Hits, Scores Runs," *Seattle Times*, July 16, 1930.

57. Peter Salvus, "Star Mermaids Will Race Here," *Seattle Times*, June 2 1930; Peter Salvus, "Crack Aquatic Stars to Swim Here Thursday," *Seattle Times*, July 8, 1930; Peter Salvus, "100 Yards Under Minute Helene's Aim Tomorrow; Seattle Girl is After One Elusive Mark," *Seattle Times*, July 9, 1930.

58. Salvus, "Star Mermaids"; Salvus, "Crack Aquatic Stars"; Salvus, "100 Yards Under Minute."

59. Peter Salvus, "Helene Tries, But Fails to Break Own World Marks; California Likes Star; Gives Her Record Gratis," *Seattle Times*, September 8, 1930; "Helene is Home From Conquests in South Waters," *Seattle Times*, September 12, 1930.

60. "Sullivan Award is Given to Jones," *Seattle Times*, December 17, 1930.

61. "Sullivan Award is Given."

62. Peter Salvus, "Fighting Heart Carries Helene to New Swim Marks; World Records Set in 440-Yard, 400-Meter Runs," *Seattle Times*, February 4, 1931.

63. Peter Salvus, "Helene Turns Down $17,500 Offer as Pro," *Seattle Times*, February 8, 1931.

64. "Helene Madison Ill; Meet Off; Billed Tuesday," *Seattle Times*, 4 March 1931, 20; "Helene Gives Up Record Assault," *Seattle Times*, March 10, 1931.

65. Peter Salvus, "Seattle's Girl Swim Team Off Tonight; Helene Heading Squad to National Meet," *Seattle Times*, April 3, 1931, 18; "Four Seattle Mermaids Near Battle Scene," *Seattle Times*, April 12, 1931, 18. Madison's teammates were Dawn Gilson, Edna McKibbon, and Lucy Schacht.

66. "W.A.C. Girls Smash 2 Swim Records; Helene Betters 50-Yard Record and Aids Relay," *Seattle Times*, April 7, 1931; "Local Natators Make Two More Aquatic Marks," *Seattle Times*, April 8, 1931; "Mark Doesn't Count, Helene Gets Speed," *Seattle Times*, April 11, 1931.

67. "Helene Retains Aquatic Honors; Local Mermaid Wins 500-Yard by Big Margin," *Seattle Times*, April 20, 1931. She also finished in third place in the backstroke, one of the few reports of Madison not winning a race.

68. Peter Salvus, "Helene, Buddies Arriving Home, to be Greeted," *Seattle Times*, May 1, 1931. Madison was interviewed about her New York experiences on KOMO radio by Ken Stuart. See "N.W. Composers' Songs to Charm on Air Tomorrow," *Seattle Times*, May 11, 1931.

69. Martha Norelius, "Beach Beauties Today, Olympic Champions Tomorrow," *Seattle Sunday Times*, May 3, 1931.

70. Norelius, "Beach Beauties Today."

71. "Helene Madison Stars at Show with Speed Spurts," *Seattle Times*, May 14, 1931; Peter Salvus, "Winged 'W' Swimmers Set Two Records; Medley Marks Chiseled by

Aquatic Squad," *Seattle Times*, May 15, 1931; Peter Salvus, "Helene Cracks World Record in 7th Attempt," *Seattle Times*, May 16, 1931.

72. "National Meet May Be Passed up by Helene," *Seattle Times*, July 7, 1931; "Paris Will See Helene in Summer," *Seattle Times*, May 30, 1931.

73. "National Meet May Be Passed"; "Paris Will See Helene." It is unclear if Madison ended up visiting Paris, as no reports were found in the *Seattle Times*.

74. George M. Varnell, "Helene Forced to Pay Freight for 2 Persons," *Seattle Times*, July 8, 1931; George M. Varnell, "$300 Shows Up From A.A.U. to Help Expenses," *Seattle Times*, July 11, 1931.

75. "Helene Seeks New Conquests," *Seattle Times*, 16 July 1931; "One Record Left for Helene," *Seattle Times*, July 18, 1931; "Helene Paces A.A.U. Title Meet Tonight," *Seattle Times*, July 15, 1931; Madison set a new record in the 1000-yard freestyle that wasn't recognized until September 1931 due to an error that delayed the AAU's recognition. See Peter Salvus, "Helene Claims All World Swim Marks, Recheck Gives Her Best Time in 1,000 Meter," *Seattle Times*, 4 September 1931, p. 25.

76. "Helene Wins; Nearly Cops Team Title," *Seattle Times*, 19 July 1931, 18; "Helene's Four Wins Land Her Third Position," *Seattle Times*, July 20. 1931.

77. George M. Varnell, "Helene Leaves Tonight, Will Try for Record at Spokane, Home-Coming Party Next," *Seattle Times*, August 4, 1931.

78. "Helene Will Swim Today at Picnic, Star to Show for Laundry Workers," *Seattle Times*, August 30, 1931.

79. "Helene Hangs up New Marks in Swim Meet," *Seattle Times*, September 14, 1931.

80. Peter Salvus, "Mermaid Helene, Greatest Feats, She's Stubborn, Money Beckons," *Seattle Times*, September 20, 1931.

81. "Helene's Quest for All Marks Virtually Over," *Seattle Times*, November 17, 1931.

82. George M. Varnell, "Sullivan Trophy Proposed for Seattle's Champion Aquatic Star; Honor is Accorded Best Athlete," *Seattle Times*, October 15, 1931; "New Honors Loom for Helene, Smashes 7 Marks; May Get A.A.U. Award," *Seattle Times*, October 15, 1931; Peter Salvus, "Miss Madison Proves Ability in Tireless Efforts at Washington A.C.; She Covers Mile For Attempt," *Seattle Times*, October 15, 1931.

83. Salvus, "Mermaid Helene."

84. George M. Varnell, "Varnell Says Hungary's Ace, Threat to Helene, Speedy in Water," *Seattle Times*, August 2, 1931. Daughters was already reported to be training two additional swimmers he thought would qualify for the Olympics, Madison's WAC teammates Dawn Gilson and Olive McKean. See George M. Varnell, "Daughters Grooms 2 New 'Champs'; Helene's Pals, Olive, Dawn to Bid for Games," *Seattle Times*, August 5, 1931.

85. George M. Varnell, "Varnell Says Another A.A.U. Joke, What Did Barney Do?, Helene More Worthy," *Seattle Times*, January 5, 1932. The East Coast bias did not stop Ray Daughters from garnering honors. He was named a member of the men's swimming committee in February 1932 and was slated to host a national men's race in the 500-yard freestyle at the WAC. See Ed Peltret, "Ray Daughters Gets Official A.A.U. Honor," *Seattle Times*, February 7, 1932. Madison was also honored in 1931 with a butter statue; see "Helene Madison's Butter Statue Shot by Watchman," *Seattle Times*, October 4, 1931.

86. "Helene Would Set New Mark," *Seattle Times*, March 18, 1932; "Helene Enters Training Meet With Her Mates," *Seattle Times*, March 6, 1932.

87. George M. Varnell, "Varnell Says Helene Cuts off 899 2–5 Seconds in Record Tries, That is Going, Seattle Mermaid's Mark-Busting Not Yet at an End," *Seattle Times*, April 13, 1932.

88. Alex Shults, "It Isn't News, But!," *Seattle Times*, February 19, 1932. Also see Ed Peltret, "Helene, Jack Medica Smash Swim Marks; W.A.C. Aces Hit Calm Water in Successful Try," *Seattle Times*, February 18, 1932. Medica was the male swimmer receiving some attention, though not nearly as much as Madison.

89. "W.A.C. Team of Swimmers Has Date to Keep," *Seattle Times*, April 17, 1932; "W.A.C. Girls Threat for Title; With Helene's Aid, Team May Win Nationals," *Seattle Times*, April 27, 1932.

90. Paul Zimmerman, "Helene Wins Again; L.A.A.C. Takes Title; Washington A.C. Ties New York; U.S. Mark Falls," *Seattle Times*, May 2, 1932.

91. George M. Varnell, "Swimmers Head to Portland, More Than 30 Natators Engage in Championships," *Seattle Times*, June 17, 1932; "Helene Breaks 50-Meter Mark; W.A.C. Natators Big Winners at Jantzen Beach," *Seattle Times*, June 19, 1932; "Helene and Dawn in Pre-Olympic Trial; Mermaids are in 2-Day Swim," *Seattle Times*, July 8, 1932.

92. George M. Varnell, "Helene's Ready to Compete; Seattle's Greatest Woman Athlete Set for Trials," *Seattle Times*, July 12, 1932.

93. "Helene Winner of 400-Meter Semifinal Try," *Seattle Times*, July 16, 1932.

94. "Helene, Miss Holm Break Swim Marks; Seattle Naiad Qualifies Again for Games Team," *Seattle Times*, July 17, 1932. For more on the swimmers in the 1932 Olympic Games, see Doris H. Pieroth, *Their Day in the Sun: Women of the 1932 Olympics* (Seattle: University of Washington Press, 1996).

95. George M. Varnell, "Helene Picked to Win Olympic Sprints; Seattle Naiad Carries Hope of U.S. Victory," *Seattle Times*, July 18, 1932; George M. Varnell, "Daughters Discovers Swim Frame-up; Olympic Coaches, Mad at Him, Conspire to Beat Helene," *Seattle Times*, August 3, 1932, p. 12; George M. Varnell, "Jessup Fails; It's Helene's Turn Now; Miss Madison's First Test Due This Saturday," *Seattle Times*, August 4, 1932, p. 14.

96. Varnell, "Jessup Fails";; "Helene Sets Swim Mark; Mrs. Seville Betters It," *Seattle Times*, August 7, 1932.

97. "Helene Faces Great Swim Field Today; Miss Madison's Semifinal Win Made in Stride," *Seattle Times*, August 8, 1932.

98. George M. Varnell, "Helene, Champ, Had Ace Up Sleeve; Seattle Girl's Swim Strategy Daughters' Idea," *Seattle Times*, August 9, 1932.

99. "Helene's Sprint to Victory Has Film Recording," *Seattle Times*, August 14, 1932.

100. "Helene to Quit Racing at Once, Says Father Charles Madison," *Seattle Times*, August 9, 1932.

101. George M. Varnell, "'Tell Seattle How Happy I Am!' Helene Sends Exultant Word Home," *Seattle Times*, August 9, 1932.

102. "Helene Wins 400-Meter Trial; Blistered Foot Fails to Hinder Seattle Queen," *Seattle Times*, August 11, 1932; "Helene Wins Fast Semifinal; Miss Poynton's Diving Mastery Wins Her First," *Seattle Times*, August 12, 1932. Also see "Movies Bar to Participation in 1932 Olympiad," *Seattle Times*, February 7, 1932.

103. "Helene Wins Final Race, Sets Record; Miss Kight Beaten by One-Tenth of Second," *Seattle Times*, August 14, 1932.

104. "Coaches Think Helene in Line to Win Trophy," *Seattle Times*, August 14, 1932.

105. Frank G. Gorrie, "Helene 'Through,' Mentor Says; Swim Champion Never Again to Reach Heights," *Seattle Times*, August 15, 1932. Also see "Daughters Due, Will Be Feted Thursday Noon," *Seattle Times*, August 15, 1932; "Helene to Talk On Her 'Movies' Bid Tomorrow," *Seattle Times*, August 15, 1932. Daughters went so far as to suggest that there were other female swimmers in Seattle "with almost as much natural ability as" Madison,

but they needed coaching (which he could offer) and many years of practice. See Alex Shults, "Daughters Goes to Work," *Seattle Times*, August 18, 1932.

106. Alex Shults, "Daughters Goes to Work."

107. "Tributes to Helene," *Seattle Times*, August 21, 1932. Editorial Page.

108. "Tributes to Helene," August 21, 1932.

109. "Tributes to Helene," August 21, 1932.

110. "Tributes to Helene," August 21, 1932.

111. George M. Varnell, "Helene to Return for Short Visit," *Seattle Times*, August 23, 1932. Also see "Home-Coming of Helene Swings in Line Today," *Seattle Times*, August 26, 1932.

112. George M. Varnell, "Royal Welcome Set for Helene," *Seattle Times*, August 24, 1932.

113. Varnell, "Royal Welcome Set."

114. Varnell, "Royal Welcome Set."

115. Varnell, "Royal Welcome Set"; Also see "Seattle Ready With Reception for her Queen," *Seattle Times*, August 25, 1932.

116. "Huge Crowd Watches Sports Parade, Helene Madison is Greatly Admired," *Seattle Times*, August 27, 1932.

117. "Gayety, Beauty Mingle at International Naval Ball," *Seattle Times*, August 27, 1932.

118. "Gayety, Beauty Mingle."

119. "Helene Admits She is Through as an Amateur," *Seattle Times*, August 27, 1932; "'Subjects' to Pay Queen Helene Homage at Park," *Seattle Times*, August 28, 1932.

120. "Seattle Ready"; "Dore to Present Auto to Helene at Park Sunday," *Seattle Times*, August 26, 1932.

121. "Swim at Park Puts Helene in 'Pro' Ranks," *Seattle Times*, August 29, 1932.

122. "Tributes to Helene," *Seattle Times*, August 28, 1932. Editorial Page.

123. "Tributes to Helene," August 28, 1932.

124. "Tributes to Helene," August 28, 1932.

125. "Tributes to Helene," August 28, 1932.

126. "Helene Signed by Sennett, Seattle Natator in Two-Reel Comedy," *Seattle Times*, November 15, 1932.

127. "Helene Drives South to Talk With Manager," *Seattle Times*, January 17, 1933.

128. George M. Varnell, "Varnell Says Helene, Vines are Nominated, Girl Deserves Sullivan Award, But Politics May Prevent It," *Seattle Times*, October 12, 1932. For one explanation of why Madison was not awarded the 1932 prize, see "It Isn't News, But!" *Seattle Times*, November 16, 1933. Torrance explains that Seattle did not have enough political clout and AAU votes to support Madison. He hoped that Seattle was on its way to establishing their ability to win the award for their next hometown hero. Don Duncan attributed Madison's inability to win the award to male chauvinism. See Duncan, "Seattle's Mark Spitz of 1932."

129. "Helene Visits; To Swim Again," *Seattle Times*, June 19, 1933.

130. "It Isn't News, But!" *Seattle Times*, June 20, 1933.

131. "It Isn't News, But!"

132. "Helene Madison Rejects Bid to Toronto Swim," *Seattle Times*, August 15, 1935.

133. "Roar of the Crowd; Helene Recalls and Yearns, A Little," *Seattle Times*, August 2, 1936. Don Duncan also recalled Madison's hot dog-selling summer of 1936 and the Parks and Recreation Department's rejection of her as a swimming instructor; see Duncan, "Green Lake."

134. "Roar of the Crowd."

135. "Roar of the Crowd."

136. "Helene Madison Nurses, Weds Power Official," *Seattle Times*, March 7, 1937.

137. For example, see George M. Varnell, "George M. Varnell Says: Helene's Record For Century is Threatened," *Seattle Times*, January 3, 1943; Emmett Watson, "Hearts Broken, and Helene's Records, Too; Miss Curtis Clicks," *Seattle Times*, May 3, 1947; Alex Shults, "From the Scorebook; U.S. Olympic Swimmers to Face Tough Opposition," *Seattle Times*, December 14, 1947. One of the first of these records to fall was in 1934; see "Madison, Holm Marks Fall; W.A.C. Stars in Busy Night of Record-Hitting," *Seattle Times*, March 16, 1934.

138. "Helene Madison Teaches Daughter to Swim," *Seattle Times*, March 28, 1943. Madison's daughter graduated from Roosevelt High School in 1956 and spent that summer helping her mother teach swimming. See Georg N. Meyers, "The Sporting Thing," *Seattle Times*, June 6, 1956. The newspaper also reported on Madison's daughter's marriage in 1960. See *Seattle Times*, November 15, 1959; "Helene Madison McIver, Jr., Becomes Bride," *Seattle Times*, June 12, 1960. The newspaper regularly reported on other Madison-related issues, including her admission to the hospital for a respiratory ailment in 1953; see "Helene Madison In Hospital With Chest Ailment," *Seattle Times*, April 7, 1953.

139. "Helene Madison to Coach Swim Team," *Seattle Times*, November 4, 1948; also see "W.A.C., Moore Swimmers to Vie in Oregon," *Seattle Times*, August 23, 1951.

140. Georg N. Meyers, "The Sporting Thing," *Seattle Times*, August 14, 1956; Advertisement for Helene Madison School of Swimming, *Seattle Times*, March 9, 1958; Louis R. Guzzo, "Words and Music; 2 Seattleites Swim Way Into Aqua Follies," *Seattle Times*, July 27, 1958.

141. Meyers, "The Sporting Thing," August 14, 1956.

142. Jack Hewins, "'Invisible Mermaid' Begins Biggest Fight," *Seattle Times*, December 13, 1968; "Helene Madison Recuperating," *Seattle Times*, January 3, 1969; "Helene Madison Resting at Home," *Seattle Times*, February 27, 1969.

143. "Athletic Club to Name Pool for Helene," *Seattle Times*, December 18, 1968.

144. Don Duncan, "Visiting with Queen Helene; Finding the Football Faithful," *Seattle Times*, September 24, 1970; "Helene Madison Succumbs at 57," *Seattle Times*, November 26, 1970; also see "Helene Madison Dies," p. 1. Related to Madison's financial problems, see "Funds Lacking, Helene Madison May Miss Trip to Hall of Fame," *Seattle Times*, December 15, 1966.

145. John Lindtwed, "Helene Madison Pool Dedicated," *Seattle Times*, January 9, 1972.

146. "Helene Madison Succumbs"; also see "Helene Madison Dies."

147. Don Duncan, "Seattle's Mark Spitz of 1932."

148. Don Duncan, "Seattle's Mark Spitz of 1932."

149. Don Duncan, "Seattle's Mark Spitz of 1932."

Chapter 9

1. Warren Moon with Don Yaeger, *Never Give Up on Your Dreams: My Journey* (Boston: Da Capo Press, 2009), p. 137; Warren Moon, lecture in class of Dr. Terry Anne Scott, University of Washington, Seattle, Washington, February 10, 2016; Warren Moon, conversation with Shafina Khaki, February 10, 2016, Seattle, Washington; Leigh Montville, "Father Moon," *Sports Illustrated*, September 27, 1993.

2. Martin Pengelly. "Richard Sherman: 'Racism Is Alive and Active' In NFL and America," *Business Insider*, May 8, 2014, accessed June 7, 2016, http://www.businessinsider.com/richard-sherman-racism-is-alive-and-active-in-nfl-2014–5; Richard Sherman,

"BOOMSDAY," *Sports Illustrated*, February 2, 2015, accessed July 10, 2016, http://www
.si.com/vault/2015/02/02/106715253/boomsday; Stephen A. Crockett Jr., "Stop Calling
Richard Sherman a Thug," *Denver Post*, January 22, 2014.

3. W. E. B. Du Bois, *The Souls of Black Folk*, (Mineola, New York: Dover Publications,
2016; first published by Chicago: A.C. McClurg, 1903), chapter one; W. E. Burghhardt
DuBois, "Strivings of the Negro People," *The Atlantic*, August 1897, accessed January 24,
2019, https://www.theatlantic.com/magazine/archive/1897/08/strivings-of-the-negro
-people/305446; John P. Pittman, "Double Consciousness," *The Stanford Encyclopedia
of Philosophy* (Summer 2016 Edition), ed. Edward N. Zalta, accessed September 9, 2017,
https://plato.stanford.edu/archives/sum2016/entries/double-consciousness.

4. Ben Goessling, "Carl Eller to Colin Kaepernick: Speak Out for Change, But Stand
for the Anthem," ESPN, August 30, 2016, accessed October 22, 2017, http://www.espn
.com/blog/minnesota-vikings/post/_/id/19967/carl-eller-to-colin-kaepernick-speak
-out-for-change-but-stand-up-for-anthem; Craig Peters, "Carl Eller, Alan Page Inspire
Future Generations," Minnesota Vikings, accessed June 12, 2018, www.vikings.com/news
/article-1/Carl-Eller-Alan-Page-Inspire-Future-Generation/05487d35-0d5a-476d-ba66
-5514f1cb3f87.

5. Charles E. Connerly, *"The Most Segregated City in America": City Planning and Civil
Rights in Birmingham, 1920–1980* (Charlottesville: University of Virginia Press, 2005), p. 43.

6. Connerly, *"The Most Segregated City in America,"* p. 43; Carl Eller, Enshrinement
Speech, Pro Football Hall of Fame Field at Fawcett Stadium, August 8, 2004, accessed
December 9, 2017, Pro Football Hall of Fame, http://www.profootballhof.com/players
/carl-eller/enshrinement; NC Department of Natural and Cultural Resources, "NFL Star
Carl Eller Born in Winston-Salem," accessed June 7, 2018, https://www.ncdcr.gov
/blog/2013/01/25/nfl-star-carl-eller-born-in-winston-salem.

7. Carl Eller, Enshrinement Speech, Pro Football Hall of Fame Field at Fawcett
Stadium, August 8, 2004, accessed December 9, 2017, Pro Football Hall of Fame, http://
www.profootballhof.com/players/carl-eller/enshrinement.

8. Jim Bruton, *Vikings 50: All-Time Greatest Players in Franchise History* (Chicago:
Triumph Books, LLC, 2012), p. 55; Ken Belson, "Carl Eller, Ex-Viking, Is Using the Super
Bowl as a Platform," *New York Times*, February 2, 2018; Mike Gastineau, Steve Rudman,
and Art Thiel, *The Great Book of Seattle Sports Lists* (Philadelphia: Running Press, 2009),
pp. 490–491.

9. Ken Belson, "Carl Eller, Ex-Viking"; Eller, Enshrinement Speech. NC Department
of Natural and Cultural Resources, "NFL Star Carl Eller Born in Winston-Salem."

10. Ben Goessling, "Carl Eller, Alan Page Educate at Vikings Black History Month
Event," ESPN, February 4, 2016, accessed on October 22, 2017, http://www.espn.com
/blog/minnesota-vikings/post/_/id/17941/carl-eller-alan-page-give-stirring-remarks-at
-vikings-black-history-month-event; Bob Temple, "Carl Eller Is Enshrined in the Hall of
Fame," Pro Football Hall of Fame, August 8, 2004, accessed October 19, 2017, http://www
.profootballhof.com/news/carl-eller-is-enshrined-in-the-hall-of-fame; Peters, "Carl Eller,
Alan Page Inspire Future Generations."

11. Sam Farmer, "It Was Safety First for UCLA, Seahawks Great Kenny Easley, Who
Is about to Enter the Pro Football Hall of Fame," *Los Angeles Times*, August 2, 2017; John
Boyle, "Jersey Retirement "Really Special" for Seahawks Legend Kenny Easley," Seattle
Seahawks, September 26, 2017, accessed September 29, 2017, http://www.seahawks.com
/news/2017/09/26/jersey-retirement-"really-special"-seahawks-legend-kenny-easley;
Clare Farnsworth, "On This Date: Kenny Easley Selected in First Round of NFL Draft,"

Seattle Seahawks, April 28, 2017, accessed September 13, 2017, http://www.seahawks
.com/news/2014/04/28/date-kenny-easley-selected-first-round-nfl-draft; Jason Woullard,
"The Enforcer: Kenny Easley," The Shadow League, October 3,2013, accessed December 17,
2017, https://www.theshadowleague.com/story/the-enforcer-kenny-easley; "Kenny
Easley," Pro Football Hall of Fame, accessed June 11, 2018, www.profootballhof.com
/players/kenny-easley.

12. See Ted Kluck, Three-Week Professionals: Inside the 1987 NFL Players' Strike
(Lanham, MD: Rowan & Littlefield, 2015); Harry Minium, "Kenny Easley: From the
Streets of South Norfolk to the Pro Football Hall of Fame," The Virginia Pilot, August 4,
2017; "Kenny Easley | Seattle Seahawks," Pro Football Hall of Fame, accessed December 4,
2017, http://www.profootballhof.com/players/kenny-easley/biography.

13. Tim Booth, "HOF Series: Hall Gets Easley after Reconciling with Seahawks," The
Washington Times, August 1, 2017, accessed December 14, 2017, https://www.washington
times.com/news/2017/aug/1/hof-series-hall-gets-easley-after-reconciling-with; Bob
Condotta, "How the 1987 NFL Strike Divided Seahawks Icons Kenny Easley and
Steve Largent," Seattle Times, October 14, 2017; Peter King, "The Surreal Strike of 1987:
Remembering a Walkout That Helped Create Today's NFL," Sports Illustrated, October 15,
2007.

14. Tim Booth, "HOF Series: Hall Gets Easley after Reconciling with Seahawks."

15. Minium, "Kenny Easley."

16. Condotta, "How the 1987 NFL Strike"; Thomas D. Wachs, No Matter What:
Learning Godly Character From Athletics (Maitland, Florida: Xulon Press, 2004), p. 19.

17. Jerry Large, "Ahead of Number Retirement, Ex-Seahawk Kenny Easley Talks
Injuries, Hits Trump on Protests," The Seattle Times, September 28, 2017, accessed
December 20, 2017, https://www.seattletimes.com/seattle-news/ahead-of-number
-retirement-ex-seahawk-kenny-easley-talks-injuries-hits-trump-on-protests; Ron
Clements, "Kenny Easley Takes Stand against Police Brutality in Hall of Fame Speech,"
Sporting News, August 5, 2017, accessed June 21, 2018, http://www.sportingnews.com/nfl
/news/kenny-easley-black-lives-matter-hall-of-fame-pfhof2017-seahawks/1pbvfsinlmsd
f1nucm3w4axdjc.

18. "Quarterback Warren Moon," Pro Football Hall of Fame, accessed June 14, 2018,
http://www.profootballhof.com/players/warren-moon; for more information on Warren
Moon, see Moon, Never Give Up.

19. Warren Moon, "Warren Moon Enshrinement Speech Transcript," Pro Football
Hall of Fame, August 5, 2006, accessed December 12, 2019, https://www.profootballhof
.com/news/warren-moon-s-enshrinement-speech-transcript/; For more information on
Warren Moon, see Moon, Never Give Up.

20. Dan Gartland, "The First Black Quarterback to Start for Each NFL Team," Sports
Illustrated, September 22, 2016; David Zirin, A People's History of Sports in the United
States: 250 Years of Politics, Protest, People, and Play (New York: The New Press, 2008),
pp. 107–108; Moon, lecture; Jason Reid, "Warren Moon Dreamed of Playing in the
NFL, But the NFL Didn't Want Moon. At Least Not at Quarterback," The Undefeated,
October 26, 2017, accessed June 14, 2018, https://theundefeated.com/features/warren
-moon-nfl-black-quarterback; A 2016 study found that if a black starting quarterback demonstrated a subpar performance, they are "1.98 to 2.46 times more likely to
be benched the next week" in comparison to white quarterbacks with similar skills.
However, these statistics should not come as a surprise. The dominant force of race in
the NFL has held sway since the league's origins. See Bryan Altman, "Study Shows Black

Quarterbacks More Than Twice As Likely To Be Benched Than White QBs," *CBS Local Sports*, November 11, 2015.

21. Moon, lecture; Reid, "Warren Moon Dreamed."

22. Moon, lecture; Moon, "Warren Moon Enshrinement Speech Transcript."

23. Moon, "Warren Moon Enshrinement Speech Transcript"; Moon, lecture.

24. Moon, lecture; "Trampling Troy: A Look at the UW-USC Rivalry," *Seattle Times*, October 23, 2003.

25. "Trampling Troy: A Look at the UW-USC Rivalry," *Seattle Times*; Moon, lecture; Moon, "Warren Moon Enshrinement Speech."

26. Moon, lecture; Moon, "Warren Moon Enshrinement Speech."

27. Moon, *Never Give Up*, pp. 137–138, p. 192, p. 143; Moon, lecture.

28. Moon, *Never Give Up*, p. 143; "Quarterback Warren Moon," Pro Football Hall of Fame.

29. Barack Obama, "Remarks by the President Honoring the Super Bowl Champion Seattle Seahawks," The White House, Office of the Press Secretary, May 21, 2014, accessed December 4, 2016; Reid Wilson, "Obama praises Seahawks' 'Legion of Boom,'" *The Washington Post*, May 21, 2014.

30. "'People Are Still Missing The Point,' of the Protests, Seahawks' Richard Sherman Says," *Seattle Times*, September 21, 2016,

31. Jill Martin, "Michael Bennett: I Can't Stand For the National Anthem,'" CNN, August 17, 2017, accessed January 2, 2018, http://www.cnn.com/2017/08/16/sport/seahawks-michael-bennett-not-standing-for-national-anthem/index.html.

32. Carol Marie Cropper, "Black Man Fatally Dragged in a Possible Racial Killing," *The New York Times*, June 10, 1998; Sheil Kapadia, "Richard Sherman Protests Shootings By Not Taking Questions at News Conference," ESPN, accessed June 14, 2018, http://www.espn.com/nfl/story/_/id/17605744/seattle-seahawks-cb-richard-sherman-protests-shootings-not-taking-questions-press-conference; Alysha Tsuji, "Richard Sherman Responds to Trump in Video: 'It's Time for the Racism and Bigotry to Go Away,'" *USA Today*, September 23, 2017, accessed December 2, 2017, http://ftw.usatoday.com/2017/09/richard-sherman-seahawks-president-donald-trump-nfl-comments-anthem-protest-white-supremacists-video-reaction; Christina Caron, "Heather Heyer, Charlottesville Victim, is Recalled as 'a Strong Woman,'" *The New York Times*, August 13, 2017.

33. "Michael Bennett: Effectiveness of anthem protests would grow with white players' involvement," ESPN, accessed December 11, 2019, https://www.espn.com/nfl/story/_/id/20363083/michael-bennett-seattle-seahawks-says-involvement-white-players-help-anthem-protests.

34. Michael-Shawn Dugar, "Pete Carroll, Doug Baldwin support message of Bennett's protest," *Seattle Post-Intelligencer*, August 15, 2017.

35. Stacy Rost, "Seahawks' Richard Sherman, Doug Baldwin say Trump's opposition to anthem protests has unified players," 710 ESPN Seattle, September 28, 2017, https://sports.mynorthwest.com/346102/seahawks-richard-sherman-doug-baldwin-say-trumps-opposition-to-anthem-protests-has-unified-players.

36. John Boyle, "Seahawks Players Discuss Decision to Not Participate in National Anthem,"Seattle Seahawks, September 24, 2017, accessed December 5, 2017, http://www.seahawks.com/news/2017/09/24/seahawks-players-discuss-decision-not-participate-national-anthem.

37. Darin Gantt, "Michael Bennett: Protest for Equality Needs a Few White Faces," Pro

Football Talk, NBC Sports, August 17, 2017, accessed September 7, 2017, http://pro
footballtalk.nbcsports.com/2017/08/17/michael-bennett-protest-for-equality-needs
-a-few-white-faces; Boyle, "Seahawks Players Discuss Decision."

38. Goessling, "Carl Eller to Colin Kaepernick."

39. Q13 News Staff, "Hall of Famer Kenny Easley says he'd take a knee if he was playing
today," Q13 Fox, October 1, 2017, accessed January 3, 2018, http://q13fox.com/2017/10/01
/hall-of-famer-kenny-easley-says-hed-take-a-knee-if-he-was-playing-today/; "Warren
Moon discusses NFL Player Protest," Kings News, accessed January 3, 2018, http://www
.kings.com/video/sports/warren-moon-discusses-nfl-player-protests/281-2740360.

40. Michael Tyson, interview with Shafina Khaki, Bellevue, Washington, June 26, 2018.

Chapter 10

1. Geoff Baker, "OVG Opens Waitlist after Seattle Puts Down 33,000 Deposits for
NHL Season Tickets," *Seattle Times*, March 1, 2018.

2. Jeff Obermeyer, *Hockey in Seattle* (Charleston, SC: Arcadia Publishing, 2004),
pp. 11–12.
Eric Zweig, *Stanley Cup: 120 Years of Hockey Supremacy* (New York: Firefly Books, 2012),
275.

3. "Canadiens" being the shortened version of the team's official name, "le Club de
hockey Canadien" which is Québécois French for "The Canadian Hockey Club"; Larry
Stone, "100 Years Ago, Seattle Won the Stanley Cup and Expanded the Reach of Pro
Hockey," *Seattle Times*, March 26, 2017.

4. "Social Section Front Page," *Seattle Times*, March 18, 1917.

5. "Social Section Front Page."

6. "Hall of Canadiens Dies of Influenza," *Seattle Times*, April 6, 1919.

7. Obermeyer, *Hockey in Seattle*, (Charleston: Arcadia Publishing, 2004), p. 10; Portus
Baxter, "World's Series Hockey Game Knocked Out by Influenza," *Seattle Times* (Seattle,
WA), April 1, 1919.

8. Wayne Norton, *Women on Ice: The Early Years of Women's Hockey in Western Canada*
(Vancouver, BC: Ronsdale Press, 2009), p. 121.

9. Information determined by author's investigation of exact newspaper articles of the
time.

10. Obermeyer, *Hockey in Seattle*, p. 15

11. Obermeyer, *Hockey in Seattle*, p. 21; Stan Fischler, *The Handy Hockey Answer Book*
(Visible Ink Press: Canton, MI, 2016), p. 63.

12. Fischler, *The Handy Hockey Answer Book,* p. 63; Lawrence Kaplan, "Inuit or Eskimo:
Which Names to Use?", Alaska Native Language Center, University of Alaska Fairbanks,
accessed December 11, 2019, https://www.uaf.edu/anlc/resources/inuit_or_eskimo.php.

13. George M. Varnell, "No Hair Pulling Girls; Act Like Ladies!," *The Seattle Daily
Times* (Seattle, WA), January 19, 1932.

14. Betty Stewart, "Knitting the Public's Whims into Payroll Dollars," *The Seattle Daily
Times* (Seattle, WA), November 24, 1929; Paul Dorpat, "The End of an Ice Age—and
Historic Mercer Arena," *Seattle Times*, May 25, 2017.

15. Jeff Obermeyer, *Seattle Totems* (Charleston, SC: Arcadia Publishing, 2015), pp. 16–17;
Ralph Slate, "Seattle Seahawks Statistics and History," The Internet Hockey Database,
accessed December 29, 2016, http://www.hockeydb.com/stte/seattle-seahawks-7961.html.

16. Quoted in Hy Zimmerman, "Ice Team Renamed Totems," *Seattle Daily Times* (Seattle, WA), August 17, 1958.

17. Lewis Kamb, "Indians Fondly Recall 'Caring,' Loyal Brando," *Seattle Post-Intelligencer* (Seattle, WA), July 2, 2004; Gabriel Chrisman, "The Fish-in Protests at Franks Landing," Seattle Civil Rights and Labor History Project, University of Washington, accessed May 29, 2018, http://depts.washington.edu/civilr/fish-ins.htm.

18. Dan Raley, *How Seattle Became a Big-League Sports Town: From George Wilson to Russell Wilson* (Seattle: Fairgreens Publishing, 2015), p. 49; Ralph Slate, "Guyle Fielder hockey stats," The Internet Hockey Database, accessed January 15, 2017, http://www.hockeydb.com/ihdb/stats/pdisplay.php?pid=1666; Ralph Slate, ed., "Jaromir Jagr hockey stats," The Internet Hockey Database, accessed February 12, 2017, http://www.hockeydb.com/ihdb/stats/pdisplay.php?filter=Y&pid=2497.

19. Jeff Obermeyer, "Seattle Totems," Seattle Hockey, accessed November 15, 2016, http://www.seattlehockey.net/Seattle_Hockey_Homepage/Totems.html.

20. "FAQ's," WHL Prospects Central, accessed November 29, 2016, http://prospects.whl.ca/prospect-central-faqs/; Obermeyer, *Hockey in Seattle*, p. 113.

21. Obermeyer, *Hockey in Seattle*, p. 114.

22. Robert T. Nelson, "Ackerley Shows Arena Plan—Sonics Owner Says He's Pursuing Hockey Franchise," *Seattle Times* (Seattle, WA), July 13, 1990.

23. "One NHL Bid Dead—Ackerley Steps Down, Another Seattle Group Steps Up," *Seattle Times* (Seattle, WA), December 5, 1990.

24. Bob Finnigan, "Seattle's NHL Bid on Ice—Officials Now Look Later Into 1990's," *Seattle Times* (Seattle, WA), December 6, 1990.

25. Quoted in Bob Finnigan, "NHL, Seattle Bidders Still Talking Expansion—Hockey Prospects Alive in Spite of Bid's Failure," *Seattle Times* (Seattle, WA), December 7, 1990.

26. David Eskenazi and Steve Rudman, "Wayback Machine: Seattle's Long Wait / Part 6,"Sportspress Northwest, February 28, 2018, accessed March 21, 2018, http://sportspressnw.com/2237640/2018/wayback-machine-seattles-long-wait-part-6.

27. Bob Finnigan, "KeyArena's Cool to Hockey, but T-Birds Call It Home," *Seattle Times*, October 30, 1995.

28. Morris Malakoff, "Kent Gets Junior-Level Expansion Hockey Team; The Crusaders," *Seattle Southside*, September 7, 2005; "NHL," *Native Hockey*, accessed March 10, 2018, http://nativehockey.com/nhl/.

29. "About WWFHA," Western Washington Female Hockey Association, accessed January 9, 2017, http://www.wwfha.com.prod.sportngin.com/about-wwfha.

30. "Northwest Sports Briefing—Everett gets WHL approval for team," *Seattle Times*, September 19, 2001.

31. Quoted in Geoff Baker, "Seattle Listed as Contender for New Pro Hockey Team," *Seattle Times*, June 24, 2015.

32. Geoff Baker, "Sodo Arena Group Seeks New Vote on Seattle Street Vacation." *Seattle Times*, Feb. 8, 2017; Matt Calkins, "There Are Reasons to Doubt KeyArena Can Be Redone for NBA and NHL," *Seattle Times*, Jan. 25, 2017.

33. Marc Stiles, "Seattle and Private Developer Outline $660 Million Plan to Redevelop KeyArena," *Puget Sound Business Journal*, Sep. 12, 2017.

34. Jeff Obermeyer, e-mail message to author, Jan. 19, 2017.

35. Geoff Baker, "OVG Opens Waitlist."

Contributors

Jaime Barnhorst earned her MA in sociology from the University of Washington in 2011 and has been working at the UW ever since. She is currently the project manager for UW's College of Arts and Sciences. Barnhorst has been connected to the roller derby community since 2006 and has played for Boston Roller Derby, Dockyard Derby Dames, and Rat City Roller Derby. She skated for seven full seasons under the name "Ethel Vermin" and collected a number of awards along the way, including Dockyard's 2010 Rookie of the Year, two home team championship trophies, and a handful of MVPs. During Barnhorst's final season on the roller derby track, she served as a captain and primary jammer for Rat City's Throttle Rockets in Seattle, Washington.

Chris Donnelly, a lifelong baseball fan, is a graduate of the College of New Jersey. He resides in Mercer County, New Jersey, with his wife, Jamie.

Shafina Khaki is a Juris Doctor candidate at the University of Washington School of Law. She serves as the communications chair for the Middle Eastern and South Asian Student Law Association. Khaki graduated with her bachelor's degree from the University of Washington in 2016. She double majored in Law, Society, and Justice and Political Science. Khaki is heavily involved in philanthropy work and organizations that focus directly on major humanitarian issues in South Asia and Africa, especially in the areas of women's rights, refugee relief, education, and health care. She served for several years as the editor for the *University of Washington Undergraduate Law Review*. Khaki was also philanthropy chair for the University of Washington South Asian Student Association and is a published writer for the global magazine *Ismaili Insight*.

Shelley Lee is an associate professor of history and Comparative American studies at Oberlin College. She is the author of two books, *Claiming the Oriental Gateway: Prewar Seattle and Japanese America* (Temple 2011) and *A New History of Asian America* (Routledge 2013)

Rita Liberti is a sports historian at California State University, East Bay, where she co-founded the Center for Sport and Social Justice in 2011. She has co-authored two award winning books: *(Re)Presenting Wilma Rudolph* (Syracuse

University, 2015) and *San Francisco Bay Area Sports: Golden Gate Athletics, Recreation, and Community* (University of Arkansas Press, 2016). They won the North American Society for Sport History best book award prizes in 2016 and 2018 respectively.

Christine S. Maggio is a longtime hockey fanatic based out of Seattle, Washington. Since receiving her BA in English literature at the University of Puget Sound, she has written and drawn comics commenting on hockey and issues of gender, race, and sexuality that arise from the surrounding culture. Her work on sports and gender inequality has also appeared in articles for *The Other Half* media, *The Sunshine Skate,* and *Fear the Fin*. She currently works in the private sector and spends much of her free time baking for her husband and spoiling her cats.

Terry Anne Scott is an associate professor of American history and the Director of African American Studies at Hood College. She earned her doctorate in history at the University of Chicago. Her research and teaching interests focus on African American social and cultural history, social and political movements, racialized social violence, and the intersection of race and sports. She completed a monograph on lynching and is the authorized biographer of the legendary National Basketball Association Hall of Fame player and coach Lenny Wilkens. Scott is heavily involved in community service and social activism and has received many awards for her community involvement. She is the director and founder of the Community Ambassadors Mentor Program, which connects college students, particularly student-athletes, with economically marginalized local youth. She is also the mother of three daughters.

Maureen M. Smith is a professor in the Department of Kinesiology and Health Science at California State University, Sacramento. She is the co-author (with Rita Liberti) of *(Re)Presenting Wilma Rudolph* (Syracuse University Press, 2015). Smith is a member of the North American Society for the Sociology of Sport, the International Society of the History of Sport and Physical Education, and the North American Society for Sport History, of which she is a past president. Her research interests include women in sports, African American sports experiences in the twentieth century, the Olympic Games, and sporting statues and material culture.

Elliot Trotter is the founder of *Skyd Magazine*, a seminal media resource for the sport of Ultimate. A former professional athlete with the Seattle Rainmakers,

Elliot has represented four countries at international championships and is a US Beach Ultimate national champion. Elliot hosts the popular travel series *Ultimate Globe Trotter,* which focuses on Ultimate communities around the world. A native of Chicago, Elliot has made Seattle home for the past decade and coaches at University Prep.

Anthony Washington is from the Central District of Seattle, Washington. He attended Garfield High School, where he played varsity basketball for the legendary Bulldogs for two years. Washington earned a basketball scholarship from the University of Washington (UW) before playing professionally overseas. He is an educator at the UW Experimental Educational Unit. Washington has been an advocate for his community for the last ten years and is a writer, and he recently founded Off the Court, a nonprofit academic training service for student-athletes pursuing college scholarships. Anthony has three children: Anthony Jr., Eniyah, and Carter. He earned his Master's in Special Education from UW.

Index